PRAISE FOR *IMAGINING THE FUTURE*

"A thorough, comprehensive and complex analysis of the origin and development of the eschatological thinking in one of the largest and most important Pentecostal denominations in the world, Assemblies of God (AG). Isgrigg offers a fascinating, constructive proposal for a contemporary pneumatological eschatology building on the huge potential of the pneumatological *imagination* which leads into a consequent eschatological imagination, as the Holy Spirit is the Spirit of the 'last days' and so the eschatological end is conceived as the future work of the Spirit."

Corneliu Constantineanu, Ph.D.
Professor of Pentecostal Theology, Aurel Vlaicu University of Arad, Romania

"This books stimulates much needed thought on eschatology within the AG and Pentecostal communities and be a blessing to both. Isgrigg combines thorough historical analysis with informed and insightful theological reflection. He writes clearly and with an irenic spirit. The result is a wonderful encouragement to the AG community to engage in much needed reflection on the contours, purpose, and impact of our eschatology."

Robert P. Menzies, Ph.D.
Director, Asia Center for Pentecostal Theology

"This fine and multi-layered study of American Assemblies of God shows how it has adjusted fundamental interpretations of its eschatology in the face of a changing world. This is a vigorous and expertly documented account that deserves to be widely read, not least because the church has a pressing need to revisit its expectations of humanity's future."

William K Kay, D.D.
Emeritus Professor, Wrexham Glyndwr University

"Isgrigg's meticulously researched and engagingly written monograph on eschatology in the Assemblies of God provides not only the first comprehensive historical and theological treatment of the development of AG eschatology throughout the movement's entire history, particularly as it relates to dispensationalism, but also makes the important theological contribution of an emphasis on *pneumatological imagination*, calling for both a *renewed focus on* and *hopeful expectation for* the Holy Spirit's work in eschatological signs. I highly recommend this book for ministers, scholars, and all who eagerly await the Blessed Hope."

Alicia R. Jackson, Ph.D.
Assistant Professor, Vanguard University

IMAGINING THE FUTURE

The Origin, Development, and Future
of Assemblies of God Eschatology

IMAGINING THE FUTURE

The Origin, Development, and Future
of Assemblies of God Eschatology

Daniel D. Isgrigg

ORU Press Monograph Series —1

ORU PRESS

Tulsa, Oklahoma USA

Copyright © 2021 Oral Roberts University Press

7777 S. Lewis Ave.
Tulsa, OK 74171 USA

ORU.edu/ORUPress

ORU Press is the book-and-journal publishing division of Oral Roberts University.

All rights reserved. No part of this publication may be reproduced, stored in a retrieval system, or transmitted in any form or by any means without the prior permission of the publisher. Brief quotation in book reviews and in scholarly publications is expected.

Cover design by Jiwon Kim
Design and Production Editor: Mark E. Roberts
Copy editor: Linda Gray

ISBN: 978-1-950971-08-4 (softcover)
ISBN: 978-1-950971-17-6 (ebook)

Printed in the United States of America

Contents

Preface ix

Part One: The Origins of Assemblies of God Eschatology

Chapter 1: The Soon Coming King 3
    The Emergence of Premillennialism 4
    The Priority of Eschatology 8
    The "Uneasy" Relationship with Dispensationalism 10
    The Development of a Doctrine 14

Chapter 2: The Landscape of Assemblies of God Eschatology 19
    Recognizing the Uneasy Tensions 19
    Critiquing Dispensational Eschatology 22
    Eschatology and Social Concern 27
    Revisioning Pentecostal Eschatology 29
    Alternative Readings of Revelation 35
    Conclusion 38

Chapter 3: The Statement of Fundamental Truths 41
    Early Doctrinal Statements 43
    The Origin of the Statement of Fundamental Truths 44
    1916 Eschatological Truths 49
    1927 Revision to the Eschatological Truths 53
    1961 Revision to the Eschatological Truths 59
    Condensed Statement of Fundamental Truths 62
    Statement of Faith in the Pentecostal Evangel 65
    World Assemblies of God Fellowship Statement of Faith 66

Chapter 4: Eschatological Controversies 69
    The Rapture and the Baptism 69
    The Scofield Reference Bible 71
    Disapproved Eschatological Errors 75

Committee on Eschatological Loopholes 79
The New Order of the Latter Rain 81
The Ecumenical Movement.. 83
The Secretary James G. Watt Controversy.. 85
Commission on Doctrinal Purity and Position Papers 87

Chapter 5: Analysis of Assemblies of God Eschatology 95
Official Inconsistencies.. 95
Shifting Emphasis from Images to Events... 96
Tribulational Diversity... 96
Hope as Resurrection 97
The Millennium and Israel 97
Dispensationalism 98

Part Two: The Development of Assemblies of God Eschatology

Chapter 6: Establishment Period (1914–1927) 101
Introduction to Popular Eschatology 101
Imminence of the Lord's Return.. 103
The Blessed Hope... 108
One Coming-Two Stages 111
The Tribulation 112
The Millennium: The Kingdom Come... 114
The Final Judgment 116
The Future of Creation 116
Eschatological Perspectives on Social Issues 118

Chapter 7: Scholastic Period (1927–1948) 125
Blessed Hope 126
The Spirit and the Script.. 128
The Rapture and the Tribulation 129
The Sign of the Jews... 131
The Millennium.. 132
Eschatological Perspectives on Social Issues 134

Chapter 8: Institutional Period (1948–1961) 137
Pentecost and Christ's Return 139

    The Jews and Israel 142
    Signs of the Tribulation 146
    The Millennial Answer.. 148

Chapter 9: Evangelical Period (1961–1985) 151
    Defending the Rapture.. 152
    Resurgence of the Spirit... 156
    Signs of the Times 159
    The Problem of Israel 161
    The Millennium... 162
    The New Creation 165

Chapter 10: Modern Period (1985–Present).. 167
    The Rapture 169
    Avoiding the Tribulation 171
    Escapism and Social Engagement 172
    The Kingdom Now and Not Yet 174

Chapter 11: Toward an Assemblies of God Eschatology.......................... 177
    A Pentecostal Eschatology 177
    Sign vs. Sigh Eschatology 181
    A Theology of Hope... 183
    Premillennialism... 184
    Modified Dispensationalism 187
    Transformationalist Eschatology 192

Part Three: The Future of Assemblies of God Eschatology

Chapter 12: Imagining the Future of Assemblies of God Eschatology ... 197
    The Crisis of Imagination 199
    The Pneumatological Imagination... 201
    The Eschatological Imagination... 204
    Images of the Spirit... 209

Chapter 13: Images of Hope: Toward a Pneumatological Eschatology .. 213
    The Spirit of Hope: Imagining Resurrection 215
    The Spirit of Peace: Imagining the Millennium 231

 The Spirit of Justice: Imagining the Final Judgment 249
 The Spirit of Life: Imagining the New Creation 257

Chapter 14: A Future for the Eschatological Fundamental Truths 265
 The Possibility of Eschatological Development 265
 Re-Imagining the Eschatological Truths 270
 The Future of the Blessed Hope 271
 The Future of the Millennial Reign 272
 The Future of the Final Judgment 273
 The Future of the New Heavens and New Earth 274

Chapter 15: Conclusion 277

Bibliography 281

Major Name and Subject Index 297

ABBREVIATIONS

Early Pentecostal Periodicals

AF	*The Apostolic Faith*
CE	*The Christian Evangel*
COGE	*The Church of God Evangel*
LRE	*The Latter Rain Evangel*
PE	*The Pentecostal Evangel*
PT	*The Pentecostal Testimony*
TP	*The Pentecost*
WE	*The Weekly Evangel*
WW	*The Word and Witness*

Other Publications

AG Heritage	*Assemblies of God Heritage*
AJPS	*Asian Journal of Pentecostal Studies*
CPT	*Centre for Pentecostal Theology*
DPCM	*Dictionary of Pentecostal and Charismatic Movements*
FPHC	*Flower Pentecostal Heritage Center (Springfield, MO)*
GC Minutes	*Minutes of the General Council of the Assemblies of God*
GP Minutes	*Minutes of the General Presbytery of the Assemblies of God*
JEPTA	*Journal of European Pentecostal Theology Association*
JPT	*Journal of Pentecostal Theology*
JPTSup	*Journal of Pentecostal Theology Supplement*
JSOTSup	*Journal of Study of Old Testament Supplement*
JSNTSup	*Journal of Study of New Testament Supplement*
NIDPCM	*The New International Dictionary of Pentecostal and Charismatic Movements*
Pneuma	*Pneuma: The Journal of the Society for Pentecostal Studies*
PTMS	*Princeton Theological Monograph Series*

Preface

Over twenty years ago, I was ordained as an Assemblies of God minister and focused my energies in the local church on teaching the Word of God. During my education at Oral Roberts University, I was grateful to be exposed to the richness of eschatology in the writings of Jürgen Moltmann and other theologians who gave great depth to my theology of the end times. This exposure also helped me examine some of my popularized end-times beliefs I gained from Pentecostal and Charismatic circles. As I reconsidered some of those beliefs, I longed for a deeper understanding of how eschatology functioned within Pentecostal theology. This quest made me more passionate about proclaiming Christ as the soon coming king.

The downside of this interest in eschatology is that it also frustrated me when I looked at the Assemblies of God Church. While the AG had eschatology as one of its four major theological pillars, I witnessed two extremes among my fellow AG ministers. On the one hand, there were those who continued the tradition of focusing on dispensational charts and trying to interpret current events. They seemed to fixate on the Rapture and speculative aspects such as the antichrist, but often seem to have no true theology of resurrection. This was troubling to me. I knew the church needed a deeper theological orientation and agreed with the growing number of Pentecostal scholars who were challenging us to re-examine our theological underpinnings. On the other hand, I also saw ministers who had grown weary of pop-eschatology and had become little more than agnostics about anything having to do with the return of Christ. These pastors simply avoided the topic altogether. This equally unfortunate that ministers avoid the very doctrine that Paul argued that if not true, it makes faith and our preaching useless. I just knew there had to be more to how the AG understood its eschatology. How could it be that, for a fellowship that placed such a large emphasis on eschatology, the only options were either obsession or avoidance?

This book is a revision of my Ph.D. dissertation completed in 2019 from Bangor University (Wales) through the Centre for Pentecostal Theology. My research was guided by a personal quest to accomplish two primary motivations. My first motivation was to discover where the AG's eschatological beliefs originated. I am someone who believes the Pentecostals have a unique theological approach to our beliefs centered in the Holy Spirit, which differentiates us from the large evangelical theological world. Because of this, I wanted to find out just how Pentecostal is AG eschatology. Did AG voices simply regurgitate evangelical positions? Or, was Pentecostal eschatology distinctly rooted in the Holy Spirit and reflective of the pneumatological orientation of this tradition? My second motivation was to cut through all the assumptions about what the AG believed and to see for myself what kind of eschatology we professed. Was it truly the type of speculation and escapism that I had perceived it to be? Was it just one failed prediction after another of world events? Or was it something else? It was these two questions that animated my reseach, not only for myself, but also for those ministers who had decided that the Second Coming was a topic that was expendable. Through this process, I let the AG voices speak for themselves and to my great delight I found what I was looking for. I discovered that my fellowship's eschatology was indeed oriented toward the type of hopeful expressions that I longed for rather than what I had seen on the Bible prophecy TV programs. I hope that this study will ignite a new passion within AG circles to see the important role that the Second Coming plays in our theology and will be stirred up to once again "love his coming."

    This book is dedicated to many people who helped me along this journey. To Amonda, Will, and Britian for sacrificing so much for me to accomplish this dream. You are my greatest joy. To my extended family for supporting me in countless ways. To my supervisors, William Kay and Chris Thomas for investing in me and guiding me on this journey. To my CPT colleagues for the encouraging conversations around the CPT table. To Darrin Rodgers and Glenn Gohr at the Flower Pentecostal Heritage Center for sharing your knowledge and passion for AG history. To my friends and colleagues Wonsuk Ma and Mark Roberts for allowing this to be the first ORU Press monograph. To Travis and Terry for being my best friends and always believing in me. To my friends Peter and Rick for sharing this journey with me as friends and fellow AG Ph.D. graduates. To the men and women of the Assemblies of God, I pray this study honors the past, encourages the present, and shapes the future.

PART ONE:

THE ORIGINS OF ASSEMBLIES OF GOD ESCHATOLOGY

1

THE SOON COMING KING

The subject of this study is the Assemblies of God-USA (AG). Formed on April 6, 1914, three hundred Pentecostal ministers and laypeople gathered in Hot Springs, Arkansas, for what would become the first General Council of the Assemblies of God.[1] The intention was not to organize a new denomination or religious sect, but to promote unity and cooperation within the Pentecostal movement.[2] They believed that the Pentecostal movement would be more effective if they were to cooperate in unity according to basic scriptural doctrine and methods.[3] For this Pentecostal group, their unity would be found in two basic tenets: the baptism in the Holy Spirit and the soon coming of Jesus. As the preamble of the constitution declares,

> For a number of years, God has been leading men to seek for a full apostolic gospel standard of experience and doctrine. . . . Almost every city and community in civilization has heard of the Latter Rain outpouring of the Holy Ghost, with many signs following. . . . Almost every country on the globe has heard the message and also the prophecy which has been predominant in this great outpouring, which is "Jesus is coming soon" to this old world in the same manner as he left it to set up His millennial kingdom and to reign over the earth in righteousness and peace for a thousand years.[4]

---

[1] *GC Minutes* (April 2–12, 1914), 1. This study concerns itself primarily with the AG in the USA, acknowledging that the World Assemblies of God Fellowship is much broader and diverse in nature.

[2] The stated purpose was fivefold: unity in message through biblical doctrine, unity in ministry through cooperation, unity in missions through organization, unity in legal matters through ministerial credentials, and unity in ministerial training through Bible schools and publishing. See *WW,* December 20, 1913, 1; *GC Minutes* (April 2–7, 1914), 4; *WW,* January 20, 1914, 4.

[3] *GC Minutes* (April 2–7, 1914), 4, declared their intention to organize around "scriptural methods and order for worship, unity, fellowship, work and business for God, and to disapprove of all unscriptural methods, doctrines and conduct and approve of all Scriptural truth and conduct, endeavoring to come into the unity of faith."

[4] *GC Minutes* (April 2–12, 1914), 1.

This early declaration articulates the way the founders valued unity in pneumatology and eschatology. As a result, the baptism in the Holy Spirit and premillennialism have been perhaps the most important doctrines of the denomination.[5] While "initial evidence" of speaking in tongues is the AG's most recognized doctrine, many scholars overlook the eschatological orientation of AG theology.[6] Yet, for over a century the Statement of Fundamental Truths, the AG's primary doctrinal statement, has devoted one quarter of its sixteen doctrinal tenets to the articulation of premillennial eschatology. This study will explore the history of the Second Coming and its importance within AG theology.

The Emergence of Premillennialism

The origins of Pentecostal commitments to eschatology reach back to the last half of the nineteenth century, when Protestant churches experienced a great awakening through the rediscovery of the Holy Spirit and an emphasis on the Second Coming of Jesus.[7] Across the evangelical theological spectrum, a restorationist emphasis on the sanctifying and empowering operations of the Holy Spirit was thrust into the forefront of theological imagination.[8] John Wesley's doctrine of sanctification shaped his eschatological beliefs, convincing him of the Holy Spirit's potential to reform culture through the power of the gospel. For Wesley, perfectionism flowed naturally toward postmillennial eschatology as believers worked to purify society through Christian social activism.[9] Coinciding with this pneumatological shift, evangelicals rediscovered the doctrine of the Second Coming of Christ and the subject of biblical prophecy.[10] Beginning in 1826, Henry Drummond hosted a yearly "Conference for the Study of Prophecy" at Albury Court in England for the

---

[5] Edith Blumhofer, *Restoring the Faith* (Urbana: University of Illinois Press, 1993), 270–71.

[6] For a discussion of the importance of the concept of initial evidence of the baptism in the Holy Spirit see, Gary B. McGee , ed., *Initial Evidence* (Eugene: Wipf & Stock, 1991).

[7] D. W. Faupel, *The Everlasting Gospel* (Sheffield: Sheffield Academic Press, 1996), 58n51.

[8] Vinson Synan, *The Holiness-Pentecostal Tradition* (Grand Rapids: Eerdmans, 1997).

[9] Donald W. Dayton, "Pentecostal Studies," *From The Margins: A Celebration of the Theological Work of Donald W. Dayton* in Christian T. Collins Winn ed., (Eugene: Pickwick Publishing, 2007), 171. Dayton sees Wesleyan perfectionism worked out socially as postmillennial eschatology as believers worked to purify society through Christian activism.

[10] Peter Prosser, *Dispensationalist Eschatology and Its Influence on American and British Religious Movements* (Lewiston: Edwin Mellen Press, 1999).

purpose of comparing eschatological views.[11] Interest in the subject of biblical prophecy shifted away from Wesley's postmillennial cultural optimism and toward premillennial pessimism.[12] Two key concepts emerged from Drummond's Albury Conferences that would contribute decisively to the shift towards premillennialism. First, attendees debated whether the condition of the world would get better or worse before Jesus' return. Drummond believed, based on the prophetic words of Jesus that the present age will end in a time of judgment upon Christendom in anticipation of the restoration of the Jews in the millennium.[13] Drummond and his fellow speaker Edward Irving taught that God would restore the true church at the end of the Church age or "dispensation" in anticipation of the Second Coming.[14] Included in this restorationist vision was the belief that "the latter rain" outpouring of the Spirit would restore the gifts of the Spirit prior to Christ's coming, including speaking in tongues.[15] One of Irving's followers testified of having a vision in which the Lord revealed to her that there would be a "secret rapture" of an exclusive group of believers prior to Christ's return to earth.[16]

[11] William K. Kay, *Pentecostalism* (London: SCM Press, 2009), 38, believes historians mistakenly point to the pessimistic view of humanity that resulted from the Civil War as the important pivot point from postmillennialism to premillennialism.

[12] Prosser, *Dispensationalist Eschatology*, 116.

[13] Henry Drummond, *A Defense of the Students of Prophecy in Answer to the Attack of the Rev. Dr. Hamilton* (London: James Nisbet, 1828), 124–25. Drummond's dispensationalism did not divide all of history, but he did emphasize that the dispensation would close with judgments on Christendom, the return of the Jewish nation, and the return of Christ to sit on his millennial throne. See also Prosser, *Dispensational Eschatology*, 137.

[14] Prosser, *Dispensationalist Eschatology*, 134–39, notes that Irving came to this conclusion after translating Manuel Lacunza, *The Coming of Messiah in Glory* (1811) from Spanish to English. The language of "dispensations" was not new to Drummond. Arnold D. Ehlert, *A Bibliographic History of Dispensationalism* (Grand Rapids: Baker, 1965), notes that Clement of Alexandria, Pelagius, Augustine, Joachim of Fiore, Jonathan Edwards, Isaac Watts, and Adam Clarke all used the language of dispensations.

[15] Donald Dayton, "From Christian Perfection to the 'Baptism of the Holy Ghost'", in Vinson Synan, ed. *Aspects of Pentecostal-Charismatic Origins* (Plainfield: Logos, 1975), 41–52. It was at Albury that Irving led attendees to pray for the latter rain the charismatic manifestations that followed led Irving to declare, "This outpouring of the Spirit, is known in scripture by 'the latter rain,' of which I deem the religious revivals of the last thirty years to be as the first droppings of the shower." Edward Irving, "Translator's Preliminary Discourse," in Juan Josafat Ben-Ezra, *The Coming of Messiah in Glory and Majesty*, translated by Edward Irving (London: L.B. Seeley and Son, 1827), v.

[16] Dave MacPherson, *The Incredible Coverup* (Plainsfield: Logos, 1975), has argued that it was one of Edward Irving's followers, Margaret Macdonald, who reportedly testified at Albury to having a vision in which the Lord revealed to her that there will be a two-phase coming of Christ in which the first phase will be a "secret rapture." However, as Paul Richard Wilkinson, *For Zion's Sake: Christian*

Believers were encouraged to be sanctified through the "baptism in the Spirit" in order to be qualified for inclusion in the bride of Christ.[17] This led to a greater emphasis on believers being prepared for Christ's coming.

One of the attendees at the Albury Conference was John Nelson Darby, a disgruntled Anglican minister who adopted three concepts from Drummond that became the hallmarks of his dispensational form of premillennialism. Darby's prophetic teachings divided time into "dispensations" terminated by a period of judgment, the restoration of national Israel in anticipation of the Second Coming of Jesus to reign on earth, and the concept of the two-phase coming of Christ that includes a secret rapture of the church before the tribulation.[18] Unlike Irving, Darby excluded restorationist aspects of the Holy Spirit from his dispensational concepts, leaning toward a cessationist paradigm.[19] Although Darby was never universally accepted, his concept of the pretribulation rapture was popularized in prophetic periodicals and was taught in prophecy conferences.[20] Many of these ideas entered the mainstream, particularly in America, through popular evangelical works such as William E. Blackstone's famous *Jesus is Coming* in 1878 and later the *Scofield Reference Bible* in 1910.[21] By the beginning of the twentieth century, the doctrine of the "Soon Coming King" had become one of the four pillars of American evangelical theology.[22]

Zionism and the Role of John Nelson Darby (Milton Keynes: Paternoster, 2007), 197, points out, some scholars dispute MacPherson's conclusions. Wilkinson documents that although Macdonald does not use the term "rapture," she does declare that believers must be filled with the Spirit in order to enter into the marriage supper of the Lamb" (262–65).

[17] Joseph A. Seiss, *The Parable of the Ten Virgins* (Philadelphia: Smith, English, 1862), popularized the connection between the Holy Spirit and the rapture in the concept of the bride. He based his teaching on the parable of the virgins where only those with "oil" in their lamps will be taken by the bridegroom to the marriage supper of the Lamb.

[18] Wilkinson, *For Zion's Sake*, 179–80, and Prosser, *Dispensational Eschatology*, 137, both attribute the term "dispensationalism" to Drummond.

[19] Wilkinson, *For Zion's Sake*, 192–97.

[20] Although Darby's views were among those discussed in the prophecy conferences, Darby's pretribulation rapture position was not widely accepted until the publication of the *Scofield Reference Bible* in 1910. Larry V. Crutchfield, *The Origins of Dispensationalism: The Darby Factor* (Lanham: University Press of America, 1992).

[21] Wilkinson, *For Zion's Sake*, 252–57.

[22] Bernie A. Van De Walle, *The Heart of the Gospel: A. B. Simpson, the Fourfold Gospel, and Late Nineteenth Century Evangelical Theology* (Eugene: Pickwick Publishing, 2009), 221–22, notes that Simpson, and many of his contemporaries such as D. L. Moody, A. J. Gordon, and A. T. Pierson, "were at once inconsistent historicists and inconsistent dispensationalists." Scott M. Gibson, *A. J. Gordon, American Premillennialist* (Lanham, MD: University Press of America, 2001), 33, shows how

This four-fold gospel, (Jesus as Savior, Sanctifier, Healer, and Soon Coming King), with the additional element of Pentecostal Spirit-baptism, became the heart of Pentecostal theology.[23]

The shift from postmillennialism to premillennialism had a cascade of effects on the way evangelicals understood Christ's coming. First, it reversed the order of the millennium and Christ's return. For postmillennialists, the kingdom is established on earth through the Church in preparation for the coming of Christ. In premillennialism, the Second Coming of Christ could be at "any moment" and the kingdom is expected in the future millennium. This shift in the timeline led to a second shift about the future and humanity's ability to affect change from optimism to pessimism.[24] Holiness revival preachers, like Jonathan Edwards, preached a postmillennial gospel of endless progress and believed that the church would usher in a golden age of missionary success and general societal progress.[25] Premillennialists, on the other hand, had a fatalistic view of the future and lost all confidence in humanity's ability to affect lasting change in a world that was ultimately doomed.[26] Prosser comments, "Dispensationalists became a self-fulfilling prophecy. In not looking for change, except for the worse, everything around them and among them would naturally tend to get worse."[27]

The third shift that took place was the shift from social engagement to an expectation of apocalyptic salvation. This "great reversal" from working to expecting was the result of emphasizing the immediacy of Christ's coming, which left little time for social reform.[28] For most of the nineteenth-century, evangelicals worked for the reversal of societal ills such as poverty, slavery, rights of women and public welfare.[29] With the shift to premillennialism, Christian activism was replaced with missionary activity, as Christians were no longer

---

A. J. Gordon was a historic premillennialist who for a short time accepted dispensationalism but later abandoned it.

[23] Donald Dayton, *Theological Roots of Pentecostalism* (Peabody: Hendrickson Publishers, 1987), 21–22; John Christopher Thomas, "Pentecostal Theology in the Twenty-First Century," *Pneuma* 20, no 1 (Spring 1998): 3–19.

[24] Prosser, *Dispensational Eschatology*, 170–71.

[25] Marsden, *Fundamentalism and American Culture*, 48–49; Kay, *Pentecostalism*, 36–37.

[26] Prosser, *Dispensational Eschatology*, 133.

[27] Prosser, *Dispensational Eschatology*, 152.

[28] Prosser, *Dispensational Eschatology*, 157.

[29] Donald W. Dayton, *Discovering an Evangelical Heritage* (New York: Harper & Row, 1976), 121–29.

trying to save society; they were focusing on saving as many souls as they could before Jesus returns.[30]

The great reversal not only changed the doctrinal stance of evangelicals; it changed the very character of the movement and set it on a course toward Fundamentalism.[31] Fundamentalism began as an intellectual reaction among evangelicals to the rise of modernistic liberalism among Protestants during the turn of the nineteenth century. The fundamentalist movement was not only a move toward restoring orthodoxy; it was also a shift away from the revivalistic character and pneumatological orientation of the late nineteenth-century.[32] Eventually, fundamentalists narrowed the boundaries of accepted biblical orthodoxy to the point that, by the 1920s, the Holiness and Pentecostal movements became targets of their critique.[33] Although some Pentecostals saw themselves essentially as Spirit-filled fundamentalists, the fundamentalists declared Pentecostalism to be a "menace" to the church because of their view of tongues and healing[34] Despite this rejection by fundamentalists and the theological differences, much of the Pentecostal movement adopted the eschatological paradigm of dispensational premillennialism.

The Priority of Eschatology

Recent studies of Pentecostal origins have demonstrated that eschatology and pneumatology were inexorably connected in the historical development of Pentecostal theology. Eschatology had such a dominant place in early Pentecostal thought that Robert Anderson commented, "in the early years at least, speaking in tongues and healing were subordinate elements."[35] William Faupel agrees with Anderson and has argued that eschatology was the central concern of the

---

[30] Dayton, "Pentecostal Studies," 170–71.

[31] Ernest R. Sandeen, *The Roots of Fundamentalism: British and American Millenarianism* (Chicago: University of Chicago Press, 1970).

[32] Dayton, *Discovering an Evangelical Heritage*, 130–31.

[33] Russell Spittler, "Are Pentecostals and Charismatics Fundamentalists," in Karla Poewe, ed., *Charismatic Christianity as a Global Culture* (Columbia: University of South Carolina Press, 1994), 108–10.

[34] Daniel D. Isgrigg, "The Pentecostal Evangelical Church: The Theological Self-identity of the Assemblies of God as Evangelical 'Plus,'" a paper presented at the 46th Meeting of the Society for Pentecostal Studies (March 9–11, 2017). See also, Gerald W. King, *Disfellowshipped: Pentecostal Responses to Fundamentalism in the United States 1906–1943* (Eugene OR: Pickwick Publishing, 2011).

[35] R. M. Anderson *Vision of the Disinherited* (New York: Oxford University Press, 1979), 80–81.

Pentecostal message.[36] The phenomenon of speaking in tongues, which accompanied the Pentecostal baptism in the Spirit, was seen as an eschatological sign of the end. They believed that the Holy Spirit was being poured out because they were in the last days.[37] Therefore, the pneumatological orientation of Pentecostalism, which is its most recognized characteristic, was firmly grounded in the eschatological realities they embraced.

The most dominant eschatological metaphor in the Pentecostal metanarrative was the restorationist concept of the "latter rain."[38] As the outpouring of the Holy Spirit began in the Azusa Street mission in Los Angeles, William Seymour declared in the October 1906 *Apostolic Faith*: "The Pentecostal Baptism Restored: the Promised Latter Rain Now Being Poured Out on God's Humble People."[39] Drawing on the analogy of the rain cycles in Israel, the latter rain concept was the expectation that prior to the Second Coming, God would send an outpouring of Pentecostal power to prepare a bride for his coming and empower an end-time harvest of souls.[40] The latter rain concept was a philosophy of history that explained the phenomenon of restoration of apostolic Christianity with signs following found in the Pentecostal movement. Early Pentecostal literature was also filled with bridal language because of its corresponding connection to the Spirit.[41] Pentecostals fused the eschatological concept of the Bridegroom coming for the bride with the pneumatological concept of baptism in the Spirit.[42] For many early Pentecostals, the baptism in the Spirit served as

---

[36] Faupel, *The Everlasting Gospel*, 20, recognizes four labels given by early leaders that describe the Pentecostal message: the Full Gospel, the Latter Rain, the Apostolic Faith, and the Pentecostal Movement.

[37] Kay, *Pentecostalism*, 246–47, remarks, "If Pentecostals were asked how they knew they stood where they did in God's calendar, they would have answered that the outpouring of the Spirit on the original day of Pentecostal was paralleled by the outpouring of the Spirit at the end of the dispensation." Tongues, then, became a sign of the end and not a separate doctrinal tenant.

[38] Daniel D. Isgrigg, "The Latter Rain Revisited: Exploring the Origins of the Central Metaphor in Pentecostalism," *Pneuma* 41, no. 3–4 (2019): 439–57.

[39] *AF*, October 1906, 1.

[40] D. W. Myland, "Latter Rain Covenant," *LRE*, June 1909, 15–22, comments, "For just as the literal early and latter rain was poured out upon Palestine, so upon the church of the First Century was poured out the spiritual early rain, and upon us today is being poured out the spiritual latter rain." See also, D. W. Myland, "Latter Rain Covenant Part Two," *LRE*, July 1909, 2–4.

[41] Faupel, *The Everlasting Gospel*, 26–27. Pentecostals often used the imagery from Matthew 25 of the ten virgins who waited with oil in their lamps for the bridegroom to arrive.

[42] Dale M. Coulter, "The Spirit and the Bride Revisited: Pentecostalism, Renewal, and the Sense of History," *JPT* 21 (2012): 301.

the seal that identified the members of the bride who are prepared for the rapture.[43]

Across most Pentecostal denominations, eschatology became a central tenet of the Pentecostal message. Pentecostals produced books, magazine articles, and dispensational charts articulating a vision of the future that was shaped by the premillennialist and dispensationalist vision inherited from their evangelical forbearers. The Assemblies of God was no different. Not only was one fourth of the statement of faith committed to eschatology, but some of its first books included *The Budding Fig Tree* (1925) by Frank Boyd, *Little Flock in the Last Days* (1927) by Alice Luce, and *Things Which Must Shortly Come to Pass* (1928) by Stanley Frodsham. Each of these books seemingly espoused a common view of the future shared with most evangelical and fundamentalist works of that time. For many, there is essentially little difference between the eschatology of Scofield and those who are Spirit-filled. It is this assumption that has the attention of many scholars.

An "Uneasy" Relationship with Eschatology

In recent decades, a segment of AG ministers and educators began re-examining the theological underpinnings of AG eschatology.[44] Long held expressions of eschatology within Pentecostal circles are losing popularity, particularly the long relationship with dispensational premillennialism.[45] William Menzies recognizes that the AG has often displayed "unevenness in eschatological emphasis" throughout the years. He comments, "In most recent years, there has been a tendency to emphasize the coming of Christ, and the cataclysmic judgment of the present order, but without depending so heavily on dispensational categories."[46] Scholars who have studied Pentecostal eschatology are questioning the adoption of dispensational forms of premillennialism because of the inherent incompatibility with Pentecostal theology. In a seminal article, former AG minister, Gerald Sheppard was the first to recognize that there are tensions that exist within

---

[43] *AF*, December 1906, 2, testifies "when we are baptized with the Holy Spirit we are sealed in the forehead until his coming. See also *AF*, February 1907, 1.

[44] Blumhofer, *Restoring the Faith*, 253.

[45] Larry D. McQueen, *Toward a Pentecostal Eschatology* (Blandford Forum, UK: Deo Publishing, 2012), 2, observes, "In recent years, this tension has increased, both in the academy and in the local church, as younger scholars have abandoned dispensational view with few resources to help replace it, and as sermons about the second coming of Jesus, not to mention the millennial reign, have become the exception."

[46] Menzies, *Anointed to Serve*, 329.

Pentecostal theology by the adoption of evangelical approaches to eschatology and hermeneutics.[47] Sheppard argued that fundamentalist dispensationalism is theologically incompatible with the earliest expressions of Pentecostal eschatology, which has created "uneasy" tensions that undermine Pentecostal theology. These tensions led him to question the rationale for the theological alliance between Pentecostalism and the Fundamentalists who have so vehemently rejected the movement. Sheppard is not alone, as other Pentecostal scholars have joined their voices to his critiques.

Matthew Thompson identifies three major ways that Pentecostal eschatology differs from the dispensationalism that was adopted by Pentecostals.[48] First, though Pentecostals were dispensationalists, they were not rigid in their categories like fundamentalist dispensationalists. Dispensationalists typically divide history into seven ages or dispensations: Innocence, Conscience, Human Government, Promise, Mosaic Law, Grace, and the Kingdom of God.[49] Instead, he argues many early Pentecostals used a three-fold dispensational model in which the church age represents the age of the Spirit. Second, whereas dispensationalists teach that the OT promises about the outpouring of the Spirit in Joel 2 will be upon future Israel, not the Church, which undermines Pentecostal claims about the baptism in the Spirit. Dispensationalists also relegate the kingdom entirely to the millennium, whereas Pentecostals believe the kingdom of God is, in some sense, present now through the demonstration of the Spirit. The third difference is related to the previous two in that the dispensational system separates the Jew and the Gentile under different dispensational covenants. These ecclesiastical and hermeneutical incompatibilities suggest to Thompson that uncritically adopting dispensationalism, at least the model popularized by C. I. Scofield, is has been detrimental to the distinctives of Pentecostal theology and its missional praxis.[50]

---

[47] Gerald T. Sheppard, "Pentecostals and the Hermeneutics of Dispensationalism: The anatomy of an uneasy relationship," *Pneuma* 6, no. 2 (Fall, 1984): 5–33. Sheppard's study has been recognized by nearly all Pentecostal scholars as an important starting point for questioning the adoption of fundamentalist dispensational eschatology.

[48] Matthew K. Thompson, *Kingdom Come: Revisioning Pentecostal Eschatology* (Dorsett, UK: Deo Publishing, 2010).

[49] C. I. Scofield, ed., *The Scofield Reference Bible* (New York: Oxford University Press, 1909), 5; John A. Bertone, "Seven Dispensations or Two-Age View of History," in Peter Althouse and Robby Waddell, eds., *Perspectives in Pentecostal Eschatologies*, 63. Crutchfield, *The Origins of Dispensationalism*, 206, argues Darby's concept of dispensations varied from Scofield's and that Scofield "took his dispensational diadem, melted it down and cast it as something quite different from the original."

[50] Thompson, *Kingdom Come*, 43–58, argues, "The adoption of Darby's and Scofield's system has generated theological confusion and awkwardness in discourse and has hamstrung Pentecostal

Just how committed to dispensational eschatology is the AG? Larry McQueen's study of early Pentecostal periodicals has demonstrated that classical dispensationalism was the only model articulated in the *Pentecostal Evangel* during the first five years of the AG.[51] He argues that from 1914–1920 AG writers followed the "standard dispensational script" without deviation.[52] McQueen also observes that the AG's Pentecostal spirituality was not a factor in shaping their core eschatological commitments.[53] When the Holy Spirit did play a role, it was usually as a means of illuminating and articulating the dispensational script rather than empowering them to transcend it.[54] As a major representative of the "finished work stream" of Pentecostalism, the AG was more inclined to adopt a rigid view of the future that did not encourage diversity in eschatological views.[55] Even when variant views were allowed, the editors carefully qualified the aspects that did not reflect the accepted position in order to ensure unity.[56]

The assessment that the AG uncritically adopted dispensational premillennialism is a source of concern for many AG scholars. In fact, a large

mission, social activism, and spiritual experience." He even suggests that dispensationalism has displaced the emphasis on the Spirit in the AG and has led to the diminishment of emphasis on Pentecostal distinctives of baptism in the Spirit and speaking in tongues. However, Thompson assumes too much of this causality.

[51] McQueen, *Toward a Pentecostal Eschatology*, 178, 198–99, 202.

[52] McQueen, *Toward a Pentecostal Eschatology*, 172. The "dispensational script" includes the secret rapture of all true believers which allows the church to escape the tribulation; the church is separated from Israel; the Jews will return to Palestine in anticipation of the tribulation when the temple is rebuilt; the Antichrist will arise during the tribulation and make a covenant with Israel, which will be a prelude to Armageddon; Christ will return at the end of the tribulation and destroy the Antichrist and Israel will come to faith; Christ will set up a millennial Jewish kingdom from Jerusalem and will rule the nations; the millennium will end with the doom of Satan and the judgment of nations to be followed by the new heavens and new earth. McQueen's assertion that the script is "without deviation" will be tested in a future chapter.

[53] McQueen, *Toward a Pentecostal Eschatology*, 150.

[54] McQueen, *Toward a Pentecostal Eschatology*, 178.

[55] McQueen, *Toward a Pentecostal Eschatology*, 141–42. Kay, *Pentecostalism*, 32, argues that two theological streams within evangelicalism were present prior to the Pentecostal movement. John Wesley, John Fletcher, and Phoebe Palmer were the theological forbearers of Holiness Pentecostalism and Charles Finney, A.J. Gordon and A. B. Simpson were the theological forbearers of the Keswick theology that became the Finished Work tradition.

[56] A good example of this is an editorial following an article by Elizabeth Sisson in which she offered a view on the resurrection in which the dead in Christ will not be resurrected until the end. While E. N. Bell admitted that they did not agree with Sisson on this point, they respected her and valued the other ideas in the article. Still, Bell corrected her view by saying, "we see the resurrection differently." *PE*, April 20, 1918, 4.

number of AG scholars who have written on eschatology have agreed with Sheppard that fundamentalist dispensationalism has stifled the pneumatological development of eschatological doctrine.[57] As a result, alternative models that are more reflective of Pentecostal commitments have been proposed.[58]

Questions about the AG's commitment to dispensational eschatology are not just limited to AG scholars. In 1993, Edith Blumhofer found that many younger ministers who received theological training outside the denominational schools were less likely to accept dispensational expressions of eschatology.[59] In 2010, Margaret Poloma and John Green studied the level of adherence among AG ministers on several positions of orthodoxy.[60] When it comes to positions on premillennialism, AG ministers score higher than clergy in most evangelical denominations, including the denominations most associated with Fundamentalism.[61] They found that 94% of AG ministers agree or strongly agree that the Bible clearly teaches a "premillennial" view of the future and 98% reported believing in the imminent "rapture" of the church.[62] However, when pressed further on the beliefs about the rapture, they found "58 percent reported accepting a dispensationalist interpretation of Scripture, 42 percent rejected this approach."[63] What Poloma and Green have recognized is that many pastors are fully committed to the AG doctrine of premillennial coming or "rapture," but are not as comfortable with the dispensational categories in which they have been expressed. Although eschatology books were some of the first doctrinal works published by the Gospel Publishing House (GPH), in recent years the number and variety of works dealing with this doctrine has diminished. Since 1975, only

---

[57] The list of scholars who have ties to the AG who have commented on such tensions will be discussed in Chapter 2.

[58] A good summary of these approaches can be found in Peter Althouse's, "Pentecostal Eschatology in Context," in Peter Althouse and Robbie Waddell, eds., *Perspectives in Pentecostal Eschatologies* (Eugene: Pickwick Publishing, 2010), 205–31.

[59] Blumhofer, *Restoring the Faith*, 270–71.

[60] Margaret Poloma and John Green, *The Assemblies of God: Godly Love and the Revitalization of American Pentecostalism* (New York: New York University Press, 2010).

[61] Poloma and Green, *The Assemblies of God*, 82.

[62] Poloma and Green, *The Assemblies of God*, 82. It should be noted that the high level of adherence could be the result of the requirement of the fellowship to adhere to the doctrine or the lack of ministers who hold such dissenting views being able to stay in the fellowship.

[63] Poloma and Green, *The Assemblies of God*, 82.

seven books on eschatology have been published by GPH.[64] The last scholarly eschatological book published by GPH was *Our Destiny: Biblical Teachings on Last Things* by Stanley Horton in 1996.[65] The lack of volumes published in this modern era by the AG suggests that eschatology is not only failing to develop, but it has also fallen into a period of neglect.

The fact that a vast number of AG scholars are studying eschatology, coupled with the lack of eschatological works within the AG, suggests that an eschatological shift is taking place in AG theology. The apparent disconnect between AG scholarship, its minsters, and the denominational structure suggests that the time for doctrinal development has arrived. The theological academy has applied itself to offering suggestions for ways eschatology in the AG could be re-visioned, but at some point, these suggestions need to be implemented at the doctrinal level in order to influence the local church, pastors, and adherents in the fellowship.[66] If dispensational premillennialism is indeed problematic for Pentecostal theology, then alternatives should be considered. However, before those conclusions can be made, a comprehensive study of AG eschatology is needed in order to test the conclusions of Sheppard, McQueen and others by using a larger volume of primary sources. By expanding McQueen's study to include the entire twentieth century, this study will reveal the ways in which AG eschatology needs to develop as the fellowship enters a new century.

The Development of a Doctrine

This study will explore the development of the AG's eschatological doctrinal positions. The goal is to explain how AG eschatology originated and developed over the last century. In order to do this, the history of AG positions will be

---

[64] Of the seven books, only two were by authors other than Stanley Horton. Without Horton's contributions, the AG would be without a book on the second coming of Christ for the past three decades.

[65] Stanley M. Horton, *Our Destiny: Biblical Teachings on Last Things* (Springfield: Gospel Publishing House, 1996).

[66] One challenge to this concept is that denominational officials often see theologians as merely agents of transmission of dogma rather than serving to explore and challenge the theological concepts that have been historically present. As Richard Dresselhaus suggests, "The work of the academy must be guided by theological and ecclesiological parameters already set in place by church dogma and tradition." Richard Dresslehaus, "What Can The Academy Do For The Church," *AJPS* 3, no. 2 (2000): 319–23.

analyzed through the methodology of doctrinal criticism.[67] Doctrine is more than just a truth statement; it has a historical location in which it developed. For Alister McGrath, doctrinal criticism can be used to identify "what specific theological insights lie behind specific doctrinal formulation, and what specific historical contingencies influenced both those insights and the manner in which they were thus articulated."[68] Doctrinal criticism not only identifies what a theological community believes, but also seeks to understand the historical, cultural, and institutional factors that shaped its expression. As Richard Heyduck points out, doctrine is a speech act of the church and the grammar by which it communicates its beliefs.[69] Doctrine provides a theological community with a theological identity that defines their place in the Christian metanarrative and articulates their particular experience of God. In this way, doctrinal expressions define the community by what it believes, but also defines its beliefs by the community.[70] This is why George Lindbeck refers to doctrine as a "cultural linguistic" or expression of theological identity.[71] In this case, the question at hand is how did the AG maintain its pneumatological commitments while at the same time hold to dispensational views that had potential to undermine its theology? Or stated another way, was AG eschatology distinctly Pentecostal in orientation or simply an uncritical adoption of evangelical eschatology?

Because AG doctrine acts as a speech act that communicates the identity of the fellowship, the sources selected for a proper "hearing" of doctrine are crucial. Therefore, this study will "listen" to four primary AG voices, each representing a different place within the larger community. The first will be the voice of the Pentecostal academy that will express the landscape of AG eschatology. Focusing on AG scholars who discuss AG eschatology, these voices will help to establish the landscape of attitudes toward AG eschatology that will identify the core commitments and possible weaknesses of these positions. This hearing will establish the baseline of questions that will be asked in the chapters that follow.

---

[67] Alister E. McGrath, *The Genesis of Doctrine: A Study in the Foundation of Doctrinal Criticism* (Grand Rapids: Eerdmans, 1997), 37. Alister McGrath proposes that there are four functions of doctrinal criticism: social demarcation, narrative, interpretation of experience, and truth claim. Each of these functions provides the means in which a doctrine functions within a particular theological community.

[68] McGrath, *The Genesis of Doctrine*, 8.

[69] Richard Heyduck, *The Recovery of Doctrine in the Contemporary Church: An Essay in Philosophical Ecclesiology* (Waco: Baylor University Press, 2002), 67.

[70] McGrath, *The Genesis of Doctrine*, 37–52.

[71] George Lindbeck, *The Nature of Doctrine* (Philadelphia: Westminster Press, 1984), 30–42.

Next, the official voice of AG eschatology will be expressed through the *Statement of Fundamental Truths* (*STF*), the statement of that has represented the accepted rule of faith for AG ministers and churches since 1916.[72] The "truth claims" in the *STF* concerning eschatology act essentially as the official dogma of the fellowship and are considered the authorized voice of the fellowship.[73] That said, since the AG is a "cooperative fellowship" in which all ministers represent the corporate body, what is truly official in the AG is not that which is determined by the magisterium, rather what is approved by the actions of the General Council.[74] The task of hearing these official statements and tracing the changes in how they have been expressed at key turning points in the denomination's history will be taken up in the chapters that follow.

In Part Two, the voice of AG ministers will be expressed through a reception history of popular expressions of these doctrines in *The Pentecostal Evangel,* which is the official organ of the AG.[75] For over a century, AG beliefs have been communicated to the fellowship through articles and testimonies on a weekly basis. Unlike academic theology, periodical literature allows ideas from across sociological, ecclesiological, and geographical locations to be expressed in ways that reflect the breadth of theological commitments within the community. By surveying a century of voices expressed in the pages of the *Evangel,* this study will give voice to individuals "on the margins" and explore the diversity of expressions of common individuals within the movement.[76] Through hearing eschatological

---

[72] The *Statement of Fundamental Truths* will be referred to as *STF* from here following when a shorter designation is warranted.

[73] McGrath, *The Genesis of Doctrine*, 9, defines dogma as "that which is declared by the church to be revealed truth as a part of the universal teaching, or thought a solemn doctrinal judgment."

[74] The principles of cooperative fellowship include voluntary cooperation of ministers, sovereign local assemblies and a Presbyterian form of leadership elected by members of the General Council. For a discussion of AG polity see Margaret M. Poloma, *Assemblies of God at the Crossroads* (Knoxville: University of Tennessee Press, 1989), 123–26; J. R. Flower, "Centralization - No! Never!," *PE*, January 30, 1915, 1; E. N. Bell, "Fostering the Spirit of Co-operation and Fellowship," *PE*, March 13, 1915, 3; A. P. Collins, "Co-operation in Fact," *PE*, November 15, 1919, 3.

[75] Reception history is a methodological approach to understanding how scripture or doctrine is received by interpreters within a particular community. See Daniel D. Isgrigg, Martin W. Mittelstadt, and Rich Wadholm, Jr., eds., *Receiving Scripture in the Pentecostal Tradition* (Cleveland, TN: CPT Press, 2020).

[76] The reception history approach of listening to the testimony of regular Pentecostal believers and how they received Scriptural texts and doctrines as expressed in periodical literature has been established by several recent studies of Pentecostal theology. See K. E. Alexander, *Pentecostal Healing: Models in Theology and Practice* (Blandford Forum: Deo Publishing, 2006) and McQueen, *Toward a Pentecostal Eschatology.*

voices expressed in the periodical literature, the narratives that framed AG eschatology can be accessed and the cultural factors led to the changing of this narrative can be identified.[77] To aid in organizing the reception history of these expressions, the primary sources will be analyzed through five periods of doctrinal development: Formative Period (1914–1926), Scholastic Period (1927–1950), Institutional Period (1950–1961), Evangelical Period (1961–1985), Modern Period (1985–Present).[78] Each period will be marked by certain turning points, or strategic moments, within the history of a particular cultural narrative, that have contributed to the articulation of certain eschatological emphases.[79] By accessing the nuanced expressions through each period of development, the true heart of AG eschatology will be revealed. Through comparing official doctrine with popular expressions, a narrative will emerge that identifies the unique doctrinal commitments, reveals the points of departure from the core narrative, and defines the various aspects that are believed, but are underdeveloped.

The final section of the book will be an attempt to draw from the AG's "own wells" in order to imagine the future of AG eschatology. As McGrath posits, the purpose of doctrinal criticism is to provide pathways for doctrinal development.[80] Based on the key commitments articulated in the historical development, the various voices of the AG community will be taken up to imagine a future of AG eschatology in a way that is faithful to the past and in conversation with contemporary scholars. The goal is to develop a pneumatic understanding of eschatology that will reinvigorate the proclamation of the four eschatological doctrines for a future generation.

---

[77] McGrath, *Genesis of Doctrine*, 52–66, argues that the "narrative function" of doctrine is the interpretive framework by which Scripture is understood. These "starting points" are conceptual frameworks for interpreting ideas and concepts in the Scripture.

[78] The structure of these periods are generally accepted and shared by several studies of AG development. Margaret Poloma, "Assemblies of God," in S. M. Burgess and E. M. van der Maas, eds., *NIDPCM* (Grand Rapids: Zondervan, 2003), 333–40, divides these periods (1914–1918), (1918–1930), (1930–1950), (1950–1985), (1985–Present). A similar structure is used by Menzies, *Anointed to Serve*, 143. However, these periods will be modified in ways that are specific to developments in eschatology.

[79] The methodology of discussing history by decisive turning points is demonstrated in Mark A. Noll, *Turning Points: Decisive Moments in the History of Christianity* (Grand Rapids: Baker Academic, 2012), 3, who argues that turning points provide the opportunity to "state more specifically why certain events may have marked an important fork in the road or signaled a new stage in the working out of Christian history."

[80] McGrath, *Genesis of Doctrine*, 8.

2

THE LANDSCAPE OF ASSEMBLIES OF GOD ESCHATOLOGY

Before surveying the official positions and popular expressions of AG eschatology, we first begin with the current conversations within Pentecostal eschatology and AG eschatology specifically. This chapter will explore the landscape of attitudes about AG eschatology within the Pentecostal academy. Unlike denominational and ministerial voices, the primary role of scholars is to critically assess theological ideas. They are not intended to be agents of the denomination who are required maintain orthodoxy on behalf of the denomination in their academic works. In this way, this chapter will look at how AG scholars have evaluated the fellowship's commitments to eschatology. It will seek to identify the key issues scholars affirm, as well as areas of potential concern within this current conversation.

Recognizing the Uneasy Tensions in AG Eschatology

The first scholar to conduct a critical assessment of AG eschatological positions was William W. Menzies. Menzies completed his Ph.D. from the University of Iowa in 1968, which was published as the first academic denominational history and was published by GPH as Anointed to Serve in 1971.[1] His voice is particularly notable because he was a pillar in AG education and was one of the first AG scholars. Menzies's study recognizes the role that eschatology has played in the denomination's self-identity and comments on a number of issues related to AG

---

[1] William W. Menzies, *Anointed to Serve: The Story of the Assemblies of God* (Springfield: Gospel Publishing House, 1971). Menzies focuses on the historical antecedents and the organizational development of the AG, adding theological depth to the telling of the AG story. Menzies completed his Ph.D. at the University of Iowa and was a noted theologian and historian of the AG. He taught at Central Bible College, Assemblies of God Theological Seminary, and Asia Pacific Theological Seminary. Menzies helped found the Society for Pentecostal Studies and served a term as President and as the editor of *Pneuma*.

positions.² First, Menzies was the first to point out that four of the sixteen fundamental truths focused on premillennial eschatology, demonstrating the high level of importance that eschatology holds in AG doctrine.³ Second, he recognizes that because the AG developed alongside Fundamentalism, it was an "easy exercise" to adopt the popular forms of dispensational eschatology as their own, but "modify" it in ways that managed the problematic elements for Pentecostal theology.⁴ He argues that early AG leaders were willing to overlook the tensions in dispensationalism by simply giving it a "proper Pentecostal baptism."⁵ Third, Menzies admits that there has often been "an unevenness in eschatological emphasis" in the history of the AG, particularly the way in which wars and world events often led to a crescendo of eschatological articles in the Evangel, only to decline once again after the conflict was over.⁶ Finally, Menzies acknowledges that a shift has been taking place in the AG towards emphasizing the coming of Christ "without depending so heavily on dispensational categories."⁷ In his mind, this shift does not undermine the core of AG eschatological commitments, because the Statement of Fundamental Truths "commits the Assemblies of God to premillennialism, but not necessarily to dispensationalism."⁸ Menzies' objective consideration of the importance of eschatology to the AG while at the same time recognizing the tensions created with the dispensational nature of AG eschatology show the level of theological maturity that was emerging in his era.⁹

Following Menzies, others began to recognize some inherent issues in dispensational eschatology. Gerald T. Sheppard offered his influential critique of

---

² Menzies makes multiple references to eschatology throughout his book. See, Menzies, *Anointed to Serve*, 27, 57, 60, 77–78, 329.

³ Menzies, *Anointed to Serve*, 77–78.

⁴ Menzies, *Anointed to Serve*, 329.

⁵ Menzies, *Anointed to Serve*, 27.

⁶ Menzies, *Anointed to Serve*, 329.

⁷ Menzies, *Anointed to Serve*, 329.

⁸ Menzies, *Anointed to Serve*, 329.

⁹ Menzies expanded on his comments on the nature of AG eschatology in his later scholarship. See William W. Menzies, "The Reformed Roots of Pentecostalism," *PentecoStudies* 6, no. 2 (2007): 78–99 and William W. Menzies, "The Influence of Fundamentalism," *AJPS* 14, no. 2 (2001): 199–211, notes that "more than 200 titles by dispensationalist-fundamentalist writers appear in the catalogs of the Gospel Publishing House during the years of the height of the Fundamentalist-Modernist controversy." Although AG eschatology is "derived directly" from Scofield, he notes that Frank Boyd and Ralph Riggs "turned dispensationalism on its head, making the Church Age the age of the Spirit." Menzies comments that Scofield's system has become a "largely-discarded system of eschatology" although it is unclear just what aspects he sees as being discarded.

Pentecostal eschatology in 1984 in which he argued that there is an "uneasy relationship" that exists between Pentecostal theology and the adoption of fundamentalist dispensationalism.[10] He observes that the original 1916 version of the AG's *Statement of Fundamental Truths* did not include the word "tribulation" or use conventional "rapture terminology." Because of this, he argues that the founding AG position was not "inherently dispensational and left room for ambiguity."[11] He comments, "Whether a precise pre-tribulational rapture was intended behind the original statement remains open to debate from the materials I have seen."[12] Furthermore, Sheppard argues that initially the AG did not share these ecclesiastical positions that existed in dispensationalism.[13] While many AG writers, such as Myer Pearlman, E. S. Williams, and Frank Boyd, accepted the dispensational distinction between the church (heavenly people) and Israel (earthly people), they did not support the idea of a postponed kingdom.[14]

Sheppard's contention is not that dispensationalism did not exist in early Pentecostalism, but that a gradual adoption of the fundamentalist hermeneutic moved Pentecostals toward a full adoption of the fundamentalist dispensational position on eschatology. He says, "My suspicions are that a number of Pentecostal denominations which came to hold to popular dispensationalism during the 1920's and the following decades are reading back into their pre-1920's statement a firm consensus on the doctrine of the pre-tribulation rapture which was not originally present among them."[15] The adoption of fundamentalist expressions of dispensationalism created an "uneasy relationship" within the Pentecostal community because the Pentecostal hermeneutic does not allow strict

---

[10] Gerald T. Sheppard, "Pentecostals and the Hermeneutics of Dispensationalism: The Anatomy of an Uneasy Relationship," *Pneuma* 6, no. 2 (Fall 1984): 5–33.

[11] Sheppard, "Pentecostals and the Hermeneutics of Dispensationalism," 8.

[12] Sheppard, "Pentecostals and the Hermeneutics of Dispensationalism," 7.

[13] Sheppard, "Pentecostals and the Hermeneutics of Dispensationalism," 6–7. Sheppard notes that the hallmarks of dispensational premillennialism are dependent upon the ecclesiological separation of the Church and Israel, including the concept of the Church Age, the pretribulation rapture, the great tribulation, and the role of Israel in the millennial kingdom. In order to demonstrate this, he surveyed the works of AG eschatology from 1930 to 1960 for the ways in which they differ from dispensational eschatology. Included in his study were *Bible Doctrines* by P. C. Nelson, *Knowing the Doctrines of the Bible* by Myer Pearlman, the three volume *Systematic Theology* by E. S. Williams, and prophecy books by Ralph Riggs and Frank Boyd.

[14] Sheppard, "Pentecostals and the Hermeneutics of Dispensationalism," 13.

[15] Sheppard, "Pentecostals and the Hermeneutics of Dispensationalism," 10.

adherence to the dispensational system.[16] Therefore, he concludes there is little that is "Pentecostal" about dispensational eschatology and that fundamentalist dispensationalism is not the best articulation of Pentecostal theology.[17]

Critiquing Dispensational Eschatology

Following Sheppard's critique, the door was opened over the next decade for a number of AG scholars to add their voices of concern and critique to the conversation.[18] Prominent voices within the AG academic community shared their own evaluations of three key issues: the extent to which early AG formulas were dispensational, the challenge of the AG adopting dispensational eschatology, and the effects these challenges had on contemporary acceptance of AG positions.

In 1993, Glen Menzies (son of William Menzies) and Gordon Anderson made the case that there has been "significant diversity" of eschatological positions in the history of the AG by looking at the eschatology of an early AG leader, D. W. Kerr.[19] Kerr is an important example because he is credited with writing the *Statement of Fundamental Truths* and yet held a unique three-fold rapture position, which he explained in a 1919 article in the *Latter Rain Evangel*.[20] Menzies and Anderson argue that Kerr's statements were intentionally ambiguous on the rapture in order to allow for eschatological diversity. The ambiguity regarding tribulation positions was intentional so that ministers with a variety of views "can affirm the wording."[21] Menzies's and Anderson's were concerned that eschatological positions were becoming too narrow and are not

---

[16] Sheppard, "Pentecostals and the Hermeneutics of Dispensationalism," 24.

[17] Sheppard, "Pentecostals and the Hermeneutics of Dispensationalism," 10.

[18] The criteria for inclusion in this section are (1) Do they hold credentials or teach at an AG university? (2) Do they hold a postgraduate degree? (3) Are they published? (4) Do they address eschatology?

[19] Glen Menzies and Gordon L. Anderson. "D. W. Kerr and Eschatological Diversity in the Assemblies of God," *Paraclete* 27, no. 1 (1993): 8–16.

[20] D. W. Kerr, "The Two Fold Aspect of Church Life: Will the Church Go Through The Tribulation," *LRE* 2.1 (October1919), 2–6. Kerr believed that only the "overcomers" will escape the tribulation through the rapture and some God will keep "through the tribulation" and others will be raptured at the end of the tribulation. Significantly, this is Kerr's only article on eschatology. Part Two of the above article was never published, which may suggest that the AG was not as comfortable with his stance as Menzies and Gordon assert.

[21] Menzies and Anderson, "D. W. Kerr and Eschatological Diversity in the Assemblies of God," 15.

allowing the type of diversity in which they were intended in the beginning of the AG.

In the same year, AG historian Edith Blumhofer, offered a more objective and critical look at AG history and theology in her book *Restoring the Faith*.[22] Blumhofer argues that premillennialism and the concept of latter rain restoration of the baptism in the Spirit have been the cardinal distinctives of AG theology throughout its history.[23] Blumhofer's main thesis is that the AG gradually left its restorationist roots as it expanded as a denomination and settled into cultural relevance as a major evangelical institution. Because of this, she argues that during the decades of the 1920s–1930s, the AG sought to gain acceptance into the broader evangelical world [24] She says, "Deemphasizing restorationism and millenarianism, they opted, rather, to perceive Pentecostalism as a 'full gospel'—fundamentalism with a difference."[25] The movement toward evangelicalism undermined the AG's Pentecostal identity and contributed to the abandonment of its restorationist roots. These concerns, coupled with the increased education level among ministers, has led some to question the ability of dispensational premillennialism to reflect Pentecostal commitments.[26] She calls on the AG to have the "courage to raise theological questions" about the challenges of historically held eschatological positions.[27]

Similarly, Zachary Tackett explores AG views toward millennialism in his Ph.D. dissertation.[28] Tackett believes that as Pentecostals moved up in society, the AG adapted to more respectable forms of evangelicalism that led to the

---

[22] Edith Blumhofer, *Restoring the Faith* (Urbana: University of Illinois Press, 1993). In *Restoring the Faith*, Blumhofer is more critical than she was allowed to be in the earlier two-volume history published by GPH. Blumhofer received criticism from the AG over her critique of the fellowship and some of its claims about the "Decade of Harvest," which is included as the last chapter. See also her denominational history Edith L. Blumhofer, *The Assemblies of God: A Chapter in the Story of American Pentecostalism* vols. 1–2, (Springfield: Gospel Publishing House, 1989).

[23] Blumhofer, *Restoring the Faith*, 270–71.

[24] Blumhofer, *Restoring the Faith*, 5–6.

[25] Blumhofer, *Restoring the Faith*, 137.

[26] Blumhofer, *Restoring the Faith*, 270–73.

[27] Blumhofer, *Restoring the Faith*, 273.

[28] Zachary Tackett, "The Embourgeoisement of the Assemblies of God: Changing Perspectives on Scripture, Millennialism, and the Roles of Women," Ph.D. thesis (Southern Baptist Theological Seminary, May 1998). Tackett is currently a professor at Southeastern University in Lakeland, Florida.

"embourgeoisement" of the AG.[29] Tackett argues that prior to WWI, Pentecostal eschatology was optimistic about the revival that would reach the world before the return of Christ. As WWI raged on in Europe, pessimism about the approaching Armageddon took over their outlook and AG writers looked to the *Scofield Reference Bible* and other fundamentalist resources for their eschatology.[30] Tackett believes that by the 1960s, the AG had fully accepted the hermeneutics, ethics, and millennial views of Fundamentalism, though now couched in their identity as Pentecostal evangelicals.[31]

During the early 2000s, the *Left Behind* novels by Tim LaHaye and Jerry B. Jenkins brought dispensationalism into the popular imagination. Several AG scholars responded with critiques. For example, Peter Althouse argued that the literal interpretation of Left Behind "is not a nuanced understanding" of premillennialism because "it gives priority to the literal" which narrows literary genres to simply "univocal propositions."[32] Although rejecting imagination in the intepretation of prophetic literature, the literal accounts of the future became the source of a new genre of eschatological fiction, which imagined the future in narrative form.[33] Similarly, Paul van der Laan cautions that the uncritical adoption of eschatological positions in *Left Behind,* which tend to make fantasy of the future and make no mention of the role of the Holy Spirit, can have real consequences for Pentecostal spirituality.[34] He says, "The *Left Behind* series should motivate us to re-think our dispensational heritage and develop an eschatology that is appealing, biblical, and relevant and is compatible with our Pentecostal identity."[35] Paul van der Laan then offers eight alternative elements he would like to see included in a true Pentecostal eschatology: (1) receive illumination from the Holy Spirit as we develop our eschatology, but do not

[29] Tackett, "The Embourgeoisement of the Assemblies of God," 2, adopts Donald Dayton's concept of embourgeoisement as "the movement of a socially and religiously marginalized group to a status in which they identify with the cultural ideals, both social and religious, of the middle classes."

[30] Tackett, "The Embourgeoisement of the Assemblies of God," 236–37.

[31] Tackett, "The Embourgeoisement of the Assemblies of God," 259.

[32] Althouse, "Left Behind—Fact or Fiction?," 194.

[33] Althouse, "Left Behind—Fact or Fiction?," 193–94.

[34] Paul van der Laan "What is Left Behind? A Pentecostal Response to Eschatological Fiction," *JEPTA* 24 (2004): 49–70. He was a professor at Southeastern University (AG).

[35] van der Laan "What is Left Behind?," 67. In response to Sheppard's attempt to prove that Pentecostals were not fundamentalists, he comments, "I do agree with him that such is certainly true with regards to Pentecostal ecclesiology; on the other hand I think that it is fair to say that the eschatological frame of mind of the early pentecostalism was shaped predominantly by a mild form of premillennial dispensationalism." (55).

claim absolute authority; (2) interpret the Bible literally, but leave room for symbolism in futuristic elements; (3) understand historical context of prophetic passages; (4) develop an eschatology in which the Holy Spirit has a prominent role; (5) concentrate on our responsibility to the now, rather than what will happen at the end; (6) relate the powers of the coming age to the revelation of the Kingdom of God through the outpouring of the Holy Spirit; (7) present the Book of Revelation as a message of hope; and (8) be careful not to be too dogmatic about Scriptures that could be meant for future generations.[36]

The most critical examination of Pentecostal eschatology came in 2010, when Matthew K. Thompson offered his critique of the popular Scofield versions of dispensational eschatology and the problems it created when Pentecostals "uncritically adopted" evangelical eschatology.[37] This adoption, says Thompson, was somewhat "a matter of happenstance" since no other options were available to them.[38] But this "ill-advised adoption" led to Pentecostals adopting Fundamentalist theology in the 1920s, which Thompson believes has allowed Pentecostal theology to devolve into a generic form of evangelicalism.[39] This move, he argues, had disastrous consequences on Pentecostal spirituality and has robbed the movement of its theological self-identity. He points out, "Many (if not most) Pentecostal academics lament the Pentecostal acceptance of dispensationalism and see it as a selling of a birthright for evangelical respectability."[40] Therefore, he argues, a "re-visioning" of Pentecostal eschatology is needed in order to be consistent with early Pentecostalism.

Thompson argues that Scofieldian dispensationalism is incompatible with Pentecostalism on three grounds. First, he argues that dispensationalism is a hermeneutical approach to interpreting Scripture that is not shared by Pentecostals. The problem with literalistic approaches to interpreting Revelation is that it fails to take into account the cultural and linguistic understanding of genre and interpretation.[41] Second, Thompson argues that dispensationalism is theologically Calvinistic and deterministic, all of which is contrary to Pentecostal

---

[36] van der Laan "What is Left Behind?," 68–69.

[37] Matthew K. Thompson, *Kingdom Come: Revisioning Pentecostal Eschatology* (Dorsett, UK: Deo Publishing, 2010).

[38] Thompson, *Kingdom Come*, 53, quotes Frank Macchia who says that Pentecostals did not "fully understand" the implications of the system. By taking this position, Thompson fails to consider the possibility that Pentecostals could have intentionally adopted the dispensationalist system.

[39] Thompson, *Kingdom Come*, 3.

[40] Thompson, *Kingdom Come*, 51.

[41] Thompson, *Kingdom Come*, 45.

theology. Third, he argues that dispensationalism cripples the mission of the church and its social concern because of a fatalistic view of the things to come. He notes that nineteenth century evangelicals engaged in social issues. But today, he says, "one more often finds evangelicals on the conservative side of these issues, maintaining the status quo, for most dispensationalists do not see the present age as the appropriate time for the manifestation of the Kingdom of God on earth."[42] More importantly, the adaptation of Fundamentalism had consequences for the pneumatological focus and practice of Pentecostalism. He says,

> Pneumatology is the last *adaptational* theological holdout against a full-fledged Pentecostal *adoption* of classical dispensationalism, at least formally. In actual practice, the process is much closer to completion, as statistics indicate a dramatic decrease in at least the Assemblies of God's adherents in practicing glossolalia.[43]

Thompson concludes that what is needed is a revisioning of Pentecostal eschatology that "remains true to the original Pentecostal points of emphasis" and "emphasizes the agency and activity of the Holy Spirit in the eschaton."[44]

However, perhaps the most important study of the relationship between dispensational eschatology and the AG came in the 2018 volume *Toward a Pentecostal Eschatology* by Larry McQueen.[45] McQueen focused his study on the primary sources of the Finished Work and Wesleyan Holiness streams of early Pentecostalism in order to understand the nuances of the eschatology of the early movement.[46] McQueen found that Wesleyan Holiness eschatology had a greater variety in eschatological positions as compared to the Finished Work stream, which had little or no variety of positions. What McQueen uncovered challenges

---

[42] Thompson, *Kingdom Come*, 47.

[43] Thompson, *Kingdom Come*, 56–57. Emphasis original.

[44] Thompson, *Kingdom Come*, 56–57. Thompson's solution is to draw on Eastern patristic theology, exemplified in the theology of Gregory of Nazianzus and the way in which he uses pneumatology to understand eschatology as a process of cosmic soteriology found in Jürgen Moltmann and Sergius Bulgakov, which he believes is theologically closer to Pentecostalism than fundamentalism (59–74, 89–108).

[45] McQueen, *Toward a Pentecostal Eschatology*.

[46] The Finished Work stream emerged in 1910 when William Durham began preaching against sanctification as a second work of grace, which resulted in a rift in the Pentecostal movement in the US. The most prominent Finished Work Pentecostal group is the AG. Edith L. Blumhofer, "William H. Durham: Years of Creativity, Years of Dissent", in James R. Goff Jr. and Grant Wacker, eds., *Portraits of a Generation* (Fayetteville: University of Arkansas Press, 2002), 123–42; Faupel, *The Everlasting Gospel*, 266–67.

Sheppard's assertions of the AG's gradual adoption of dispensational by demonstrating that AG was decidedly committed to dispensationalism both before and after the adoption of the *Statement of Fundamental Truths*.[47]

McQueen found that nearly all Finished Work periodical literature up until 1920 follows the standard dispensational script of the secret rapture, tribulation, return of Jews, the antichrist, the revelation of Jesus and the battle of Armageddon, the millennium, and the eternal state.[48] He notes that AG literature follows the basic plan of future events without much variety. McQueen proposes that Finished Work soteriology asserted considerable influence on the eschatological positions and explains why the AG was so highly committed to dispensational eschatology.[49] He says, "The view of Christ's work as 'finished' or complete lends force to the resistance in the *Pentecostal Evangel* toward allowing any open-ended questions with regard to the future."[50] For the AG, future events are "fixed" and prophecy is simply "history written in advance." McQueen believes the uniform approach to eschatology also had to do with the cooperative polity of the AG.[51] Dissenting eschatological views were viewed as detrimental to maintaining unity, which meant that commentary on eschatological issues were restricted to the leadership. McQueen, therefore, argues that Pentecostals should re-capture the Wesleyan openness to more transformative expressions.

Eschatology and Social Concern

One major concern scholars have with dispensational eschatology is its lack of emphasis on social engagement. A major voice of this view is AG educator and ethicist, Murray Dempster, who calls dispensational eschatology the primary "theological factor that has sparked and perpetuated the controversy over the social involvement of the church."[52] He notes that eschatological fervor grew

---

[47] McQueen, *Toward a Pentecostal Eschatology*, 162–79.

[48] McQueen, *Toward a Pentecostal Eschatology*, 171–72. This is contra Sheppard's assumption that dispensationalism did not become fully engrained until the 1920s. Sheppard, "Pentecostals and the Hermeneutics of Dispensationalism," 10.

[49] McQueen, *Toward a Pentecostal Eschatology*, 294, comments, "The fact that classical dispensationalism was the only model articulated in this stream suggests that Finished Work soteriology is inherently compatible with a dispensational eschatology."

[50] McQueen, *Toward a Pentecostal Eschatology*, 179.

[51] McQueen, *Toward a Pentecostal Eschatology*, 178.

[52] Murray W. Dempster, "Eschatology, Spirit Baptism, and Inclusiveness: An Exploration into the Hallmarks of a Pentecostal Social Ethic," in Althouse and Waddell, eds., *Perspectives in Pentecostal Eschatology*, 155.

with expectation of imminence was the primary force for the missional impulse among Pentecostals. However, this impulse to save people while there was still time also promoted the fear that social justice might "sidetrack" the church from its mission. While acknowledging this tendency, Dempster offers three ironies to this narrative of quietism that Pentecostals fail to recognize. First, missionaries were at the forefront of social ministry through creating orphanages, feeding programs, and rescue homes.[53] Second, he notes that the Pentecostal movement has impacted the world's social, political, and human situations, often lifting up marginalized people in society. Third, he argues that tensions still remain within Pentecostal circles, but the AG has attempted to recapture the compassion impulse.[54] Further, Dempster points to the Lukan orientation of Pentecostal theology as a model of Spirit empowerment that includes the social mission alongside the evangelistic. He says, "Belief in the triumphant return of Jesus Christ, when it is grounded in Jesus' own message about the kingdom of God, actually entails an eschatological warrant and a moral mandate for the church's engagement with society."[55]

In much the same way, Robby Waddell is concerned about the impact of apocalypticism on Pentecostal views of ecology.[56] Because Pentecostals have often been "hopelessly otherworldly" and have focused on the soul of the individual more than all creation, Waddell fears this has led to a lack of "ecological concern." He notes that Pentecostals often fall into either premillennial apocalypticism or an over-realized postmillennial eschatology such as is found in the hyper-faith movement that emphasizes the here and now. Pentecostal scholars tend to reject both extremes, advocating an already/not yet eschatology in which the new creation should be rightly understood as "*ex vetera* (out of the old)" rather than *ex nihilo*.[57] He concludes, "By addressing the ecological crisis, Pentecostals will find their efforts intersecting with other social ministries, because environmental degradation and poverty go hand-in-hand."[58]

---

[53] Dempster, "Eschatology, Spirit Baptism, and Inclusiveness," 158.

[54] In 2009, the Assemblies of God changed its reasons for being to include "demonstrating love and compassion for the world." See *GC Minutes* (August 4–7, 2009), 49–52; Dempster, "Eschatology, Spirit Baptism, and Inclusiveness," 159–60.

[55] Dempster, "Eschatology, Spirit Baptism, and Inclusiveness," 155–56.

[56] Robby Waddell, "Apocalyptic Sustainability," in Althouse and Waddell, eds., *Perspectives in Pentecostal Eschatology*, 95–110.

[57] Waddell, "Apocalyptic Sustainability," 101.

[58] Waddell, "Apocalyptic Sustainability," 110.

Another critique of the social consequences of AG eschatology has to do with the abandonment of Pentecostal pacifism found in early AG leaders. In his book *Peace to War,* Paul Alexander examines the shift in AG views of war, peace, and passivism.[59] Alexander documents the AG's journey from an early commitment to pacifism through the shifts toward full endorsement of war and nationalism. Alexander argues that dispensational eschatology shaped AG views of war because they believed that God was re-aligning the nations through WWI in order to bring about the conditions predicted in Bible prophecy.[60] By WWII, the AG came to believe war was an inherent part of living in this world.[61] He says, "Regrettably, Spirit-empowered peace witness denigrated into mere verbal proclamation, and eschatology helped them accept Christian participation in 'war, wickedness, and violence' as inevitable and necessary."[62] As a result, support for the government and the growth of military chaplaincy has placed the AG in the position of supporting war rather than prophetically critiquing it based on the ethics of Jesus.[63]

Revisioning Pentecostal Eschatology

Beginning in late 1990s, Pentecostal eschatology began to emerge as a major theological topic for Pentecostal scholars. The problematic relationship with dispensationalism led to a number of calls for Pentecostal eschatology to be "revisioned" to reflect more faithfully Pentecostal concerns.[64] Several Pentecostal theologians turned to the eschatological works of leading Protestant eschatological scholar, Jürgen Moltmann, particularly his pneumatological emphasis in his seminal work Theology of Hope.[65] Moltmann's transformationalist eschatology,

---

[59] Paul Alexander, *Peace to War: Shifting Allegiances in the Assemblies of God* (Telfor, PA: Cascadia Publishing House, 2009).

[60] Alexander, *Peace to War,* 110–12.

[61] Alexander, *Peace to War,* 274–75.

[62] Alexander, *Peace to War,* 330–31.

[63] Alexander, *Peace to War,* 333.

[64] The term "re-vision" is used in several recent studies of Pentecostal eschatology by scholars who have offered eschatological alternatives to the dispensationalist eschatology for Pentecostals. Peter Althouse, *Spirit of the Last Days: Pentecostal Eschatology in Conversation with Jürgen Moltmann* (London: T&T Clark International, 2003), 1, says "revision in this book means to "re-envision" or create a new way of looking at something." Thompson, *Kingdom Come,* 3, says, "What is needed is a re-visioning of Pentecostal eschatology along the line more consistent with its early witness and with what is still says it believes." Cf. Frank D. Macchia, "Theology, Pentecostal," *NIDPCM,* 1138–40.

[65] Jürgen Moltmann, *Theology of Hope* (Minneapolis: Fortress Press, 1993).

which emphasized a Spirit-inspired hope for the coming of Jesus rather than pessimism, was a welcome message to Pentecostal academy.[66] This section will focus on three of the AG's premier theologians writing on eschatology: Peter Althouse, Frank Macchia, and Amos Yong.

Peter Althouse

In recognition of Moltmann's influence upon Pentecostals, Peter Althouse proposed "revisioning" Pentecostal eschatology by engaging in a dialogue with Moltmann's eschatology in his monograph, *Spirit of the Last Days* (2003).[67] Following Sheppard's thesis, Althouse believes early Pentecostal latter rain eschatology was not fundamentalist in nature and that Fundamentalism slowly infiltrated Pentecostal eschatology, especially in the AG.[68] Althouse argues that fundamentalist dispensationalism "is not the best articulation of Pentecostal eschatology, even though Fundamentalism has made its way into the mainstream of Pentecostal dogmatic formulations."[69] In response to the loss of a distinctive Pentecostal eschatology, Althouse calls for a revision of Pentecostal commitments to eschatology. He says, "Neither a simple re-institution of the doctrines of the early movement, nor the wholesale abandoning of Pentecostal heritage is helpful, but rather a re-thinking of Pentecostal eschatology in a contemporary way which does justice to both."[70]

In order to "revision" Pentecostal eschatology, Althouse engages with the Moltmann's transformationist eschatology. For Althouse, the advantage of Moltmann is the emphasis on the hope of God's coming beyond just hope heaven. The coming of Jesus provides an alternative vision for the present in anticipation of the future that makes transformation possible.[71] Moltmann's eschatology is millenarian in that, like Pentecostals, he maintains a belief in a

---

[66] This is illustrated by the invitation to Moltmann to participate in several dialogues with Pentecostal scholars. See Jürgen Moltmann, "A Pentecostal Theology of Life," *Journal of Pentecostal Theology* 4, no. 9 (October 1996), 3–15, Jürgen Moltmann, "The Blessing of Hope: The Theology of Hope and the Full Gospel Life," *JPT* 13, no. 2 (April 2005): 147–61, and the 2008 annual meeting for the Society for Pentecostal Studies featured the theme, "Signs, Sighs, and Significance" with plenary addresses by Moltmann.

[67] Peter Althouse, *Spirit of the Last Days: Pentecostal Eschatology in Conversation with Jürgen Moltmann* (London: T&T Clark International, 2003).

[68] Althouse, *Spirit of the Last Days*, 41.

[69] Althouse, "Left Behind—Fact or Fiction," 206.

[70] Althouse, *Spirit of the Last Days*, 61.

[71] Althouse, *Spirit of the Last Days*, 120.

future messianic kingdom.[72] Furthermore, Moltmann draws on the work of the "Spirit of Life" to empower the church to engage the world and to do the work of liberation, drawing the world toward the coming kingdom. It is this "Spirit of the last days" that unites, orders, and preserves the "eschatological community" in the world.[73] Finally, Althouse believes that Moltmann's eschatology emphasizes the cosmological dimension of the eschaton in that the present creation is renewed and liberated by the Spirit in the coming "new creation."[74] All of these eschatological turns encourage engagement in social transformation through the kingdom and resists passivity and escape.

These distinctives of Moltmann's eschatology, Althouse argues, are already present in Pentecostal scholars such as Steven Land, Eldin Villafane, Miroslav Volf, and Frank Macchia. Althouse notes that Moltmaan and his theology of hope is a basis for enriching a uniquely Pentecostal eschatology found in all four Pentecostal scholars. Each emphasizes the Spirit, which renews and liberates not only individuals, but also all of creation from bondage of oppression.[75] Althouse says,

> The theological revisions offered by the aforementioned Pentecostals are an effort to retain the eschatological and pneumatological fervor of the early movement, while contextualizing Pentecostal theology within the contemporary context. These revisions not only critique the alliance Pentecostals made with fundamentalism, but also re-evaluate the more prophetic vision of the early Pentecostalism as a critique of current social-political conditions.[76]

While there are certainly points of departure Pentecostals would have with Moltmann, Althouse demonstrates that a consistent pneumatological eschatology should include all of these dimensions.

Frank Macchia

Frank Macchia's *Baptism in the Spirit: A Global Pentecostal Theology* seeks to expand the metaphor of baptism in the Spirit in order to pneumatologically

---

[72] Althouse, *Spirit of the Last Days*, 118–24.
[73] Althouse, *Spirit of the Last Days*, 135.
[74] Althouse, *Spirit of the Last Days*, 150–57.
[75] Althouse, *Spirit of the Last Days*, 186–92.
[76] Althouse, *Spirit of the Last Days*, 158.

orient all of Pentecostal theology.[77] Macchia believes Pentecostal theology needs to recapture the "latter rain" understanding of the Spirit, one that sees the Spirit preparing the world for his coming.[78] Because Pentecostalism is eschatological and pneumatological in orientation, Macchia argues that the Pentecostal distinctive of Spirit-baptism has the opportunity to be re-invigorated by exploring its eschatological function present in early Pentecostalism.[79] He says,

> I find Spirit baptism to be a useful metaphor for getting at the pneumatological substance of eschatology. Eschatology is helpful for showing the expansive reach of pneumatology, because eschatology implies a participation in God that is both purifying and empowering, presently at work and still unfulfilled, and life-transforming and demanding in terms of how we will respond to the reign of God in our times.[80]

Speaking in tongues serves an eschatological sign of God's presence that is a foretaste of the future in which the King will be present on earth.[81] But Spirit-baptism also has a cosmic and eschatological dimension when all of creation is liberated in the kingdom of God. He says, "We are filled with the Spirit as a foreshadow of the divine indwelling in all of creation."[82]

Therefore, he believes that the task of re-orienting Spirit-baptism as an eschatological concept will in turn create the "possibility of revitalizing eschatology as a richly pneumatological concept."[83] He fears that the apocalyptic nature of Pentecostal eschatology has created an "otherworldliness" that is contrary to the holistic impulse found in its doctrine of healing. Pentecostals have often ignored the "sighs" of those within societal structures of oppression and poverty.[84] Instead, Macchia argues for a "prophetic" eschatology, one that is oriented "toward historical fulfillment of God's will in a way that involves human participation on a level more profound and more genuinely human than mere yielding by faith to

---

[77] Frank D. Macchia, *Baptized in the Spirit: A Global Pentecostal Theology* (Grand Rapids: Zondervan, 2006). Macchia is a professor of theology at Vanguard University and has been very active in the area Pentecostal systematics.

[78] Macchia, *Baptized in the Spirit*, 17.

[79] Macchia, *Baptized in the Spirit*, 40.

[80] Macchia, *Baptized in the Spirit*, 41.

[81] Frank D. Macchia, "Tongues as a Sign: Towards a Sacramental Understanding of Pentecostal Experience," *Pneuma* 15, no. 1 (1993): 61–76.

[82] Macchia, *Baptized in the Spirit*, 104.

[83] Macchia, *Baptized in the Spirit*, 48.

[84] Macchia, *Baptized in the Spirit*, 280.

supernatural interventions 'from above.'"[85] While Macchia doesn't engage the eschatology of Fundamentalist dispensationalism that has been so prevalent in Pentecostalism, he does note that Pentecostals have differentiated themselves from the Fundamentalist hermeneutic and modernist obsession with scientific objectivity.[86]

Amos Yong

Amos Yong is one of the movement's premier theologians doing constructive systematic theology from a pneumatological foundation.[87] In his treatise on political theology called *In the Days of Caesar*, Yong uses the theological structure of the five-fold gospel in order to demonstrate the "many tongues" of expression of political theology within the global Pentecostal movement, which is grounded in eschatological categories.[88] Yong identifies three problematic characteristics of Pentecostal eschatology: its dispensational view of the end centered on the nation of Israel (tribulationism), its escapist and futurist tendencies (futurism), and its apocalyptic mentality (apocalypticism).[89] These dispensational tendencies were adopted by first generation Pentecostals but were "uncritically absorbed" from a dispensationalist hermeneutic.[90] Yong notes that in some ways, dispensational understandings are not uncharacteristic of a Pentecostal way of reading the Scripture.[91] Yong believes there are two misguided notions within Pentecostal eschatology that affect the way in which they engage in political theology: the concept of the secret rapture which leads to escapism that takes no responsibility for the world and futurism that relegates God's response to issues in the culture only to the coming kingdom. In response, he argues that these concepts are incompatible with Pentecostal spirituality. Therefore, he argues, "I think there

---

[85] Macchia, *Baptized in the Spirit*, 278.

[86] Macchia, *Baptized in the Spirit*, 52–53, believes that Pentecostals were "not originally part of the modernist debate" and were not as interested in the Fundamentalist approach to historical-critical investigation that alienated the reader from the text.

[87] Yong is a prolific author who has held credentials with the AG and has served as faculty at Bethany College of the Assemblies of God, Regent University, and is now a professor at Fuller Theological Seminary.

[88] Amos Yong, *In the Days of Caesar* (Grand Rapids: Eerdmans, 2010), 316–17.

[89] Yong, *In the Days of Caesar*, 317–18.

[90] Yong, *In the Days of Caesar*, 321.

[91] The narrative orientation of early Pentecostals naturally fit with their Lukan hermeneutic that of "this is that" as well as applying that principle to Revelation and current events. Yong, *In the Days of Caesar*, 321.

are resources from within the pentecostal experience to articulate a counter-eschatology to the one that they have inherited from dispensationalism."[92]

Yong offers three moves that are necessary to re-orient Pentecostal eschatology towards these inner pneumatological resources. First, he urges a fundamental shift away from futuristic apocalypticism that sees the present world as headed for destruction toward a pneumatological apocalypticism in which the last days are characterized by signs, wonders, and the outpouring of the Spirit.[93] Second, he argues that the distinction between Israel and the church should be re-oriented in light of the Spirit being poured out on all flesh. Redemption is a matter of historical distinction in which salvation is a future reality for Israel and a present reality for Gentiles. The Spirit has poured out on the Jewish diaspora as well as every nation with the goal of universal salvation.[94] Third, Yong believes a pneumatological orientation recognizes the way in which the Spirit is renewing creation and producing ecological concern in those in the Kingdom of God in anticipation of the coming eschatological renewal.[95] In conclusion, unlike the escapism of dispensational eschatology, Yong believes that a pneumatological eschatology will shape the affections of believers in a way that engages culture, politics, the environment, and global conflict through suffering and hope.[96]

Similarly, Yong offers a renewalist eschatology based on the World Assemblies of God statement of faith is in his systematic theology called *Renewing Christian Theology*.[97] He departs from traditional systematics by placing his chapters on eschatology and pneumatology at the beginning of his study. This reversal is reflective of the character of the movement that is Christological,

---

[92] Yong, *In the Days of Caesar*, 327.

[93] Yong, *In the Days of Caesar*, 327–32.

[94] Yong, *In the Days of Caesar*, 332–42. Universal salvation is not the universalism that holds that all will be saved. It is the "present redemption of the ends of the earth, including its inhabitants regardless of where they are to be found, what language they speak, what spaces or places they populate, or what barriers keep them from being reconciled to others. In short, because of the Spirit's outpouring and the gift of many tongues, forgiveness can be elicited not only in human hearts, but also in human history." (341)

[95] Yong, *In the Days of Caesar*, 343–47.

[96] Yong, *In the Days of Caesar*, 358.

[97] Amos Yong, *Renewing Christian Theology: Systematics for a Global Christianity* (Waco, TX: Baylor University Press, 2014). It is interesting to note that Yong uses the WAGF statement, which condenses eschatological tenants, rather than the North American AG *SFT*, which has four eschatological articles. His stated purpose is that the WAGF represents a global theology. But one might wonder if the shortened statement, which lacks a tribulational position and does not mention the restoration of Israel, is also a more palatable and inclusive formulation of AG eschatology.

pneumatological, and eschatological, which "celebrated the salvation inaugurated in the incarnational and pentecostal events but not yet culminated until the restoration of all things in the age to come."[98]

Yong notes that there is nothing "distinctive" to renewal Christianity contained in the WAGF article on eschatology.[99] However, Yong does offer four suggestions from a renewal perspective that could contribute to renewal eschatology. First, the belief in the imminence of Christ's personal return anticipates a desire for reunion with a person rather than events to come. Second, this emphasis should create a longing in the Spirit for the presence of Messiah within the bride of Christ. Third, although the exact nature of the millennium may not be fully understood or agreed upon, whatever the nature of the millennium, believers ought to be working in anticipation of the coming King Most importantly, renewal eschatology should recognize that the last days began with the outpouring of the Holy Spirit. Instead of speculation about events, eschatological doctrines should point believers to the goal of participating in the "eschatological work of God manifest in Christ and poured out in the Spirit."[100] In contrast to Yong's pneumatological approach to eschatology, his chapters on pneumatology fail to place the experience of the Holy Spirit in the same eschatological orientation on which his book is framed. He discusses the various issues of apostolicity, charismata in the church, and even the doctrine of evidential tongues. Yet the only mention of any eschatological significance of pneumatology is in passing.[101]

Alternative Readings of Revelation

New Testament and Revelation scholar, Robby Waddell, has offered two works that address eschatology from a Pentecostal perspective that challenge traditional dispensational understandings of Revelation. The first work is his monograph, *The Spirit of the Book of Revelation,* in which he offers an alternative reading of

---

[98] Yong, *Renewing Christian Theology*, 15–16.
[99] Yong, *Renewing Christian Theology*, 49–56.
[100] Yong, *Renewing Christian Theology*, 51–52.
[101] Yong, *Renewing Christian Theology*, 97. He says, "The Lukan sign of glossolalia heralds the pneumatological and eschatological in-breaking of the reign of God while empowering the mission of the people of God in hastening its inauguration."

Revelation to the apocalyptic approach to which Pentecostals are accustomed.[102] He uses literary theory and intertextuality in order to craft a Spirit-led hermeneutic that interprets Revelation through emphasizing an encounter with the Spirit rather than via modernist approaches.[103] He argues that a true Pentecostal reading of Revelation consists of the Pentecostal community "hearing what the Spirit is saying" about the Apocalypse.[104] The second work is an article in which Waddell engages in a discussion of the relationship between time and eschatology.[105] He believes that instead of reading Revelation for themselves, Pentecostals have often adopted dispensational ideas that have been "regrettable and problematic."[106] Waddell admits that Pentecostal eschatology is "not inconsistent" with dispensationalism, but neither is it "dependent on its eschatology."[107] This has caused two problems in Pentecostal eschatology. First, they are often guilty of overemphasizing the futurist position, which minimizes Revelation's value for present day believers. He argues that the way in which dispensationalists suspend time between the sixty-ninth and seventieth week allows "self-proclaimed prophecy experts to argue *ad infinitum* over the details of end time events."[108] Second, for many Pentecostal scholars, dispensational teachings are simply a "patchwork of biblical texts" that do not hold up to critical engagement. Waddell argues that the Pentecostal belief in healing and power over evil is most congruent with inaugurated eschatology because God is and at the same time still yet to come.[109] He concludes that most recent Pentecostal scholars prefer the inaugurated position to the futurist position because it offers an eschatology that is transformational of the present and hopeful of the future.

---

[102] Robby C. Waddell, *The Spirit of the Book of Revelation* (Dorsett, UK: Deo Publishing, 2006). Waddell is ordained Church of God, but is a professor of NT at Southeastern AG University in Lakeland, Florida.

[103] Waddell, *The Spirit of the Book of Revelation*, 113.

[104] Waddell, *The Spirit of the Book of Revelation*, 125, comments, "I am proposing that the only interpretation that a Pentecostal community will endorse is an interpretation which is centered on Jesus Christ."

[105] Robby Waddell, "What Time is it? Half-past Three: How to Calculate Eschatological Time," *JEPTA* 2 (2011): 141–52.

[106] Waddell, "What Time is it?," 142.

[107] Waddell, "What Time is it?," 146. Like most, Waddell follows Sheppard on this.

[108] Waddell, "What Time is it?," 145.

[109] Waddell, "What Time is it?," 147, argues there are three views on the kingdom: the apocalyptic position which expects an abrupt end, the realized position which sees the kingdom fully present, and the inaugurated position that emphasizes the kingdom being present but not yet consummated.

In the *Two Horizons Revelation Commentary*, Frank D. Macchia and fellow Pentecostal biblical scholar John Christopher Thomas[110] team up to offer a biblical and theological commentary on Revelation.[111] Macchia's account is not specifically Pentecostal eschatology, with the only overt mention of Pentecostal themes is the eschatological nature of glossolalia.[112] However, this volume is filled with pneumatological themes of redemption, renewal, prophetic witness, and the liberating Spirit of the gospel. The Spirit is the key to his understanding and to the revelation of the truth of the coming of God in the eschaton. Macchia believes all of eschatology is ultimately about God's plan for reversing the dominance of wickedness and sin in humanity as well as its effects on all creation. The redemptive victory won by the Lamb means victory for believers in the present, but also the victory still yet to come.[113] During the "now," the church plays a role in the fulfillment of the promised "not yet."[114]

Ecclesiologically, Macchia sees the Church as the "eschatological Israel" in a way that is closer than most dispensational understandings. The church does not replace Israel; Israel's election ultimately finds its fulfillment in Christ.[115]. He says, "There is no Israel ultimately without the Church and the nations to whom the church as the eschatological Israel of the Lamb is called to bear witness."[116] Through the Spirit, who is the "global Spirit," the followers of the Lamb are moved toward global witness to every nation, tribe, and tongue.

The coming millennium will not be a demonstration of the human ability of the church to reign; it will be the reign of the Lamb, his justice, and his liberty in which the nations will be given the opportunity to repent. The millennium is also a time of Sabbath rest for the creation before the rebirth of the heavens and the earth.[117] A simple futuristic understanding of Revelation fails to recognize the

---

[110] Thomas' Revelation commentary is the most extensive commentary by a Pentecostal scholar. See J.C. Thomas, *The Apocalypse: A Literary and Theological Commentary* (Cleveland, TN: CPT Press, 2012).

[111] John Christopher Thomas and Frank D. Macchia, *Revelation* (Grand Rapids: Eerdmans, 2016). As an AG scholar, this survey will focus on Macchia's contribution to this volume, which is found in the theological portion.

[112] Thomas and Macchia, *Revelation*, 622.

[113] Thomas and Macchia, *Revelation*, 586.

[114] Thomas and Macchia, *Revelation*, 501.

[115] Thomas and Macchia, *Revelation*, 534–35. Macchia solves the ecclesiastical tension by showing that "Israel and the church find their destiny in him." The crucified Lamb is the "fulfillment of Israel's mission," which the church prophetically proclaims to the nations.

[116] Thomas and Macchia, *Revelation*, 502.

[117] Thomas and Macchia, *Revelation*, 619.

overlap of the past, present, and future found in the drama of the one who was, is, and is to come.[118] The return of Christ is the climax, but not the end of redemption. Christ's return establishes the kingdom on earth in which Christ reigns for one thousand years.[119] After Christ brings the present earth under his total reign, he will rule in justice over the nations and will bring about the final judgment. The present earth will be transformed, as a new city from heaven will complete the transformation of the new creation.

Conclusions

According to this survey, AG scholars recognize a number of fundamental issues inherent in AG eschatological positions. First, scholars universally recognize the central role eschatology has played in Pentecostal theology from the very beginning. Pentecostals linked their eschatology to their pneumatology in that the latter rain outpouring of the Spirit and the phenomenon of speaking in tongues were seen as eschatological signs, which pointed to the imminence of the return of the Lord. The message that "Jesus is coming soon" filled their preaching and was the key to the movement's self-understanding, their hermeneutic, and their philosophy of history. The AG is certainly an eschatological community.

Second, scholars disagree on how early dispensational forms of premillennialism were present in Pentecostal thought. There is a dominant stream of interpreters that agree with Sheppard that in the 1920s, that when Pentecostals identified with Fundamentalism, that dispensationalism was uncritically adopted, especially in the AG.[120] This "gradual adoption" of dispensationalism has resulted in "uneasy tensions" in Pentecostal theology and is believed to have undermined the original pneumatological foundation.[121] The primary issues of incompatibility can be found in a different hermeneutical approach to Scripture, belief in the supernatural, and ecclesiastical separation of

---

[118] Thomas and Macchia, *Revelation*, 589.

[119] Thomas and Macchia, *Revelation*, 591. He points out that the reader notes that the number of years of Christ's reign will tower over the amount of time the saints will suffer in waiting the kingdom.

[120] Sheppard, "Pentecostals and the Hermeneutics of Dispensationalism," 10; Althouse, *Spirit of the Last Days*, 41; Althouse, "The Landscape of Pentecostal and Charismatic Eschatology," 15; Tackett "The Embourgeoisement of the Assemblies of God," 239; Thompson, *Kingdom Come*, 51

[121] Althouse, "The Landscape of Pentecostal and Charismatic Eschatology," 15; Althouse, *Spirit of the Last Days*, 48.

the Church and Israel in order to postpone the kingdom.[122] These tensions and contradictions have convinced scholars that fundamentalist dispensationalism is not the best articulation for Pentecostal eschatology.[123] The fact that there is no particular pneumatological orientation leads scholars to believe there is nothing "Pentecostal" about AG eschatology.[124] However, there are several minority dissenting positions. William Menzies argued before Sheppard that the AG held a "modified dispensationalism" from the beginning, of which they intentionally managed or resolved the pneumatological tensions.[125]

Perhaps an even more substantial challenge to this thesis is McQueen's recent study, which demonstrates that the Finished Work tradition was dispensational from the beginning without any variance, a fact that is particularly the case with the AG. In light of McQueen's study, scholars will have to re-assess the narrative that Pentecostals gradually adopted dispensationalism, at least for the finished work tradition.[126] Although McQueen found a greater variety in the Wesleyan holiness stream, all Pentecostals used the basic elements of dispensational premillennialism.

Third, scholars are concerned that the combination literalist apocalyptic visions of the future and the fundamentalist ethic of withdrawal from culture have caused an attitude of social quietism and indifference to meeting the social needs of society.[127] Scholars believe the expectations of the imminent premillennial return of Christ led Pentecostals to focus more on saving souls than social welfare.[128] This has led to calls Pentecostal approaches to eschatology that are grounded in the concept of the kingdom of God that move people toward action and social concern, including care for creation.[129]

Finally, there is nearly unanimous interest by Pentecostal and AG scholars for revisioning an alternative Pentecostal eschatology that is distinct from fundamentalist dispensationalism and is pneumatologically compatible with the

---

[122] Thompson, *Kingdom Come*, 25–32.

[123] Althouse, "Left Behind—Fact or Fiction," 206.

[124] Sheppard, "Pentecostals and the Hermeneutics of Dispensationalism," 10; Tackett "The Embourgeoisement of the Assemblies of God," 315; McQueen, *Toward a Pentecostal Eschatology*, 294.

[125] Menzies, *Anointed to Serve*, 329.

[126] It should also be noted that van der Laan, "What is Left Behind?," 55, does not accept Sheppard's thesis because the *Scofield Reference Bible* was so influential on the AG.

[127] Macchia, *Baptized in the Spirit*, 280.

[128] Alexander, *Peace to War*, 112.

[129] Robeck, "Faith, Hope, Love, and the Eschaton," 5.

distinctive characteristics found in Pentecostal theology.[130] The most common alternative is the "already/not yet" inaugurated eschatology that understands the kingdom to be present now by the Spirit as well as expected to be fully consummated in the future. All of the scholars who have argued for an alternative vision have, to various degrees, been influenced by the eschatology of Jürgen Moltmann. They do so in order to argue for a premillennial eschatology that is pneumatological, Trinitarian, and rooted in the kingdom of God. What these suggestions demonstrate is that there are other models available to the AG that supports the possibility of developing a uniquely Pentecostal eschatology.

In the next chapters, the official doctrine of the AG and the popular expressions in the *Pentecostal Evangel* will be surveyed in order to test these five conclusions about AG eschatology.

---

[130] Althouse, *Spirit of the Last Days,* 61; Thompson, *Kingdom Come,* 56–57; van der Laan "What is Left Behind?," 68–69; Yong, *In the Days of Caesar,* 327.

3

THE STATEMENT OF FUNDAMENTAL TRUTHS

The theology of the Assemblies of God is best summarized by the four cardinal doctrines: Salvation, Spirit-baptism, Healing, and Second Coming of Christ.[1] These four core beliefs are more than doctrines or religious experiences; they reflect a Christological orientation in that Jesus is proclaimed as the Savior, Healer, Baptizer in the Spirit, and the soon coming King.[2] Rivaled only by the doctrine of Spirit-baptism and initial physical evidence of speaking in tongues, the doctrine of the return of Jesus has been one of the most important emphases in the history of the local AG church. Although the popularity of end times teaching has waned in recent years, it still remains an important subject in AG churches.[3]

This chapter will explore the official eschatological positions as expressed in the *Statement of Fundamental Truths* (*SFT*). Since 1916, this doctrinal statement has served as the theological foundation of the fellowship.[4] As important as spirituality was to early Pentecostals, proper understanding of biblical doctrine was equally important to the unity and integrity of the movement.[5] Written in 1916, the *SFT* is one of the earliest formal statements of faith within the

---

[1] The General Council reemphasized the four core doctrinal beliefs in 2009. Each of the four doctrines were presented and discussed by the Executive Presbytery in a special emphasis called "iVALUE" on the ""Four Core Beliefs" of the Assemblies of God: Salvation, Baptism in the Holy Spirit, Divine Healing and the Second Coming of Christ." http://ag.org/top/Beliefs/Our_Core_Doctrines/index.cfm (accessed 1 April 2017).

[2] George O. Wood, *Core Values* (Springfield: Gospel Publishing House, 2007).

[3] Poloma and Green, *The Assemblies of God*, 82.

[4] *The Statement of Fundamental Truths* will be referred to as *SFT.*

[5] Two out of the five rationales for organizing the first General Council in 1914 had to do with Pentecostal ministers uniting in sound doctrine. "General Convention of Pentecostal Churches of God in Christ," *WW,* December 20, 1913, 1. See also, *GC Minutes* (April 2, 1914), 4. The five purposes were unity in doctrine, cooperation in ministry, organization of missions efforts, legitimacy in legal matters and the need for a Bible school for training ministers and a literature department for publishing endeavors.

Pentecostal movement.[6] J. R. Flower describes the *SFT* as the "skeleton structure" of AG doctrine, being representative of those beliefs "held in common by many other prominent evangelical groups, and therefore is fundamental and orthodox."[7] The *SFT* provides positions on the Trinity, salvation, sanctification, baptism in the Spirit, healing, ordinances, ministry, and eschatology.[8]

The story behind the formation of the *SFT* has been well documented.[9] However, few studies have made a significant effort to look at the changes made to the statement beyond the first few years, particularly with regard to the eschatological truths. Although the specific doctrines addressed by this document have remained the same, revisions to the titles, wording, and content took place in 1917, 1920, 1921, 1927, 1961, and 1969.[10] Ministers are required to affirm on a yearly basis their support for the doctrine contained in this statement.[11]

This chapter will take a fresh look at the story from an eschatological perspective. It will survey of the various changes made to the eschatological fundamental truths (EFT) in order to understand the way in which AG eschatology has been modified or developed. This survey will also include some

---

[6] For example, the Church of God (Cleveland, TN) had a statement of "teachings" as early as 1910, but the Statement of Faith was not codified until 1948. See, "The Church of God," *Church of God Evangel*, August 15, 1910, 3. The Pentecostal Holiness Church predated the Pentecostal movement and had adopted a statement of faith but modified it to reflect Pentecostal doctrine.

[7] J. R. Flower, *The Origin and Development of the Assemblies of God* (Springfield: Gospel Publishing House, 1938), 18.

[8] At the same time, this statement is missing key elements of the pillars of Fundamentalism such as the virgin birth, miracles of Jesus, and the resurrection of Jesus. The exclusion of these pillars of fundamentalist doctrine suggests that the "fundamentals" were not necessarily the blueprint for the *SFT*.

[9] Menzies, *Anointed to Serve*, 106–21; Brumback, *Suddenly … From Heaven*, 204–10; Blumhofer, *The Assemblies of God* vol. 1, 205–39. Most of these histories discuss the origin of the *Statement of Fundamental Truths* but do not discuss the changes made throughout its history. Glenn W. Gohr, "Historical Development of the Statement of Fundamental Truths," *AG Heritage* 32 (2012): 61–66, is the only article that charts the changes made over the last century, though it does not concern itself with the specific changes to eschatological doctrine.

[10] Glenn Gohr, "The Historical Development of the Statement of Fundamental Truths," *AG Heritage* 32 (2012): 61–66.

[11] *GC Minutes* (October 1–7, 1916), 13–14, states, "In as much as unity among ministers is dependent upon their speaking the same thing on all fundamental matters (1 Cor. 1:10), the Credential Committee is hereby instructed to ask each applicant of the ministry for credentials or for a Certificate of Fellowship whether he recognizes and accepts the truth in the Statement of Fundamentals to the extent that he will endeavor with all lowliness and meekness and loving forbearance, to keep the unity of the Spirit in the bond of peace."

additional declarations of faith that have surfaced in recent years in order to see how these expressions may differ.

Early Doctrinal Statements

The SFT was not the first doctrinal statement that AG leaders promoted to the members of the fellowship. Immediately following the first General Council, E. N. Bell expressed the doctrinal identity of the new fellowship with a list of nine doctrinal commitments: salvation from sin, baptism with the Holy Ghost, no "holy rolling," spiritual gifts, the local Church, the ordinances of baptism and the Lord's supper, the soon coming of Jesus, missions, and divine healing.[12] Although not an official statement passed by the members of the General Council, Bell believed he was speaking authoritatively for the new fellowship. Bell's statement about the Second Coming contains the basic framework for what would eventually become the SFT. He says, "We believe in the pre-millennial coming of the Lord Jesus to reign with the saints 1000 years, Rev. chapters 19 and 20. In the new heaven and new earth as here promised."[13]

A second early doctrinal statement came from A. P. Collins in August of 1915. Collins and Bell were fellow Baptist pastors and close friends who served together on the committee that called the first General Council. Collins was elected the second chairman of the General Council in 1914. Because of the "various issues" facing the fellowship, Collins felt compelled to write a personal declaration of faith to share with the *Pentecostal Evangel* readers in anticipation of the October 1915 Council.[14] It reads:

> A DECLARATION OF FAITH
>
> I hereby affirm, declare and avow my belief in God the Father, Son and Holy Ghost, and these three are one. That the Bible is the inspired Word of God, the only rule of faith and practice. That men are saved from sin upon repentance toward God and faith in the Lord Jesus Christ whose blood cleanses from all sin. That baptism in water according to Matthew 28:19, and the Lord's Supper

---

[12] "For Strangers. Who Are We?," *WW*, May 20, 1914, 1–2. Bell expressed some of the early AG attitudes toward the holiness movement, commenting, "We have never been in any way associated with the real Unholy Rollers wrongly called holy, nor do we practice or believe in such shame and folly as rolling from one side of the house to the other. This is nonsense and dishonoring to God."

[13] "For Strangers. Who Are We?," 1. This is the first mention of the new heaven and new earth prior to the *SFT*.

[14] "General Council Meets October First," *WE*, August 28, 1915, 1.

are to be observed by all believers. That the baptism in the Holy Spirit is the privilege of the believer who obeys Jesus. That Jesus is coming to earth again with the saints to reign a thousand years. We love God and all His children. – Arch. P. Collins.[15]

With this brief statement, Collins set the stage for the AG to clarify its position on the Trinity, since debate over the baptismal formula was already causing division. Collins's statement differs from that of Bell in that he begins with more traditional evangelical concerns such as the Trinity and inspiration, but does not include healing, sanctification, or the church. Both affirm basic premillennial doctrine but make no mention of a two-phase coming, tribulation, or rapture.

Following the October 1915 General Council, Collins again took to the *Pentecostal Evangel* to provide readers with a list of eight core doctrines that he believed defined the Pentecostal movement: the Bible, salvation for all, the church, baptism in the Holy Spirit, healing for the body, ordinances of the Church, and the end times.[16] Instead of emphasizing that Jesus is coming soon, Collins declares, "we are nearing the close of the dispensation" and warns of coming judgment. This list of doctrines was "compiled for distribution," but just a few months later it was determined that the *SFT* was needed and the tract never made it into print. Although Collins was not a member of the committee that proposed the *SFT*, his role in the leadership makes this document very likely to be the foundation of the statement that developed.

The core doctrinal commitments expressed by Bell and Collins provided fourteen of the seventeen foundational elements that would be included in the *SFT* less than a year later. The only doctrines not found in these early lists, remarkably, are speaking in tongues, entire sanctification, and eternal punishment. But the similarities point to these two early statements being at least the starting point for the *SFT*.

The Origin of the Statement of Fundamental Truths

When the AG began in 1914, they intended for the fellowship to provide a way for Pentecostal ministers to cooperate together to accomplish the great commission and to conserve foreign missions efforts.[17] The preamble of the AG Constitution made it clear that they did not believe in establishing themselves as

---

[15] A. P. Collins, "Declaration of Faith," *WE*, August 28, 1915, 1.

[16] A. P. Collins, "Who We Are," *WE*, November 27, 1915, 3.

[17] *WW*, December 1913, 1.

a new sect or creating laws that would establish "unscriptural lines of fellowship and which separates itself from other members of the Assembly."[18] A. P. Collins argued, "It would be better to dissolve the council and the Presbytery" than to give in to any sort of organizational centralization.[19] D. W. Kerr believed the General Council model would only work if each individual assembly maintained the ability to be sovereign and self-determined, as long as people managed themselves well under Scripture's authority.[20] However, the grand experiment of cooperation and unity without a doctrinal basis was short lived, lasting only 1914–1916. As controversy over the "New Issue" of baptismal formula arose, they recognized that cooperation demanded some sense of unity on basic Bible truths.[21] J. R. Flower commented, "We are fully determined that centralization will not be allowed to present itself in any form.... At the same time, we are determined to get back to Apostolic standards of order, both in doctrine and in ministry."[22] The need for unity in sound doctrine motivated the council to give itself jurisdiction to "disapprove of all unscriptural methods, doctrines and conduct" which might hinder the unity of faith.[23]

On the opening day of the 1916 General Council, E. N. Bell, S. A. Jamieson, T. K. Leonard, D. W. Kerr, and Stanley Frodsham were appointed to a committee charged with crafting resolutions for the Council.[24] The resolution committee recommended to the Council a list of seventeen "Fundamental Truths" that they believed set forth a "clear statement of the things most surely believed among us" considered essential to unity.[25] The preamble captures the spirit in which they crafted this list of doctrines.

---

[18] *GC Minutes* (April 2–12, 1914), 4.

[19] A. P. Collins, "Centralization? No! Never!," *PE,* January 30, 1915, 1.

[20] D. W. Kerr, "He That Ruleth His Spirit," *CE,* December 12, 1914, 3.

[21] Blumhofer, *Restoring the Faith,* 127–35; E. N. Bell, "The 'Acts' on Baptism in Christ's Name Only," *PE,* June 12, 1915, 1–3; "Preliminary Statement Concerning the Principles Involved in the New Issue by the Presbytery," *WW,* June 1915, 1. Since baptizing in "Jesus' Name" was considered to be a "Bible method" of baptism and since several AG leaders had accepted the teaching, the early position was to allow the differences to remain in order to promote unity. However, others within the AG were expressing concerns that it undermined the orthodox understanding of the Trinity. The Presbytery was more concerned with claims of "new revelations" than they were with the theological implications of baptizing in Jesus' name only.

[22] J. R. Flower, "Editorial Note," *CE,* January 30, 1915, 1.

[23] *GC Minutes* (April 2–12, 1914), 4.

[24] *GC Minutes* (October 1916), 4.

[25] S. H. Frodsham, "Notes From an Eyewitness Account," *PE,* October 21, 1916, 4.

> This Statement of Fundamental Truths is not intended as a creed for the Church, nor as a basis of fellowship among Christians, but only as a basis of unity for the ministry alone (i.e., that we all speak the same thing, 1 Cor. 1:10; Acts 2:42). The human phraseology employed in such statement is not inspired nor contended for, but the truth set forth in such phraseology is held to be essential to a Full Gospel ministry. No claim is made that it contains all truth in the Bible, only that it covers our present needs as to these fundamental matters.[26]

Over the next three days, the Council of ministers discussed, revised, and passed each of the seventeen statements separately.[27] The statement that emerged contained a core list of evangelical doctrines (Bible, God, Trinity, Deity of Christ, Fall of Man, Salvation, Ordinances), Pentecostal distinctives (Baptism in the Holy Spirit, Tongues as Evidence, Sanctification, Church, Ministry, Divine Healing), and premillennial doctrine (The Blessed Hope, Millennial Reign, Final Judgment, New Heavens and New Earth).[28]

In many of the histories of the AG, Daniel W. Kerr is credited with being the architect of the *SFT*.[29] D. W. Kerr was a respected minister and associate of A. B. Simpson in the Christian & Missionary Alliance before joining the Pentecostal movement. He was a staunch defender of the Trinity, evidential tongues, and was highly involved in the doctrinal controversy that led to the creation of the *SFT*.[30] Kerr's role in the creation of the *SFT* has led most historians to assume that AG eschatology is also reflective of Kerr's eschatology. What makes this assumption significant is that Kerr wrote an article in the *Latter Rain Evangel* in 1919 that argues for a three-fold rapture.[31] Glen Menzies and Gordon Anderson present Kerr's eschatology as a case study to argue that the *SFT* was created to be intentionally ambiguous on rapture positions, which should demonstrate that

---

[26] *GC Minutes* (October 1916), 10.

[27] *GC Minutes* (October 1916), 7; Frodsham, "Notes From an Eyewitness Account," 4. The details concerning the discussion or revision of each item was not recorded in the minutes so it is unknown what debates may have taken place considering the wording.

[28] *GC Minutes* (October 1916), 10–13.

[29] S.H. Frodsham, "Notes From an Eyewitness Account," *PE*, October 21, 1916, 4.; "With Christ Which is Far Better," *PE*, April 16, 1927, 4; Menzies, *Anointed to Serve*, 119; Brumback, *Like a River*, 55; Blumhofer, *The Assemblies of God*, 236.

[30] "Tributes to Brother Kerr," *PE*, April 16, 1927, 4; Kerr, "We All Agree," 6–7.

[31] D. W. Kerr, "The Two Fold Aspect of Church Life: Will the Church Go Through The Tribulation?," *LRE*, October 1919, 2–6. This was part one of two articles that Kerr was supposed to write. Part two was never published.

eschatological diversity was widely tolerated early in the fellowship.[32] They comment, "While there is significant diversity of opinion regarding eschatology in the Assemblies of God today, a review of the Movement's history shows that this has always been the case."[33] Menzies and Anderson convincingly argue that because the author of the *SFT* had a different position on the rapture than is found in the official position, then there should be room for eschatological diversity within the fellowship today.

Although I agree with their conclusion, a weakness in their argument comes from the fact that the *SFT* was not the creation of one man, as is commonly thought. It was the result of a five-member committee that included E. N. Bell, Stanley Frodsham, S. A. Jamieson, and T. K. Leonard. It is certain that Kerr's largest contribution to the *SFT* wa the doctrines of God and the Trinity, but how important was he to the eschatological truths? As Menzies and Anderson point out, Kerr held to a view of multiple raptures that was more diverse than what ended up in the statement.[34] However, it is interesting to note that Kerr only wrote one significant article on eschatology, which was not in the *Pentecostal Evangel*, rather it was published in the regional paper *The Latter Rain Evangel* more than three years after the creation of the *SFT*. Furthermore, the follow up article that was advertised, which would likely have further clarified his position, never made it to print.[35] It is very possible that the second article was in fact censured because Kerr was a presbyter and the first article was considered to be a deviation from accepted AG positions. Perhaps more telling is Kerr's Central Bible College correspondence course called "Fundamentals of the Faith 'Plus,'" which contains no lesson on eschatological doctrine at all.[36] It seems that Kerr was censured in his eschatology.

---

[32] Menzies and Anderson, "D. W. Kerr and Eschatological Diversity," 12.

[33] Menzies and Anderson, "D. W. Kerr and Eschatological Diversity," 12. The argument that there was "significant diversity of opinion" in the early years of the AG is exaggerated. Outside of Kerr and Sisson, there are very few leaders who have documented positions that do not follow the basic script.

[34] Menzies and Anderson, "D. W. Kerr and Eschatological Diversity," 12. The view that there will be multiples raptures was not uncommon in the early days of the Pentecostal movement, but the AG rejected this position and avoided taking a position on who is included in the rapture.

[35] Kerr, "The Two Fold Aspect of Church Life: Will the Church Go Through The Tribulation?," *LRE*, October 1919, 2–6.

[36] D. W. Kerr, "Fundamentals of the Faith 'Plus,'" CBI Correspondence Course 8, 1926, Flower Pentecostal Heritage Center, Springfield, Missouri. Furthermore, in D. W. Kerr and Willard C. Pierce, "Outline Studies in the Chart of the Ages," (Central Bible College, 1924), 16–18, contains a chart

Therefore, I contend his controversial positions on eschatology likely restricted his ability to influence the "official" statements on eschatological truth for the AG. This suggests to me that Bell, Jamieson, and Frodsham were more likely to have provided the bulk of the eschatological statements that made the final document that was approved by the General Council.[37] As was pointed out earlier, Bell's early doctrinal statement, which included statements on the premillennial coming and new heavens and new earth, likely became the template for creating the *SFT*. Bell was a prophecy enthusiast who regularly fielded questions on end-times subjects in his column "Questions and Answers" in the *Pentecostal Evangel*. Frodsham wrote one of the first AG books on eschatology and regularly commented on eschatological topics and current events because of his role as editor of the *Pentecostal Evangel*. Similarly, Jamieson wrote one of the first AG books on doctrine, which included a chapter on eschatology and authored the only article in the *Pentecostal Evangel* specifically on the new heavens and new earth.[38]

Regardless of who wrote the statement, the case of Kerr's eschatology does reveal one of the reasons that AG eschatology perhaps was not crafted in more distinctively "Pentecostal" terms. Many early Pentecostals were debating about who would be included in the bride and thus qualified for the rapture. This is precisely the sort of categorization of believers reflected in Kerr's concept of the three raptures. Because of this debate, the AG chose to adopt a more widely accepted premillennial position with no initial statement about bridal or rapture theology. The AG was not so much interested in arguing about who would be included in the rapture as they were in simply affirm the basics of the Second Coming and millennial reign. Furthermore, they understood that they did not want to alienate themselves from the evangelical community by claiming Spirit-filled exclusivity for inclusion in the rapture. For the sake of unity and ecumenical appeal, the AG chose to mute eschatological positions that were distinctly Pentecostal. This sort of inclusivity within accepted premillennial boundaries was necessary because of the ecclesiastical structure of the fellowship.

---

that is credited to Kerr that includes a pretribulation rapture and a post-tribulation rapture similar to his article.

[37] T. K. Leonard was also on the committee, but he contributed very little to AG doctrine, failing to contribute even a single doctrinal article to the *Pentecostal Evangel*. Leonard was most notable for his leadership in promoting the name "assembly of God" for the fellowship and lending his facilities in Findlay, OH as the first home for the Gospel Publishing House.

[38] S. A. Jamieson, *Pillars of Truth* (Springfield: Gospel Publishing House, 1925); S. A. Jamieson, "A New Heaven and a New Earth," *PE*, September 30, 1922, 6.

1916 Eschatological Fundamental Truths

Of the original seventeen statements in the SFT, four were focused on eschatology. This means more attention was given to eschatology than other "distinctive" doctrines, such as baptism in the Spirit. Although it might seem disproportionate that eschatology would occupy a fourth of the statements, it is reflective of the foundational eschatological emphasis in the introduction to the 1914 constitution and bylaws:

> Almost every country on the globe has heard the message and also the prophecy which has been predominant in this great outpouring, which is "Jesus is coming soon" to this old world in the same manner as he left it to set up His millennial kingdom and to reign over the earth in righteous and peace for a thousand years.[39]

Considering the premillennial and latter rain language was present two years before the SFT and the stance on initial evidence, it could be argued that eschatology was the AG's original "distinctive doctrine."

One common narrative in AG literature is that the *SFT* has endured with only "minor" changes throughout its existence.[40] While it is true that no additional doctrines have been added in the past century, there have been significant changes to the wording and emphasis of the doctrines, particularly the Eschatological Fundamental Truths.[41] The original 1916 *SFT* contained a list of seventeen statements.

The four original 1916 statements articulating the AG positions passed by the General Council contain the basics of premillennial eschatology including the rapture of the church, literal thousand-year reign of Christ, eternal punishment, and the new heavens and new earth. They were written as follows:

> 14. THE BLESSED HOPE: The Resurrection of those who have fallen asleep in Christ, the rapture of believers which are alive and remain, and the translation

---

[39] *GC Minutes* (April 1914), 1.

[40] For example, Menzies, *Anointed to Serve*, 317, states that "no changes whatsoever were made until the General Council in 1961," and the changes were only a "minor rewording."

[41] I am grateful to Glenn Gohr, Archivist at the Flower Pentecostal Heritage Center, for sharing with me a list of changes he complied for the General Secretary's office. Glenn Gohr, "The Statement of Fundamental Truths: Chronological History compiled by Glenn Gohr," 2000, IFPHC, Springfield, MO.

of the true church, this is the blessed hope set before all believers. 1 Thess. 4:16, 17; Rom. 8:23; Tit. 2:13.

15. THE IMMINENT COMING AND MILLENIAL REIGN OF JESUS:[42] The premillennial and imminent coming of the Lord to gather His people unto Himself, and to judge the world in righteousness while reigning on earth for a thousand years is the expectation of the true Church of Christ.

16. LAKE OF FIRE: The devil and his angels, the Beast and the false prophet, and whosoever is not found written in the Book of Life, the fearful and unbelieving, and the abominable and murderers and whoremongers, and sorcerers, and idolaters and all liars shall be consigned to everlasting punishment in the lake which burneth with fire and brimstone, which is the second death.

17. THE NEW HEAVENS AND NEW EARTH: We look for new heavens and a new earth wherein dwelleth righteousness. 2 Pet. 3:13; Rev. 21 and 22.[43]

The title of the first truth, "The Blessed Hope," represents a biblical title for the Second Coming doctrine found in Tit. 2:3. But, perhaps more importantly, it was written in a way that pushes against the negative connotations of Christ's coming by appealing to the affective dimension in the concept of "hope." Note that it says that when Jesus returns, the dead in Christ will be "resurrected" and the living will be "raptured." What makes this event "blessed" is the promise of the resurrection of the body, which inspires a sense of hope and anticipation for the future. It is interesting that there is no stated tribulational position, although it does use the term "rapture." While it is likely that a pretribulation position was in their minds, that position was not made explicit.[44] Second, it says together believers will be "translated" but there is no mention of the destination of the believers after they are "translated." It was common for Pentecostals to emphasize the rapture as the invitation to the Marriage Supper of the Lamb, but this statement leaves the ultimate destination ambiguous. It is clear that the main emphasis of this doctrine is the hope that is engendered from the promise of Christ's return and the resurrection of believers.

The second statement, "Imminent and Premillennial Coming of Christ," was written as a summary of premillennial eschatology. Because it contains both the

---

[42] From 1916–1925, "millennial reign" was misspelled "millenial." It was corrected in the 1927 revision.

[43] *GC Minutes* (October 1–7, 1916), 13.

[44] This agrees with Sheppard, "Pentecostals and the Hermeneutics of Dispensationalism," 8, that the writers may have "implied" a pretribulation rapture, but the statement was left ambiguous.

Second Coming of Christ and the millennial reign, it is likely it may have been the original statement proposed by the committee and the other three truths were later additions during the deliberation process. Nevertheless, this statement emphasizes two aspects of Christ's Second Coming: his imminent coming to gather his people and the establishment of a literal millennial kingdom on earth. Like the "Blessed Hope," this statement lacks any reference to tribulation or the two-phases (rapture and revelation) as part of this vision of the future, though perhaps it is implied. Menzies and Anderson note that although a pretribulation position is likely, both pretribulation and post-tribulation adherents could conceivably affirm the somewhat general premillennial statement.[45] There is a "this worldly" orientation to the way the Millennium is crafted considering the strong sense of hope welcoming Christ's kingdom to earth rather than hope that believers will escape the earth.

In the same way the first two statements frame Christ's return in terms of hopeful anticipation, the final judgment is also seen as an event that inspires hope. The title, "The Lake of Fire," focuses on the final destination of God's ancient foes: the Devil, the Beast, and the False Prophet. It assures that there will be a day in which justice will be done, God's enemies will finally be defeated, and evil will finally be removed from the creation. It also includes a warning that those who align with these ancient foes by committing the sins mentioned in Revelation 20 will share their fate.[46] Since many AG ministers came from Charles Parham's network, it was important to include a strong statement that this judgment will be "everlasting" so as to warn against those who might hold his doctrine of annihilationism.[47]

The final statement, "The New Heavens and New Earth," is a partial quotation of 2 Pet. 3:13 and lacks any commentary or explanation. Its inclusion, beyond just a literalist approach to Revelation, was likely because it was already present in Bell's early doctrinal statement, which mentions the new heavens and

---

[45] Menzies and Anderson, "D. W. Kerr and Eschatological Diversity," 15. They also note that the ambiguity in the statement likely led to the 1937 resolution to disapprove post-millennialism and to instruct AG ministers to refrain from preaching it (12).

[46] *GC Minutes* (October1–7, 1916), 11. The inclusion of specific sins that will result in judgment is also a confirmation the AG's position on entire sanctification "without which no man shall see the Lord."

[47] Charles F. Parham, *The Everlasting Gospel*, (Baxter Springs, KS: n.p., 1911), 112, rejected the notion of the immortality of the damned. He argued that the love of God will spare the wicked from an everlasting hell by "utterly destroying" the wicked in a hell that is "hotter than orthodoxy teaches."

new earth.[48] However, it also shows that for early AG ministers there is a cosmological orientation to the AG vision of the future. Once Christ has reigned in righteousness and evil is purged through the final judgment, they expected a new heavens and earth where righteousness will "dwell." It is unclear from this statement if there is an expectation of a completely new earth or a renewed earth.

What do we make of these early statements? It is clear that these statements affirm a premillennial eschatology. With that, we also see that although there are certainly dispensational elements in these statements, it should not be assumed that it is their primary orientation. The term "rapture," which is employed in the first statement, is used as a synonym for resurrection rather than seeking to identify its relation to the tribulation. In fact, there is a lack of a stated position on the tribulation at all, which suggests that escape from tribulation was not their primary concern. Furthermore, the way these are written certainly demonstrates that these doctrines are more than just a list of the events to come; they thematically encapsulate what AG ministers look forward to.[49] Being expressed as somewhat fluid concepts, each of the four statements affirm a vision of the future based on the hope of the resurrection, the coming reign of Christ on earth, a future judgment for God's enemies, and a coming renewal of creation. Or put another way, they communicate the hopeful expectation of the renewal of all things in the resurrection, the millennium, the judgment, and the renewed creation. In this way, I see the "Blessed Hope" as an overarching theme for the other three tenets (See Figure 1). This hopeful and thematic orientation was their fundamental starting point for expressing their Pentecostal hope for the future.

FIGURE 1: 1916 THEMATIC EMPHASIS ON HOPE

Resurrection	Reign of Christ
Final Justice	Renewed Creation

(with **Hope** at the center)

---

[48] Bell, "For Strangers. Who Are We?," *WW,* May 20, 1914, 1–2, says "We believe in the premillennial coming of the Lord Jesus to reign with the saints 1000 years, Rev. chapters 19 and 20. In the new heaven and new earth as here promised."

[49] I am grateful to William K. Kay, "Premillennial Tensions: What Pentecostal Ministers Look Forward To," *Journal for Contemporary Religion* 14, no. 3 (1999): 361–73, for this concept from the subtitle of his article.

1927 Revision to the Eschatological Truths

Although the preamble of the AG constitution was adopted in 1914, the actual constitution was not fully written until 1925. But first, in 1920, the SFT was revised and the number of statements was shortened from seventeen to sixteen when the "Essentials of the Godhead" was moved to the end as an addendum.[50] In addition, several sections were also reorganized and moved in order to reflect the AG *ordo salutis*, or the order of salvation.[51] The only change made to the eschatological truths was the addition of support verses for the "Lake of Fire" (Rev 19:20; 20:10–15).

The 1920 version continued until 1925 when the General Council commissioned a full review and revision of the *SFT*. Chairman J. W. Welch and J. R. Flower proposed to the Council that the various resolutions from the previous decade be complied into a formal constitution.[52] The Presbytery appointed a committee for this task consisting of J. Narver Gortner, E. S. Williams, A. G. Ward, S. A. Jamieson, and Frank Boyd.[53] In conjunction with the work on the constitution, Welch asked D. W. Kerr to draft a revision of the *SFT*; only, the committee decided to propose its own revisions instead.[54] Many in the Council were uncomfortable with moving toward being formally organized. The resistance was so great that when the Constitution was introduced at the 1925 Council, Welch and Flower were voted out of office and the Council

---

[50] *GC Combined Minutes* (1914–1920), 15. There is no record of GC action to revise the statement in 1920. However, there is a resolution for the Executive Presbytery to revise minutes as needed.

[51] It is interesting to note that although the baptism in the Holy Spirit sections were moved in these early revisions, the section on "Entire Sanctification" always followed. This suggests that the reordering in 1920 was intended to follow a non-Wesleyan pattern of sin, salvation, ordinances, baptism in the Spirit, and then sanctification.

[52] Menzies, *Anointed to Serve*, 143.

[53] See "Final Report of Revision Committee on Essential Resolutions," *GC Minutes* (September 16–22, 1927); *PE*, October 8, 1927, 1–7.

[54] D. W. Kerr to J. W. Welch," July 22, 1925, Flower Pentecostal Heritage Center, Springfield MO. (Transcription by Daniel D. Isgrigg, October 2015). Kerr reported to Welch, "I have at last succeeded in completing the recasting of the Fundamentals herewith enclosed. Look it over and make such changes as will be necessary for clearness of expression, and correctness of doctrinal statements." Kerr became ill in early 1927 and died in April. In the meantime, J. W. Welch was replaced by W. T. Gaston as general superintendent at the 1927 Council and none of Kerr's suggested revisions were included in the new version. This draft is mistaken by some as a draft of Kerr's 1916 original version.

was now in the hands of a new generation of leaders.⁵⁵ Two years later, much of the tension had diminished, and the leadership revisited the proposed constitution and revision of the *SFT*, where it passed without opposition.

The version of the *SFT* contained several significant changes, including changing the title of "Full Consummation of the Baptism in the Holy Ghost" in the 1927 revision to "The Evidence of the Baptism in the Holy Ghost."⁵⁶ But the committee's most significant changes were in the wording of the four eschatological fundamental truths.

The Blessed Hope

13. THE BLESSED HOPE (1916–1925)⁵⁷

The Resurrection of those who have fallen asleep in Christ, the rapture of believers which are alive and remain, and the translation of the true church, this is the blessed hope set before all believers. 1 Thess. 4:16; Rom. 8:23; Tit 2:13.

13. THE BLESSED HOPE (1927)⁵⁸

The resurrection of those who have fallen asleep in Christ ~~the rapture of believers which are alive and remain~~ and their translation **together with those who are alive and remain unto the coming of the Lord** is the **imminent and** blessed hope **of the Church**. (1 Thess. 4:16, 17; Rom. 8:23; Titus 2:13; **1 Cor. 15:51, 52**).

The 1927 revision of "The Blessed Hope" contains several significant changes from the 1916 version. In 1916, the wording stated that deceased believers will be "resurrected" and living believers will be "raptured." The 1927 version removed the term "rapture" and reworded the language to indicate that the living and the dead will be "translated" together.⁵⁹ This surprising development was likely due to the fact that different rapture positions were held among the

---

⁵⁵ By 1927, Bell, Collins, and Kerr had passed away, Welch and Flower were pastoring in other states, and W. T. Gaston, J. R. Evans, David McDowell, and E. S. Williams assumed the leadership. Menzies, *Anointed to Serve*, 149–50.

⁵⁶ *GC Minutes* (September 16–22, 1927), 5–8.

⁵⁷ *GC Combined Minutes* (1914–1925), 13.

⁵⁸ *GC Minutes* (September 16–22, 1927), 8. The words that have been omitted from the earlier version have been stricken and the words in bold were added from the earlier version.

⁵⁹ The term "rapture" did not reappear until it was added to the article "The Millennial Reign of Christ" in 1961.

leadership and they preferred to use the biblical term "translation" rather than "rapture." This move would seem to contradict the conclusions made by Sheppard and others, that during the 1920s, the AG had moved to fully adopt fundamentalist dispensationalism.[60] On the contrary, the revised statement and removal of the distinctive dispensational term "rapture" further supported an ambiguous tribulational position and wording that both historic and dispensational premillennialists could conceivably affirm. They also added the word "imminent" to the phrase "blessed hope", which they moved from the "Millennial Reign," and strengthened the importance on the resurrection of the body by adding the supporting verse (1 Cor. 15:51, 52).

The Millennial Reign

> 14. THE IMMINENT COMING AND MILLENNIAL REIGN OF JESUS (1916–1925)[61]
>
> The premillennial and imminent coming of the Lord to gather His people unto Himself, and to judge the world in righteousness while reigning on the earth for a thousand years is the expectation of the true Church of Christ.
>
> 14. THE MILLENNIAL REIGN OF JESUS CHRIST (1927)[62]
>
> The revelation of the Lord Jesus Christ from heaven, the salvation of national Israel, and the millennial reign of Christ on the earth is the Scriptural promise and the world's hope. (2 Thess. 1:7; Rev. 19:11–14; Rom. 11:26, 27; Rev. 20:1–7).

Unlike the Blessed Hope, which became more inclusive in this revision, the rewrite of Millennial Reign in 1927 took a somewhat dispensational turn.[63] Whereas the 1916 version was a summary of several concepts of premillennial eschatology, the 1927 version focused on key elements of the Millennium. They removed the word "imminent" because the second phase of Christ's return is not imminent and can only take place after the tribulation. Also, the phrase "revelation of the Lord Jesus Christ from heaven" was added to identify this coming with Christ's return to earth

---

[60] Sheppard, "Pentecostals and the Hermeneutics of Dispensationalism," 10; Althouse, *Spirit of the Last Days,* 41; Althouse, "The Landscape of Pentecostal and Charismatic Eschatology," 15.

[61] *GC Combined Minutes* (1914–1925), 13.

[62] *GC Minutes* (September 16–22, 1927), 8.

[63] The turn toward a clearer dispensational formula is likely the influence of Frank Boyd and J. Narver Gortner.

to initiate the millennium (Rev. 19:11–14). However, it is also interesting to note that the 1927 version omits the literal thousand-year that is explicit in the 1925 version.

The most controversial change to some was the insertion of the clause "the salvation of national Israel." What was originally a vague concept of the church-centered millennium shifted to an Israel-centered millennium.[64] The biggest factor that contributed to this shift toward Israel instead of the church was the increasing support for a Jewish State in Palestine following the Balfour Declaration in 1917.[65] This monumental development captured the AG's eschatological imagination and fueled apocalyptic rhetoric.[66] They believed it was necessary for Israel to become a political state in order for the spiritual restoration to take place during the millennium (Rom. 11:26–27).[67] For the AG, the addition of salvation of national Israel is a theological statement about the messianic nature of the millennium. While the differentiation between the church and Israel features prominently in dispensational theology, it should be noted that it is not exclusive to dispensationalism and was held by many post-tribulational historic premillennialists.[68]

---

[64] David H. McDowell, "The Purpose of the Second Coming," *PE*, May 2, 1925, 2–3, argues that the return of the Jews and the establishment of the Messianic kingdom is not part of the program, "It is THE PROGRAM ITSELF." In his mind, the whole purpose of the outpouring of Spirit is to "fill out the details that are necessary to make possible the coming of the Lord Jesus Christ."

[65] "Preparations for the Return to Palestine," *WW*, August 1915, 2, comments, "One of the reasons that we as Pentecostal people are interested in the present war, raging in Europe and Asia, is that it is closely connected with the return of the Jews to their beloved land, Palestine." See also, "A Prophetic Creed," *WE*, March 11, 1916, 9; Newberg, *The Pentecostal Mission in Palestine*, 74.

[66] Philip Jenkins, *The Great and Holy War* (San Francisco: HarperOne, 2014), 18–19, notes, "The most intense era of spiritual excitement probably came in late 1917, when apocalyptic hopes ran high. As signs of the times accumulated—the crescendo of slaughter on the western front."

[67] Raymond L. Gannon, *The Shifting Romance with Israel* (Shippensburg, PA: Destiny Image, 2012), 169, comments, "Since the Assemblies of God could not ignore the literal interpretation of Scripture, they felt obliged to take it at face value that the promises of Israel's ultimate restoration and salvation." An example of this is John Goben, "Millennial Reign of Christ," *PE*, February 21, 1925, 2, in which he outlines all of the verses in the OT about the future millennium.

[68] Craig L. Bloomberg and Sung Wook Chung, eds., *The Case for Historic Premillennialism* (Grand Rapids: Baker Academic, 2009). Historic premillennialists do not divide the return of Christ into two comings.

The Lake of Fire

15. THE LAKE OF FIRE. (1916–1925).[69]

The devil and his angels, the Beast and the false prophet, and whosoever is not found written in the Book of Life, and the fearful and unbelieving, and abominable and murderers and whoremongers, and sorcerers, and idolaters and all liars shall be consigned to the everlasting punishment in the lake which burneth with fire and brimstone, which is the second death.

15. THE LAKE OF FIRE. (1927).[70]

The devil and his angels, the Beast and the false prophet, and whosoever is not found written in the Book of Life, ~~and the fearful and unbelieving, and abominable and murderers and whoremongers, and sorcerers, and idolaters and all liars~~ shall be consigned to the everlasting punishment in the lake which burneth with fire and brimstone, which is the second death. (Rev. 19:20; Rev 20:10–15).

The 1927 version of the Lake of Fire saw only a few minor revisions. The most significant is the list of sins from Revelation 20 was removed. This change meant that, rather than focusing on the sinful acts of humanity, this statement narrows the qualifications for judgment only to include whether one's name is recorded in the book of life. It also clarified that that main importance of this doctrine was that judgment was "everlasting" and not temporal.[71] The only other change was the addition of support texts (Rev. 19:20, Rev. 20:10–15).

The New Heavens and New Earth

16. THE NEW HEAVENS AND NEW EARTH. (1916–1925)[72]

We look for the new heavens and a new earth wherein dwelleth righteousness. 2 Pet. 3:13; Rev. 21 and 22.

---

[69] *GC Combined Minutes* (1914–1925), 13.

[70] *GC Minutes* (September 16–22, 1927), 8.

[71] E. N. Bell, "Questions and Answers," *WE*, August 23, 1919, 5, says, "The Council does not fuss over whether the lake of fire now exists or will start up after the final judgment. It does not teach that the wicked at death will be at once cast into the lake of fire. But it does hold they will be cast into such lake of fire at the Great White Throne judgment and shall be punished for ever and ever—not annihilated."

[72] *GC Combined Minutes* (1914–1925), 13.

16. THE NEW HEAVENS AND NEW EARTH. (1927)[73]

We, "*according to His promise,* look for the new heavens and a new earth wherein dwelleth righteousness." 2 Pet. 3:13; Rev. 21, 22.

The 1927 revision of the New Heavens and New Earth was the only revision in the statement's history. Since the 1916 version was a partial quote of 2 Pet. 3:13, this version added an additional phrase "according to the promise" from the verse and set it off in quotation marks. It is unclear what motivated the addition of the phrase other than reflecting that it is a quote. This somewhat insignificant revision signaled the pattern of lack of attention and development of this doctrine.

1927 Summary

The original 1916 EFT made four general and somewhat overlapping statements about premillennial eschatology, which were thematically oriented. The 1927 version shifted the emphasis from thematic and general statements toward chronological statements (see Figure 2). The committee who revised the EFT, consisting of J. N. Gortner, A. G. Ward, and Frank Boyd, were prophecy enthusiasts and who wrote prophecy books. However, the changes made in 1927 actually resulted in a less dispensational Blessed Hope by removing the term "rapture", but a more dispensational Millennial Reign in regards to the role of Israel. However, both statements remained ambiguous on the subject of the tribulation and could be affirmed by dispensational and non-dispensational premillennialists.

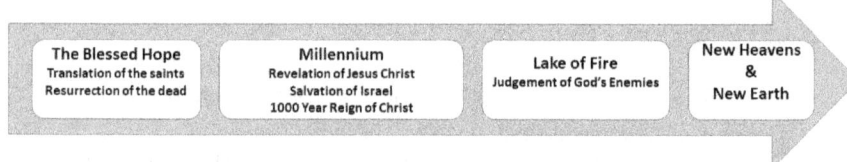

FIGURE 2: 1927- CHRONOLOGICAL EMPHASIS

What is clear is that the image orientation of 1916 statement turned chronological in the 1927 revision. The "Blessed Hope" is the first event, in which the dead in Christ will be resurrected and the living translated to be with the Lord. The "Millennial Reign" is the next event, in which Jesus will be "revealed" to Israel when he returns with the saints. As a result, Israel will be saved and the Kingdom will be established on earth for a thousand years. At the end of

---

[73] *GC Minutes* (September 16–22, 1927), 8.

the millennium, the Devil, beast, and false prophet will be judged and placed in the "Lake of Fire." This final judgment will usher in a new era in which the "New Heaven and New Earth" will be established as the eternal state. The attempt to clarify the events of their premillennial script in some ways detracted from the thematic expression of the original version. Most of the elements are still present, but the focus shifted from a sense of hopeful expectation to a sense of chronological specificity in the script.

1961 Revision to the Eschatological Fundamental Truths

The next major revision to the SFT came in 1961 during a time when the AG was rising to a level of prominence in the National Association of Evangelicals (NAE).[74] Although this may have played a role in shaping how the statements were expressed, the revision was initiated over concerns about the AG's eschatology. In 1959, a resolution by Ralph Salzman of Southern California was sent to all the District Councils, which contended that the SFT failed to include some "vital doctrinal terms and beliefs" that specifically pertained to the eschatological truths.[75] In response, the Executive Presbytery appointed a "Tenets of Faith Revision Committee" charged with preparing a "thorough and inclusive Statement of Fundamental Truths which shall include some truths surely believed among us but which are not recorded in the present Statement of Fundamental Truths."[76] After meeting for a year, the committee recommended to the Presbytery what they deemed as "minor changes" in wording for several of the tenets.[77] In reality, what

---

[74] Blumhofer, *Restoring the Faith*, 243 and C. M. Robeck, "An Emerging Magisterium," *Pneuma* 25, no. 2 (Fall 2003): 198, both contend that the 1961 revision was the result of a desire to conform to that of the NAE in an effort to further "evangelicalize" the denomination. The committee who proposed the revision did not indicate that such motivation existed. If there is any similarity to the NAE statement, it is what Gary B. McGee, "Historical Background," in Stanley M. Horton, ed., *Systematic Theology* (Springfield MO: Logion Press, 1995), 30, pertains to the language of sanctification and biblical inspiration.

[75] "Resolution 9: Statement of Fundamental Truths," presented to the 28th General Council (August 26–September 1, 1959); *GG Minutes* (August 26–September 1, 1959), 45–46.

[76] *GC Minutes* (August 26–September 1, 1959), 45–46. See also, "Committee Appointed to Study the Statement of Fundamental Truths," *PE*, February 7, 1960, 8. *GG Minutes* (August 23–29, 1961), 19–21. Members of the committee were E. S. Williams, Ralph Riggs, J. R. Flower, Stanley Horton, G. Raymond Carlson, Milton T. Wells, and D. H. McLaughlin.

[77] *AG Minister Letter*, November 6, 1961, 2, records Thomas Zimmerman's comments. "Nothing short of a miracle occurred in the adoption of the report of the Committee on Tenets of Faith. The six-man committee presented its report with the result that after only slight editing it was adopted unanimously by the convention. It does appear that a miracle of God's Holy Spirit was wrought when

they proposed were substantial changes to the Millennial Reign and minor changes to the Lake of Fire.[78] Although the Millennial Reign had already received a full revision in 1927, the committee wanted to correct the "missing elements" by "outlining the order of the events of the end-time" that were considered "vital" to their premillennial position.[79]

The Millennial Reign

14. THE MILLENNIAL REIGN OF JESUS CHRIST (1927)[80]

The revelation of the Lord Jesus Christ from heaven, the salvation of national Israel, and the millennial reign of Christ on the earth is the Scriptural promise and the world's hope. (2 Thess. 1:7; Rev. 19:11–14; Rom. 11:26, 27; Rev. 20:1–7).

14. THE MILLENNIAL REIGN OF JESUS CHRIST (1961)[81]

The second coming of Christ includes the rapture of the saints, which is our blessed hope, followed by the visible return of Christ with His saints to reign on the earth for one thousand years (Zech. 14:5; Matt. 24:27, 30; Revelation 1:7; 19:11–14; 20:1–6). This millennial reign will bring the salvation of national Israel (Ezekiel 37:21, 22; Zephaniah 3:19–20; Romans 11:26, 27) and the establishment of universal peace (Isaiah 11:6–9; Psalm 72:3–8; Micah 4:3, 4).

First, there was a concern that the statement contained no clear position on the rapture, which left a sense of ambiguity. By restoring the term "rapture" to the EFT in the Millennial Reign, they were able to differentiate the first coming for the saints from the "visible return" of Christ when he comes with his saints, while using

---

so many people from varied locations could so quickly agree on its most important piece of business. By this action the General Council of the Assemblies of God has told the world that its faith in the Full Gospel as declared forty-five years ago is still unchanged and unwavering."

[78] *GC Minutes* (August 23–29, 1961), 23. The only notable change to the New Heavens and New Earth article is an error in the Scripture support verse. The committee changed (Rev 21, 22), meaning all the full chapters, to (Rev 21:22), which is a verse about the Lamb and the Temple. That error was corrected in during the 1973 council. *GC Minutes* (August 16–21, 1972), 122.

[79] "Introductory Comments of Committee on Tenets of Faith Revision," Proposed Revised Statement of Fundamental Truths Article V. at General Council, June 14, 1961, comments, "Because of the intrusion of A-Millennial doctrine into our midst, we have outlined the events of the end-time that lead up to the millennium along with firming up of our belief in the one thousand year reign of Christ on this earth."

[80] *GC Minutes* (September 16–22, 1927), 8.

[81] *GC Minutes* (August 23–29, 1961), 23.

the term "Second Coming" to describe both of the phases.[82] Even with this clarification, the committee did not take a position on the tribulation. The result is a version that is similar to the 1916 version, which integrates the elements of the Blessed Hope and the Millennial Reign but focuses on outlining the future events. The second major change included the further clarification of the 1927 affirmation of the salvation of national Israel by adding OT verses that predicted a messianic kingdom of universal peace.[83] This was an important clarification as proponents of amillennialism were accused of spiritualizing the millennium and applying it to the church.[84] It is clear that they believed the future universal reign of peace on earth was a source of hope for the Church and Israel.

The Lake of Fire

15. THE LAKE OF FIRE (1927)[85]

The devil and his angels, the Beast and the false prophet, and whosoever is not found written in the Book of Life, shall be consigned to the everlasting punishment in the lake which burneth with fire and brimstone, which is the second death. (Rev. 19:20; Rev 20:10–15).

15. THE FINAL JUDGMENT (1961)[86]

There will be a final judgment in which the wicked dead will be raised and judged according to their works. Whosoever is not found written in the Book of Life, together with the devil and his angels, the beast and the false prophet, will be consigned to everlasting punishment in the lake which burneth with fire and brimstone, which is the second death (Matt 25:46; Mark 9:43–48; Revelation 19:20; 20:11–15; 21:8).

The 1961 version changed the title "The Lake of Fire" to "The Final Judgment," which was consistent with the chronological emphasis, considering the "final judgment" is an event and "the lake of fire" is a place (Figure 3). The

---

[82] William W. Menzies and Stanley M. Horton, *Bible Doctrines: A Biblical Perspective* (Springfield: Logion Press, 1993), 216; Menzies, *Understanding Our Doctrine*, 65.

[83] Menzies and Horton, *Bible Doctrines*, 238, says, "The premillennial view is the only one that has a place for the restoration of Israel and for the literal fulfillment of the prophecies of peace and blessing."

[84] Menzies and Horton, *Bible Doctrines*, 233, contend that the greatest problem with the amillennial position is that there is "no room in their theological system for any restoration of an earthly Israel."

[85] *GC Minutes* (September 16–22, 1927), 8.

[86] *GC Minutes* (August 23–29, 1961), 23.

rearrangement of the wording and additional sentence helped to clarify that the resurrection of the wicked dead will take place at the end of the millennium (Rev. 20:12). This version also reemphasizes the judgment of the wicked based on works that was deemphasized in 1927. Whereas, in the 1916 version the lake of fire is the place for God's enemies, the 1927 version reverses that emphasis and places the judgment primarily on the wicked and the judgment of God's enemies secondary. By reversing the order, they reversed the emphasis on the final judgment from God's cosmic enemies to sinful humanity.

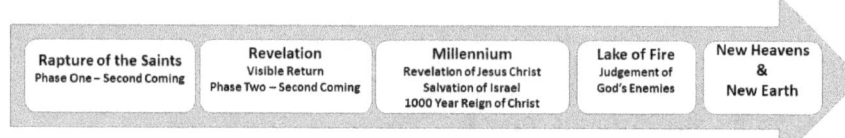

FIGURE 3 - 1961 CHRONOLOGICAL EMPHASIS

Condensed Statement of Fundamental Truths

In the first decade of the twenty-first century, the AG began using a "condensed" statement of truths on their website and as a pamphlet for distribution in the local church called "Assemblies of God Fundamental Truths Condensed" (FTC).[87] This version added the phrase "We Believe" to the statements but did not give supporting verses. Rather than being simply statements of Bible truths like the SFT, this edition suggests this statement is intended to be a more dogmatic declaration of denominational beliefs.[88] Whereas most of the articles are drastically reduced in size, the eschatological truths remain full statements, but deviate in language and emphasis from the current full statements.

---

[87] "Assemblies of God Fundamental Truths condensed" http://ag.org/top/Beliefs/Statement_of_Fundamental_Truths/sft_short.cfm (accessed 11 January 2017). The origin of this statement is unknown and there is no record in the General Secretary office of its origin. It appears to have been created sometime in the 2000s by the Office of Public Relations for a pamphlet called "Our 16 Doctrines," Springfield MO: Office of Public Relations, 2004. It will be referred to as *FTC*.

[88] Bernard Lonergan, *Method in Theology* (New York: Seabury Press, 1979), 319, says, "Doctrines are not just doctrines. They are constitutive of both the individual Christian and of the Christian community." Heyduck, *The Recovery of Doctrine*, 51–96, argues that dogma is the speech act of the community and gives form to the community. It is contextual in that is applies to the specific context in which the doctrine is being declared.

The Blessed Hope

13. The Blessed Hope (2015)[89]

The resurrection of those who have fallen asleep in Christ and their translation together with those who are alive and remain unto the coming of the Lord is the imminent and blessed hope of the Church (1 Thessalonians 4:16,17; Romans 8:23; Titus 2:13; 1 Corinthians 15:51,52).

13. WE BELIEVE ... in The Blessed Hope—When Jesus Raptures His Church Prior to His Return to Earth (the second coming). At this future moment in time all believers who have died will rise from their graves and will meet the Lord in the air, and Christians who are alive will be caught up with them, to be with the Lord forever. [1 of 4 cardinal doctrines of the AG]

Although intended to be a shortened statement, the Blessed Hope is actually longer and more detailed. The language of this "condensed" statement departs in that the FTC replaces the word "resurrection" with the term "rapture" in the Blessed Hope, referring to the rapture as the Blessed Hope rather than the resurrection. This change gives a different feeling to the formula when it is coupled with the phrase "caught up" later in the statement. It is also interesting that this coming is not imminent, but it is a "future moment." While interpreted as the same thing, it lessens the longstanding importance of the immediacy of Christ's return.

The Millennial Reign

14. The Millennial Reign of Christ (2015)

The second coming of Christ includes the rapture of the saints, which is our blessed hope, followed by the visible return of Christ with His saints to reign on the earth for one thousand years (Zechariah 14:5; Matthew 24:27, 30; Revelation 1:7; 19:11–14; 20:1–6). This millennial reign will bring the salvation of national Israel (Ezekiel 37:21, 22; Zephaniah 3:19, 20; Romans 11:26, 27) and the establishment of universal peace (Isaiah 11:6–9; Psalm 72:3–8; Micah 4:3, 4).

14. WE BELIEVE ... in The Millennial Reign of Christ when Jesus returns with His saints at His second coming and begins His benevolent rule over earth for 1,000 years. This millennial reign will bring the salvation of national Israel and the establishment of universal peace.

[89] *GC Minutes* (August 3–7, 2015), 99–100.

The reworded millennium article changes the meaning of the term "second coming" from how it is defined in the SFT, which uses the term to describe both phases of the return of Christ. The FTC uses "second coming" to denote only the visible return at the beginning of the millennium. The other details about the millennium are similar in nature and tone.

The Final Judgment

> 15. The Final Judgment (2015)
>
> There will be a final judgment in which the wicked dead will be raised and judged according to their works. Whosoever is not found written in the Book of Life, together with the devil and his angels, the beast and the false prophet, will be consigned to everlasting punishment in the lake which burneth with fire and brimstone, which is the second death (Matthew 25:46; Mark 9:43–48; Revelation 19:20; 20:11–15; 21:8).
>
> 15. WE BELIEVE ... A Final Judgment Will Take Place for those who have rejected Christ. They will be judged for their sin and consigned to eternal punishment in a punishing lake of fire.

The article on the final judgment also differs markedly from the SFT, especially when compared to the 1916 version. In the FTC, the shift in emphasis from judgment of God's enemies to the judgment of humanity is complete. The final judgment is no longer a source of hope for humanity in which cosmic justice is finally executed on the Devil and his agents. Instead, God's justice is aimed solely at humanity with the promise of wrath and the lake of fire. The only justice done in this version is the eternal punishment of those who have rejected Christ.[90]

The New Heavens and New Earth

> 16. The New Heavens and the New Earth (2015)

---

[90] An example of this move was demonstrated by a recent Ph.D. dissertation by Alicia R. Jackson, "Ezekiel's Two Sticks and Eschatological Violence in the Pentecostal Tradition: An Intertextual Literary Analysis," Ph.D. dissertation, University of Birmingham, 2018, which examines the role of eschatological violence in Pentecostal literature. Jackson argues that dispensational interpretations of Ezekiel had the effect of justifying the dehumanization of nations that are interpreted as eschatological enemies of God. Jackson's dissertation was not available to the author until the completion of this study.

"We, according to His promise, look for new heavens and a new earth, wherein dwelleth righteousness" (2 Peter 3:13; Revelation 21, 22).

16. WE BELIEVE ... and look forward to the perfect New Heavens and a New Earth that Christ is preparing for all people, of all time, who have accepted Him. We will live and dwell with Him there forever following His millennial reign on Earth. "And so shall we forever be with the Lord!"

Nearly a century after it was written, the "New Heavens and New Earth" finally received some attention in the FTC. This surprisingly hopeful revision is twice as long as the original and is helpful in giving insight into the purpose of this doctrine. Note that the new creation is being "prepared" by Christ as a future home for Christ to live and dwell with believers for eternity following the millennium. Although not explicit, this language implies an awareness of the eternality of the creation and the earth itself as the future home for resurrected believers.

While the eschatological statements found in the condensed statement are similar to the *SFT*, they do not necessarily portray the AG's position. These revisions were not approved by the General Council and based on the rules of polity should not be considered to be authoritative. The fact that the *FTC* has been used for the credentialing of ministers is potentially problematic and could lead to reasons for objections by the ministers who are asked to affirm their belief in these tenets.

Statement of Faith in the *Pentecostal Evangel*

In addition to the SFT, a short "We Believe" statement of faith was published weekly in the Pentecostal Evangel beginning in 1956, adapted from the National Association of Evangelicals magazine.[91] The modification of the NAE statement demonstrates that the AG had continuity with the NAE but also wanted it to

---

[91] Robert Cunningham, "We Believe: Robert C. Cunningham Recalls the Origin of the Doctrinal Statement That Appears Regularly in the Pentecostal Evangel," *AG Heritage* 15, no. 3 (Fall 1995): 15, explains where the statement came from. "I noticed there was a statement titled, 'This We Believe,' in each issue of the *United Evangelical Action*, the official magazine of the National Association of Evangelicals, of which the Assemblies of God has been a member from the beginning. It occurred to me that a statement of this kind was needed in the *Pentecostal Evangel* so that anyone picking up the magazine for the first time might be assured that our doctrine is biblically sound. So I offered this suggestion to Brother Flower. He favored the idea and suggested we should pattern our statement on that of the N.A.E. magazine. This we did, using the same phraseology in most of the sentences, but we added two sentences."

conform to the standards of AG Pentecostal positions.[92] The eschatological statements are as follows:

> *We believe* in the deity of our Lord Jesus Christ, in His virgin birth, in His sinless life, in His miracles, in His vicarious and atoning death, in His bodily resurrection, in His ascension to the right hand of the Father, and in His personal future return to this earth in power and glory to rule a thousand years. *We believe* in the blessed hope, which is the Rapture of the Church at Christ's coming. . . . *We believe* in the resurrection of both the saved and the lost, the one to everlasting life and the other to everlasting damnation.[93]

It is noteworthy that the sentence, "[We believe] in the blessed hope—the rapture of the Church at Christ's coming" was not in the NAE statement; it was added in 1963 at the request of the readers who felt the eschatological tenets were incomplete.[94] This suggests that the eschatological revisions are directly a result of maintaining Pentecostal positions even while seeking evangelical identity. The statement takes a general premillennial position, which does not differentiate between the rapture and the revelation. It is also missing any mention of the restoration of Israel or the new heavens and new earth. Like the SFT, there is no position on the tribulation. In many ways, this statement is not truly reflecting AG positions, yet was seen as instructive to thousands of weekly readers. The fact that he was able to publish a statement is surprising considering it was not formally approved by any official AG body.

World Assemblies of God Fellowship Statement of Faith

In 1988, J. Phillip Hogan gathered together general superintendents from forty of the world's AG national fellowships for the purpose of promoting greater cooperation in missions and fellowship. In August of 1989, delegates met to form the World Pentecostal Assemblies of God Fellowship (WAGF) and drafted a constitution and bylaws. For a statement of faith, they decided to adopt the

---

[92] The assertion made by Blumhofer, *Restoring the Faith*, 243, that the *SFT* was modified in 1961 to reflect the NAE was most likely mistakenly attributed to this origin of the *Pentecostal Evangel* statement. As was demonstrated earlier, the 1961 revision was initiated because of questions over eschatological clarity.

[93] "This We Believe," *PE*, September 15, 1963, 7.

[94] Cunningham, "We Believe," 15.

statement found in the Pentecostal Evangel, not the SFT.[95] The WAGF statement was expanded in 2000 to the current formulation.

Whereas the *SFT* has four articles on eschatology, the WAGF has only one article with two statements:

11. The End of Time.[96]

We believe in the premillennial, imminent, and personal return of our Lord Jesus Christ to gather His people unto Himself. Having this blessed hope and earnest expectation, we purify ourselves, even as He is pure, so that we may be ready to meet Him when He comes (John 14:1–3; Titus 2:13; 1 Thessalonians 4:15–17; 1 John 3:2–3; Revelation 20:1–6).

We believe in the bodily resurrection of all humanity, the everlasting conscious bliss of all who truly believe in our Lord Jesus Christ, and that everlasting conscious punishment is the portion of all whose names are not written in the Book of Life (John 5:28–29; 1 Corinthians 15:22–24; Revelation 20:10–15).

The WAGF statement concisely combined the Blessed Hope, Millennial Reign, and final judgment into one article. The first statement is similar to SFT Millennial Reign doctrine but without the emphasis on the restoration of Israel. The second statement closely mirrors the British AoG statement with slightly modified language.[97] The inclusive and general wording of this statement was for cultivating universal agreement by the various national fellowships, many of which do not take firm stances on eschatology.[98] Like the SFT, there is no position on the tribulation. In the WAGF, the reference to resurrection is part of the final judgment in which righteous believers receive "everlasting bliss" and the wicked receive "everlasting punishment." This wording could imply a simultaneous resurrection of the righteous and the wicked as described by Jesus in Jn 5:28–29, which does not suggest a two-phase coming.[99] This statement also contains the admonition to

---

[95] William Molenaar, "The World Assemblies of God Fellowship: United in the Missionary Spirit," *AG Heritage* 31 (2011): 43.

[96] World Assemblies of God Fellowship Constitution and Bylaws, August 2014, 6.

[97] The British Assemblies of God Statement of Faith has only one eschatological tenet, which reads, "We believe in the bodily resurrection of all men, the everlasting conscious bliss of all who truly believe in our Lord Jesus Christ and the everlasting conscious punishment of all whose names are not written in the Book of Life." www.aog.org.uk/about-us/what-we-believe (accessed 17 March 2018).

[98] William Kay, *Pentecostals in Britain* (Carlisle: Paternoster Press, 2002).

[99] "Do not be amazed at this, for a time is coming when all who are in their graves will hear his voice and come out—those who have done what is good will rise to live, and those who have done what is evil will rise to be condemned" (Jn. 5:28–29).

prepare for his coming through sanctification, which is something that is not present in any of the AG statements.

4

ESCHATOLOGICAL CONTROVERSIES

Over the past century, a number of eschatological controversies emerged that forced the General Council to seriously consider the boundaries of what eschatological views would be allowed within the fellowship. In this section, we will look at each of these controversies and how the leadership of the AG responded.

The Rapture and the Baptism

One of the most common eschatological metaphors of the Pentecostal Movement was the concept of the "Bride of Christ." Early Pentecostals fused the eschatological concept of the Bridegroom coming for the bride with the pneumatological concept of baptism in the Holy Spirit.[1] Several testimonies in the Apostolic Faith talked of individuals who were baptized in the Spirit as being "sealed as one of the bride" and in which the "sign" of that seal was speaking in tongues.[2] In this way, they believed only Spirit-filled believers would be included in the rapture. Those who are not prepared will be left behind to endure the tribulation while the bride celebrates the Wedding Supper of the Lamb in heaven. For many Pentecostals, the Spirit and the bride were intimately connected, particularly in the cry of the Spirit to hasten the Lord's return. As one writer said, "To emphasize the cry, God has given the bride a new tongue to utter it."[3]

Although there were some in the AG that held the exclusive bridal rapture doctrine, the majority of early leaders such as Bell, Flower, and Jamieson were expressing their discomfort with Spirit-baptism as the minimum requirement for

---

[1] Dale M. Coulter, "The Spirit and the Bride Revisited: Pentecostalism, Renewal, and the Sense of History," *JPT* 21 (2012): 301.

[2] *AF* 1.4 (December 1906), 2, testifies "when we are baptized with the Holy Spirit we are sealed in the forehead until his coming." See also *AF*, February 1907, 1. See also *AF*, October 1906, 3; A. A. Boddy, "'Tongues' as a Seal of 'Pentecost,'" *Confidence*, April 1908, 18; McQueen, *Toward a Pentecostal Eschatology*, 68–69.

[3] "They Shall Speak With New Tongues," *PE*, December 27, 1919, 3.

the rapture.⁴ Many others shared this sentiment as well. When Bertha Dixon outlined her "essentials for the rapture," she criticized the doctrine of the exclusive rapture as a "subtle form of spiritual pride" and ultimately a form of "fanaticism."⁵ Dixon believed the parable of the foolish virgins describes backslidden Christians instead of those who weren't filled with the Spirit. She concludes, "If the church includes all true believers in Jesus, so also does the bride, so also does the body, and so also does the rapture."⁶ J. T. Boddy declared, "The Lord is coming back for his entire family, not just certain members of it."⁷ J. N. Gortner said in 1931, "The people who will go up when Jesus comes will be the people who love the Lord and will be found loving Him at the time of His appearance."⁸

During the controversy with the New Order of the Latter Rain, the bridal rapture doctrine began to reemerge. In a time when the AG was gaining acceptance in the broader evangelical community as a part of the NAE, they could not afford to support such an exclusivist and elitist view.⁹ As a result, in 1946 the General Presbyters passed a resolution declaring that Spirit-baptism was not a qualification for the rapture.

> Whereas, word has been brought to the General Presbyters that contention is arising in some sections by those who are strongly teaching that a person must have the Baptism with the Holy Ghost, speaking with other tongues in order to be ready for the rapture, and whereas, it is the belief of this body that those who are born of the Spirit and walking in the light have the promise of being ready when Jesus comes, therefore be it resolved, that we disapprove of extreme teaching which only tends to breed controversy instead of unity and fellowship.¹⁰

---

⁴ J. R. Flower, "The Bride of Christ," *TP,* November 1910, 10; "As a Presbyterian Now Sees It," *CE,* October 31, 1914, 1–2; E. N. Bell, "Questions and Answers," *CE,* August 24, 1918, 9.

⁵ B. P. Dixon, "What is the Essential Preparation for the Rapture," *PE,* November 1, 1919, 14, says, "Walking in the light whether it means one definite experience or another, is essential to perfect justification and therefore to a preparation for the rapture."

⁶ Dixon, "What is the Essential Preparation for the Rapture," 14.

⁷ J. T. Boddy, "Who Will be in the Rapture," *PE,* April 16, 1921, 5.

⁸ J. N. Gortner, "Who Will Constitute the Bride?," *PE,* January 3, 1931, 3.

⁹ Earlier that year, J. R. Flower urged the AG members to embrace the opportunity to cooperate with evangelicals through the NAE. He said, "This is not the time to draw back into a shell of exclusiveness. We need to go forward, make contacts, mingle with Christians of other faiths in every cause of righteousness, which would not involve a compromise." *AG Minister Letter,* March 1, 1946.

¹⁰ *AG Minister Letter,* October 22, 1946.

Despite the declaration, the issue reemerged again during the Charismatic Renewal in the 1960s. In 1961, Ralph Riggs addressed the ongoing bridal theology controversy over the nature of the bride and declared that speculation about which groups are part of the bride "destroyed the beautiful significance" of the Second Coming.[11] Riggs argued that the parable of the virgins is a "figure of speech" that was intended to be interpreted generally rather than as specific details. Riggs says, "I therefore conclude that the Bride of the Lamb will include all God's holy saints from Abel to the last one converted before the Rapture."[12] In downplaying the emphasis on the Spirit in the rapture they succeeded in avoiding the charge of exclusivity but they also successfully purged a uniquely Pentecostal modification of the rapture doctrine.

The Scofield Reference Bible

One of the most influential resources on eschatology in the AG was the popular Scofield Reference Bible published in 1909.[13] Cyrus I. Scofield's Bible was a marvel of its time containing a system of topical references, book introductions, indexed scriptures, and extensive notes that harmonize and explain the dispensational structure. The Scofield Reference Bible is credited with popularizing Darby's dispensational model, though direct influences are hard to prove and there is little to suggest that he intended to popularize Darby's teachings.[14]

The *Scofield Reference Bible* made its first appearance in the *Pentecostal Evangel* in 1914 where it was highly recommended by the editors and was the primary Bible promoted to members of the AG.[15] The editors called it "a wonderful Bible" that has "gained universal favor with Pentecostal people."[16] By 1917, the paper regularly contained a nearly full-page advertisement.[17] However, the Bible

---

[11] Ralph Riggs, "Christ Takes A Bride," *PE,* November 19, 1961, 10–11.

[12] Riggs, "Christ Takes A Bride," 11.

[13] C. I. Scofield, ed., *The Scofield Reference Bible* (New York: Oxford University Press, 1909).

[14] Prosser, *Dispensational Eschatology,* 245–62, comments "Darby did not succeed in promulgating his doctrine in the way that his later disciple, Cyrus I. Scofield, did in 1909." However, as R. Todd Mangum and Mark S. Sweetnam, *The Scofield Bible: Its History and Impact on the Evangelical Church* (Colorado Springs: Paternoster, 2009), 79–81, point out, Scofield relied heavily on James Brookes and his distinctive brand of dispensationalism that simplified the separation of Israel and the Church.

[15] *CE,* August 8, 1914, 3; McQueen, *Toward a Pentecostal Eschatology,* 294; Thompson, *Kingdom Come,* 38–39, 49–58.

[16] *WE,* December 9, 1916, 16.

[17] *WE,* September 15, 1917, 16.

was not without controversy. In 1917, W. W. Simpson wrote to Scofield and asked him to defend his views on the topic of speaking in tongues since it was not made clear in the commentary of his Bible.[18] Scofield chose not to engage with Simpson, which prompted Simpson to write a scathing critique of Scofield's position in the *Pentecostal Evangel*. In an editorial response, Flower tried to minimize Simpson's assertion that Scofield's Bible was anti-Pentecostal.

> The Scofield Reference Bible, which contains no attacks on the Pentecostal or any other movement, is still highly esteemed among us. The Scofield Bible is found in the hands of hundreds of Pentecostal preachers, workers and Bible students, who take advantage of its clear teachings and rejoice in the aid which its use affords. We continue in our recommendation of the Scofield Bible as the best work of its kind that has ever been published.[19]

In the same issue as Simpson's critique, Flower wrote a glowing recommendation of the Bible and testified that it was finding "happy homes" in many Pentecostal families because of its "condensed Pentecostal truths."[20] Bell reassured readers who may have been worried that the Bible would contribute to a loss of belief in Pentecostal distinctives. He comments,

> While there are splendid helps in the Scofield Bible and others which we can most certainly heartily endorse, yet the fact remains that almost any special translation or any Bible with special notes in it, has some objectionable features. . . . Our Pentecostal people are so well taught on these lines of the Baptism with the Spirit, surely none of them would follow Scofield's wrong conclusions on this matter. Rather, take the many good things in his Bible, and pass these mistakes up to his ignorance of full Pentecostal light.[21]

The Bible continued to be advertised with the full assurance Flower and Bell that it was acceptable to Pentecostal believers.

As attacks by Fundamentalists grew in the 1920s, the controversy over the *Scofield Bible* resurfaced. In 1924, concerns about the Scofield's position on

---

[18] W. W. Simpson, "The Baptism in the Spirit—A Defense," *WE*, July 14, 1917, 2–6; See also McQueen, *Toward a Pentecostal Eschatology*, 164–65.

[19] *WE*, July 14, 1917, 6.

[20] J. R. Flower, "Scofield Bibles Finding Many Happy Homes," *WE*, July 14, 1917, 7–8. Flower notes, "One brother received his Bible and wrote: 'The work is a marvel of condensed Pentecostal truths brought out more clearly than I have seen anywhere else. I am very thankful for the privilege of possessing a copy.'" Cf. *WE*, August 19, 1916, 2.

[21] E. N. Bell, "Notes on Modern Bibles," *CE*, June 1, 1918, 5.

Spirit-baptism resulted in a decision by the AG Executive Presbytery to remove the Bible from their advertisements.[22] However, the ban on this popular Bible didn't last long. Just two years later J. R. Evans asked the Executive Presbytery to reinstate the Bible, arguing that its extremely helpful notes were better than any other Bible.[23] They agreed to sell it again with the concession that it must be accompanied by a list of Scofield's teachings that were considered out of harmony with their Pentecostal views. The first was Scofield's dispensational belief that the Sermon on the Mount was "pure law" for Israel and not the Church.[24] Second, they rejected Scofield's theory that the kingdom was "postponed" and not present during the Church age. Third, they note that Scofield advocated a "somewhat extreme teaching on eternal security" that had already been disapproved by the General Council. The greatest disagreement was with Scofield's opinion that "every believer is baptized in the Spirit," which was in contradiction with the distinctive testimony of Pentecostals. Still, the overall value of the dispensational framework in the Bible was of such great importance that they overlooked what they considered as minor points of difference on the Holy Spirit, the kingdom, and ecclesiology.[25] The Executive Presbyters concluded that the *Scofield Bible* was "perfectly sound" and would once again sell the Bible as long as it was accompanied by the list of issues of disagreement.[26] Support for the *Scofield Bible* continued over the next few decades with the similar endorsement and caveats.[27]

---

[22] Gary B. McGee, "Historical Background" in Stanley M. Horton, ed., *Systematic Theology* (Springfield: Logion Press, 1995), 22. There is no record of official action to remove the *Scofield Bible* from circulation in the *Pentecostal Evangel*.

[23] "A Great Move Forward," *PE,* May 1, 1926, 3.

[24] For Scofield, Jesus proclaimed the Kingdom of God through the Sermon on the Mount. But the Jews rejected Jesus and therefore rejected the Kingdom of God. Though the principles are true for the Christian, he says, "For these reasons the Sermon on the Mount in its primary application gives neither the privilege nor the duty of the Church." *The Scofield Reference Bible*, 999–1000.

[25] It is interesting to note that Scofield had very limited notes on 1 Thessalonians 4 and does not refer to this event as the rapture or explain its connection to the dispensation that would follow. The word "rapture" does not regularly occur in the Bible's notes and is not included in the topical index. *The Scofield Reference Bible*, 1269.

[26] "A Great Move Forward," *PE,* May 1, 1926, 3.

[27] *PE,* June 8, 1935, 15, Stanley Frodsham commented, "For the past 18 years I have been using a Scofield Bible with great profit. . . . There are some foot notes in the Bible I do not like, noticeably a note on the Sermon on the Mount, some notes concerning what Scofield calls 'the postponed kingdom,' and his notes on the second chapter of Acts. But apart from these his notes are most valuable and quite spiritual."

The fact that the leadership was willing to accommodate disagreements on Pentecostal doctrine for the sake of Scofield's eschatology is certainly perplexing to scholars today. However, it is important to note there were a number of ambiguities on important Pentecostal topics in the *Scofield Reference Bible* that allowed the AG to manage such tensions.[28] First, his commentary on Acts 2 was not hostile toward Pentecostal positions, even if he did not affirm them. His position on the Day of Pentecost was that the outpouring of the Spirit was given first to the Jew and then later to the Gentiles and is "permanent for the entire church-age."[29] Second, like many late nineteenth-century evangelicals, Scofield taught the need for a subsequent "filling with the Spirit" that was separate from conversion.[30] In fact, he argued, "the N.T. distinguishes between having the Spirit, which is true of all believers, and being filled with the Spirit."[31] Scofield also believed that the Holy Spirit is the source of power for the Church that enables the gifts in the Church.[32] It is true that Scofield believed that the "power gifts" mentioned in 1 Corinthians 12 were for only for the "primitive church" and believed that ultimately "tongues and the sign gifts are to cease," but he was somewhat ambiguous about when or why that cessation would take place. Scofield was also notably silent on his position on divine healing and simply avoided commentary on passages that affirmed such beliefs.[33] It is therefore safe to say that, although Scofield disagreed with Pentecostals, Scofield's Bible was not openly hostile toward Pentecostal theology any more than earlier evangelical resources. In fact, Scofield commented in his *Plain Papers on the Holy Spirit,* He says, "No Christian should be willing to perform the slightest act in the service of Christ until he is definitely filled with the Holy Spirit." [34] As Bell noted,

---

[28] Menzies, *Anointed to Serve*, 329.

[29] *The Scofield Reference Bible*, 1149.

[30] Thompson, *Kingdom Come,* 56, asserts "the Scofieldian system focuses almost exclusively on Christ to the exclusion of the Spirit." While that may be true of his end-time scenario, Scofield focuses on the Spirit in the present ministry of the Church during the present dispensation.

[31] *The Scofield Reference Bible*, 1149.

[32] *The Scofield Reference Bible*, 1150, says, "The Spirit forms the church" by baptizing believers into the body of Christ and "imparts gifts for service to every member of that body (I Cor. 12:7–11, 27, 30)," and "gives power to serve."

[33] Some examples are Mt. 8:17, Jas. 5:14, Mk. 16:17, 1 Pet. 2:24, and limited comment on 1 Corinthians 12–14.

[34] C. I. Scofield, *Plain Papers on the Doctrine of the Holy Spirit* (Westwood, NJ: Revell, 1899), 78. Like other evangelicals of his time, he fully embraced the concept of Spirit Baptism (salvation) and being filled with the Spirit (empowerment). Likewise he says of gifts, "We quench the Spirit when we

Pentecostals should be secure enough to overlook the differences and appreciate what they considered to be an otherwise significant Bible.[35]

Disapproved Eschatological Errors

The introduction to the AG Constitution gave the General Council the ability to "disapprove all unscriptural methods, doctrines, and conduct" in order to maintain unity within the fellowship."[36] Beginning in 1917, a number of eschatological "heresies" were addressed by the General Council.[37] Pentecostals took notice when the U.S. entered WWI and Britain took control of Palestine in 1917.[38] These significant events, coupled with the relative frequency of visions about the return of Christ, raised the level of speculation about the date of the Lord's return.[39] Arthur Frodsham commented, "This year therefore has some special claims to be considered as a very principal starting point of the times of the Gentiles, which measured from that period, run out in A.D. 1917. The latest date they could terminate would be 1934."[40] In response, the General Council passed a resolution against preaching or publishing a fixed time of the Second Coming.[41]

> Setting a date for the Lord's return. It is unwise to teach that the Lord will come at some specified time, thereby setting a date for His appearing (Mark 13:32, 33; Luke 12:37–40; 1 Thessalonians 5:2). It is also unwise to give out from the platform, or publish, visions of numbers and dates fixing the time of the second coming of the Lord.[42]

---

consent to such arrangements in the life or organization as give no liberty for the ministry of the various gifts of the Spirit, thus imposing silence or inactivity on others."(58)

[35] E. N. Bell, "Notes on Modern Bibles," *CE*, June 1, 1918, 5.

[36] *GC Minutes* (April 2–12, 1914), 4.

[37] *GC Minutes* (September 9–14, 1917), 17.

[38] "The Great War," *WE*, April 6, 1918, 6.

[39] A perfect example of this is, "War! War! War!," *WE*, September 23, 1916, 16, which declares, "Did you know that this world-war is a fulfillment of prophecy?'

[40] J. R. Flower, *WE*, March 28, 1917, 4, notes that many were having visions of the Lord returning in 1917. One of the sources for this date setting was the chronology by Dr. H. Grattan Guinness, which was used in several articles in 1917. See *WE*, July 28, 1917, 5; *WE*, September 8, 1917, 3; A. W. F. "1917," *WE*, December 22, 1917, 7.

[41] *GC Minutes* (September 9–14, 1917), 17. The management of the paper apologized for publishing the articles and commented that they "never meant to set a date for His coming again. So we are all agreed on this."

[42] *GC Minutes* (August 3–7, 2015), 132.

In 1920, the Council passed another resolution that disapproved of eternal security and Seventh Day Adventist teaching.[43] In 1925, the council added the disapproval of the universalist doctrine of the "restitution of all things" taught by Charles Pridgeon.[44] Pridgeon was a popular teacher in Pentecostal circles but became a controversial figure when he combined his Pentecostal faith with a form of universalism that taught that judgment would be temporal until God restored all things in Christ in the eschaton.[45] As "Pridgeonism" became more popular in AG circles, the 1925 Council condemned the teaching as heretical and added it to the list of disapproved doctrines.[46]

> a. The restitution of all things. The Assemblies of God understands the teaching of Acts 3:21 to limit the restoration to that of which the prophets have spoken, thus denying the universal redemption theory. We are opposed to all forms of universalism (Matthew 25:46; Revelation 20:10).[47]

Post-Tribulation Rapture

The early Pentecostal exclusive rapture position on the left open the possibility that some Christians would have to endure the tribulation. As a result, in 1936 the General Presbytery decided to address the AG position on whether Christians will go through the tribulation.[48] They crafted a resolution for the 1937 General Council warning against ministers teaching post-tribulationism.[49] The resolution addressed two matters of concern to the Council. First, they were concerned about the way in which the post-tribulation rapture undermines the doctrine of imminence. Post-tribulationists held that the events depicted in Revelation must transpire before the rapture occurs, which the AG believed discouraged believers

---

[43] *Combined GC Minutes* (1914–1920), 30. E. N. Bell, "Seventh Day Trouble," *PE*, January 11, 1919, 9, mentions that Advent teaching was "disturbing the mind of the saints." The AG rejected Adventist views of the Sabbath. Cf. "Warnings," *WW*, July 1915, 4; D. M. Canright, "Adventism Refuted," *PE*, June 28, 1919, 6. They also rejected Adventism for its history of date setting by founder William Miller.

[44] Gary B. McGee, "Historical Background," in Stanley M. Horton, ed., *Systematic Theology*, 24–25.

[45] G.B. McGee, "Pridgeon, Charles Hamilton," in *DPCM*, 727.

[46] *GC Minutes* (September 16–22, 1927), 31.

[47] *GC Minutes* (August 3–7, 2015), 132.

[48] McGee, "Historical Background," 25. Around 1930, Executive Presbyter J. Narver Gortner was asked by ministers to publish a series of lectures given at Glad Tidings Bible Institute in San Francisco, California. This resulted in J. N. Gortner, *Are the Saints Scheduled to Go Through the Tribulation?* (Springfield: Gospel Publishing House, 1930). See *PE*, November 29, 1930, 4–5.

[49] *GC Minutes* (September 2–9, 1937), 46.

from being prepared for his coming. The second objection to post-tribulationism was that disagreements about which groups had to go through the tribulation were causing "confusion and division."[50] J. N. Gortner argued that if Christians must go through the tribulation, how would Christ's coming be a blessed hope? He comments,

> If the saints are going to have to go through the tribulation it would be better for us to die than to live until Jesus comes. . . . And if it is indeed true that the saints are going to have to go through the tribulation, I pray, let me not live until Jesus comes! Let me die before the rapture! . . . It will be better for me than for those who live and go through those awful days.[51]

The Presbytery was reluctant to declare a definitive position on the tribulation, but felt it was necessary because ministers were making it an issue for the Council.[52] In the end they decided to condemn post-tribulationism, but with the caveat that allowed ministers to hold a personal belief in the post-tribulation rapture if they refrained from preaching and teaching it. It was added to the list of disapproved doctrines, and its wording remains essentially the same as the original.

> b. Post-Tribulation Rapture. The General Council of the Assemblies of God has declared itself in the Statement of Fundamental Truths that it holds to the belief in the imminent coming of the Lord as the blessed hope of the Church; and since the teaching that the Church must go through the Tribulation tends to bring confusion and division among the saints, it is recommended that all our ministers teach the imminent coming of Christ, warning all to be prepared for that coming, which may occur at any time, and not lull their minds into complacency by any teaching that would cause them to feel that specific Tribulation events must occur before the rapture of the saints.[53]

Amillennialism

During the 1960s, some AG ministers were earning advanced degrees from Protestant schools where they were exposed to other millennial views. At the same time, the Pentecostal movement gained an influx of people from other Christian

---

[50] *GC Minutes* (September 2–9, 1937), 70.

[51] Gortner, *Are the Saints Scheduled to Go Through the Tribulation*, 9.

[52] Superintendent E. S. Williams declared, "We are not bringing up these differences; it is being done by other brethren, and the responsibility for these differences all rests upon these brethren." *GC Minutes* (September 2–9, 1937), 70.

[53] *GC Minutes* (August 3–7, 2015), 132.

traditions who were baptized in the Spirit during the Charismatic Renewal.[54] As amillennialism was becoming more popular, AG leaders felt they needed to address the issue. A resolution was offered at the 1969 General Council added amillennialism to the list of "Eschatological Errors" because ministers were "actively espousing the divisive doctrine of Amillennialism, a position in direct opposition to our historical premillennial teaching." [55] They considered amillennialism to be erroneous because it denied the premillennial coming and defined the Church dispensation as the "spiritual millennium." After some discussion by the Council, the matter was referred to a study committee. The next year, a resolution was approved that added amillennialism to the list of eschatological errors.[56]

> c. Amillennialism. The General Council of the Assemblies of God disapproves of the amillennial teaching and its attendant erroneous philosophy which denies the fact of a literal 1,000-year reign of Christ on the earth, and substitutes for it the theory that this Christian or Church dispensation is the spiritual Millennium of which, its proponents say, the Bible writers prophesied. [57]

The Allowance Clause on Eschatological Errors

The post-tribulational controversy of 1937 forced the AG to reluctantly take a position on the tribulation. However, by establishing the allowance clause, they protected the individual's right to hold variant views as long as they "refrain from preaching and teaching it." In 1967, a committee was appointed to revise, clarify, and expand the list of disapproved doctrines.[58] In 1969, the list of "disapproved doctrines" was reorganized and placed under the heading "Eschatological Errors."[59] The reorganization effort resulted in moving the allowance clause, which originally only applied to the post-tribulation controversy, to the end of the list making it applicable to all eschatological errors.

> d. Credentials jeopardized if made an issue. We recommend that those ministers who embrace any of the foregoing eschatological errors refrain from preaching or teaching them. Should they persist in emphasizing these doctrines to the

---

[54] Blumhofer, *Restoring the* Faith, 223–38.
[55] *GC Minutes* (August 21–26, 1969), 81–82.
[56] *GC Minutes* (August 19–24, 1971), 14–15.
[57] *GC Minutes* (August 3–7, 2015), 132.
[58] *GC Minutes* (August 24–29, 1967), 40–41; *PE,* October 15, 1967, 19.
[59] *GC Minutes* (August 21–26, 1969), 116; *GC Minutes* (August 19–24, 1971), 14–15.

point of making them an issue, their standing in the Fellowship will be seriously affected (Luke 21:34–36; 1 Thessalonians 5:9, 10; 2 Thessalonians 1:4–10; Revelation 3:10, 19, 20).[60]

In moving the allowance clause, it gave ministers the opportunity to affirm that the AG as a denomination affirms the pre and mid-tribulational views, but also permits privately held post-tribulational and amillennial views as long as they do not make an issue of them. This created a legal difference between a minister who may personally embrace a disapproved position and a minister who preaches/teaches a disapproved position whose credentials are in jeopardy or "may be seriously affected."

Committee on Eschatological Loopholes

In 1979, J. Philip Hogan raised concerns with General Presbytery that missionary candidates were failing to take a "precise position" on the issue of the rapture in relation to the tribulation.[61] Hogan believed that the "allowance clause" in the SFT created an "eschatological loophole" that eroded doctrinal purity. Hogan was also critical of AG college faculty who he believed were not defending AG positions. Hogan persuaded the General Presbytery to appoint a "committee on loopholes" in order to investigate the possible gaps the SFT, the bylaws, and the credentialing questionnaires that allowed ministers to skirt doctrinal conformity.[62]

In 1980, the committee reported back to the Presbytery that they had indeed found a number of loopholes that they deemed necessary for the Council to address.[63] First, they felt the allowance clause needed firmer language and suggested substituting "we therefore instruct" in place of "we recommend." Second, they asserted that the founders believed in a pretribulation rapture and

---

[60] *GC Minutes* (August 3–7, 2015), 132.

[61] *GP Minutes* (August 13–15, 1979); Blumhofer, *Assemblies of God*, Vol. 2, 183–85.

[62] *GP Minutes* (August 18–20, 1980). The General Presbytery defined the word loophole as "a small or narrow opening, an outlet or means of escape, an evasion." Appointed to that committee were Assistant General Superintendent Raymond Carlson, Joseph Flower, Paul Lowenberg, R. D. E. Smith, and Dwight McLaughlin.

[63] *GP Minutes* (August 18–20, 1980). The committee identified three reasons why AG ministers could be holding other eschatological positions. First, they believe some ministers had not had enough exposure to AG doctrine and felt that the position papers needed to be emphasized to a greater degree. Second, they believed that some ministers who have studied the subject either in colleges or in their own studies had changed their position from what they once held. Third, they believed that there were those who innocently interpreted the language of the *SFT* differently than the original intent, which was the result of imprecise language.

therefore the position was implied even though the *SFT* has no "definite statement on the time of the rapture." They also recommended that the minister questionnaire require candidates to write out a statement of their position. The report concluded, "We must avoid the drifting of individuals into unreasonable and untenable positions. To hold a balanced position requires the discipline of real scholarship. We strongly recommend that our schools, colleges, and districts keep careful watch on these controversial matters."[64] When it came to a vote, the Presbytery decided to accept the report, but chose not to act on it. Instead, they ordered a further investigation and expanded the number of members on the committee with the commission to report its findings at the next General Presbyter meeting.[65]

The expanded committee met several times throughout that year and prepared a report of their findings for the 1981 General Presbyter meeting. This time, the committee came to two very different conclusions about the problem of loopholes in eschatological commitments than was highlighted by the original committee.[66] First, the 1981 committee did not share any of the concerns of Hogan or the 1980 committee, despite the fact that half of the members were a part of both. Ironically, Hogan's original concern about faculty failing to teach and support the pretribulation position was not addressed or even mentioned in the 1981 report. This committee report concluded the AG's position was sufficiently represented by the existing doctrinal statements and reported, "When it comes to eschatological matters we are in good order to not go beyond the bylaws."[67] They concluded that the bylaws that were sufficient enough to deal with any ministers who might insist on making an issue of the matter.

Second, because the *SFT* maintained that its language was "not inspired or contended for", the committee concluded that that the doctrine presented within it was "large enough to retain reasonable people in the fellowship." They also concluded that the allowance clause, which "recommended" that ministers refrain from teaching other views, was sufficient and that more forceful language was not needed. By keeping the allowance clause in place, they accepted that some ministers were going to hold differing tribulational positions. The

---

[64] *GP Minutes* (August 18–20, 1980). Although the committee noted possible issues with initial physical evidence, baptism, divine healing, eternal security, and sanctification, the bulk of the committee's attention was given to eschatological issues. Blumhofer, *Assemblies of God*, Vol. 2, 183–85, omits the committee's conclusions about the eschatological issues.

[65] Added to the committee were Lowell C. Ashbrook, Edward B. Berkey, Charles E. Crank, W. Earl Cummings and Robert K. Schmidgall.

[66] *GP Minutes* (August 17–19, 1981).

[67] *GP Minutes* (August 17–19, 1981).

committee concluded that better vetting at the district credentialing level would go further to assure that positions on eschatology were maintained rather than narrowing eschatological definitions. Since there were no recommendations for changes to the bylaws, *SFT*, or the credential process, no action was needed and no resolution on the matter was brought to the 1981 General Council. The fact that the committee decided against recommending further eschatological precision is a surprising result. In a time when the General Presbytery was seeking to add more precise definitions on doctrinal positions through position papers, they intentionally preserved the attitude of eschatological diversity that characterized the early years.

The New Order of the Latter Rain

During the 1930s and 1940s, Pentecostal denominations were gaining legitimacy and influence within the broader evangelical movement, but some thought they were losing their spiritual vitality. As a result, a new revivalist movement called the New Order of the Latter Rain began, which sought to recapture the latter rain and revivalist characteristics of the early movement. Latter Rain advocates believed that a latter rain revival was even more powerful than the beginnings of the Pentecostal movement was still to come and would fully restore the apostolic faith to the church. The Latter Rain blamed the waning of power in the Pentecostal movement on the efforts to organize, particularly within the AG.[68]

At first, many members of the AG were open to the revivalist nature of the movement. However, concerns over what were thought of as extreme doctrines necessitated a response by AG leadership. E. S. Williams and J. R. Flower, both veterans of the movement, attended a meeting of the Latter Rain in St. Louis in order to investigate what the adherents were teaching. After meeting with the Presbytery in April 1949, they sent a letter to ministers outlining their concerns.

> It is being claimed that the Pentecostal Movement is passing through a new era, that now we are receiving the Latter Rain, whereas forty years ago the outpouring of the Spirit was merely the Former Rain; now we are receiving an enduement of power "after that" the Holy Ghost has come upon us, whereas forty years ago we received merely an anointing of the Spirit; that this enduement of power is received through the laying on of hands; that now, through the laying on of hands and prophecy, the nine gifts of the Spirit are

---

[68] Blumhofer, *Restoring the Faith*, 207.

bestowed upon or confirmed to believers, and calls to service in home and foreign fields are given and confirmed.[69]

The Presbytery assured minister that what the Latter Rain claimed was "new" was not new at all, after all, the practice of laying on of hands and prophetic ministry was present in the movement from the beginning. However, the Presbytery thought the practice of laying of hands for ordination and impartation of gifts was excessive. They also rejected the claim that this new order was somehow the true manifestation of the latter rain. They cautioned, "That showers of Latter Rain must be confined to a particular mold is unthinkable."[70] Still, they were willing to welcome any group that would pray for an increase of the latter rain of the Spirit that anticipated the soon coming of the Lord.

As the year progressed, more ministers were drawn into the Latter Rain movement, including *Pentecostal Evangel* editor Stanley Frodsham. As a consistent voice in the AG for the latter rain orientation of the movement, Frodsham became a popular speaker at Latter Rain meetings and eventually decided that staying with the AG would limit his ministry among this new movement.[71] Losing Frodsham hurt the Presbytery dearly and only further convinced them that the Latter Rain was a clear threat to the fellowship and was as a tool of the adversary to bring division. At the 1949 General Council, a resolution was adopted that disapproved of the New Order of the Latter Rain and particularly the doctrines of overemphasis on impartation, present-day apostles and prophets, confession of sin to man, impartation of missionary languages, and imparting spiritual gifts.[72] Despite the painful departures and criticisms, Flower wanted to assure AG ministers that Pentecostal movement was still alive and well, yet they must stay committed to their message.

> Our church fellowship is the product of a truly great revival, a latter-rain outpouring of the Holy Spirit that has played a great part in flattening out the wave of last-days humanistic opposition to historic Bible religion. The fires of evangelical, Holy Ghost salvation must be kept burning. For us there must be

---

[69] *AG Minister Letter*, (April 20, 1949).

[70] *AG Minister Letter*, (April 20, 1949).

[71] Frodsham's resignation was included in the *AG Minister Letter*, December 20, 1949, in which he told of his regret that he must leave brethren whom he does "highly esteem and love." *GC Minutes* (September 9–14, 1949), 24.

[72] *GC Minutes* (September 9–14, 1949), 26–27.

no retreat from the full message or the high standards that have been ours from the very beginning of this Pentecostal visitation.[73]

Peter Althouse argues the Latter Rain controversy essentially ended the use of the concept for many Pentecostal groups and pushed the AG to cast their unique understanding of eschatology into more fundamentalist categories.[74] However, as we will see in later chapters, leaders within the AG did not abandon the latter rain concept, rather, they avoided the terminology. Many continued to characterize the AG as a latter rain movement and believed that it was still benefiting from the last days outpouring. For example, Narciso Dionson says, "The outpouring of the Spirit is God's timepiece. It ushered in the Christian age 1900 years ago and there is strong Biblical evidence that it signals the close of the age as well."[75] Assistant General Superintendent Raymond Carlson said the outpouring of the latter rain in the Charismatic movement was "one of the greatest signs" of the soon return of Christ. He says, "The nearer we get to the Second Coming, the greater will be the outpouring of the Holy Spirit."[76] Although the controversy was detrimental to the unity of the AG, it did renew their sense of identity as an eschatological and pneumatological movement during a critical time when they were also seeking to identify with the evangelical community.[77]

The Ecumenical Movement

When the Second Ecumenical Council (Vatican II) was called in 1962, the religious world entered a new era of ecumenical cooperation with the Roman Catholic Church. But AG leaders were skeptical of such endeavors. Robert Cunningham, editor of the Pentecostal Evangel, commented, "Clearly the ecumenical movement among spiritually-dead churches is headed toward that ecclesiastical union called Babylon which is described in Revelation 17 and 18."[78] Frank Boyd echoed this sentiment. "Many evangelical leaders feel that what is going on in the ecumenical movement today is leading to the specific fulfillment

[73] *AG Minister Letter*, June 2, 1952.

[74] Althouse, *Spirit of the Last Days*, 48. See also, Thompson, *Kingdom Come*, 50–51.

[75] Narcisco Dionson, "Pentecost—God's Time Piece," *PE*, January 4, 1970, 3.

[76] G. Raymond Carlson "The Charismatic Movement Today," *PE*, March 30, 1975, 8–11. See also Robert C. Cunningham, "Get Your Share of the Great Outpouring," *PE*, February 19, 1984, 14.

[77] Blumhofer, *Restoring the Faith*, 219.

[78] Robert C. Cunningham, "The Ecumenical Fever," *PE*, March 11, 1962, 3; Robert C. Cunningham, "Scriptural Unity," *PE*, October 7, 1962, 2.

of a biblical prophecy—the emergence of a superchurch."[79] Growing unity between the World Council of Churches and the Roman Catholic Church only heightened fears of a world religious power structure. The Ecumenical movement fed into their Universalist fears and fueled their anti-Catholic bias.[80]

In August of 1963, Dr. George Ford, the director of the NAE, spoke at the 1963 General Council about the dangers of "Communism, Catholicism, and Liberalism" and urged the AG to stand with the NAE in refraining from "participating in this effort to establish a world church."[81] As a result, the General Presbytery decided to make a public stand against the movement and crafted a resolution asking ministers to refrain from participating.[82] The resolution was adopted at the 1963 General Council and was added to the list of disapproved doctrines and discouraged ministers from participating out of fears that "the combination of many religious organizations into a World Super Church will culminate in the Religious Babylon of Revelation 17 and 18."[83]

Ironically, in a time when the AG was seeking acceptance in the evangelical community, they were also shunning ecumenical cooperation with the global church that was opening up to the Spirit through the Charismatic Renewal. The AG's eschatological belief in a coming apostate world church ultimately fueled their bias against ecumenism. This is demonstrated by the dismissal of David du Plessis, one of the AG's most notable world ambassadors for Pentecostalism.[84] Because of his leadership in the Charismatic Renewal, du Plessis was invited to participate in discussions with the World Council of Churches, which he saw an opportunity for Pentecostals to be accepted and to dialogue with the global church. However, the AG forbid du Plessis from participating over fears that he was cooperating with apostate churches. After multiple attempts to reconcile the differences, du Plessis resigned his credentials.[85] The sad irony was that the AG was more interested in acceptance with evangelical churches in the NAE than with the Spirit-baptized people from all denominations in the Charismatic Renewal.

[79] Frank Boyd, "Ecumenicity—False and True," *PE*, October 7, 1962, 4.

[80] Boyd, "Ecumenicity—False and True," 19, commented, "these groups are universalist—they believe that all men of whatever race, creed, or color are brothers; that men are not 'lost' but 'not saved yet;' and 'all roads lead to heaven.'"

[81] *GC Minutes* (August 21–26, 1963), 20.

[82] *AG Minister Letter*, October 15, 1962.

[83] *GC Minutes* (August 21–26, 1963), 52–53, 120.

[84] For the complete story see Joshua R. Ziefle, *David du Plessis and the Assemblies of God* (Boston: Brill, 2013).

[85] *AG Minister Letter* (October 15, 1962); Blumhofer, *The Assemblies of God*, vol. 2, 90–106.

The Secretary James G. Watt Controversy

One criticism of dispensational eschatology is that it is not interested in the care of creation. No situation demonstrated this stereotype more poignantly than the controversy surrounding James G. Watt, a member of an AG church who served as Secretary of Interior under Ronald Reagan. Knowing that Watt was a Pentecostal, the House committee asked the potential Secretary how his eschatology would affect his attitude toward the preservation of natural resources. Watt's reported response by media outlets was, "I don't know how many future generations we can count on before the Lord returns."[86] Not surprisingly, this quote drew criticism from various groups[87] and even some Christian scholars.[88] However, Watt's comment that made headlines was only a partial quote, which was intended to make him sound careless toward the environment because of his eschatology.[89] The statement was part of the House Confirmation Hearings for Watt's appointment to Secretary of the interior. The full context is as follows:

> **Mr. Weaver**: I wonder if you agree, also, in the general statement that we should leave some of our resources—I am now talking about scenic areas or preservation, but scenic resources for our children? Not just gobble them up all at once?
>
> **Secretary Watt**: Absolutely. That is the delicate balance the Secretary of the Interior must have, to be steward for the natural resources for this generation as well as future generations. I do not know how many future generations we can count on before the Lord returns, whatever it is we have to manage with skill to leave the resources needed for future generations.[90]

---

[86] There were multiple sources carrying this quote according to Susan P. Bratton, "The Ecotheology of James Watt," *Environmental Ethics* 5 (1983): 225–35.

[87] "The Legacy of James Watt," *Time Magazine*, October 24, 1983, 25.

[88] George Marsden, "Lord of the Interior," *The Reformed Journal* 31, no. 6 (Jun 1981): 2–3, criticized Watt's understanding of eschatology that he felt he was using for political convenience to pass certain economic policies. Miroslav Volf, "On Loving with Hope: Eschatology and Social Responsibility," *Transformation* 7, no. 3 (1990): 28–31.

[89] Bratton, "The Ecotheology of James Watt," 227. Bratton concludes that his "political and economic policy" were the primary sources of his interior policy rather than his eschatology and "charismatic" theology.

[90] *United States and James G. Watt. Briefing by the Secretary of the Interior: Oversight Hearing Before the Committee on Interior and Insular Affairs, House of Representatives; Ninety-Seventh Congress, First Session; on Briefing by the Secretary of the Interior; Hearing Held in Washington, D.C.; February 5, 1981* (Washington: Government Printing Office, 1981).

The legend of Watt's supposed anti-environmental attitudes became even more exaggerated when PBS personality Bill Moyers falsely revised the statement and claimed Mr. Watt said, "After the last tree is fell, Christ will come back."[91] Watt responded to Moyers false claim, "I never said it. Never believed it. Never even thought it. I know no Christian who believes or preaches such error. The Bible commands conservation—that we as Christians be careful stewards of the land and resources entrusted to us by the Creator."[92] Watt was unashamed of his Christian eschatological beliefs, but that same faith also led him to feel a responsibility to carefully steward creation. Watt later commented,

> We don't know when He is coming, so we have a stewardship responsibility to see that people are provided for until He does come and a new order is put in place. So we cannot waste or despoil that which we've been given in the Earth because we don't know our tenure here.[93]

Furthermore, Watt said,

> We Americans are blessed with the human and natural resources to build a great nation. This blessing carries with it a responsibility for good stewardship. This earth that sustains mankind must provide for untold generations to come. This generation must leave the world in better condition than we found it. . . . We must see that natural resources are not wasted and are not squandered.[94]

Watt demonstrated that his Pentecostal eschatology did not lead him neglect the environment, yet only a few in the media were willing set the record straight.[95]

---

[91] Joe Strupp, "Bill Moyers Apologizes to James Watt for Apocryphal Quote," http://www.editorandpublisher.com/news/bill-moyers-apologizes-to-james-watt-for-apocryphal-quote/ (accessed 13 August 2017).

[92] James G. Watt, "The Religious Left's Lies," *Washington Post*, May 21, 2005, http://www.washingtonpost.com/wp-dyn/content/article/2005/05/20/AR2005052001333.html (accessed 15 August 2017).

[93] Les Line, "Etcetera," *Audubon* 83, no. 3 (May 1981): 5, quoted in Bratton, "The Ecotheology of James Watt," 227.

[94] James Watt, "Ours is the Earth," *Saturday Evening Post*, January-February 1982, 74–75, 104.

[95] Duane Larson, "An Ecumenical 'Council' Revisited", *Dialogue* 44, no. 4 (Winter 2005): 389–400, admits that he unjustly used this characterization. He says, "In fact, as the full record states, Mr. Watt insisted and insists that Christians are obligated to care for God's creation, no matter whether Christ's return is indeed soon or a long time yet away. I apologize for my having not checked out the source (Mr. Watt) directly,"

Commission on Doctrinal Purity and Position Papers

Because the SFT contains only short statements on AG doctrine, the General Presbytery felt that a series of "position papers" were needed in order to clarify important doctrinal matters. In each case, when controversies arose, the Presbytery appointed a committee to study the matter and would report their findings and recommendations. Although these papers came from the top leaders in the AG, because the General Council has not ratified the papers, they are not considered authoritative or enforceable.[96] In 1979, the General Council created a "Commission on Doctrinal Purity," which took over the responsibility for creating Position Papers. The purpose was to give "careful attention to preventing deviations from the Statement of Fundamental Truths and proliferation of unscriptural teachings."[97] Since 1970, the General Presbytery has approved a total of twenty-five Position Papers on various doctrinal positions.[98]

As Cecil Robeck has pointed out, the presence of these papers has shifted the responsibility for the determination of AG doctrine from the General Council and the *SFT* truths to a magisterium of the General Presbytery and the ten-member Commission on Doctrinal Purity.[99] This group has been given the power to expand the definitions on AG positions beyond the positions accepted by the General Council in the *STF.* Consolidation of power to a small group was exactly what the founders were trying to avoid. The establishment of a magisterium which controls the doctrinal direction of the fellowship does so without the consent of the members of the General Council.[100] Their commentary has increasingly become a source of authoritative dogma even when it is in contradiction to earlier declarations. Charles Nestor objects, "These

---

[96] For a history of the Position Papers and the procedures for their acceptance, see *GC Minutes* (August 6–11, 1991), 57–60. The committee also reported to the 1993 Council that "it would be an exercise in futility" to try to pass the papers in the General Council. Therefore, they recommended the papers be non-binding in the same way as the *SFT. GC Minutes* (August 10–15, 1993), 20–21.

[97] *GC Minutes* (August 16–21, 1979), 26–27.

[98] http://ag.org/top/beliefs/position_papers/ (accessed 25 January 2017). Some of the topics include Inerrancy of Scripture (1970), Divorce and Remarriage (1973), Divine Healing (1974), Eternal Punishment (1976), Abortion (1985), Women in Ministry (1990), and Initial Evidence (2000) were bound in a volume called *Where We Stand* (Springfield: Gospel Publishing House, 2001) that has been revised and republished as various papers have been added or edited.

[99] C. M. Robeck, "An Emerging Magisterium," *Pneuma* 25, no. 2 (Fall 2003): 170; Charles Nestor, "Position Papers," *Agora* 2, no. 3 (Winter 1979): 10–11.

[100] Robeck, "An Emerging Magisterium," 214, warns that if the lines of differentiation between the ruling class and the council continue to erode the sense of cooperation and fellowship.

'positions' may well become an 'official' commentary imposed on the established doctrines and positions of the fellowship much in the manner of canon laws in the Roman Catholic Church or the Jewish Talmud."[101] This section will look at three eschatological position papers in order to understand the effect they have on the perception of AG eschatology.

Eternal Punishment Position Paper (1976)

The SFT had made a firm statement about eternal punishment because of the teachings of Charles Parham. However, in the 1970s, a resurgence among evangelicals of the doctrine of annihilationism prompted the Presbytery to issue a position paper in 1976.[102] Advocates of annihilationism were arguing that the love of God would not allow for an eternal punishment and that the wicked would be destroyed out of God's mercy. The position paper appealed to the words of Jesus in which he affirmed in multiple places in the gospels that the fire would be eternal. They agreed with annihilationists that "hades" will be an intermediate state, but argued "this is to be distinguished from eternal fire." The paper retorts, "The punishment will be as eternal as the eternal life. This leaves no room for any later restoration for the wicked." The eternal nature of the fire meant that annihilation was not a possibility. The Presbytery concluded, "None of these passages indicates any promise of rehabilitation or restoration once the final judgment is pronounced."

Rapture Position Paper (1979)

Prompted by the eschatological issues addressed during the 1979 General Council that led to the Committee on Eschatological Loopholes, the Presbytery approved a position paper on "The Rapture of the Church."[103] The paper focuses most of its attention on clarifying the definition of the Second Coming, the difference between the rapture and the revelation, and reasons why believers will be spared from the tribulation. It begins by affirming the doctrine of the imminence of the rapture and warns believers to be ready and expecting the Second Coming of

---

[101] Charles Nestor, "Position Papers," *Agora* 2, no. 3 (Winter 1979): 10–11.

[102] "Eternal Punishment," *Where We Stand: Official Position Papers of the Assemblies of God* (Springfield: Gospel Publishing House, 2001), 83–86.

[103] "The Rapture of the Church," General Council of the Assemblies of God, 1979, 4. Limiting itself to clarification of the "Blessed Hope" fundamental truth, it does not engage the other eschatological concepts such as the millennial position, the final judgment, or the new heavens and new earth.

Christ, which will "happen suddenly without warning."[104] It re-affirmed the prohibition in the bylaws against teaching that certain signs or events that must take place before the rapture.[105] The paper also gives considerable attention to the differentiation between the rapture of the Church and the revelation of Jesus Christ. The difference between these two events is explained by their relationship to the saints. It says, "Passages which pertain to the Rapture describe the coming of the Lord for His people. Passages which refer to the revelation of Christ describe the coming of the Lord with His people."[106]

This five-page paper lacks an artful defense of these positions that one would expect in a dogmatic declaration on a matter of official doctrine. It is more of a simply constructed apologetic of rationales and proof texts that support the pretribulation rapture position. Although the *SFT* contains no position on the tribulation or its purpose, more than half of the position paper is devoted to defending the pretribulation rapture. It says, "We believe it is scripturally correct to assume that the intervening period between the two (phases of Christ's coming) is the time when the world will experience the Great Tribulation."[107] The length of the tribulation is not of concern in this paper, but the purpose of the tribulation is instrumental to the argument. The primary purpose of the rapture is to remove believers from earth before the tribulation while the wicked will be left behind to endure judgment. The Antichrist, who will rule during the tribulation, will appear only after the restraining power of the Spirit is removed, which is the Spirit that is working in the Church. After the tribulation, Jesus will return with his saints in order to execute final judgment upon the earth.

The Rapture Position Paper is an example of the dilemma presented by such a document. While endeavoring to clarify the *SFT*, this paper differs significantly from official AG positions, particularly in that it neglects the primary emphasis of hopeful aspects within the resurrection. Instead, this paper engages in a dogmatic defense of the pretribulation rapture, a topic that is absent from the *SFT*. Although the pretribulation rapture is accepted within the pale of AG orthodoxy, it is not the central tenet of official doctrine. By virtue of the fact that the General Presbytery approved the paper, it in some sense codifies a definitive pretribulation rapture position, something the General Council and the Constitution and Bylaws have refrained from doing so on multiple occasions. In this case, the fears of the critics of Position Papers are justified. The Rapture

---

[104] "The Rapture of the Church," 2.
[105] "The Rapture of the Church," 4.
[106] "The Rapture of the Church," 3.
[107] "The Rapture of the Church," 3.

Position Paper provided a way for those on the Commission on Doctrinal Purity to undermine the non-specific position on the tribulation without having to gain permission from the General Council. Even though the paper is non-binding, it nevertheless obscures what the AG has historically held and has the potential to be used as a weapon of enforcement based on popular and accepted teaching, but not official doctrine.[108]

The Kingdom of God Position Paper (1989)

The decade of the 1980s brought new Pentecostal visibility through the medium of television. Several popular AG ministers took advantage of the medium of television to spread Pentecostal teaching. The rise of independent Charismatic evangelists also spread popular and sometimes controversial ideas including the proliferation of eschatological teaching that became popular in the AG. The biggest attention came from Hal Lindsey's *Late Great Planet Earth* and other teachers who spread end times teachings through television and Christian books. This was particularly true in 1988 when prophetic speculation about the forty-year anniversary (one generation) of Israel's founding led some to expect Christ's return in 1988. The AG avoided adding fuel to the eschatological frenzy during in that they did not publish a single article on the return of Christ or Israel in 1988.[109] Speculation about the return of Christ has been disapproved since 1920, yet, once again, the Council needed to address the practice of ministers to set dates for the Lord's return. So in 1989, the General Council re-affirmed their disapproval of any ministers preaching or publishing a date for Christ's return.[110]

The second 1980s eschatological issue came from t the "Kingdom Now" theology. Popular pastor and televangelist Earl Paulk, Jr. promoted on his television program a restorationist theology called "Kingdom Now" or "Dominion Theology," which emphasized the authority of believers to establish the Kingdom of God on earth through the Spirit.[111] The Kingdom Now emphasis focused too much on the establishment of the kingdom in the present and not enough of the kingdom that is "not yet." However, Paulk criticized the AG's doctrine of the rapture because he believed that it encouraged escapism. As a result, several AG leaders provided rebuttals in the *Pentecostal Evangel*.[112] Paul

---

[108] Robeck, "An Emerging Magisterium," 170; Nestor, "Position Papers," 10.

[109] This compares to the average of six articles per year in the years surrounding 1988.

[110] *GC Minutes* (August 8–13, 1989), 114–15.

[111] Althouse, *Spirit of the Last Days*, 58–59.

Lowenberg, an executive presbyter, fired back at Paulk and other "purveyors of religious novelties," arguing that the belief in the coming of Christ has not encouraged Christian escapism; it has "stirred many lethargic Christians to zealous discipleship, the comfortable to a life of sacrifice, the self-satisfied to living and loving witness of the truth." [113] Meanwhile, another restorationist controversy sprang up from the Shepherding Movement, which was an ecclesiastical movement among Charismatics that emphasized the restoration of the five-fold offices of the church and encouraged church members to submit to apostolic authority. [114] As a restorationist eschatology, critics found it overly triumphalist and postmillennial and undermined the expectation of the imminent return of Christ. [115]

In response to these two extreme positions on the Kingdom of God, the presbytery produced a position paper in 1989. [116] This carefully crafted paper shows a level of theological development not present to this point. The first thing the paper points out is that there is no difference between the terms "kingdom of God" and "kingdom of heaven," a concept that was promoted by dispensationalists who relegate the kingdom of God entirely to the future. For the AG, the kingdom of God is defined as "the sphere of God's rule" in two contexts: the believer's present realm in the Spirit and the believer's future apocalyptic order at the end of the age. [117] The AG resisted the postmillennial notion of establishing the kingdom now, but this controversy caused the AG to mature its concept of the kingdom in the "already/not yet." [118] The Paper declares, "As Pentecostals we recognize the role of

---

[112] For example, Dwight Fearing, "The Kingdom: Now or Later?," *PE*, October 30, 1988, 13, criticized Kingdom Now theology for wanting to have a Christian president, congress, and nation in order for Jesus to have a kingdom to which to return. See also, David Allen, "It's here-and it's Coming," *PE*, February 7, 1988, 6–7.

[113] Paul Lowenberg, "Message under Siege," *PE*, July 5, 1987, 6–8, says, "Purveyors of religious novelties, like hucksters at a bazaar, peddle schismatic trinkets with high-sounding titles."

[114] David Moore, "Discerning the Times: The Victorious Eschatology of the Shepherding Movement," in Althouse and Waddell, eds., *Perspectives in Pentecostal Eschatology Perspectives in Pentecostal Eschatologies*, 273–92.

[115] Althouse, *Spirit of the Last Days*, 60, argues that what connects early Pentecostals, the New Order of the Latter Rain, and these independent Charismatic groups is the common restorationist commitment to the renewal of apostolic Christianity in eschatological dimensions.

[116] "The Kingdom of God as Described in Holy Scripture," *Where We Stand: Official Position Papers of the Assemblies of God* (Springfield: Gospel Publishing House, 2001), 171–80. *GC Minutes* (August 8–13, 1989), 114–15. The Paper was also published in *PE*, February 11, 1990, 6–7, 20–21.

[117] "The Kingdom of God as Described in Holy Scripture," 173.

[118] McGee, "Historical Background," 32–35.

the Holy Spirit in inauguration and ongoing ministry of the Kingdom."[119] Through the baptism in the Spirit, "the power of the Kingdom, manifest in the Cross, the Resurrection, and the Ascension" is manifest. Pentecostal signs, wonders, and miracles are indicators that the kingdom of God is already breaking into this present age. It says, "Biblical charismata, anointed proclamation of the Word, and confirming signs and wonders are the distinguishing marks of the kingdom of God at work now."[120] And yet, the kingdom is a future reality.

Although the work of the Spirit through the Church establishes the kingdom, the church is not the entire expression of the kingdom; it existed before the Church was created and will reign after the Church is completed. This distinction is important because of the way in which dominion theology seeks to establish the kingdom on earth through establishing a Christian dominion over society, culture, and political structures. Though members of the AG are encouraged to participate in society, the paper reminds the reader, "the kingdom of God may operate within, but is not to be identified with, any present political system."[121] Christians therefore engage in society as kingdom people but are not deceived into believing that the world will be saved through social efforts. At the same time, the Church has a responsibility to bring the kingdom of God in the present age by the Spirit. The paper declares, "Filled with the Spirit, and given the opportunity to influence society, [Christians] are impelled to denounce unjust laws (Isaiah 10:1, 2) and to seek justice and goodness (Micah 6:8; Amos 5:14, 15)." Ultimately, "Kingdom Now" theology is erroneous because, although Christians have victory in this life, the work of the kingdom also involves suffering and, at times, deprivation. Dominion theology "discounts or destroys the important biblical themes of suffering, cross-bearing, and self-denial or assumes an elitist attitude toward Christians who suffer economic deprivation."[122]

This paper demonstrates a new level of maturity in AG eschatological views. It contains the types of nuances, with regard to the kingdom and the intersection of the Spirit with the already/not yet, that is reflective of modern eschatological scholarship. This Pentecostal approach to the kingdom of God allows expression of the work of the Spirit in the present age as well as points to the coming age in fulfillment in the millennium. It rejects dispensationalism's relegation of the kingdom only to the future but also gives place to the restoration of Israel and the future Kingdom of God on earth. It empowers believers to work for the

---

[119] "The Kingdom of God as Described in Holy Scripture," 175.
[120] "The Kingdom of God as Described in Holy Scripture," 175.
[121] "The Kingdom of God as Described in Holy Scripture," 177.
[122] "The Kingdom of God as Described in Holy Scripture," 179.

Kingdom in social engagement with the poor and marginalized. At the same time, it recognizes that only through the future apocalyptic establishment of Christ's rule will there be true transformation of the present order. It affirms a long held rejection of postmillennial triumphalism that would equate the kingdom of this world with the kingdom of God.

5

ANALYSIS OF ASSEMBLIES OF GOD ESCHATOLOGY

For over a century, the AG has sought to provide its ministers and members a proper biblical understanding of their position on eschatology. They have done so through (1) the Statement of Fundamental Truths, which have been modified and clarified, (2) supplemental statements of faith, (3) disapproved "eschatological errors," and (4) position papers. Throughout these various mediums, a number of points of diversity and continuity are expressed. In this section, some conclusions can be considered about the AG's official positions on eschatology.

Official Inconsistencies

Over the past century, AG expressions of eschatology have not only been varied but have often been contradictory, especially when comparing the SFT to the various other supplemental statements. For example, the definition of the Second Coming is sometimes used for both phases of Christ's return and sometimes is used only for the visible return with the saints. The doctrine of the Second Coming is also inconsistent with regards to the rapture and tribulation, particularly compared to the position papers and other supplemental statements. The imprecise nature of these various statements inevitably gives the impression of confusion as to what the AG exactly believes. While this may be preferred by those who hope for more ambiguity and diversity, the failure to precisely and consistently articulate these doctrines is undoubtedly problematic for ensuring doctrinal unity.

Second, this survey has demonstrated that the *SFT* has not only changed, but also at times the EFT have been completely rewritten. The articles that received the most revision and development are the Blessed Hope and Millennial Reign. The Millennial Reign has seen the biggest revisions as leaders worked to define not only the events surrounding the millennium but also to clarify the purpose of the Millennial Reign pertaining to Israel. These revisions have led to different wording and different emphases. The only truth not touched by the revisions was the New Heavens and New Earth, which has experienced a century of neglect.

Being simply a partial quotation of Scripture, there have been no editorial or explanatory statements of its importance except in the *Fundamental Truths Condensed*. The statements found in both the WAGF and the *Pentecostal Evangel* omit this doctrine completely. This demonstrates a complete lack of importance placed on a doctrine that was deemed "fundamental" by the original statement.

Shifting Emphasis from Images to Events

One of the most important results of this survey is that there has been a shift in emphasis from the thematic emphasis to the chronological emphasis on end-times. In the original version, hope was the unifying factor by which each doctrine was expressed. The rapture was expressed as the hope of resurrection. The millennium was the hope of Christ's righteous rule on earth. The final judgment was the hope of justice over God's enemies and the effects of sin. The new heavens and new earth were the hope of a renewed creation. However, the 1927 revision was a move toward a chronological description of end time events by clarifying its position on the millennium and the role of Israel. The revision of 1961 further fossilized this chronological orientation when the millennium was revised, and the "Lake of Fire" shifted emphasis toward the judgment of humanity. Because of the various doctrinal controversies and revisions, the statements grew increasingly focused on the order of events and how they fit within the script rather than focusing on the meaning of the doctrines. In doing so, the thematic elements that were part of the original statements have been lost. The result is a dogmatic statement of AG eschatology whose script is indistinguishable from dispensational theology, even if the theology behind the script may differ.

Tribulational Diversity

This survey has confirmed the assertion of Sheppard, as well as Menzies and Anderson, that the AG does not officially endorse a tribulational position.[1] The only document that does is the rapture position paper, which is officially endorsed but not binding and is not representative of the will of General Council. In each of the official statements and throughout each of the revisions, there has remained no official declaration that the pretribulation position is the official AG position. It is also seen that throughout the various eschatological controversies, the AG repeatedly declined to declare an official position on the tribulation. This intention was demonstrated during the decisions concerning "eschatological

---

[1] Sheppard, "Pentecostals and the Hermeneutics of Dispensationalism," 8; Menzies and Anderson, "D. W. Kerr and Eschatological Diversity," 15.

loopholes" in 1980. For nearly a century, the allowance clause has governed how the General Council should view those who hold to various tribulational positions. The resistance by the AG leadership to make an issue of the tribulation speaks to the level of diversity that the AG has intended to foster. As J. R. Flower commented, "There is so much room for speculation here that is behooves none of us to be dogmatic."[2] This suggest that there should be room in the AG for people who have different views as long as they seek to keep the unity of the fellowship.

Hope as Resurrection

One prominent eschatological emphasis is the connection between hope and resurrection. The title of article 13 is not "The Rapture." Instead, for a century it has remained "The Blessed Hope." Robeck notes that for many Pentecostals the Blessed Hope is "that Christians will not have to suffer such a devastation," which has often been used as a threat to motivate believers.[3] But, this is not the emphasis in the AG position on the Second Coming. Hope for the AG is not found in going to heaven, escaping tribulation, or avoiding apocalyptic eschatological events. True hope is grounded in the resurrection of the body and the establishment of the Messianic kingdom on earth. The Blessed Hope is a longing for full salvation in the resurrection not longing for escape. Hope is also relational as it is longing to be with Jesus in a physical sense, a hope that is rooted in the believer's destiny to reign with Christ on earth.

The Millennium and Israel

The millennium place an important role in AG eschatology. It was the expectation that Christians would reign on earth with Christ. However, the AG shifted its doctrine of the millennium in conjunction with the political realities playing out in Israel. The AG was interested in the return of the Jews as a harbinger of the things to come. However, the by the 1920s, Zionist efforts to expand Israel's claim to the land raised the expectation that the return was at hand. Consequently, the AG added the expectation of the "salvation of Israel" in 1927 to reflect this

---

[2] This ambiguous position is reflected ably by J. R. Flower, "Living in Momentous Days," *WE*, July 14, 1917, 8, where he notes that there are different interpretations of whether the rapture will happen at the beginning of the tribulation. He says, "Whether this event takes place at the beginning of the seven-year period or in the middle of the period, depends on the interpretation of the 8th verse of 2 Thess. 2." Flower concedes that the coming could be at the beginning or middle of the tribulation.

[3] Robeck, "Faith, Hope, Love, and the Eschaton," 3.

conviction. The millennium began to be seen as the fulfillment of the promise to Israel of the Messiah's kingdom. By 1961, the AG's position concerning the coming salvation of the Jews closely mirrored a dispensational understanding of Israel's role in the future. Though support for Israel was theologically motivated, it ultimately led to political consequences in the way in which the AG approached the political situation.

Dispensationalism

In terms of the eschatological events in official statements, AG eschatology certainly correlates with dispensationalism. The dispensational script is followed in a general sense in that there is often a two-fold coming, the return of Jews to Israel, a literal thousand-year kingdom, a final judgment, and the eternal states. But there are also many details that are missing, such as the role of antichrist and the battle of Armageddon. It is certainly reasonable to state an implicit adherence to these positions, but it also does not explicitly promote dispensationalism. Considering there is no official tribulational position, I would have to agree with Sheppard that the AG position is not "inherently dispensational" and has left the matter intentionally ambiguous.[4]

Although this chapter questions the assumption that the AG was co-opted by fundamentalist dispensationalism, there certainly is some concern about the overall pneumatic orientation of official AG doctrine. It is striking that there is no position on the Holy Spirit in any of the official statements. Anyone reading these statements would find it hard to distinguish them from fundamentalist statements. Outside of "The Kingdom" position paper, which affirmed a Pentecostal understanding of the kingdom being present in the Spirit while at the same time expecting the full consummation, the AG simply did not prioritize the Spirit in their expression of eschatological doctrine.

This chapter set out to hear the official voice of the AG concerning its position on eschatology. In the next chapter, this study will look at the popular expressions of AG eschatology found in the pages of the *Pentecostal Evangel*.

[4] Sheppard, "Pentecostals and the Hermeneutics of Dispensationalism," 8.

PART TWO:

THE DEVELOPMENT OF ASSEMBLIES OF GOD ESCHATOLOGY

6

ESTABLISHMENT PERIOD (1914–1927)

Introduction to Popular Eschatology

In this section of the book, we will seek to understand the development eschatology through the lens of the popular expressions by individuals in the AG. While many of the eschatology books from Gospel Publishing House could be analyzed, this section will focus on the periodical literature in the official organ, The Pentecostal Evangel. As the oldest and most exhaustive source for AG doctrine, it was a consistent source of news from the fellowship, editorials on important issues, missionary reports, articles on Pentecostal beliefs, and testimonies of the Pentecostal life and ministry. By surveying a century of voices expressed in the paper, this section will give voice to individuals on the margins and explore the diversity of expressions of ordinary individuals within the movement.[1] Unlike academic theology, periodical literature allows ideas from across sociological, ecclesiological, and geographical locations to be expressed in ways that reflect the breadth of theological commitments within the community. These articles provide the best opportunity to understand how the official positions have been understood by members of the fellowship throughout the history of the AG. This section will attempt to craft this narrative through five phases of doctrinal development: Establishment Period (1914–1927), Scholastic Period (1928–1950), Institutional Period (1950–1961), Evangelical Period (1961–1985), and Modern Period (1980–Present).[2]

---

[1] Jeff Astley and Leslie J. Francis, eds., *Exploring Ordinary Theology* (Farnham, Surrey, England: Ashgate Publishing, 2013), 1, defines ordinary (or popular) theology as "the theological beliefs and processes of believing that find expression in the God-talk of those believers who have received no scholarly theological education." This type of theology is an empirical/practical theology approach that allows church members to reflect on their theology rather than academics and ecclesiastical officials. See also, Mark J. Cartledge, *Testimony in the Spirit: Rescripting Ordinary Pentecostal Theology* (Farnham, Surrey, England: Ashgate Publishing, 2010).

[2] The structure of these periods is generally accepted and shared by several studies of AG development. Margaret Poloma "Assemblies of God," in S. M. Burgess, and E. M. van der Maas, eds.,

The *Pentecostal Evangel* began as the *Christian Evangel* in 1913 by J. R. Flower in order to help unify the Pentecostal movement and disseminate its message. After the first General Council, Flower was named General Secretary and the *Christian Evangel* was chosen as the official organ. E. N. Bell, who was elected as the first General Chairman, also operated a paper called *Word and Witness*. The two papers merged in 1916 and *The Pentecostal Evangel* emerged as the official organ of the Assemblies of God for the next 100 years.[3] Bell and Flower had a vision to chronicle "news of what the Holy Spirit is actually doing in these days as these glorious truths are tried and demonstrated and proved to be practical in the lives of those who dare to trust God."[4] The formula of Pentecostal news, doctrine, and testimonies became a consistent template throughout its publication until it ceased in 2015. While doctrinal books were primarily influential upon Bible school students and ministers receiving credentials, the *Pentecostal Evangel* was read by a broad spectrum of pastors and church members. Coupled with the frequency of publication, the *Pentecostal Evangel* provides a valuable glimpse into the landscape of eschatological commitments within the AG.

For the first few years, the *Pentecostal Evangel* solicited articles from "sweet, pure, sensible Spirit-filled saints" in order to "allow the rich experience of some of our readers to be given to bless others."[5] J. W. Welch noted that articles "that did not agree entirely" with the editors were acceptable as long as "no vital principle of truth" was questioned.[6] Following the controversy with the New Issue and the formation of an official doctrinal statement, the *Pentecostal Evangel* began to serve a more dogmatic function for the preservation of the doctrine of the fellowship and operated with an editorial policy of "unity through

---

NIDPCM (Grand Rapids: Zondervan, 2003), 333–40, divides these periods (1914–1918), (1918–1930), (1930–1950), (1950–1985), (1985–Present). A similar structure is used by Menzies, *Anointed to Serve*, 143. However, these periods will be modified in ways that are specific to developments in eschatology and corresponding periods of developments to the *SFT*.

[3] Though the paper changed names several times in the early years, for the sake of simplicity, this periodical will be referred by the generic name *Pentecostal Evangel*.

[4] *WE*, August 22, 1914, 2.

[5] E. N. Bell, "Good Articles Solicited," *CE*, March 6, 1915, 2.

[6] *WE*, January 8, 1916, 3, reports, "We expect that there will be (and in fact there has already been) some things in the various articles published that did not agree entirely with the thoughts of either of the Editors. We realize, however, that others are subject to light as well as we, and it is more than possible that where there is no vital principle of truth involved, it is better to have liberty among us to express our things in our own peculiar manner, rather than for one or two minds to shape the style of all that goes into the paper."

uniformity."[7] Welch's earlier toleration was replaced by his stated responsibility to "shape the policy of the paper to agree with the purpose of THE GENERAL COUNCIL OF THE ASSEMBLIES OF GOD SO LONG AS IT IS THE RECOGNIZED ORGAN OF THE COUNCIL."[8] Therefore the eschatology in these articles, while not official, should certainly be understood as vetted and acceptable within the pale of AG dogma.

The Establishment Period begins with the organization of the AG on April 2, 1914, and ends with the ratification of the Constitution and Bylaws and revision of the *SFT* in 1927.[9] Since the first books articulating and expounding on AG doctrine did not come until 1925, the *Pentecostal Evangel* became the primary medium for doctrinal explanation.[10] During this period, there were four special editions specifically devoted to articles about the Second Coming of Christ.[11]

Imminence of the Lord's Return

For the first few months following the founding of the General Council, the topic of the return of the Lord was only occasionally addressed.[12] However, when WWI began in July 1914, immediately the editors took note.[13] The very next week, a front page article commented on the prophetic significance of the war.

> We are convinced that the time for the return of the Lord is near at hand, added to which this great conflict which is breaking out amongst the strongest nations of the world and which will go far to weaken them and awaken them to God's plan for the coming age, more than assures us that we are not mistaken and the

---

[7] McQueen, *Toward a Pentecostal Eschatology*, 162–63, describes the editorial policy as "unity through uniformity."

[8] *WE*, January 8, 1916, 3. Emphasis original.

[9] W. Menzies *Anointed to Serve*, 143, refers to this period as the "formative years" and the "stabilizing years."

[10] The first editor of the *Evangel* was J. R. Flower until E. N. Bell became the managing editor as the first Chairman. J. W. Welch served as the editor from 1915–1918 and J. T. Boddy 1919–1921. In 1921 the General Council appointed Stanley Frodsham to be the editor and he held the position for twenty-seven years. Stanley Frodsham, "Future of the Evangel," *PE*, September 23, 1921, 4.

[11] *WE*, April 10, 1917; *CE*, March 23, 1918; Second Coming Supplement, *PE*, July 10, 1920; *PE*, December 15, 1923.

[12] "He is Coming," *CE*, October 3, 1914, 1; J. S. Seerist, "Jesus is Coming Soon," *CE*, October 10, 1914), 3.

[13] J. R. Flower, "Rumors of Wars," *PE*, August 8, 1914, 2.

Lord is coming soon, sooner than we realize. It is possible that when the war is at its height, the rapture of the saints may take place.[14]

Over the next four months, in nearly every issue, articles on WWI were prominently featured on the front page.[15] The picture these articles paint of the present and future conditions were quite pessimistic.[16] Contributors watched as the world was declining morally, economically, and politically, while human attempts to create a better world failed to the point that the whole world was embroiled in war.[17] Even after WWI ended, attempts by nations to "reconstruct" the world were seen as vain attempts to bring human peace and were nothing more than the spirit of the antichrist.[18] The signs were everywhere that the return of Jesus was near.[19] One article observes, "Jesus is coming. The skies are darkening. The clouds are lowering. The lightnings are flashing. The thunders are rolling. The signs are multiplying that proclaim the birththroes of the new creation are at hand."[20] Many also testified to seeing astronomical phenomenon and proclaimed them as "signs in the heavens."[21] The rapidly changing world could only mean that the present dispensation was coming to an end.[22]

---

[14] "War! War!! War!!!," *CE*, August 15, 1914, 1.

[15] J. R. Flower, "Prophetic War Horses Sent Out," *CE*, August 29, 1914, 1; "Take WARning," *CE*, September 5, 1914, 1; George Carlyle, "The Great Tribulation," *CE*, September 5, 1914, 1; Burt McCaffrey, "Someone is Coming," *CE*, September 12, 1914, 1; "The Second Coming Near," *CE*, September 12, 1914, 3; "He is Coming," *CE*, October 3, 1914, 1; "A Voice From England," *CE*, October 3, 1914, 1; "The Destiny of Our Nation," *CE*, October 10, 1914, 1.

[16] "The Great War and the Speedy Return of our Lord," *WE*, April 10, 1917, 2. To the charges that the end times views were too pessimistic, the writer comments, "'A very pessimistic picture,' you say. Perhaps so, but it is not one of my own invention, but of God's revelation." This same argument was made verbatim in "This Present Crisis," *WE*, July 1, 1916, 7.

[17] "A Voice From England," *CE*, October 3, 1914, 1, describes the war as "a shame on England" and a judgment from God for her "pleasure seeking, covetousness and sin." See also, "Is the World Growing Better or Worse?," *PE*, May 1, 1915, 3; R. M. Russell, "Prophecy and Present Day Events," *PE*, April 16, 1921, 8; "The Good News of the Lord's Appearing," *PE*, July 23, 1921, 8.

[18] "The Spirit of Antichrist: Are the Post-Millennialists Anti-Christian?," *PE*, September 3, 1921, 1.

[19] *WE*, April 10, 1915, 1; "Signs of the Approaching End," *WE*, September 8, 1917, 8; James McAlister, "Startling Signs of the End," *PE*, Second Coming Supplement, September 10, 1920, 1–3; "Signs of the Times," *PE*, December 15, 1923, 8.

[20] *WE*, January 13, 1917, 3.

[21] *WW*, January 20, 1914, 1; *PE*, August 4, 1917, 11; *PE*, August 18, 1917, 13; *PE*, August 25, 1917, 11; *PE*, May 25, 1929, 11; *PE*, February 24, 1940, 3.

[22] James McAlister, "Startling Signs of the End," *PE*, Second Coming Supplement, September 10, 1920, 1, comments, "We know by its very rapidity of movement that the age is ending. Slowness is the characteristic of the beginning of the age, and rapidity of its end."

By the end of WWI, the Second Coming was taking center stage in their theology. According to D. H. McDowell, everything that was distinctive about the Pentecostal movement functioned as a sign of the Lord's return.

> The second coming of the Lord Jesus Christ is not a feature of a program but it is THE program. The preaching of regeneration, the restoration of man back to God, the outpouring and the Baptism of the Holy Spirit upon believers, the working of signs and wonders and in the earth, are features of this program, leading up to its grand and glorious fulfillment.[23]

Therefore, in their minds, their pneumatology was fundamentally dependent upon their eschatology. The Second Coming of Jesus was not just another important doctrine to be believed, it was an imminent reality that was being confirmed by the Spirit. As one writer wrote, "The most important of all messages, and one which the Holy Ghost emphasizes above everything else is this: 'Jesus is coming soon.'"[24] The knowledge that Jesus was coming soon meant that the world as they experienced it was not out of control; it was following God's plan for the ages. He notes, "Christ [is] unfolding the purposes and plans of God, and the Holy Spirit [is] bringing home the revelation."[25]

Despite their pessimism about the conditions of the world, they were experiencing the power of the Holy Spirit, which made them optimistic about their future. J. N. Gortner comments,

> One of the greatest evidences of the near coming of Jesus is this wonderful Latter Rain which God is pouring out in these days upon the earth. Men and women and little children; thousands of them, all over the earth, are being baptized with the Holy Ghost at the beginning. Thank God for the fact that Jesus is coming![26]

The Pentecostal outpouring of the Spirit was thought to be the prelude to the true fulfillment of Joel's prophecy that the Spirit will be poured out on Israel during the millennium.[27] Therefore, the latter rain outpouring in the Pentecostal movement

---

[23] D. H. McDowell, "The Purpose of the Coming of the Lord," *PE,* May 2, 1925, 2.
[24] "How Long," *WE,* April 20, 1918, 8.
[25] "How Long," 8.
[26] J. N. Gortner, "Some Last Things," *PE,* January 22, 1921, 2–3.
[27] W. B. McCafferty, "Joel's Prophecy of the Holy Ghost," *PE,* May 15, 1920, 3, comments, "The last days of the Jews is still in the future." This view, common in dispensational premillennialism, believes the OT promises will have their ultimate fulfillment in Israel, not the Church.

was the beginning of the promise of the "restitution of all things" to Israel (Acts 3:21).[28] Stanley Frodsham explains,

> Peter spoke of "Pentecost" as the "last days," and it would have been the last days had the children of Israel accepted their Lord. But God has stretched over, held over, the promise until the last of the last days, so the latter rain, due and overdue, is and will be manifested to herald the Husbandman.[29]

In the concept of the latter rain, the Spirit was simultaneously preparing the church for the Second Coming and preparing the land of Israel for the Lord's return.[30]

The renewed interest in studying the return of Christ and ability to interpret the "signs of the times" was itself a function of the outpouring of the Spirit.[31] Frank Bartleman comments, "Today the Holy Spirit is leading us into the Book of Daniel and Revelation, unfolding their meaning. The time for their opening has come."[32] It was God himself that was leading ministers to study the subject, produce literature, and hold conferences on the "soon coming of Christ."[33] The study of prophecy was seen as a particularly Pentecostal endeavor because of the special openness to the gift of prophecy. The Latter Rain opened up special revelation to believers who are "in the Spirit" and will "show in a particular manner" the things to come.[34] However, the increase in prophecy teaching did come with cautions against being too preoccupied with the details. Alice Luce

---

[28] Stanley Frodsham, "The Coming Revival and the Coming Christ," *PE*, May 17, 1924, 4, says, "Christ is retained in heaven until the revival, the restitution, has come and has accomplished its work. Retained, held back, detained, till God's grace, love, mercy, has been showered down, sent forth, and spent, and has accomplished its purpose ... and he is being retained in heaven till the Father says, that all is fulfilled; that it is finished." Cf. J. W. Welch, "Looking for the Glorious Hope," *WE*, November 13, 1915, 2.

[29] Frodsham, "The Coming Revival and the Coming Christ," 4.

[30] Arthur W. Frodsham, "Why Does He Tarry?," *WE*, April 20, 1918, 5. Frodsham, "The Coming Revival and the Coming Christ," 4.

[31] "An Appeal to Pentecostal People," *CE*, August 24, 1918, 1, declares, "As never before in the history of the church, the promises concerning the Lord's Second Coming are being diligently and reverently studied. And the Spirit is enlightening and quickening the saints as never before."

[32] Frank Bartleman, "Present Day Conditions," *WE*, June 5, 1915, 3.

[33] "The Spirit of Antichrist," *PE*, September 3, 1921, 1, 7, explains, "God ... is working on the hearts of His people and they are holding conferences on the Lord's coming. Literature on the subject is being poured forth from the presses. There is even controversy on the subject at the ministerial convocations. The subject is debated, and by some rejected, yet the truth is being disseminated that the coming of the Lord draweth nigh ... It is the Spirit, the Spirit in advance, heralding the coming of the Lord."

[34] "Signs of the Approaching End," *WE*, September 8, 1917, 8.

advises, "Surely it is time that a warning was sounded against too much public discussion of the details of interpretation which are not revealed in the Word, and a plea for more plain, unvarnished preaching of the simple truth: "Jesus is coming soon: let us get ready to meet Him!""[35]

The promise that God will pour out the Spirit in Acts 2 was accompanied by a promise that God would give "visions" and "dreams," which many early AG members testified to having.[36] During a 1917 Maria Woodworth-Etter meeting, an attendee noted there were "strong messages given in the Spirit in other languages, with clear interpretation relative to the imminent appearing of our Lord, and the urgent need of the bride to make herself ready."[37] There were also testimonies of visions in which the Spirit revealed the details of the coming events that often reinforced commonly accepted interpretations of prophetic texts.[38]

Another practice the AG recognized was prayer to "hasten" the Lord's return. Since the latter rain was an eschatological event, they understood that the prayer for the latter rain to fall was also a prayer for Jesus to return.[39] On two occasions, the *Pentecostal Evangel* made appeals for Pentecostal people throughout the world "to invite Jesus to come back" by praying that "a rushing mighty wind" would come in order "to catch away believers."[40] They believed the experience of the baptism in the Spirit was itself the source of this prayer to hasten the Lord's return. As Arthur Frodsham points out, "The first word spoken through many by the Holy Spirit is "Jesus is coming quickly", which is often followed by the

[35] Alice Luce, "God is Soon To Speak," *PE,* January 10, 1920, 1.

[36] *PE,* December 15, 1923, 3; *PE,* May 12, 1917, 4; *PE,* September 15, 1917, 15; *PE,* November 11, 1922, 14. Such testimonies disappear after the mid-1920s.

[37] "Mighty Warnings of the Imminence of the Lord's Coming at the Woodworth-Etter Meetings in Los Angeles, Cal.," *WE,* April 21, 1917, 14.

[38] "Prophetic Vision of the Lord's Second Coming, the Great Tribulation and the End of the World," *PE,* May 1, 1920, 1–3; J. N. Gortner, "666," *CE,* April 19, 1919, 1–2; *CE,* May 17, 1919, 3; "Remarkable Visions of Things to Come," *PE,* December 15, 1923, 3. It is interesting to note that in each of these visions, the events described did not deviate from common premillennial and dispensational script.

[39] Arthur W. Frodsham, "Why Does He Tarry?," *WE,* April 20, 1918, 5.

[40] "An Appeal to Pentecostal People Throughout the World to Observe Sunday, Nov. 3rd and Monday, Nov. 4, 1918 in United Prayer Inviting Jesus, Our Heavenly Bridegroom, to Come Back," *CE,* August 24, 1918, 1, notes that after a similar appeal was made in 1912, a series of six events took place to hasten the Lord's return which included the following: the declaration of war by Greece, Bulgaria, Serbia, and Montenegro against Turkey in 1912, Britain's taking of Jerusalem from Turkey in 1917, America's joining the war in 1917, and the inauguration of a Zionist government in Jerusalem in 1918. See also A. W. Frodsham, "The Lord's Return," *PE,* March 31, 1917, 6; A. W. Frodsham, "Heading for a Crisis," *PE,* December 15, 1923, 5.

"immediate response in every Spirit-filled saint, "Even so, come, Lord Jesus'."[41] The practice of "hastening" the Lord's return through prayer was a common phenomenon among Pentecostals. When they prayed in tongues they believed they were praying for the return of the Lord by longing and groaning in the Spirit.[42] As one writer argues, "The King has to come back. And He has to be invited, and the Holy Ghost is the prompter, the rehearser, and He will put the words in your heart and mouth, 'Even so, come, Lord Jesus.' . . . Send out distress signals to heaven, and heaven will respond quickly."[43] So common was the practice among Pentecostals that Lillian Yeomans comments, "never since the world began was there such a volume of prayer for the soon return of the Lord Jesus Christ ascending to the throne as is going up now. And He longs to come."[44] One writer testified that practice of "hastening" had three benefits: it gratifies the heart of Jesus, it quickens the saints to right praying, and it convinces the unconverted.[45] This shows how even prayer had an eschatological orientation.

The Blessed Hope

When the SFT was created in 1916, the AG labeled the doctrine concerning the Second Coming of Jesus as "the blessed hope." That label was not only biblical, but it was also the primary sentiment they associated with his coming. Like most premillennialists, they rejected the optimism of postmillennialism and believed the world was getting worse.[46] At the same time, the Holy Spirit instilled in them a sense of hope for the future. J.W. Welch declared that through the Holy Spirit, "God becomes to us the God of hope, Rom. 15:13. For He establishes in us the glorious hope, thus making Himself the God of Hope to us."[47] But, what where they hoping for? Was it escape the horrors of the tribulation? Although present in this period, this was not the primary motivation for their hope.[48]

[41] "How Long," *WE*, April 20, 1918, 8.
[42] Yeomans, "Behold He Cometh," 2.
[43] "How Long," *WE*, April 20, 1918, 9.
[44] Lilian B. Yeomans, "Behold He Cometh," *PE*, December 15, 1923, 2.
[45] "How Long," *WE*, April 20, 1918, 8.
[46] Russell, "Prophecy and Present Day Events," 8.
[47] J. W. Welch, "Looking for the Glorious Hope," *WE*, November 13, 1915, 2.
[48] Some examples of articles that focused only on being left behind are Lelia Mayan Conway, "He is Near—Even at the Door," *WE*, March 25, 1916, 6–7; Arthur Booth-Clibborn, "Nigh, Even At The Door," *CE*, September 7, 1918, 1; Alice Luce, "God is Soon To Speak," *PE*, January 10, 1920, 1.

During the Establishment Period, the hope of Christ's return was expressed in three primary ways.[49] First, they saw the rapture as the culmination of the Spirit's ministry in preparing a bride for Jesus.[50] The rapture was seen as a "wedding ceremony" in which the bride will be delivered to heaven to celebrate the marriage supper of the Lamb.[51] Through the baptism in the Spirit, believers are "commencing the transforming process, preparatory to the catching up of His Bride."[52] AG ministers held various views about the "requirements" for inclusion in the bride. Some followed the holiness-Pentecostal interpretation of the baptism in the Holy Ghost as the sealing of the Bride.[53] However, fears over the exclusionary nature of this doctrine led several of leading voices in the AG to hold an inclusive view in which the bride consists of all "true Christians."[54] For example, J. R. Flower comments,

> At first the general opinion seemed to be that it was only those who had been baptized into the Holy Ghost who should be of that number. . . . The Lord wants to deliver us from any such spirit of classification or measuring ourselves by ourselves, for they that do this thing are not wise. Much harm came to the Pentecostal work in the beginning because some unwise leaders took the stand that they were prepared for the bridehood, having received the baptism in the Holy Spirit and spoken in tongues, while all those who were simply sanctified were not in it and would be left behind at the coming of Jesus.[55]

---

[49] "The Good News of Christ's Coming," *PE*, July 23, 1921, 8.

[50] J. W. Welch, "Looking for the Glorious Hope," *WE*, November 13, 1915, 2, comments,

[51] Although several articles acknowledge the marriage supper, few articles give any details about the event. E. N. Bell, "Questions and Answers," *WE*, December 9, 1916, 9; E. N. Bell, "Questions and Answers," *WE*, March 30, 1918, 9; J. N. Gortner, "666," *CE*, April 19, 1919, 1; John Goben, "The Millennial Reign," *PE*, February 21, 1925, 2.

[52] "The Invitation," *PE*, January 22, 1921, 3.

[53] Lelia Mayan Conway, "He is Near—Even at the Door," *WE*, March 25, 1916, 6–7; E. N. Bell, "Questions and Answers," *WE*, December 9, 1916, 9; Elizabeth Sisson, "That Blessed Hope," *PE*, Second Coming Supplement, September 10, 1920, 6–8; H. W. M., "Shut In or Shut Out," *PE*, Second Coming Supplement, September 10, 1920, 4.

[54] "As a Presbyterian Now Sees It," *CE*, October 31, 1914, 1–2; B. P. Dixon, "What is the Essential Preparation for the Rapture," *PE*, November 1, 1919, 14; J. T. Boddy, "Who Will Be In The Rapture?," *PE*, April 16, 1921), 5; John Coxe, "The Rapture—Who Will Be Taken?," *PE*, January 21, 1922, 3.

[55] Flower, "The Bride of Christ," *TP*, November 1910, 10.

Bell argued that being filled with the Spirit could not be the requirement because "thousands in the past have died in Christ who have never had the Latter Rain."[56]

Second, they hoped for their salvation to be complete in the resurrection of the body. In their belief in Christ's return, the body is not neglected in favor of spiritual bliss in heaven. J. N. Gortner comments, "God is interested in our bodies while we live here amid these scenes of time, and He does not forget them when our spirits take their departure from this world. They are His bodies now, and even though they may die they will be His bodies still."[57] This hope was commonly understood in light of Paul's connection of the Spirit and resurrection in Rom. 8:22–24. Lillian Yeomans echoes this verse, adding that the church has been "longing, praying, and sighing" since the beginning.[58] The connection between the Spirit and the resurrection of the body was important because the power needed for God to bring about the resurrection was present in the baptism in the Spirit.[59] The hope inspired by the resurrection is a reality in the "here and now" for those who wait for the return of the Lord.[60] This hope also "creates a sanctifying character" in believers as they wait for his return.[61]

The third aspect of hope they emphasized was an expectation that Christ will establish his rule on earth.[62] Although the rapture will lift the resurrected body to heaven for the marriage supper of the Lamb, that journey will only be temporary.[63] They did not consider heaven to be their final destination. Instead, they understood that resurrected bodies were necessary for the coming reign of Christ and his saints on earth in the millennial kingdom. The topic of heaven was not prominent in their minds; instead, they favored the earth-centered concepts of the resurrection of the physical body and the hope of the establishment of the earthly reign of the Messiah. The "this world" emphasis

[56] E. N. Bell, "Questions and Answers," *CE*, August 24, 1918, 9.

[57] J. N. Gortner, "Some Last Things," *PE*, January 22, 1921, 2–3.

[58] Lillian B. Yeomans, "Behold He Cometh," *PE*, December 15, 1923, 2.

[59] John Coxe, "The Rapture—Who Will Be Taken?," *PE*, January 21, 1922, 2.

[60] "The Good News of the Lord's Appearing," *PE*, July 23, 1921, 8.

[61] J. Stuart Holden, "Maranatha!," *WE*, March 23, 1918, 9, "You cannot find any exhortation to holiness, to self-sacrifice, to identification with the Lord Jesus in His death and life, that is not based upon the great and glorious fact to which we humbly bear our witness today—that the Lord is coming." Cf. Dinsdale T. Young, "The Practical Issue of the Coming of Christ," *WE*, March 23, 1918, 6–8; "Certainties," *WE*, March 23, 1918, 9.

[62] G. C. Morgan, "The Coming Revelation of the Lord Jesus Christ," *WE*, March 23, 1918, 4–5.

[63] E. N. Bell, "Questions and Answers," *WE*, November 24, 1917, 8, says the marriage supper "takes place after the Rapture and in the air (heaven), before Jesus comes on earth to take possession." Also, "The Future Life," *CE*, September 6, 1919, 12.

acted as a buffer to the pull to be "otherworldly," which also meant they were interested in the future of the earth before and after the coming of Christ.[64] Much of the eschatology in the Establishment Period conveyed an overwhelming sense of hope that was grounded in the resurrection of the dead and the transformation of the living at Christ's coming.

One Coming-Two Stages

Belief in the soon coming of Jesus, when explained in more detail, was most often articulated using the dispensational teaching that there are two phases of Christ's coming. E. N. Bell explains, "So the coming of the Lord is one coming, called His SECOND COMING, but it is by two steps in two stages."[65] The relationship of Jesus to his people differentiated the first and second phases. W. T. Gaston says, "There is a double aspect of the Lord's coming. He is to come as a thief, and He is to come as a King, as a Judge. He is to come as a Bridegroom, and He is to come as a Warrior. He is to come for the saints, and He is to come with the saints."[66] The first stage of Christ's coming is the rapture of the church, which is the "first resurrection" of believers. In this coming, "When Jesus comes for the saints, for the church, for the bride, for those who have made themselves ready, He does not touch the earth; but they are caught up from the earth and meet Him in the air."[67] The reason they are caught up, as was mentioned earlier, is to prepare the bride to come back to earth to reign with Christ. The second phase of the coming of the Lord was his appearing or revelation from heaven, at which point he will establish his kingdom on earth.[68] Only this time when he comes, he comes "to make war."[69] The revelation of Christ will be both a time of judgment and "a purging, a cleansing, preparing the way for the restitution."[70]

The two-phase coming was also necessary to explain their dispensational concept of the latter rain. Stanley Frodsham argued that when the Jews rejected

---

[64] Grant Wacker, *Heaven Below* (Cambridge, MA: Harvard University Press, 2003), argues that Pentecostals managed the tensions between "this-worldly" and "otherworldly" attitudes, believing the Holy Spirit was working in the world to create "Heaven Below."

[65] E. N. Bell, "Questions and Answers," *CE*, March 30, 1918, 9.

[66] W. T. Gaston, "Coming For and With His Saints," *PE*, September 27, 1924, 2.

[67] Gaston, "Coming For and With His Saints," 2.

[68] Gaston, "Coming For and With His Saints," 2.

[69] Gaston, "Coming For and With His Saints," 2; John Goben, "The Millennial Reign," *PE*, February 21, 1925, 2.

[70] "The Soon Coming of Christ," *WE*, November 24, 1917, 4.

the Messiah, the kingdom of God that was promised was "set aside" and opened up a "parenthesis" in which Gentiles were given "the operations of the Spirit."[71] Through the Gentiles, God held over the promised kingdom until the end of the age.[72] As the dispensation of the Spirit comes to a close, the latter rain prepares the church for the Messianic kingdom to be fully realized. Frodsham comments,

> The restoration of the Kingdom is linked up and closely connected with the working of the Spirit of God. First there must be a powerful witnessing and when the witnessing power and demonstration of the Spirit is completed, then you may look for the restoration of the Kingdom. The former and latter rain, the dispensation of the Gentiles, the dispensation of the Spirit, are to precede the restoring again of the Kingdom of Israel.[73]

The latter rain and the experience of the baptism in the Holy Spirit was God's way of heralding the message that "Jesus is coming soon!"[74] They believed the latter rain was "ripening" the harvest of souls that were being prepared to fill out the eschatological body of Christ (the bride) in preparation for the coming reign of Christ.[75]

The Tribulation

In Chapter 3, it was noted that the AG did not take an official position on the tribulation until 1937, which even then was not a positive affirmation of pretribulation rapture. However, the majority position in the Pentecostal Evangel was that the rapture would take place before the tribulation.[76] But this does not mean that it was the only position within the AG. E. N. Bell pointed out to readers that there were some within the fellowship that taught that the rapture would take place in the middle of the seven-year tribulation when the manchild is taken to

---

[71] "God's Grace to the Gentiles," *CE*, September 6, 1919, 4.

[72] Stanley Frodsham, "The Coming Revival and the Coming Christ," *PE*, May 17, 1924, 4.

[73] "God's Grace to the Gentiles," 4.

[74] "How Long," *WE*, April 20, 1918, 8.

[75] Reader Harris, "Nearing the End of the Pentecostal Age," *PE*, July 15, 1916, 7; "The Preparation of the Bride for the Return of Her Lord," *PE*, September 15, 1917, 8.

[76] E. N. Bell, "Questions and Answers," *WE* February 8, 1919, 5, comments, "It is 'generally agreed' among us, though not unanimously, that the saints go up about the beginning of the great tribulation." See also Lelia Mayan Conway, "He is Near—Even at the Door," *WE*, March 25, 1916, 6–7; James McAlister, "Startling Signs of the End," *PE*, Second Coming Supplement, September 10, 1920, 1; "Shut In or Shut Out," *PE*, Second Coming Supplement, September 10, 1920, 4.

heaven (Rev. 12:5).[77] Bell admitted that he himself held to a mid-tribulational position.[78] Bell believed Christians will go through the first three and one-half years of the tribulation, but will be raptured before the Great Tribulation.[79] Bell wasn't the only one during this period that held a mid-tribulational position.[80] D. W. Kerr and Elizabeth Sisson also held to multiple rapture positions based on different classifications of believers.[81] G. C. Garrison also supported the mid-tribulational position based on his interpretation of Jesus' apocalyptic discourse.[82] Garrison argued that when Jesus commanded the disciples to "flee to the mountains," he was referring to Christians "fleeing" to heaven in the rapture. In an editorial note on Garrison's article, Bell comments that they included the article because it represented a "middle view" between two extremes on the subject.[83] Bell notes that though most believe that "all saved people" will be taken in rapture prior to the tribulation, others take the opposite extreme view that Christians will "go entirely through the tribulation." Bell concludes, "Any view taken should leave us free to obey Jesus in continually looking for his return."[84]

Similar to Bell, J. R. Flower believed the issue of when the rapture takes place in relation to the tribulation was up for debate.[85] Flower notes that if one interprets the removal of the hinderer in 2 Thess. 2:7–9 as the Holy Spirit within the saints, then the "wicked one," whom Daniel prophesies will arise in the second half of the tribulation, will be revealed immediately following. Flower concludes, "There is so much room for speculation here that it behooves none of us to be dogmatic."[86] So while a pretribulation position was the most common, the articles in the *Pentecostal Evangel* during the Establishment Period confirm the early orientation toward tribulational diversity and support the ambiguity found in the *SFT*.

[77] E. N. Bell, "Questions and Answers," *WE*, February 8, 1919, 5.

[78] E. N. Bell, "Questions and Answers," *WE*, March 30, 1918, 9. Cf. E. N. Bell, "Questions and Answers," *WE*, December 9, 1916, 9; E. N. Bell, Questions and Answers," *WE*, February 8, 1919, 5. This is also suggested by S. A. Jamieson, "Second Coming of Christ," *WE*, February 26, 1916, 5.

[79] E. N. Bell, "Questions and Answers," *WE*, 216 (November 24, 1917), 8.

[80] McQueen, *Toward a Pentecostal Eschatology*, 164, acknowledges this fact yet does not consider it to be significant enough to challenge his argument of uniformity.

[81] D. W. Kerr, "The Two Fold Aspect of Church Life: Will the Church Go Through The Tribulation," *LRE*, October 1919, 2–6; Elizabeth Sisson, "Philadelphia, Laodicea," *PE*, May 15, 1920, 5.

[82] G.C. Garrison, "At What Point Will Rapture Occur?," *PE*, July 9, 1921, 21.

[83] "Note as to the Rapture," *PE*, July 9, 1921, 21. The editors announce that this topic would be taken up at the General Council so that the matter may be "cleared up."

[84] "Note as to the Rapture," 21.

[85] J. R. Flower, "Living in Momentous Days," *PE*, July 14, 1917, 8.

[86] Flower, "Living in Momentous Days," 8.

The Millennium: The Kingdom Come

In the same way, the AG understood the Second Coming to have two phases, the kingdom of God was also understood in two dispensational phases. The first phase is the invisible kingdom in the "hearts of believers" through the Holy Spirit.[87] Because the Jews rejected Jesus as the Messiah, the kingdom was postponed to the future, but not entirely.[88] Believers enter into the invisible aspect of kingdom through being born of the Spirit. In turn, believers proclaim the kingdom by the power of the Spirit, which is confirmed with signs and wonders.[89] When Pentecostals proclaim the gospel of the kingdom, they are proclaiming that the kingdom of God is present through "salvation, baptism in the Holy Ghost, healing for the sick, and spiritual gifts."[90] In this way, they understood the manifestations of the Spirit to be the sign that the kingdom is already present.

In addition to the spiritual aspects, the kingdom will be a literal kingdom that will exercise authority over injustice and oppression in the dominions of this world. What is foreshadowed now through the power of the Spirit will be brought into its global fullness when Jesus reigns. Alice Luce says,

> When He comes whose right it is to reign, he will take the kingdoms of the world into his control and then every oppressor will be punished, every wrong righted, and the earth filled with righteousness and peace.[91]

This kingdom will be a one thousand year "millennium" in which Christ rules with his saints from Israel, which will be restored prior to the millennium in anticipation of the revelation of Jesus from heaven.[92]

Despite their firm conviction that a literal kingdom was coming, the details of the millennium are not clearly articulated. Visions of the millennium follow two trajectories based on their vision of Christ's rule. In the first trajectory, the millennium is portrayed in terms of "renewal" of the earth and "reconstruction"

---

[87] J. T. Boddy, "The Antichrist," *PE*, January 20, 1917, 4; "The Kingdom," *PE*, Second Coming Supplement, September 10, 1920, 5.

[88] "God's Grace to the Gentiles," *CE*, September 6, 1919, 4.

[89] "The Kingdom," *PE*, Second Coming Supplement, September 10, 1920, 5.

[90] C. W. Doney, "The Gospel of the Kingdom," *WW*, March 1914, 2.

[91] Alice Luce, "God is Soon To Speak," *PE*, January 10, 1920, 1.

[92] "Preparations for the Return of the Jews," *WW*, August 1915, 2; Reader Harris, "Nearing the End of the Pentecostal Age," *PE*, July 15, 1916, 9; "The Budding Fig Tree," *WE*, May 26, 1917, 11; E. L. Langston, "Signs of the Times," *PE*, March 3, 1923, 2–3, 8.

of the present order under the lordship of Jesus through peace and justice.[93] In this kingdom, the un-regenerate nations will undergo "a purging, a cleansing, preparing the way for the restitution."[94] Under Christ's perfect reign sin will be restrained, the curse will be lifted, and the nations will be able to conform to his rule.[95] This vision of the millennium presents an interesting anthropological situation in which both glorified and un-glorified people will coexist. Bell says, "Men will not be immortal during the Millennium, but under those ideal conditions some may live the whole thousand years."[96]

The second trajectory paints a different picture of Jesus' rule. In contrast to expecting Jesus to reign as the Prince of Peace, this vision portrays Jesus as one who "is coming to make war."[97] The millennium will be a time of judgment based on Jesus' teaching on the sheep and the goats (Matt. 25:31).[98] In fact, some in the AG believed that the onset of WWI was the beginning of Christ's judgment upon the nations.[99] Gaston argued that Christ's millennial work will be "grappling with

---

[93] "The Shaking of the Nations, *PE*, Second Coming Supplement, September 10, 1920, 8; J. T. Boddy, "The Kingdom," *PE*, Second Coming Supplement, September 10, 1920, 5; D. H. McDowell, "The Purpose of the Coming of the Lord," *PE*, May 2, 1925, 3.

[94] "The Soon Coming of Christ," *WE*, November 24, 1917, 4.

[95] E. N. Bell, "Questions and Answers," *WE*, March 30, 1918, 9, comments, "The remnants of the living nations will live on in the flesh and prosper as never before in the history of the world under the personal righteous and wise reign of Christ as King."

[96] E. N. Bell, "Questions and Answers," *CE*, September 7, 1918, 9.

[97] John Goben, "The Millennial Reign," *PE*, February 21, 1925, 2.

[98] S. A. Jamieson, "The Five Judgments," *WE*, March 11, 1916, 6; Goben, "The Millennial Reign," 2. However, as one article points out, Jesus is not so much judging political entities as he is judging individuals. For example, "The Future Life," *CE*, September 6, 1919, 12, comments, "A nation consists of individuals, and . . . the Lord will render to every man according to his deeds. We believe that this passage teaching personal as well as national judgment."

[99] Frank Bartleman, "Present Day Conditions," *WE*, June 5, 1915, 3, comments, "The nations are being judged. Belgium for her Congo atrocities, France for her infidelity and devil worship, Germany for her materialism and militarism, England for her hypocrisy, bullyism over weaker nations, and her overwhelming pride." He did not spare his criticism of America saying, "The United States has a score of kings where European countries have but one. That is about the only difference. We are ruled by the money gods." See a similar characterization of the nations in James Gray, "A Voice from England," *CE*, October 3, 1914, 1; "The Great War and the Speedy Return of our Lord," *WE*, Second Coming Supplement, April 10, 1917, 2. Several years later after America joined the war, E. N. Bell retracted this article and subsequently printed tracts because it was "entirely too radical for war times" and asked everyone "not to reprint it" and to "burn all their old supply of this tract" in order to not draw criticism to the fellowship of being disloyal. E. N. Bell, "Destroy This Tract," *CE*, August 24, 1918, 4.

conditions, rebuking nations, dealing with wicked men" and will ultimately "smite the whole system, to break it in pieces like a potter's vessel."[100]

The Final Judgment

The doctrine of the final judgment receives little attention during this period. When the final judgment was discussed, it was consistent with the SFT doctrine of the "Lake of Fire" that focused on the fate of Satan and the enemies of God. The AG makes it clear that everlasting fire was "not made for man"; it was made for the Devil and his angels.[101] The subject of hell was rarely a topic in these early articles. They were not overly preoccupied with emphasizing the "fire and brimstone" pronouncements of judgment of God. As one writer admonishes believers, "Do not be occupied so much with impending judgment. Gaze more on the hope."[102] They saw the final judgment as a source of hope in that Satan, who was deemed the source of all suffering, will finally receive justice for his oppression of humanity. J. N. Gortner expresses it this way,

> I am ready for God to send Satan to hell. Satan has been back of all the devilishness of all the ages. All the wars and all the sufferings, all the heartaches, the miseries, the wretchedness, the woes of humanity—Satan has been the real instigator of them all. There can be no permanent peace in the world until Satan shall have been removed from the theater of action.[103]

The final judgment of sin, wickedness, and the Devil will be God's long-awaited answer on the issues of injustice and suffering in world. As Alice Luce observes, "God is soon to speak," and he will have the final word on injustice in response to the "pitiful cries of homeless and mutilated little children in Belgium, and the dying groans of thousands of slaughtered Armenians."[104]

The Future of Creation

The subject of the new heavens and new earth is one that is mentioned only a few times during this period, but the most common position on the future of creation

---

[100] W. T. Gaston, "Coming For and With His Saints," *PE*, September 27, 1924, 2.

[101] "The Future Life," *CE*, September 6, 1919, 12; "The Kingdom," *PE*, Second Coming Supplement, September 10, 1920, 5.

[102] "The Impending World Judgment," *CE*, January 25, 1919, 9.

[103] J. N. Gortner, "Some Last Things," *PE*, January 22, 1921, 3.

[104] Alice Luce, "God is Soon To Speak," *PE*, January 10, 1920, 1.

was that the new creation would replace the old creation. One article records a vision in which the writer testifies, "Then I beheld a new earth which was very beautiful, and I saw a new heaven take the place of that one which had passed away."[105] Another article declares, "If God was well pleased to make a better, a new heaven and new earth, and the one is going to exceed the other as much as grace exceeds law.... The old earth will serve its time till the better one come (sic) in."[106]

However, others during this period recognized continuity between the first creation and the new creation, which will be transformed rather than abandoned in favor of a new one. For example, S. A. Jamieson argues,

> The planet on which we live is by no means to be annihilated.... As sinful man has been delivered by the redemption of Jesus Christ, so this sin-cursed earth is also to share in that redemption. It is to be transformed, renewed, glorified and made a fit place for the habitation of God's redeemed people.[107]

The process of restoration will begin during the millennium when Christ and his saints will establish political and ecological peace.[108] What is initiated in the millennium will be consummated as the ultimate act of salvation in the complete redemption of the heavens and the earth. The goal of history was to restore the earthly fellowship between God and man as it was in the Garden of Eden.[109]

> God has been a stranger and an outcast to His own garden because of the usurper, but the Son of the Father undertook to deal with the usurper and will not leave off till He has completed the work given to Him by His Father, so that God once more can visit His garden.[110]

When Christ returns, he will reverse the curse on the earth, and it will be restored to its pristine state at creation. G. D. Watson proposed that Noah's flood "knocked the earth out of joint," which has affected the length of life and the balance of creation.[111] The physical judgments that are coming in the tribulation will serve a redemptive purpose in that God will "knock the earth back again into its original

---

[105] "Prophetic Vision of the Lord's Second Coming, The Great Tribulation and the End of the World, Part Two," *PE,* May 1, 1920, 1–3.

[106] "New Heavens and A New Earth," *WE,* February 9, 1918, 5.

[107] S. A. Jamieson, "A New Heavens and A New Earth," *PE,* September 30, 1922, 5.

[108] "The Soon Coming of Christ," *WE,* November 24, 1917, 4.

[109] "New Heavens and A New Earth," *WE,* February 9, 1918, 5.

[110] "The Soon Coming of Christ," *WE,* November 24, 1917, 4.

[111] G. D. Watson, "Knocking the Earth Into Place," *PE,* February 19, 1921, 15.

position with the north star and the sun, and that will eliminate all these curses from our earthly system and restore the earth back to its primitive condition."[112]

Eschatological Perspectives on Social Issues

Intermingled with the doctrine of the return of Christ are a variety of perspectives on political and social issues that were important to early adherents. AG writers often interpreted various societal issues through an eschatological lens. Like most premillennialists, they objected to the perceived apostasy in the Federation of Churches,[113] the vain work of prohibition,[114] laxity in social morals,[115] and labor unions as signs of the times.[116] They weren't just critical of the moral state of the world, they were also critical of church relying on human efforts to reform society.

> Saved men become better fathers, better neighbors, better businessmen, better citizens, and there is a trend of world life toward kingdom righteousness. Indeed, this is the shortest path for all great reforms, hence Paul did not pause in his gospel efforts to organize anti-slavery societies or even temperance leagues. The gospel effort that saves the individual will as a byproduct save society.[117]

Furthermore, prayer and waiting on the Lord was seen as much more valuable than social work. A. G. Ward comments, "More things are wrought through prayer than by all this fleshly activity on the part of believers on a lower plane of grace."[118]

Their reluctance to work for social change did not mean that they ignored social issues taking place around them. In fact, they were very interested in documenting all social regress as a validation of their conviction that the return

---

[112] Watson, "Knocking the Earth Into Place," 15.

[113] *CE*, April 10, 1915, 1.

[114] "When the Son of Man Comes," *PE*, April 21, 1928, 2.

[115] *WW*, June 1915, 2.

[116] "The Mark of the Beast," *PE*, December 25, 1920, 3 says, "The very minute you sign up with an [labor] organization that has not the glory of God for its purpose, . . . you have sown the seed of the spirit that will develop into the application of the mark of the beast."

[117] R. M. Russell, "Prophecy and Present Events," *PE*, April 16, 1921, 9.

[118] A. G. Ward, "Soul Food for Hungry Saints," *PE*, August 23, 1919, 1. Ward further comments, "If you are tempted at times when you are alone waiting on God and you hear a voice urging you to get up and do something, if you are tempted to feel that you ought to be doing what other folk are doing, will you please just remember that your Bridegroom is much more concerned about your waiting upon Him and satisfying His heart than He is about your going around working in your own energy."

of Christ was near.[119] One social issue they recognized was income inequality. The advent of industrialization in America created a new set of economic realities in which individuals were acquiring unprecedented wealth. But Pentecostals were not impressed, nor did they aspire to attain worldly things. The wealth that people gained was nothing more than "miseries for rich men" that was being "hoarded for the last days."[120] They were particularly critical of the rich because wealth was included as a "sign of the times" in James 5:1–8, which prophesied that wealth would be gained at the expense of the poor. One writer notes, "The growth and multiplicity of the millionaires in every land, even in poverty-stricken Germany, proves conclusively that we are in the last days."[121]

At the same time that the rich were gaining unprecedented wealth, the latter rain of the Spirit was falling on the poor. As one writer said, "The phenomenon of the Latter Rain coincides with the phenomenon of the increasing world riches; the early harvest ripening, despite the warning of the final crash and the destruction."[122] Riches were seen as a sign of judgment, but the outpouring of the Spirit was interpreted as God's answer to economic equality.[123]

> The Spirit of God takes aside the down-trodden, the defrauded, the cheated; and you who have little or nothing upon which the cancer and the rust can operate, you spoiled ones, having little, are to have the dew of heaven instead of the wrath of God.[124]

Through the Spirit, these marginalized believers felt empowered and were promised a destiny in which they would "inherit the earth." The AG not only

---

[119] The most common approach to Bible prophecy was a sign-based empirical approach, which attempted to prove the nearness of the return of Christ by correlating the signs of the times from Jesus' apocalyptic discourse in Matthew 24 with current events. This approach can be seen in Frank Boyd, *The Budding Fig Tree* (Springfield: Gospel Publishing House, 1925); Stanley Frodsham, *Things Which Must Shortly Come To Pass*, (Springfield: Gospel Publishing House, 1928); Frank Boyd, *Signs of the Times* (Springfield: Gospel Publishing House, 1950); C. M. Ward, *Waiting* ... (Springfield: Gospel Publishing House, 1959).

[120] "Miseries for Rich Men," *PE*, November 27, 1926, 4–5. Similarly, S. A. Jamieson, "Seven Fears," *PE*, February 13, 1926, 3, blamed the "greed and corruption" of the government and the banking industry for the rising poverty in America.

[121] "Significant Signs of the Times," *PE*, January 8, 1927, 5.

[122] "Significant Signs of the Times," 5.

[123] "Significant Signs of the Times," 5, "The Lord says, 'Upon my servants, I will pour out my Spirit!' Handmaidens! In the millionaire's home is it the millionaire of the cook who goes to the Pentecostal meeting? Judge yourselves."

[124] "Significant Signs of the Times," 5.

recognized the plight of the poor, but some also worked to serve the victims of economic injustice. A Sunday school lesson reminded readers that "the inheritors of the Kingdom will be those who have given Christ food and drink and have taken Him into their houses, visited Him when sick and when in prison."[125] Also, several early AG missionaries opened orphanages in various parts of the world and in the US.[126]

Industrialization not only created economic inequality; there were also growing issues surrounding racial inequality.[127] The Pentecostal Movement was founded on the alternative vision that when the Spirit was poured out on all flesh, the blood washed away all social and racial distinctions.[128] But a decade after Azusa, the fact that the AG withdrew from under C. H. Mason as members of the Church of God in Christ raises questions about racial attitudes within the AG.[129] Although there is little overtly racist language in AG literature, there also is a complete absence of the type of racial vision present at Azusa Street.[130] In contrast to the AG's silence on racism and black slavery, the growing problem of the "white slave trade" did receive attention.[131] The "white slave trade" was name given to the trafficking of women across state lines for the purpose of

---

[125] "The Future Life," *CE*, September 6, 1919, 12.

[126] "Pentecostal Orphanage in Alabama," *PE*, May 1, 1920, 10.

[127] Brian Donovan, *White Slave Crusades: Race, Gender, and Anti-vice Activism 1887–1917* (Chicago: University of Illinois Press, 2005), points out that during the turn of the century, fears surrounding growing immigration and industrialization led to concepts of "whiteness" and "colored."

[128] Estrelda Alexander, *Black Fire: One Hundred Years of African American Pentecostalism* (Downers Grov: Intervarsity Press, 2011).

[129] I agree with David D. Daniels, "Charles Harrison Mason: The Interracial Impulse," in James R. Goff and Grant Wacker, eds., *Portraits of a Generation* (Fayetteville: University of Arkansas Press, 2002), 254–70, that there could be polity reasons rather than racial reasons for the separation of the AG. It is likely that the AG did not want to identify with Mason's holiness organization rather than his racial identity. The association with Mason that began in 1910 was prior to the Finished Work controversy. But by 1913, there was a need for a new fellowship that was not identified as holiness.

[130] One example of white supremacy was by W. F. Carothers, "Attitude of Pentecostal Whites to the Colored Brethren in the South," *CE*, August 14, 1915, 2. Carothers was a close associate of Parham who shared his views against racial mixing. Carothers argued that different races were "God's intention," a claim he believed was not motivated by "prejudice nor any other evil intent" but was intended to "preserve racial purity and integrity." He argued that the South "selfishly" mixed the races for their own financial gain, which ultimately instituted the racial tensions in America.

[131] See Daniel D. Isgrigg, "'Rescued women:' Early Pentecostal Responses to Sex Trafficking," a paper presented at the 50th Annual Meeting of the Society for Pentecostal Studies, Southlake Texas, March 2021.

prostitution.¹³² E. N. Bell considered human trafficking grave moral crisis.¹³³ Though the exaggerated claims made by the producers of "white slave" literature were intended to create moral panic, AG members used these narratives as justification that the coming of the Lord was near.¹³⁴ What is noteworthy about this controversial issue is that the AG was motivated to bring help and recovery to trafficking victims. In 1913, Bell and Howard Goss took over leadership of a rescue home in Arkansas for girls who had come out of the white slave trade. Bell encouraged his readers to give offerings, donations of food, and clothing in order to "help save girls and send them to the Home where they can get saved and get on their feet again and lead a clean life."¹³⁵

A second aspect of social engagement that significantly shaped their eschatology was their outlook on politics. In 1917, Woodrow Wilson told congress of his intention to enter the WWI against Germany in order to make the world "safe for democracy." Wilson believed the promotion of democracy was a divine global mission given to America to save the nations and promote liberty, prosperity, order, and justice.¹³⁶ The AG unequivocally disagreed. Many discerned that the elevation of democracy as a divine idea was just a secular form of postmillennialism. James McAlister comments, "Democracy means to govern without Christ, and will therefore prove the biggest failure of all forms of government. It will land this world in a welter of blood and death

---

¹³² Donovan, *White Slave Crusades*, provides a telling account of the "white slavery" campaigns, which sought to protect women and the "morality and purity" of American Culture during a time when the age of industrialization was producing racial and social anxiety. Dramatic stories of white women being lured into prostitution rings were often exaggerated and repeated in various books and even films. The unintended consequences of this movement was the emergence of racial designations of "colored" and "white" as well as the rise of white masculinity and degradation of femininity. Much of the "morality and purity" literature surrounding this issue came out of Chicago, a center for Mid-West Pentecostals.

¹³³ E. N. Bell, "Questions and Answers," *CE*, April 14, 1917, 9; "White Slave Craft," *WW*, January 1914, 3; "An Experience of Divine Guidance," *Christ's Ambassadors*, June 1926, 1.

¹³⁴ Donovan, *White Slave Crusades*, 19. One AG pastor propagating these exaggerated claims was Willard Pope, "Morphine Tablets of Hell," *LRE*, December 1918, 5. See also Willard Pope, "The Crying Need of the Hour," *LRE*, November 1931, 9–12.

¹³⁵ "Bethel Rescue Home," *WW*, June 1913, 1. The Bethel Rescue Home's mission was to "rescue girls that are in the 'White Slave prisons.'" The home was operated by a Sister Chambers who had twenty-five years of experience as a nurse and in rescue work.

¹³⁶ Steven M. Studebaker, *A Pentecostal Political Theology for American Renewal: Spirit of the Kingdoms, Citizens of the Cities* (New York: Palgrave McMillan, 2016), 33–37, points out that Wilson's vision was indicative of the postmillennial belief in Manifest Destiny of America.

unparalleled."[137] Because of the corruption in government, Stanley Frodsham believed that the democratic value of exercising voting rights was often fruitless and antithetical to basic Christian convictions. He says, "The world says: 'Of two evils, choose the lesser.' The saint says: 'Seeing two evils, avoid both.'"[138] They understood that the political realm belonged to the kingdoms of the world and not the kingdom of God. W. T. Gaston declared,

> Oh, brother, I am going to vote for Jesus. You can go on with this political situation if you want to, you can throw your hat and make yourself foolish about industrial situations, but I am going to sing and shout and vote for Jesus, I have no enthusiasm for anybody else.[139]

The AG's apolitical eschatological orientation can also be seen in their pacifist stance.[140] Since political institutions and governments were considered tools of the beast, they were appalled at the way American society celebrated "those who invent the most violent gun and the most violent explosive."[141] As one writer says, "The War belongs to the world, and it has served to illustrate the association of the highest civilization with the deepest wickedness."[142] When Germany and Britain used their identities as "Christian nations" as justification for WWI, the AG argued that truly "Christian nations" would have "made such a war impossible."[143] In fact, the AG leaders rejected the notion that any nation could be classified as a "Christian nation" since the Church is scattered throughout all nations. As one author noted,

> A little clear and logical thinking, accompanied by an intelligent knowledge of God's Word, will easily dispose of the fallacy that this war is being waged between

---

[137] James McAlister, "Startling Signs of the End," *PE*, Second Coming Supplement, September 10, 1920, 1. See also Reader Harris, "Nearing the End of the Pentecostal Age," *PE*, July 15, 1916, 9; "The Good News of the Lord's Appearing," *PE*, July 23, 1921, 8.

[138] S. H. Frodsham, "Politics From The Pentecostal Viewpoint," *PE*, October 30, 1920, 3.

[139] W. T. Gaston, "Coming For and With His Saints," *PE*, September 27, 1924, 3.

[140] Alexander, *Peace to War* and Tackett, "The Embourgeoisement of the Assemblies of God," 226–30.

[141] "The Impending World Judgment and the Only Place of Shelter," *CE*, January 25, 1919, 9.

[142] "The Good News of the Lord's Appearing," *PE*, July 23, 1921, 8.

[143] Cf. Phillip Jenkins, *The Great and Holy War* (San Francisco: HarperOne, 2014).

Christian nations, for it is impossible for us to find in this dispensation a whole Christian town, village or congregation, not to mention a Christian Nation.[144]

On the one hand, they understood that war was inevitable because Jesus prophesied that it would be a sign of the times.[145] On the other hand, the AG believed Spirit-filled Christians were not "those who delight in war," but those who are so "permeated by the Spirit of the Prince of Peace."[146] These tumultuous early days would be followed by a new period of stability, as we will cover in the next chapter.

---

[144] "Light on the Present Crisis," *PE*, July 1, 1916, 6–9. The author further declares, "In this great European war the strife is not between two companies of God's people, but between various world powers whose doom is sealed."

[145] John Goben, "The Millennial Reign," *PE*, February 21, 1925, 2, declares, "I don't like war: but, my brother, there will be war as long as the devil is loose and rules in the hearts of men." Also, "The Great War and the Speedy Return of Jesus," *WE*, Second Coming Supplement, April 10, 1917, 1.

[146] "Crisis," *WE*, April 21, 1917, 7.

7

SCHOLASTIC PERIOD (1927–1948)

The period of 1927–1948 was a period of relative tranquility where the AG was "untroubled by internal conflict and isolated from the larger church world."[1] The adoption of the constitution in 1927 ushered in an era of stability as the AG was beginning to build its institution framework. Several new departments were added to the General Council including Sunday School, Department of Home Missions, and the expansion of Bible Schools to include liberal arts education. Douglas Jacobsen has labeled this period as the "Scholastic Period" because of the way Pentecostals sought to articulate Pentecostal theology to a new generation of ministers.[2]

Culturally, the new mediums of radio and television increased awareness among Pentecostals of world events.[3] This new awareness was expressed in the *Pentecostal Evangel,* which became a regular source for news and information about the world often through the lens of eschatology. Readers were regularly exposed to information about the rise of fascism, communism, religious persecution, and the rapid move toward a state for Israel. Prior to 1930, the *Pentecostal Evangel* carried two regular columns highlighting missionary news called "Gospel in Foreign Lands" and "In the Whitened Harvest Fields." When

---

[1] Menzies, *Anointed to Serve*, 145.

[2] Douglas Jacobsen, "Knowing the Doctrine of Pentecostals: The Scholastic Theology of the Assemblies of God," in Edith L. Blumhofer, Russell P. Spittler, and Grant A. Wacker, eds., *Pentecostal Currents in American Protestantism* (Urbana: University of Illinois Press, 1999), coined the term "Scholastic Period," which has been adopted for this period of time when AG leaders codified doctrine for a second generation of Pentecostals in doctrinal books published by GPH. Stephen M. Studebaker, "Pentecostal Soteriology and Pneumatology," *JPT* 11, no. 2 (2003), 248–70, argues that Pentecostal theology borrowed from Protestant scholasticism to categorize its theological positions. However, the term "scholastic" may be a mischaracterization of this period. Scholasticism is a theological method that uses dialectical reasoning to attempt to resolve the conflicts between theological views, a methodology that is not characteristic of the literature from this period. See also Macchia, "The Struggle for Global Witness: Shifting Paradigms in Pentecostal Theology," 9.

[3] Stewart P. MacLennan, "Air-Mindedness, Is it a Sign of the Times?," *PE*, November 14, 1931, 1.

Stanley Frodsham returned to his duties as Editor in January 1930, Frodsham started a regular editorial column called "Editor's Notebook," in which he occasionally highlighted news and notes from around the world. The practice of commenting on world events eventually led to the addition of a regular column in that began at the end of 1932 called, "The Passing and the Permanent," which was intended to be a "weekly survey of passing events viewed in the light of the permanent Word."[4] Consequently, this period saw an increase in commentary on world events interpreted as "signs of the times."

Blessed Hope

Early members of the AG expected Christ to return at any moment. However, a decade later, the delay in Christ's return was beginning to dampen their eschatological fervor. One writer comments, "In the early days of the Latter Rain outpouring the message was, 'The Lord is coming soon.' But there has been a softening of that cry. It has been a muzzled cry. While the bridegroom tarried they all slumbered."[5] First-generation AG ministers looked to the parable of ten virgins to awaken people to the baptism in the Spirit so they would be prepared for the rapture. As Christ's coming tarried, the second generation turned once again to this parable for the encouragement to stay ready with a full portion of oil even in a long delay.[6] Some were growing concerned that American Pentecostals were becoming too comfortable in this life.[7] They feared that if eschatological urgency waned, so would the impulse of the Spirit to reach the lost. J. N. Gortner comments, "It is to be feared that our ardor has cooled off a bit; that we are not quite as zealous as we once were; that we are not putting forth as great an effort to give the gospel to the ends of the earth, and that we should be over the prospect of the coming of the Lord."[8] Even worse, some feared believers were losing the incentive to live a life of holiness.[9] Multiple warnings were issued to the Pentecostal

---

[4] *PE*, December 31, 1931, 5.

[5] "Even So, Come, Lord Jesus," *PE*, February 1, 1930, 5.

[6] "Preparing for the Bridegroom," *PE*, February 22, 1930, 9, comments, "Lack of response in the bride shows declension. Many are lamenting, 'We have not the same zeal, fire and manifestation in our meetings as in the early days of Pentecost.' It is true. It is to be lamented."

[7] W. E. Long, "Signs of the Times," *PE*, December 13, 1941, 3, comments, "We in America are not so anxious to have Him come. We have good jobs, we live in luxury, we have comfortable homes, we still enjoy peace."

[8] J. N. Gortner, "Christ Will Come Again," *PE*, January 29, 1927, 5.

[9] Dinsdale T. Young, "The Coming of the Son of Man," *PE*, November 3, 1928, 7.

faithful to recapture the unction to encourage others to receive the baptism in the Spirit.[10]

For the first few years of the Scholastic Period, articles continued to see the return of Christ in terms of the hope of the resurrection. As W. T. Gaston comments, "We are not here considering carnal hopes nor optimistic tendencies . . . but that divine, Spirit-breathed hope that abides inherent in the new nature and is therefore natural and spontaneous in every normal Christian."[11] As restorationists, they drew from the historical importance apostolic Christianity had placed on the doctrine of the resurrection. As Harvey McAlister notes in 1929, "With the apostles and with Christians who lived in their days, death was, so to speak, left behind; while the resurrection or rather the coming of Him whom they knew to be the 'resurrection and the life,' was their one joyful, triumphant hope."[12] Drawing on the "finished work" concept of salvation, E. S. Williams calls the resurrection of the body the "finished" aspect of salvation.[13] By receiving the "seal of the Spirit," it not only guaranteed the resurrection of the body of believers, but also insured the salvation of all creation.[14]

Even among fears that the revival was waning, they continued to be convinced that the latter rain outpouring of the Spirit was still in effect. After all, the latter rain was a "limitless reservoir" of God's Spirit for his people.[15] Faithful believers need not be deterred by the delay in Christ's return, for as long as latter rain was still falling, Christ's return was still imminent. Pentecostals were encouraged to continue to embrace the manifestations of the Spirit, especially the eschatological sign of speaking in tongues, which had been given to the bride to herald the coming Bridegroom.[16] Whenever one speaks in tongues they "ward, herald,

---

[10] "When the Son of Man Comes," *PE*, April 21, 1928, 2; "Return! Come!," *PE*, January 25, 1930, 9; E. S. Williams, "Knowing the Time," *PE*, August 18, 1934, 7.

[11] W. T. Gaston, "Looking for That Blessed Hope," *PE*, August 27, 1927, 1.

[12] Harvey McAlister, "Will Christ Come Again?," *PE*, October 5, 1929, 2.

[13] E. S. Williams, "Knowing the Time," *PE*, August 18, 1934, 1. "You will notice here that salvation has a *finished* and an *unfinished* aspect. We rejoice *now* in the salvation of our *souls,* but ours will not be *perfect* until we have the redemption of *our bodies."*

[14] E. S. Williams, "Sealed Unto the Day of Redemption," *PE,* February 24, 1940, 2.

[15] "Limitless Pentecostal Reservoirs," *PE*, March 8, 1930, 7, comments, "God is opening up the realm of the Spirit in these last days and He is pouring out from the divine reservoir, so that you may drink abundantly and be satisfied as never before."

[16] "Signs of Christ's Coming," *PE*, September 26, 1930, 8, declares "To the cry, He has given the bride a tongue to utter it, yea to whisper it, so the world shall not hear it and the enemy cannot understand it."

point to, and invite" the one who is coming.[17] Instead of waning manifestations, E. S. Williams expected signs, wonders, and miracles to continue to increase until the ultimate act of the Holy Spirit; the translation of the saints.[18]

The Spirit and the Script

As a second generation of Pentecostals emerged, the connection between the Spirit and the return of Christ began to be tested. For early Pentecostals, the latter rain outpouring and accompanying manifestations were considered the eschatological signs of the end. Because the AG settled on an inclusive doctrine of the rapture, they turned their attention to identifying physical signs in the world. William Long describes this shift:

> A few years ago I used to preach on the Antichrist. I knew who he was then, but today I am not so sure. At that time I knew who the 144,000 were, and the Man-child, and just about everything else there was to know—at least, I thought I knew. . . . I believe the devil has used these wild, weird ideas to blind the people so that the "signs of the time" would not be preached any more. . . . The Bible does give us definitive, distinct signs of the times.[19]

Instead of Spirit helping the believer discern the identity of the bride, 144,000, or the manchild, they began to emphasize the role of the Spirit in illuminating, explaining, and unfolding the end-time script from the Word of God.[20] This shift meant they focused less on the Spirit and more on the end time script.[21] As one writer comments, "The newspaper will help you if you read it in the light of the Lord's own Word."[22] By shifting their gaze from what was happening in the altars of the local assemblies to what was happening in the newspapers, they ultimately shifted from relying upon the Spirit as the Sign to using the Spirit to interpret the

---

[17] "The Latter-Day Pentecost a Prelude to Christ's Coming," *PE*, January 15, 1927, 1, 14.

[18] E. S. Williams, "Sealed Unto the Day of Redemption," *PE*, February 24, 1940, 3, comments, "The greatest display of the work of the Holy Spirit of God will take place. In a moment, in the twinkling of an eye, at the last trump, we shall be caught up to meet the Lord in the Air." A similar thought is found in Elizabeth Sisson, "The Coming Glory," *PE*, November 26, 1927, 3.

[19] W. E. Long, "Signs of the Times," *PE*, December 13, 1941, 2.

[20] Long, "Signs of the Times," 3; "The Signs of Christ," *PE*, December 7, 1940, 5.

[21] For example, Frank Boyd did a series of regular articles in 1934 that went into detail about each sign of the times mentioned by Jesus in his apocalyptic discourses. See, *PE*, May 26, 1934, 3; *PE*, June 2, 1934, 6; *PE*, June 9, 1934, 6; *PE*, June 16, 1934, 6; *PE*, June 30, 1934, 6; *PE*, July 7, 1934, 6; *PE*, July 14, 1934, 5.

[22] Dinsdale T. Young, "The Coming of the Son of Man," *PE*, November 3, 1928, 1.

signs. In their minds, nothing is more Pentecostal than allowing the Spirit to interpret the signs of the times to shape their understanding of the world.[23] The Spirit, therefore, was the key that empowered believers to "interpret the Word in light of happenings around in the world."[24] As one writer expressed,

> Last days need last-day truths. There are hidden, obscure passages regarding the Lord's coming, which can be explained by the Holy Spirit; and these explanations unlock the book of the world which is printed daily and known as the press.[25]

In shifting from discerning the Bride to discerning the world, they eventually became more concerned with escaping the world. As Zelma Argue puts it, "The expectation of deliverance has long been the cherished 'hope' of the church."[26] Throughout the decade of the 1930s, the hope of Christ's coming began shifting from an emphasis on resurrection to removal.[27] E. S. Williams declares, "To those of God's saints in this age who are counted worthy, a complete escape is to be granted from the disasters, political, terrestrial, and planetary, in which humanity at large is to be involved at the close of this age."[28]

The Rapture and the Tribulation

During the Scholastic Period, the emphasis between the two phases of Christ's coming became more pronounced as the AG sought to more carefully define their position. J. N. Hoover declares, "The second coming of Christ, though one grand event, is in two parts. First: He comes in the air for His saints, the church, the bride, at which time occurs the first resurrection. The resurrection of the righteous is

---

[23] "Signs of Christ's Coming," *PE,* July 26, 1930, 8, argues Jesus "gave a complete, minute, exhaustive description. But in later days He can and will give later information. But there must first be the asking, 'When shall these things be?' and the Holy Spirit is waiting to give the answer. 'He shall show you things to come.' The majority of the Church of Christ have kept the Holy Spirit inactive by not asking Him to exercise His office in showing things to come."

[24] "Last Day's Truths," *PE,* August 13, 1927, 2.

[25] "Last Day's Truths," 2.

[26] Zelma Argue, "The Time Is Fulfilled," *PE,* January 16, 1932, 3.

[27] E. S. Williams, "Behold He Cometh," *PE,* September 9, 1933, 2. "Our only hope, of escape, from that time of tribulation judgments to which the world is hastening is the gospel of the grace of God. . . . Although sorrow, tribulation, and judgment are coming, the church of Jesus Christ has promise of escape."

[28] E. S. Williams, "The Great Removal," *PE* July 10, 1937, 5.

completed at His coming to earth to reign."[29] A greater emphasis on the two phases meant they needed to better define the details of the period between the two comings, which meant more attention was given to the tribulation. As E. S. Williams describes it,

> This blessed hope is known as the Rapture, or catching away. As Bridegroom, our great Redeemer comes to some place in midair where His bride meets Him. . . . It is a distinct event from the Revelation when His feet shall stand upon the Mount of Olives (Zech 14:4), and takes place before the Tribulation, while the Revelation does not occur until the Tribulation has finished its course.[30]

The diversity of opinions on the tribulation that were common in the Establishment Period became less common in this second generation. While there was still a debate, H. J. Steil acknowledges, "a great majority of Spirit-filled saints believe He shall come for his saints before the Tribulation."[31]

The shift in emphasis from resurrection to tribulation meant that articles majored on the negative aspects of the world as "signs of the times."[32] They lamented the rampant apostasy, moral decline, modernism, and evolution as harbingers of the conditions needed for the antichrist to arise during the tribulation.[33] Fears that Mussolini, Stalin, and Hitler could revive the Roman Empire and become the autocratic ruler captured their imagination and fueled speculation about the identity of the antichrist.[34] In its spiritual aspect, the apostasy of the church will reach its zenith; in its political aspect, the rule of man (democracy) will have its zenith. But they were convinced that the antichrist would only be revealed once the "hinderer" was removed, which they interpreted

---

[29] J. N. Hoover, "The Second Coming of Christ," *PE*, January 26, 1929, 8.

[30] E. S. Williams, "Rapture and Revelation," *PE*, July 27, 1929, 2.

[31] Harry J. Steil, "The Trend Toward Armageddon," *PE*, July 18, 1936, 2.

[32] Those who wrote about the tribulation often included the judgments of God, the rise of the Antichrist, and the battle of Armageddon. J. N. Hoover, "The Second Coming of Christ," *PE*, January 26, 1929, 8; E. S. Williams, "Be Ye Ready," *PE*, April 1, 1933, 2; Harvey McAlister, "Bethlehem and Armageddon," *PE*, December 20, 1941, 2, 7.

[33] Hoover, "The Second Coming of Christ," 9, says, "It is during this heated season, this reign of the Antichrist, in which flourish all forms of evolution, modern theology, unbelief in Jesus Christ and in the inspiration of the Holy Scriptures."

[34] J. N. Hoover, "Mussolini: Is the World Preparing for Antichrist?" *PE*, 724 (November 26, 1927), 1; E. S. Williams, "Be Ye Ready," *PE*, April 1, 1933, 2; Harry J. Steil, "The End of Human Government," *PE*, July 30, 1938, 11.

as the Holy Spirit in Spirit-filled believers.[35] So while they rejected the view that only Pentecostals will be raptured, they also equated the "hinderer" with Spirit-filled believers, which in turn buttressed their support for a pretribulation rapture.

The Sign of the Jews

One of the greatest signs the AG believed was being illuminated by the Spirit was the restoration of Israel. As they watched the political situation in Palestine unfold, they were convinced it was a sign of the nearness of Christ's return. J. N. Hoover declared, "The reclaiming and rebuilding of Palestine seems to be not only a reasonable evidence of God's renewing His dealings with Israel, but of the near approach of the return of Jesus Christ and of the glorious meeting in the air."[36] In 1928, F. E. Howett wrote an article outlining in great detail the events that were leading to the establishment of the Jewish state.[37] The recovery of Jewish identity, language, and customs were all steps closer to this reality.[38] There were also expectations in the 1930s that the Jews would rebuild the temple and begin the restoration of the sacrificial system.[39] These signs surely pointed to the fulfillment of the promise of "the millennial reign of our Lord Jesus Christ after His advent in glory, with the Jews as His restored and ransomed people."[40]

The increased emphasis on the state of Israel as a sovereign work of God also gave rise to philosemitism.[41] As one article comments, "When I hear some speak with disregard and disparagement against this nation, whom God loves with an everlasting love, I feel like sounding out a warning. Take heed lest you find yourselves taking an exactly opposite attitude to what God takes."[42] William Long

---

[35] E. S. Williams, "Rapture and Revelation," *PE,* July 27, 1929, 3, comments, "This Hinderer to the consummation of the iniquity must be none other than the Holy Spirit who will withdraw His restraint when the church, the salt of the earth, is caught away." See also Zelma Argue, "The Time Is Fulfilled," *PE,* January 16, 1932, 8.

[36] J. N. Hoover, "The Jews," *PE,* January 31, 1931, 5.

[37] F. E. Howett, "Israel and Other Lands," *PE,* March 10, 1928, 2–3, 9.

[38] R. H. Boughton, "The National Restoration of the Jews," *PE,* June 30, 1934, 1, 3.

[39] Eva Morton, "Behold the Fig Tree," *PE,* August 13, 1927, 6; "Rebuilding the Temple," *PE,* January 25, 1930, 5; "Will the Temple Soon Be Rebuilt?," *PE,* February 1, 1930, 4.

[40] Boughton, "The National Restoration of the Jews," 3.

[41] Philosemitism is a term used by Newberg, *Pentecostal Mission in Palestine,* xii, to describe the "support or admiration for the Jewish people by non-Jews" and the overall favoring of Israel above other national states.

[42] "God's Attitude Toward Israel," *PE,* June 30, 1934, 4.

reminds readers that "God's hand has been upon them and still is, and nations that curse the Jews shall be cursed—the Bible says so."[43] Support for Israel did not mean that the AG was not committed to the evangelization of Jews.[44] Stanley Frodsham proclaimed, "It is the duty of the Church to evangelize the Jews."[45] A Jewish missionary also proclaimed, "millions of Jews and Gentiles at home, and unnumbered millions abroad, await the glad sound of the gospel as proclaimed through a revived and re-empowered church."[46] In fact, one evangelist testified that Jews were being converted "in larger numbers today than any time since the crucifixion of Jesus, but not without isolation, humiliation, and suffering."[47] The downside of a growing sentiment for Israel was that some expressed an anti-Arab sentiment.[48] Stanley Frodsham noted the Balfour Declaration had created a situation where "Arabs have a great hatred for the Jews" and resisted with protests and disturbances.[49] Frodsham interpreted resistance as a way God could be creating the circumstances whereby Israel will destroy of the Mosque of Oman from the Temple Mount through military force.[50]

The Millennium

During the Scholastic Period, the millennium received only slight treatment. As writers focused on the details of the tribulation, details about the millennium decreased and talk of heaven increased. However, the millennium was still important. Similar to the Establishment Period, the millennium was expected to be the institution of Christ's rule on earth and the end of all human

---

[43] William E. Long, "Signs of the Times," *PE*, December 13, 1941, 2.

[44] Eva Morton, "Behold the Fig Tree," *PE*, August 13, 1927, 5.

[45] S. H. Frodsham, "Israel's Spiritual Need," *PE*, December 31, 1932, 5.

[46] "God's Sovereign Grace in Christ," *PE*, January 26, 1929, 9.

[47] J. N. Hoover, "The Jews," *PE*, January 31, 1931, 7.

[48] Eric Newberg, *The Pentecostal Mission in Palestine* (Eugene: Pickwick Publishing, 2012), 127–53. Newberg argues that presence of Pentecostal Missionaries in Palestine contributed to philosemitism enabled by the importation of eschatological Zionism and by exporting Islamophobia to the US through missionary reports. This led to a shift in Pentecostal missionary activity from evangelizing Jews and Muslims in favor of neglecting outreach to Muslims, evangelizing Arab Christians, and supporting Jews instead of evangelizing them. This argument will be explored further in the next chapter.

[49] "Will the Temple Soon Be Rebuilt?," *PE*, February 1, 1930, 4, notes "The national organ of the Arabs threatens that unless the Balfour Declaration is repealed Palestine will in the future be the scene of incessant disturbances and insecurity, riots, and bloodshed."

[50] "Will the Temple Soon Be Rebuilt?," 5.

government.⁵¹ In one of the few articles about the millennium, P. C. Nelson imagines some of the details in this way.⁵² When Christ returns, the Jews will gather in Israel and accept him as Messiah. Christ will lift the curse from creation and humanity will enjoy long life on a fruitful earth. In Christ's government, there will be no need for armies and military resources will be repurposed for agricultural use. Finally, the Holy Spirit will be poured out in its latter rain fullness and the glory of the Lord will fill the earth. Nelson rejoices,

> O glorious day! for which a million hearts have longed; for which the oppressed, the sorrowing, the suffering of earth have cried; for the animal creation in its suffering moans; for with all natures waits—the day of the personal, glorious reign of our Lord and Saviour Jesus Christ with His saints.⁵³

For Nelson, the millennium is the crowning event of salvation. Others saw the millennium in less optimistic terms. Rhoda Lantz compared the millennium with the levitical procedure for dealing with leprosy as a "marvelous antitype" of the way in which the kingdom will play out.⁵⁴ During the millennium, Christ will attempt to renovate the world by a work of the Spirit.⁵⁵ However, the ideal conditions will be compulsory and when there is a reoccurrence of leprosy (the rebellion of Satan at the end of the millennium) and the world will have to be "totally destroyed beyond cure." In Lantz's mind, the millennium will be a failed project that will replaced by a new heavens and new earth.⁵⁶

---

⁵¹ Harry J. Steil, "The End of Human Government," *PE,* July 30, 1938, 1, uses Daniel's image of the statue, which is built of gradually decreasing grades of metals, to illustrate the "end of human government" through the appearing of Christ. He comments, "No longer will there be democracy or autocracy, but instead of these forms of government (or misgovernment) a new form of righteous government will be instituted."

⁵² P. C. Nelson, "The Millennial Reign of Jesus," *PE,* November 30, 1929, 5.

⁵³ Nelson, "The Millennial Reign of Jesus," 5.

⁵⁴ Rhoda Lantz, "Our Lord's Unveiling of Things to Come," *PE,* September 22, 1928, 3. She argues that the present world of sin will be inspected by Christ the priest, and will be quarantined for seven days (tribulation). Afterwards he will enter the house (world) and will remove the old structures of the sin and rebuild the walls of the house (millennium).

⁵⁵ Lantz, "Our Lord's Unveiling of Things to Come," 3, says, "The world will be renovated but not rebuilt; it is scraped and replastered, but not recreated; it is made righteous, not by inherent sinlessness, but by the omnipotent compulsions of God. It is the regeneration (Matt. 19:28) in which a divine Spirit breathes a new life through the earth."

⁵⁶ The only article that discussed the new heavens and new earth specifically was "A New Heavens and a New Earth," *PE,* May 26, 1945, 7, which was a reprint of "New Heavens and A New Earth," *WE* February 9, 1918, 5.

Eschatological Perspectives Social Issues

After WWI ended, the increased awareness of societal issues at home and abroad in the Pentecostal Evangel meant that more articles were focused on processing the eschatological ramifications of societal issues. As one writer proclaimed,

> Today a cry of injustice, cruelty, despair, anguish, is going up, summarized in the newspapers in the reports of divorce, banditry, murder, suicide. The cry has come up to God, an unprecedented cry because of crimes, the operation of unpitied poverty, and it demands divine investigation and intervention.[57]

One such injustice that caught the AG's attention was the prevalence of poverty, worker exploitation, and injustice that resulted from the Great Depression.[58] Some saw the Great Depression as a judgment on the rich, as millionaires were "reduced to poverty in a matter of days."[59] Other writers drew attention to various ways the wealthy had encouraged the systematic institutional exploitation of the vulnerable. One article had scathing condemnation for crooked salesman, bankers, stockbrokers, and large industrialized farm corporations that were driving local farmers into poverty.[60] Even with a growing sense of permanence within the movement, the AG struggled to push for greater social justice because they believed God's "intervention" would be coming soon in the millennial kingdom.

During the 1930s–1940s, AG churches were operating out of storefronts and temporary tabernacles populated by lower class populations.[61] But with growth came new challenges as members moved up in the social strata and were forced to wrestle with the eschatological implications of wealth. What they once interpreted as a "sign of the times," they now saw in terms of issues of stewardship. If one has wealth, as one minister points out, it is ok as long as they

---

[57] "When the Son of Man Comes," *PE*, April 21, 1928, 2.

[58] S. H. Frodsham, "The Coming of Christ and Our Gathering To Him," *PE*, June 2, 1928, 1, recalls that during prayer a man had become overwhelmed in the Spirit about a "coming crash" that would bring sorrow to people all over the world. Frodsham expects the fulfillment of this vision to be the coming Tribulation period. However, it was a little over a year later that the "Black Monday" stock market crash happened in October 1929 that led to the Great Depression. And yet nothing was said of that prophecy by Frodsham after the crash happened. His commitment to his vision of the tribulation kept him from recognizing a potentially prophetic word about current circumstances.

[59] "The Uncertainty of Riches," *PE*, April 1, 1933, 2, comments, "As the ruthless hand of passing events strips the veil of illusion from earthly prosperity, the child of God will rejoice in the fact that he has laid up a treasure in heaven that no person and no circumstance can take from him."

[60] "When the Son of Man Comes," *PE*, April 21, 1928, 2.

[61] Menzies, *Anointed to Serve*, 144–49.

heed the words of Jesus and "sell all he has" in order to "lend to the poor," lest he be called "thou fool!" by God on judgment day.[62] The shift is seen much clearer in a 1944 re-print of an article from John Wesley in which Christians are encouraged to "gain all they can and save all they can" so that they can "give all they can" to the gospel.[63] This more positive perspective on wealth was shared by Superintendent E. S. Williams, who says, "It is wrong when people frown on persons just because they are rich. Some of them are the most beautiful of characters. God bless them."[64] Instead of seeing wealth as a "sign of the times," which will receive the judgment of God, wealth was seen as a matter of responsibility and a means to advance the Christian mission. A shift away from eschatological interpretation of wealth enabled the AG to place more emphasis on stewardship, giving to the poor and needy, and supporting the work of the gospel.

During this period, prophetic interpretations continued to shape their engagement with societal structures. When some in the AG started to look to inject themselves in matters of political reform, E. S. Williams cautioned readers otherwise.

> We do not hear the apostle to the Gentiles denouncing the rulers of the Roman Empire, nor Peter, to whom was given a ministry of circumcision, denouncing national injustice in Israel. Corruption in government was plentiful, but they had not come to set such abuses right by carnal pressure, but to proclaim a new Kingdom which would bring no threat to "the powers that be," but which could uplift through the infusion of a new power or viewpoint.[65]

In their minds, the concept of "gradual reform," even if cast in Christian principles, was nothing more than political evolutionary theory and should never be substituted for belief in the Blessed Hope.[66] Williams believed that all human governments were tools of the "Beast" and the means by which the antichrist will

---

[62] "The Man God Calls A Fool," *PE*, December 23, 1944, 1, 4–5.

[63] "Wesley on Wealth," *PE*, July 1, 1944, 9. Wesley notes that true religion naturally promotes "both industry and frugality" and yet, "wherever riches have increased . . . the essence of religion has decreased in the same proportion." Wesley saw wealth as a means, if used correctly, to advance the gospel.

[64] E. S. Williams, "Jesus Advises a Rich Man," *PE*, December 13, 1947, 5.

[65] E. S. Williams, "The Christian and Politics," *PE*, June 24, 1939, 2.

[66] W. T. Gaston, "Looking for That Blessed Hope," *PE*, August 27, 1927, 9; Dinsdale T. Young, "The Coming of the Son of Man," *PE*, November 3, 1928, 7.

gain power.[67] Therefore, Williams encouraged Christians to be a prophetic witness for the Kingdom of God, not immersed in trying to reform the state based on political opinions. Williams says, "If we believe in the separation of church and state then let the Church abide in its own and useful sphere of getting men to God and showing forth the excellences of God's Kingdom."[68]

---

[67] Williams, "Rapture and Revelation," 3, comments, "This political period of Gentile dominion will completely fill its cup of iniquity under the government of the beast."

[68] Williams, "The Christian and Politics," 2, believes that Christians should not use their voice for advocating or denouncing political issues that they are "too uniformed" to speak to. However, they can be confident in voicing their perspectives on the kingdom of God.

8

INSTITUTIONAL PERIOD (1948–1961)

During the period of 1948–1961, the AG was becoming less of a revival movement and more an established institution as two significant developments took place. The first was the AG's acceptance into the National Association of Evangelicals (NAE). During the 1930s, the AG was isolated from the evangelical world because of Fundamentalism's rejection of Pentecostals.[1] The opportunity to join the NAE represented a new chapter in the quest to be identified as part of the wider evangelical world. Over the next two decades, the AG leadership not only thrived in this environment, but several AG officials were elected to positions of leadership.[2] Shortly after joining the NAE, fellowship opportunities opened up with Pentecostal groups through the Pentecostal Fellowship of North America and the Pentecostal World Conference. The AG had not only revived the vision of cooperation and fellowship, but were leading from the front.[3] Whereas, during the Scholastic Period the AG was concerned with promoting Pentecostal doctrine to a second generation of adherents, the Institutional Period was the beginning of Pentecostal influence upon the larger evangelical church.[4] The rise of the healing movement, the Charismatic Renewal, and the emergence of influential AG leaders meant that Pentecostal theology was becoming mainstream.

As the AG sought to broaden their identity within evangelicalism, they also worked to narrow their place as a Pentecostal institution/denomination. In previous generations, AG ministers referred to themselves as Pentecostals in order to avoid being labeled as a sect or denomination. By the 1950s, identification as "Assemblies of God" became more prominent and often beliefs were articulated as specifically AG beliefs. For example, Keith Munday declared, "The glorious

---

[1] Menzies, *Anointed to Serve*, 177–82.

[2] AG leaders who held positions in the NAE include, J. R. Flower, Ralph Harris, Thomas Zimmerman, Noel Perkin, E. S. Williams, Fred Vogler, and J. Phillip Hogan, *PE*, May 10, 1947, 6–7; "Four A/G Officials Elected to NAE Posts," *PE*, June 8, 1969, 27.

[3] Blumhofer, *Restoring the Faith*, 197, notes that the AG "discovered advantages in cooperation." However, considering the nearly four-decade quest for identification, I would argue that they revived the original vision I outline in Isgrigg, "The Pentecostal Evangelical Church."

[4] Blumhofer, *Restoring the Faith*, 180–219.

truth that the Lord Jesus Christ will one day return to the earth as its rightful King is surely believed among us in the Assemblies of God."[5] Although belief in the Second Coming was still important, leaders struggled to maintain an emphasis on the soon return of Christ while at the same time developing sense of permanence as a distinct denominational body. Ralph Riggs describes this tension:

> Some of our own people have said: "We can't go to Bible School for Jesus is coming soon. We can't build a church. What is the use of a building? Jesus is coming soon." How utterly contrary to common sense that is. It is logic in reverse. If Jesus is coming soon, then we must get up and work with intense activity. . . . Let us not retire to some upper room to congratulate ourselves that we are different from other people. Instead let us intensify our missionary and evangelistic program to go into all the world.[6]

The tensions that were created by balancing efforts to maintain their identity as a movement and the desire to be seen as a valid evangelical institution had to be carefully navigated. On the one hand, they were seeing the beginning of a revival in the AG, primarily as a result of new interest in the Holy Spirit in the Healing Movement and Charismatic Renewal. At the same time, articles during this period focused on more traditional dispensational concerns that were popular in evangelicalism.

The final factor that shaped AG eschatology was the founding of a physical state of Israel in 1948. With few exceptions, nearly every article emphasized the nearness of Christ's coming established by the reality of the new nation. The absolute certainty that came from this reality could not help but supplant the outpouring of the Holy Spirit as the primary sign of the nearness of Christ's coming. Ralph Riggs comments, "The Spirit says He is coming. The Bible says he is coming. The Jews say he is coming."[7] The rise of Russia, the atomic age, and communism also became major themes in charting out the immediate future. Visions of the end were becoming more apocalyptic as the prospect of world annihilation was now conceivable. The final result was more emphasis on the rapture as a way of escape rather than a fulfillment of salvation through the resurrection of the body.

---

[5] Keith W. Munday, "The Coming of the King," *PE*, January 25, 1959, 4–5.
[6] R. M. Riggs, "Pentecost and Christ's Return," *PE*, September 30, 1951, 15.
[7] Riggs, "Pentecost and Christ's Return," 4.

Pentecost and Christ's Return

Early in the 1950s, the AG began to experience a renewed emphasis on the Spirit and the coming of Jesus. The desire for revival during the decades of the 1940s was met with a renewed emphasis among AG leaders on the two pillars of the early years: the baptism in the Holy Spirit and the soon return of Jesus. Ralph Riggs reminds readers,

> One of the main emphases of the Pentecostal message is the truth that Jesus is coming soon. The Lord Jesus said that when the Spirit of Truth was come, He would show us things to come. (John 16:13). The Holy Spirit has come and where he is honored and allowed to have His right of way, He lays definite emphasis upon the return of our Lord and Savior Jesus Christ. Many of the messages in the Spirit are a warning and a promise that Jesus is coming soon.[8]

The fact that Christ's expected return was not realized in previous generations was no reason to stop proclaiming his imminent return. Riggs commented, "The Holy Ghost did not lie. The Holy Ghost did not build up a false hope. The Holy Ghost told the truth. Jesus is coming soon."[9] Yet decades of speculation caused many ministers to stop proclaiming the Blessed Hope. Riggs encourages, "You say you made a mistake when you prophesied that Mussolini would be the Antichrist? That is no reason why you should stop preaching that Jesus is coming. Keep off those extreme limbs of interpretation. Keep on the solid Word of God and keep on preaching that Jesus is coming."[10]

During the Institutional Period, Christ's coming was understood in three ways. First, as in previous generations, the coming of Jesus was to be accompanied by a final salvific act of resurrection of the body. Caleb Smith says, "Jesus provided full salvation for the body as well as the soul. Until we have our glorified bodies at Christ's return, however, our redemption will not be complete."[11] Although emphasis on the resurrection was in decline, it was still very much in their minds. Second, there was more emphasis on the rapture as being "with Jesus." Articles called for the AG faithful to recapture their love "for his appearing."[12] True

---

[8] Ralph Riggs, "The Second Coming of Christ," *PE*, March 4, 1950, 2.

[9] Riggs, "Pentecost and Christ's Return," 3.

[10] Riggs, "Pentecost and Christ's Return," 15.

[11] Caleb V. Smith, "7 Reasons for Loving His Appearing," *PE*, October 18, 1953, 3.

[12] Riggs, "Pentecost and Christ's Return," 16; Smith, "7 Reasons for Loving His Appearing," 3, 20; Gayle F. Lewis, "Watch," *PE*, January 15, 1956, 3, 13; A. W. Pettet, "Loving the Lord and Looking for Him," *PE*, January 25, 1959, 18–19.

Christians are known by their love for God, and no greater expression of that love can be found than wanting to "see him face to face" at his coming. In this affective dimension, love for Jesus produces love for his coming, because as Riggs comments, "the whole objective of the resurrection and translation is to meet the Lord in the air and to be with Him forevermore, a grand reunion with One whom we love dearer than life itself."[13] The third emphasis accompanied the other two, in that to "be with the Lord" was preferred to being "left behind." A. W. Pettit comments, "To those who are prepared to meet Him and who will not be ashamed before Him at His coming it is a Blessed Hope, a joyous prospect. To those who do not love Him it will be a stroke of doom. Our individual reaction *then* will depend upon our attitude toward Him."[14] The hope of Christ's coming was that faithful believers will be privileged to escape the horror of things to come.[15] Dismayed at the current conditions of the world, Clay Cooper declared, "There is only one way out; that is up! It's either Christ or chaos! revival or ruin! now or never!"[16] The combined emphasis on being with Jesus and escaping the world led to a growing sense that heaven was their eternal home.[17] Prior to the 1950s, heaven was not commonly emphasized as the eschatological destination of the saints. Heaven was a temporary destination as believers waited for the Second Coming and establishment of the kingdom on earth.

Because of the controversy surrounding the New Order of the Latter Rain, the AG avoided latter rain language when discussing the movement, but didn't lessen their emphasis on the Spirit.[18] They continued to see the Pentecostal

---

[13] Riggs, "The Second Coming of Christ," 2.

[14] Pettet, "Loving the Lord and Looking for Him," 19.

[15] Charles W. Scott, "Skywatchers," *PE*, August 22, 1952, 3–4; R.M. Riggs, "Will the Saints Escape the Tribulation?," *PE*, April 6, 1952, 3, 13–14; Gayle F. Lewis, "Watch," *PE*, January 15, 1956, 3.

[16] Clay Cooper, "It Is Later Than You Think," *PE*, 1 August 12, 1950, 3.

[17] There are few articles in each decade prior to 1950 that emphasized heaven as a final home. One early example is W. T. Gaston, "A Glimpse of Our Future Home," *PE*, February 7, 1925, 2–3, 5, which describes heaven based on Revelation 20–21, but ultimately understands heaven to be on earth. In the 1940s–1950s, heaven as a final home for believers became a regular subject of articles. See A. H. Argue, "Heaven—The Future Home of the Saints," *PE*, March 8, 1959, 6–7; Frank Insensee, "Our Heavenly Inheritance," *PE*, June 17, 1951, 6; *PE*, April 26, 1953, 10; *PE*, January 17, 1954, 12; E. S. Williams, "Our Heavenly Inheritance," *PE*, June 1, 1958, 12; "I'll Be Home Soon," *PE*, June 12, 1960, 24.

[18] This is contra Althouse, *Spirit of the Last Days*, 48, who believes the New Order controversy essentially ended the use of the concept for many Pentecostal groups and pushed the AG to cast their unique understanding of eschatology in more fundamentalist categories.

movement as a last days outpouring at the end of the Gentile age.[19] With the growing evil in the world, leaders proclaimed that the power of the Holy Spirit was needed more than ever to stem the tides of apostasy, atheistic communism, and political unrest at home and abroad.

> While Christ has been publicly rejected by the leaders in Russia, the same spirit is subtly yet definitely working in our own country. The evolutionistic, atheistic teachings in our institutions of learning, the decision of the Supreme Court ruling religious training out of our school, the power of organized labor in all countries which are considered "free," governmental control of industry, restoration of life in Israel—these are all definite indications of the approach of the end of the present age.[20]

They believed the best way to resist the tide of deterioration was a renewed emphasis on the baptism in the Spirit. Although they maintained their belief that Christianity cannot gradually reform culture, Spirit-filled people were expected to be a restraining influence on society. Riggs comments, "In the particular stress and strain of the present distress, as we approach the time of the world's greatest tribulation, God has provided the proper counterbalance, and counteraction, and recompense for us in this glorious Baptism of the Holy Spirit."[21] Articles tended to emphasize the Holy Spirit as a force for societal preservation more so than fuel for world evangelism.[22] As S. S. Scull, comments, "It is the Spirit-filled Church that is the great restraining influence in the world. We are the salt of the earth, saving it from corruption."[23] Williams comments, "God has reinforced the church in these last days with the visitation of the Holy Ghost outpouring. The

---

[19] E. S. Williams, "Living in Light of His Coming," *PE*, January 7, 1951, 3–5; Riggs, "Pentecost and Christ's Return," 3; Charles W. Scott, "Skywatchers," *PE*, August 22, 1952, 3–4; S. S. Scull, "Will The Spirit Be Withdrawn?," *PE*, August 28, 1955, 5, 11; "Young Church Shows Amazing Growth," *PE*, September 23, 1956, 2–4.

[20] Williams, "Living in Light of His Coming," 3–5

[21] "Young Church Shows Amazing Growth," 4.

[22] Being "salt" and restraining influence carried political tones and was likely influenced by the NAE playing a greater role in political influence. Blumhofer, *Restoring the Faith*, 189, notes that NAE and Harold Ockenga's vision for reclaiming America's Christian heritage was influential on AG leadership. Blumhofer claims this was a position that the AG had always held. However, this study has demonstrated that interest in America as a chosen or Christian nation was objectionable to early AG leaders.

[23] Scull, "Will The Spirit Be Withdrawn," 5.

purpose is to fortify us with spiritual power; to have a people in the right place at the right time, a people with the saving salt."[24]

The emphasis on the "restraining influence" of Spirit-filled Christians naturally fit their eschatological belief in the pretribulation rapture. They understood the "restrainer" to be the Holy Spirit (or Spirit-filled people) who will be "taken out of the way" before the antichrist is revealed. Williams comments, "My conviction is that when the Church is caught away, the Spirit's restraint on iniquity will be removed, making way for the manifestation of the man of Sin."[25] The removal of this restraining influence in the rapture will allow the antichrist to have full reign in the earth; a process they believed had already started.[26] So while they could not reform society through the Spirit, they could restrain the forces of evil that were accelerating conditions of the tribulation. Although the Holy Spirit will be taken out of the way, Scull argued that because the Holy Spirit is God, there could be no way the Spirit would be absent from the tribulation.[27] This is demonstrated in the expectation that the Spirit will be working in the two witnesses, who will minister in the power of the Spirit, be reanimated by the Spirit, and caught up to heaven. The power of the Spirit will be "unparalleled" when the resurrection of the dead takes place at the rapture.[28] The Spirit will also be present to offer repentance for those left behind, power to resist the mark of the beast, and endurance to be faithful to martyrdom. The work of the Spirit is not diminished during the tribulation; it will just shift from the church to the elect of the Jewish nation.

The Jews and Israel

On May 14, 1948, the efforts to partition Palestine by The United Nations became a reality when Britain withdrew their control of Palestine and Israel proclaimed itself a sovereign nation for the first time in 2,000 years. News of the re-establishment of a political nation of Israel was heralded as a fulfillment of prophecy. Harry Steil declares,

> My friend, you and I have lived to witness the greatest resurrection miracle since the resurrection of Christ. A nation, dead for almost two thousand years, has

[24] Williams, "Living in Light of His Coming," 3–5.
[25] E. S. Williams, "Your Questions," *PE*, November 3, 1957, 13.
[26] Riggs, "Will the Saints Escape the Tribulation?," 13.
[27] Scull, "Will The Spirit Be Withdrawn," 5.
[28] Scull, "Will The Spirit Be Withdrawn," 5.

been raised from the dead! The God of all power, who predicted and decreed the national death and burial and by whose divine oversight it was carried out, also predicted He would raise the nation from the dead.[29]

The founding of the political state of Israel in 1948 became a new empirically-verified sign that Christ was coming soon. From that point on, nearly every article on the return of Jesus listed this new political reality as the surest sign of the times. The absolute certainty of this sign eventually supplanted the outpouring of the Holy Spirit as the primary sign of the nearness of Christ's coming.

Support for the restoration of Israel was strong during this period, yet many in the AG were unsure as to what extent God was involved in directing the circumstances that created the new state. Two weeks before it became official, a Hebrew Christian named Morris Zeidman questioned the legitimacy of Israel's claim the land because they came in unbelief. He comments, "From the religious point of view and the Bible, the Jewish people have little or nothing in their favor for claiming Palestine as their land."[30] He also expressed concern with the UN decision to partition Palestine, which was leading to a growing emboldened response of the Jewish people against Arabs.[31] In his mind, the problem with Israel was that it seemed to be a military and political creation rather than a divine creation.[32] Others saw Israel's move toward nationhood as nothing more than a human attempt to fulfill God's plan. As one article critiques,

> Israel is trying to restore herself. It is not God's plan and not God's time. The restoration must come from God's appointed Restorer, Him who must restore all things. See Acts 3:19-21. Any plan for the restoration apart from the Lord Jesus Christ is futile, and will be brought to naught.[33]

The AG believed that only through the return of Jesus would God "restore the kingdom to Israel" (Acts 1:7). Zeidman comments, "Instead of looking to the United Nations at Lake Success for the gift of a State for Jewish people, the Jews should have given the United Nations the Gift of God, which is Jesus Christ. Instead of clamoring for a world State, let the Jewish leaders cry for the Kingdom

---

[29] Harry J. Steil, "A Million Signs of the Times," *PE,* July 28, 1957, 5–7.

[30] Zeidman, "Restoration of the Kingdom," 12.

[31] Morris Zeidman, "Restoration of the Kingdom," *PE,* May 1, 1948, 2.

[32] Zeidman, "Restoration of the Kingdom," 2, comments, "One cannot find any passage that would indicate that the Lord God Jehovah ever intended the Jewish people to be a fighting nation." See also, Zeidman, "Commonwealth of Israel," *PE,* November 13, 1948, 2.

[33] "God's Future Plans for Israel," *PE,* May 29, 1948, 4.

of God first."³⁴ In clamoring for a political kingdom, AG ministers felt that they were subverting God's plan to restore the promised kingdom under the true King.³⁵ Others argued that the government could not be "theocratic" since Israel was prophesied that they would return in unbelief.³⁶ Much of the conflict Israel was experiencing was because of their refusal to accept Jesus as messiah. As one writer comments, "As long as they refuse to recognize the Prophet of whom Moses spoke, and whom Peter rightly referred to as Jesus Christ, so long will the Jew suffer."³⁷ But, for the most part, AG members believed the true restoration of Israel would only come through spiritual awakening to Jesus the Messiah.

Because Israel was established in unbelief, it not only raised biblical questions about its legitimacy as an act of God, but there were also a host of other concerns. AG members were forced to deal with the tensions between interpreting prophecy and the theological issues that the restoration represented. One writer contemplated the theological difficulty of God allowing the Jews to restore their religious system. He says, "If they are contemplating a restoration of sacrifices, will they restore these and ignore the fact that Jesus of Nazareth has come as the 'Lamb of God, which taketh away the sins of the world?'"³⁸ Since the Muslim Arabs had control of Jerusalem, he was convinced that God was not allowing them to return to the old sacrificial system. As another article comments, "The site of the ancient Temple is still in Arabs hands. Would the Jews in their impatience and impulsiveness proceed to build their new Temple at some other spot in Jerusalem?"³⁹ Still others argued that the Jews must remain in unbelief and establish the temple in order to fulfill the prophecies that the antichrist will stand in the Temple and deceive Israel into accepting him as Messiah.⁴⁰

Support for Israel did not mean they believed that Jews were already saved. Readers were often encouraged to pray for Jews and Arabs that they might come to Christ. The hostility of the Jews in Israel to Christianity and missionaries was

---

³⁴ Zeidman, "Restoration of the Kingdom," 2.

³⁵ Louis Hauff, "A Sign of the Times," *PE*, February 5, 1956, 6–7, says, "They are not returning to Palestine in order to worship God, but are hoping to find safety and security in their own homeland. The spiritual awakening will come later. I believe that their lack of spiritual life and godliness is prophetically foretold."

³⁶ L. Sale-Harrison, "Has Israel Come to Stay?," *PE*, March 4, 1950, 3.

³⁷ "God's Future Plans for Israel," *PE*, May 29, 1948, 4.

³⁸ "Jews Challenged to Rebuild Temple," *PE*, August 28, 1955, 14.

³⁹ "Jews Challenged to Rebuild Temple," 14.

⁴⁰ Hauff, "A Sign of the Times," 6–7.

of gravest concern.⁴¹ The editor of the *Pentecostal Evangel*, Robert Cunningham, sums up the attitude toward missions efforts:

> We need to pray for the people of Israel, that more and more of them will repent and call on the Lord for personal salvation. As individuals, they are no more privileged than others. There is no difference in God's sight between a Jewish sinner and a Gentile sinner. . . . All human beings alike need to accept Jesus Christ as their Saviour and Lord, otherwise they are eternally lost. And this, after all, is Israel's greatest predicament.⁴²

So while they understood there to be a dispensational distinction between Jews and Gentiles, they did not believe there was a soteriological distinction. Herbert Bruhn, the head of the AG Jewish Mission department insists,

> There are those that propound the unscriptural idea that this is the time when God is gathering out a Gentile Church. There is no such thing in all the Scriptures. The only church spoken of in the Word of God is THE CHURCH, where both Jew and Gentile sit together in heavenly places in Christ Jesus, both rejoicing in the same salvation, trusting in the same Savior.⁴³

At the same time, he does not deny that there are different ethnic destinies in God's plan.⁴⁴ The "salvation" of national Israel during the millennium will be the culmination of the work of the gospel that began in this dispensation. Until that time, missionaries were encouraged to keep working to convert Jews, while believers were encouraged to pray for their conversion. One missionary instructed those who desired to witness to Jewish people must be in love with Jesus, a student of the word, a lover of Jews, patient, and be particularly sensitive to the feelings and needs of Jewish people.⁴⁵

---

⁴¹ "The Gravest Danger," *PE,* October 16, 1948), 9, comments, "the gravest danger is neither physical nor psychological, but spiritual … Pray that missionaries may reach them with the Gospel in spite of prevailing conditions." Cf. Robert C. Cunningham, "God's Plan for Palestine," *PE,* December 2, 1956, 2; Zeidman, "Restoration of the Kingdom," 12.

⁴² Robert C. Cunningham, "Israel's Greatest Predicament," *PE,* March 3, 1957, 2.

⁴³ Herbert Bruhn, "Why Evangelize the Jew?," *PE,* January 27, 1957, 14.

⁴⁴ This position is what has been labeled in recent years as progressive dispensationalism, where there is an ethnic distinction but not a soteriological distinction between Jew and Gentile. The fact that this is the position for the AG's head of Jewish missions signifies the level of agreement with this progressive dispensational position.

⁴⁵ Herbert Bruhn, "How To Win Jews To Christianity," *PE,* August 12, 1956, 14–15.

A second concern the AG had with the State of Israel was how the government was responding to the resistance by Arabs. Even though they supported Israel's return, several articles were critical of Israel's actions toward Arabs in disputed territories.

> As much as our sympathies are with the Jewish people, and we believe that their cause and desire for the Holy Land as their rightful inheritance is just, yet we cannot approve the murder and assassination even in righteous cause—no, not even in "self-defense against the Arabs."[46]

The Israeli removal of Arabs from occupied territories was becoming a humanitarian crisis. One visitor to Israel reports of the plight of Arabs:

> Wretched, sprawling camps of Arab refugees who fled from Israel at the time of partition are a constant source of friction, and Communism finds a fertile field among them. The presence of 500,000 refugees burdened with poverty and blighted hopes lends a spirit of impermanence to the whole social structure of the area. Israel is hated by the Arabs and the age-old enmity has reached white heat.[47]

The editor assured readers that they were not going to "take sides" in the political and humanitarian conflict between Arabs and Jews.[48]

Signs of the Tribulation

In 1950, AG superintendent Ralph Riggs declared, "We live in a frightening age."[49] Following World War II, a host of threats caught the attention of students of prophecy and fostered a spirit of eschatological fear that characterized the eschatology of the period. C. M. Ward comments,

> That the foundations of civilization are in the process of being destroyed can hardly be a matter of dispute. Prophecy allows no room for optimism as regards

---

[46] Morris Zeidman, "Restoration of the Kingdom," *PE*, May 1, 1948, 2; Morris Zeidman, "Commonwealth of Israel," *PE*, November 13, 1948, 2.

[47] G. H. Carmichael, "The Strategic Middle East," *PE*, December 30, 1956, 14–15.

[48] Cunningham, "God's Plan for Palestine," 2, comments, "Without entering into politics and without approving the tactics used by either side, it is possible for the Christian to look ahead and see the final outcome. The Bible says that God has a plan for Palestine. In His own good time, His program will be carried out."

[49] Ralph M. Riggs, "The Present World Situation in Light of Bible Prophecy," *PE*, September 23, 1950, 3, 12.

to world conditions in general. The picture is the same in every major national field, religiously, morally, economically and politically. Everywhere may be seen the signs of crumbling foundations—foundations laid by men who leave God out of account.[50]

Never before in human history had there been more potential for disaster on such a global scale. During the beginnings of the Cold War in the 1950s, Russia was emerging as a world military power that was seeking to rival the United States. Russia's atheism, communism, and intention of world domination led several articles to identify Russia as Gog and Magog of Ezekiel 38 and 39.[51] Hart Armstrong comments, "Never in history has a nation so horribly outraged God, defied His Word, tormented and destroyed His people. Certainly, God is against them!"[52] AG writers easily imagined that Russia would invade Israel during the Tribulation, only to be destroyed by the coming of Jesus.

Another great fear was the growing nuclear threat. Images of America dropping the atomic bomb on Hiroshima and Nagasaki left an indelible mark in the imaginations of AG members.[53] For the next decade, speculation about the role of nuclear weapons permeated eschatological articles. The atomic bomb was condemned as a "monstrosity" that had unlimited potential for destruction.[54] Northcote Deck laments, "Of late the atomic bomb has come as a new specter, so that increasingly today, no life, no city, no continent is safe from annihilation."[55] Some feared the prophecy in 1 Peter, that "the elements will be dissolved," was becoming an imminent possibility of atomic annihilation.[56] D. P. Holloway comments, "The word for unloose there is the Greek *luo*, the same word Peter used. So, the elements are not *dissolved*, as we interpret the word, but unloosed, disengaged, as in an untying. This is an exact statement of what occurs

---

[50] C. M. Ward, "The Cold War," *PE*, 14 Jun 1959, 3–5.

[51] Frank M. Boyd, "Russia in Prophecy," *PE*, June 10, 1950, 5, 13; H. A. Armstrong, "Night Before Morning," *PE*, July 22, 1950, 3–4; Riggs, "Pentecost and Christ's Return," 16; F. W. Hoffman, "Perhaps Today," *PE*, January 4, 1953, 5.

[52] Armstrong, "Night Before Morning," 3.

[53] During this period, eschatology articles regularly included pictures of atomic explosions.

[54] Clay Cooper, "It Is Later Than You Think," *PE*, August 12, 1950, 3.

[55] Northcote Deck, "Sign of the Times," *PE*, February 25, 1951, 4.

[56] Charles E. Blair, "Minutes to Midnight," *PE*, August 26, 1956, 3, 21–24; A. A. Wilson, "Is This the End Time," *PE*, August 28, 1955, 3–4.

to an atom in the explosion: the parts (protons, neutrons, and electrons) are loosed from their principles of control."[57]

Another factor that projected a bleak picture of the future was a growing recognition of ecological and environmental crises. Climate change caught the attention of some AG ministers who warned of the growing threat to humanity. M. L. Davidson says,

> Some time ago a vast blanket of fog strangely covered thousands of square miles of the Pacific Ocean. Meteorologists are wondering if the wind currents of the atmosphere are not being altered. Our mean temperature is rising. Ice at the North Pole is melting too fast. The equilibrium of our globe may be disturbed.[58]

Maynard James also noted the rise of global temperatures and its apocalyptic consequences. "A rise in temperature of two degrees throughout the U.S.A. may not seem significant. But according to scientists, an increase of only two degrees all over the world would be enough to melt every particle of ice at both the North and South poles."[59] James believed that God was reserving the water from the flood in the polar ice for his own purposes until "the time of trouble, against the day of battle and war" (i.e., the Great Tribulation).[60] He imagined that during the tribulation, nuclear conflagration will "return the water to the atmosphere" to prepare for the new age.[61] One article predicted that the impact of a hydrogen bomb could alter the tilt of the earth's axis to the point that it would usher in Tribulation-like calamities.[62] In each case, ecological disasters were both acknowledged and interpreted through the lenses of eschatology.

The Millennial Answer

While AG ministers tried to understand ecological issues in light of prophecy, they did not let humanity off the hook for their role in ecological crises. They believed people were to blame for the damage to the environment, but they were pessimistic about humans possessing the ability to solve these crises. As Ralph Riggs comments, "To work for political legislation, to strive for social reform, to substitute education and physical welfare for the blessings of real Christianity, are

[57] D. P. Holloway, "The Approaching Day of Doom," *PE*, August 15, 1954, 3–4.
[58] M. L. Davidson, "Are You Ready For Christ's Return," *PE*, June 6, 1954, 3–4.
[59] Maynard G. James, "The Changing Climate: Is it a Sign of the Times?," *PE*, August 26, 1956, 5.
[60] James, "The Changing Climate: Is it a Sign of the Times?," 5.
[61] James, "The Changing Climate: Is it a Sign of the Times?," 5.
[62] *PE*, December 2, 1956, 10.

the natural results of losing sight of the blessed hope of the Church."[63] Caleb Smith argued that true hope comes only from Christ's ability to reverse what humanity has done to the world.

> When the Lord Jesus returns to the earth, creation will be delivered from its age-long curse. When man fell, God said, "Cursed is the ground for thy sake . . . thorns also and thistles shall it bring forth to thee" (Gen. 3:17, 18). Because of sin "the whole creation groaneth and travaileth in pain together until now" (Rom. 8:22). The sounds of nature, the cries of animals, and the songs of birds are all pitched in a minor key. Earth, sea, and sky are full of fierce pursuit and crude capture, breathless escape and haunting fear. But then the misery of nature will be transformed into a jubilee.[64]

The increase in world conflicts only strengthened their belief that the millennium was the answer. C. M. Ward comments,

> In the Millennium, the devil will be bound, justice will be established, agricultural problems will be settled, animals will be domesticated, safety and security, life expectancy will increase, war will be abolished, evangelism will be accomplished, Christians will be in government, the Jewish question will be settled (restoration), Jerusalem will be the center of the world, Jesus will reign literally, universal joy and happiness.[65]

The Millennium was seen as Christ's opportunity to set things right for humanity and injustices. Frank Boyd emphasized that Christ's rule will "mete out justice for the needy and the poor, to preserve them from deceit and violence."[66] Although the threats of world destruction were real, John Meredith assured readers that the world was valuable to God and would not be destroyed. He says, "The whole idea is that of transition and not extinction. Marvelous changes are due to come to this earth. Earthly conditions will be destroyed, but the earth will be renovated, cleansed, changed."[67] W. B. McCafferty argued the gift of tongues foreshadowed the millennial reunification of humanity under one language. After that, "tongues

---

[63] Ralph Riggs, "The Second Coming of Christ," *PE*, March 4, 1950, 2; "Editorially Speaking," *PE*, May 20, 1951, 2, Robert Cunningham comments, "If a man is called to preach, he ought to stick to his job and leave politics in the hands of those to whom the high calling is not given."

[64] Smith, "7 Reasons for Loving His Appearing," 3, 20.

[65] C. M. Ward, "A Change in Government," *PE*, May 22, 1960, 3, 22–23.

[66] Frank Boyd, "Questions and Answers," *PE*, March 4, 1951, 13.

[67] John L. Meredith, "Does the Second Coming of Christ Mean the End of the World?," *PE*, August 26, 1956, 15.

will cease when the perfect comes," which for McCafferty will be during the millennium. He says, "In the 'restitution of all things' (Acts 3:20, 21) in the great Millennium, God will restore the language, and turn to the people a pure language."[68]

---

[68] W. B. McCafferty, "The Millennial Language," *PE*, August 28, 1955, 4.

9

EVANGELICAL PERIOD (1961–1985)

During the years 1961–1985, the AG was growing and becoming a prosperous denomination as it adapted to the broader culture of American evangelicalism.[1] With the appointment of AG General Superintendent, Thomas F. Zimmerman, to the head of the NAE in 1960, the Pentecostal movement had officially emerged from marginalization and isolation to the top of the most prominent evangelical association in the world.[2] The AG was not only an established evangelical institution; AG theology was beginning to mature as AG ministers with seminary education in evangelical theological institutions began to produce doctrinal materials. The AG employed some of their most educated ministers to address several eschatological controversies by drafting position papers on Amillennialism in 1969 and the Rapture in 1979.[3] However, there were also a growing number of educated ministers in the AG who were dissatisfied with dispensational views.[4] During the 1970s, AG writers were growing weary of the accelerated level of prophetic speculation associated with the popularized eschatology of Hal Lindsey's The Late Great Planet Earth and movies depicting the horrors of who will be "left behind." Raymond Cox warned AG believers to be wary of such fictionalization and "fancies" of popular Bible prophecy teachers.

> What about the chain of calamities that sermon, books and films imagine as concurrent with Christ's coming? "Pilotless planes will crash. Driverless cars will careen in collision." That is how some dramatize the consequences of the sudden disappearances of Christian believers. Is this fact or fancy?[5]

---

[1] Blumhofer, *Restoring the Faith*, 253–60.

[2] See Isgrigg, "The Pentecostal Evangelical Church," 6–10, for discussion of the AG's quest for evangelical identity. Cf. "Assemblies Superintendent Named NAE Head," *PE,* July 7, 1960, 14.

[3] See Chapter 4 on eschatological controversies.

[4] Menzies, *Anointed to Serve*, 329; Blumhofer, *Restoring the Faith*, 270–73.

[5] Cox, "Rapture Facts and Fancies," 5.

Instead of fiction and speculation, Cox admonished readers to focus on the one thing they know to be true: Jesus is coming soon. He concludes, "The next time you read a book, see a film, or hear a discussion of this subject, divide the truth from fiction. You'll profit if you filter facts from fancies. Actually, the facts are exciting enough!"[6] Daniel Johnson pushed back against the apocalyptic visions and "survivalist mentality" that was being pushed by prophecy teachers who were telling people to stock up on food and flee to the countryside.[7]

> We are promised economic chaos, social upheaval, and persecution. We are made to feel almost guilty if we are happy. We are given explicit instructions on the fine art of survival: move to smaller towns or rural areas; dig a well; plant a garden; simplify your life-style. The problem is compounded by the confusion. Like the witnesses against our Lord, these prophets agree not among themselves.[8]

Fatigued by the speculation, exaggeration, fictionalization, and distractions of prophecy teaching, AG ministers called for a return to the simple message that Jesus is coming soon, and believers should be ready.[9] Forrest Smith comments, "The field of eschatology is overrun with gentleman farmers, each reaping a different harvest. There seems to be a fear that God might thoughtlessly do something that someone didn't predict!"[10] One writer even searched through his library of prophecy books and found "25 different predictions of the exact time of Christ's coming. All have long since proved to be false."[11] Charles Crabtree sums up the attitudes of this era, "We need to return to basics whereby the Christian can view the prophecies as wonderful promises, not as worrisome problems. Prophecy is given to us not for controversy but to confirm our faith and give us a hope."[12]

Defending the Rapture

During the Evangelical Period, AG ministers devoted considerable effort to re-emphasizing the importance of the teaching of the Second Coming. However, the

---

[6] Cox, "Rapture Facts and Fancies," 5.

[7] Daniel E. Johnson, "Please Don't Tamper With the Blessed Hope," *PE*, August 24, 1980, 4.

[8] Johnson, "Please Don't Tamper With The Blessed Hope," 4.

[9] Forrest Smith, "So Many Kinds of Voices," *PE*, March 9, 1975, 10–11; Johnson, "Please Don't Tamper With The Blessed Hope," 4; "Ready for His Any Moment Coming," *PE*, December 26, 1982, 3–4.

[10] Forrest Smith, "So Many Kinds of Voices," *PE*, March 9, 1975, 10–11.

[11] M. L. Davidson, "Ready for His Any-Moment Coming," *PE*, December 26, 1982, 3–4.

[12] Charles Crabtree, "Our Blessed Hope," *PE*, April 1, 1984, 4.

primary way they attempted to do that was to defend the pretribulation rapture.[13] Attacks from "scoffers" led the AG to defend the Second Coming with articles titled "Why I Believe in the Second Coming" and "What the Rapture Means to Me." Raymond Cox notes,

> After years in which eschatology endured a relative eclipse (perhaps because of reckless excesses by self-styled prophetic experts) there has exploded tremendous interest in the subject. This excitement may be dismissed in some circles as a "cop-out," an escape from the realities of present problems. However, it reflects an attitude the New Testament recommends. Believers are exhorted to be "looking for that blessed hope."[14]

Though often not scholarly, many of these articles took a scholastic approach in which writers often engaged opposing viewpoints.[15] For example, Ian MacPherson presented four ways Christians have historically understood the Tribulation, but argued that the futurist position was the strongest biblical position.[16] Another article gave seven reasons, ranging from the practical to the scriptural, for why Christians will escape wrath.[17]

Writers during this period used three approaches to defending the rapture. The first approach was to emphasize the dispensational aspects of the two-phase coming. Harry J. Steil accomplished this by comparing the different functions of Christ's coming based on the different dispensational divisions between the Church, the Jews, and the Gentiles.

> To the Church, He is coming as the Bridegroom (Ephesians 5:29–32). To the Jew, He is coming as Messiah (Zechariah 12:10. 13:16). To the Gentiles (the two-thirds who survive the tribulation judgments) He is coming as King of kings (see: Matthew 25:31–34: Revelation 19:11–16: Zechariah 14:9)....This

---

[13] As seen in Chapter 3, the revision of the *SFT* in 1961 was in direct response to AG leadership feeling like the AG position on the rapture was not clear enough.

[14] Raymond L. Cox, "Rapture Facts and Fancies," *PE,* August 18, 1974, 4.

[15] In previous generations, articles did not typically present the various positions on theological issues, assuming AG doctrine to be simply Bible doctrine. However, during the Evangelical Period, authors often took a dialectical approach to AG positions. See for example, Ralph M. Riggs, "Looking for that Blessed Hope," *PE,* September 12, 1965, 2–4.

[16] Ian MacPherson, "The Great Tribulation," *PE,* May 25, 1975, 8–10, offers four views of the tribulation: destruction of Jerusalem in AD 70, the whole church age, the time between the birth of Jesus and AD 70, and futurist interpretation of seven years before the millennium. He discusses both preterism and futurism and cites scholars from both positions.

[17] Ernest F. Kalapathy, "Not Appointed to Wrath," *PE,* 1 January 19, 1975, 6–7.

is the divine order for the end time events. The church first; Israel next; and then the Gentiles.[18]

The divisions between peoples not only explained the functional difference between the rapture and the revelation, also the corresponding affective response. Forest Smith explains, "Jesus told his disciples 'I will come again…' Isn't that exciting? To the world it means judgment. To Israel it means tribulation. But to us who are saved it means eternal happiness."[19] For those who are ready for his return, his coming is a hopeful event; for those who are not, it is somber warning.[20]

A second approach to defending the rapture was to argue that it was a reasonable, biblical, and practical doctrine. Robert Larter defended the historical precedent, retorting, "Christ predicted it," "the apostles taught it," and "all Evangelical Christians believe it."[21] Another article lists "Twelve Certainties of Christ's Coming," in which twelve text verses are given as proof to support the two-phase coming.[22] Some, like Earnest Kalapathy, focused on defending the rapture by giving seven scriptural and logical reasons why he believes the church will escape the tribulation.[23] Still others appealed to experience and emotion in order to argue for the doctrine of the rapture.[24] With the emergence in the 1970s of rapture fiction, some capitalized on the fear those who "missed the rapture" would experience.[25] Ruth Copeland says, "If you miss the rapture, you will find most of your best spiritual helpers have gone."[26] C. M. Ward argued that the finished work of Christ is not compatible with the belief that Christians need to suffer the wrath of the tribulation. For Ward, believing that Christians must go

---

[18] H. J. Steil, "The End of the Age," *PE*, May 10, 1964, 2.

[19] Forrest Smith, "What the Rapture Means to Me," *PE*, November 16, 1975, 4.

[20] F. Helen Jarvis, "Our Blessed Hope," *PE*, August 25, 1963, 3; "Coming Soon," *PE*, May 4, 1980, 10; R. C. Champion, "When is the Thief Coming," *PE*, August 1, 1982, 6–7; Charles Crabtree, "Our Blessed Hope," *PE*, April 1, 1984, 4.

[21] Charles Larter, "Why I Believe in the Second Coming," *PE*, January 7, 1968, 5.

[22] "Twelve Certainties Concerning the Return of Our Lord," *PE*, March 24, 1963, 8.

[23] Ernest F. Kalapathy, "Not Appointed to Wrath," *PE*, January 19, 1975, 6–7.

[24] Forrest Smith, "What the Rapture Means to Me," *PE*, November 16, 1975, 4, argued that the appeal of the rapture is seeing Jesus face to face, seeing loved ones again, and being free from bodily ailments.

[25] Shortly after the movie was released in 1971, R. C. Champion, editor of the *Evangel*, capitalized on its popularity with "When Will the Thief Come," *PE*, May 2, 1971, 4–5.

[26] Ruth Copeland, "If You Miss the Rapture," *PE*, August 15, 1976, 4–5, mentions the rapture taking away parents, teachers, pastors, police officers, postal workers, and innocent children.

through the Tribulation is nothing more than a "protestant purgatory" because it is based on Christians failing to perform.[27]

> It all adds to an attack on Calvary. It questions the strength of salvation. It doubts whether or not the cross and the open tomb are sufficient. If salvation cannot do more than save us from the lake of fire, and if the qualification for the first resurrection depends upon our attainments, full salvation is no longer of grace through faith; it is also of works.[28]

By appealing to the "finished work" of Christ on the cross, Ward exempts Christians from the wrath of tribulation. In each of these cases, they appealed to something other than Scripture to defend their position on the rapture.

A third approach to defending the rapture was through interpreting key Greek words in eschatological passages. Because more educated ministers were raising hermeneutical issues with dispensationalism, the AG appealed to the most notable scholar of the era, Stanley Horton to provide a reply.[29] Horton used his education and knowledge of biblical languages to defend his eschatological positions.[30] For example, Horton used a Greek word study to differentiate between the tribulation Christians might experience in this life and the Great Tribulation.[31] He also appealed to the Greek language to defend against the criticisms of the "left behind" interpretation.[32] Horton was not the only one to use Greek word study to lend force to their arguments. J. S. Eastman argued that the key to understanding the phases of Christ's coming is found in understanding the Greek words used in the Scriptures. He says,

---

[27] C. M. Ward, "Must Believers Go Through the Tribulation," *PE*, August 29, 1971, 22.

[28] Ward, "Must Believers Go Through the Tribulation," 22.

[29] Lois E. Olena, *Stanley M. Horton: Shaper of Pentecostal Theology* (Springfield: Gospel Publishing House, 2009).

[30] Stanley M. Horton, "Counted Worthy to Escape," *PE*, August 15, 1976, 6, 11, says, "Many have told me they appreciate the help that comes from the Greek and Hebrew. The study of the Greek especially does often give shades of meaning that clarify or intensify the thought."

[31] Stanley M. Horton, "Tribulation Now," *PE*, January 19, 1975, 9, says, "At first glance it appears as if Jesus is saying that tribulation is a necessity. But the meaning is not 'must have,' but 'do have.' Jesus is just recognizing that tribulation is a fact of life. We can understand this better when we see the meaning of the word *tribulation*. . . . In everyday Greek it was used of literal pressing or pressure."

[32] Stanley Horton, "One is Taken; One is Left," *PE*, September 16, 1973, 4. Horton counters those who say the left behind passage in Matt. 24.40 teaches the wicked will be taken by arguing the Greek word for "taken" means "to take to oneself," but that the word "took" referring to the judgment upon the people in Noah's day is to "remove" in judgment is a different Greek word.

> At His coming there will be a *parousia*, for He shall come personally for us. There will be an *epiphania*, for we shall see Him in His excellent glory. There will be an apocalypse (*apokalupsis*), for He shall reveal Himself to us. And there will be an *harpazo*, for we shall be caught up to meet Him in the air.[33]

The appeal to Greek words shows the maturation in the way doctrine was defended. But it was also intended to give the impression of scholarly legitimacy for these doctrines. In each of these three approaches to defending the rapture, the necessary element was a defense of the doctrine of the tribulation. This meant that on a popular level, to believe in the soon coming of Christ is to believe in the pretribulation rapture in its dispensational expression without the nuances of earlier Pentecostal expressions.

Resurgence of the Spirit

The strong identification with the NAE during the Evangelical Period did not diminish the AG's commitment to Pentecostal distinctives.[34] After a decade of downplaying latter rain language because of the "New Order" controversy, the latter rain emphasis reemerged as the AG witnessed more interest in the Holy Spirit through the Charismatic Movement. The resurgence in pneumatological emphasis reaffirmed that they were still in the midst of the outpouring of the latter rain that signaled the nearness of Christ's return. Superintendent Thomas Zimmerman comments,

> In my opinion, this broadening of the work of the Spirit in our day is significant because it indicates God's desire to reach all circles of humanity. God is pouring out the latter rain in order to prepare the Church for the end-time harvest. He is raising up Spirit-filled witnesses of His grace and power.[35]

Although the AG had reservations about the ecumenical nature of the Charismatic Movement, they could not deny that AG churches were benefitting from the outpouring of the Spirit that was taking place. Roy Sapp noted, "Praise God, it is

---

[33] J. S. Eastman, "The Rapture of the Church," *PE*, April 29, 1973, 30.

[34] Blumhofer, *Restoring the Faith*, 240–60, and Thompson, *Kingdom Come*, 56–57, have suggested the opposite on this point. Thompson claims a "dramatic decrease" in the AG's cherished distinctives as a result. However, one of the primary reasons expressed by the AG for joining the NAE was cooperation without compromising positions on Pentecostal doctrine. See J. R. Flower, "Why We Joined the NAE," *PE*, March 29, 1947, 12.

[35] "Apostolic Christianity," *PE*, May 21, 1961, 4–5.

bringing to the Assemblies of God a fresh flow of anointing and power–a new sense of purpose and direction."[36]

With the reemergence of latter rain emphasis, there also came a reestablishment of the connection between the Spirit and the Second Coming. In a 1961 article called "The Holy Spirit and the Blessed Hope," Michael Horban outlined five ways the Holy Spirit functions in relation to the Blessed Hope.[37] These five functions were also shared by various others and serve as an outline of some of the major connections between the Spirit and the Second Coming in this period. First, the Holy Spirit nurtures in believers a love for Christ's appearing. Belief in the propositional truth of the Second Coming was not enough; that truth should produce an affective response of "loving" Christ's coming.[38] Horban says, "The indwelling Spirit inspires in the believer a constant prayer, an ardent urge for Christ's return. . . . It is the Holy Spirit who nurtures this fond yearning and directs the heart of the Church."[39]

Second, the Spirit is the essential element that empowers believers to be patient and wait for Christ's return. Several articles appealed once again to Romans 8 to connect the Spirit with the "sighs" for the redemption of the body and creation.[40] As one writer comments, "In the days of primitive Christianity it would have been deemed a kind of apostasy not to sigh for the return of the Lord."[41] The Spirit within the believer longs for full redemption all the while "the inward man is renewed and strengthened by the Spirit to wait patiently."[42] Belief in the kingdom requires dependence on the Spirit for patience to navigate the tension of the "already-not yet." As Melvin Hodges describes,

---

[36] Roy G. Sapp, "Five Reasons Why God is Pouring Out His Spirit Today," *PE*, October 3, 1971, 2–3, 10. Sapp recognized that the revival was providential and gave five reasons for the resurgence of the latter rain outpouring: 1) The Holy Spirit is increasing because the wickedness of the world is increasing, 2) counteracting the increase in false prophets who are deceiving the world, 3) revealing the truth amidst a growing end-time deception, 4) preparing the Bride for the Bridegroom, 5) bringing in a harvest of souls.

[37] Michael Horban, "Holy Spirit and the Blessed Hope," *PE*, May 21, 1961, 22–23.

[38] Horban, "Holy Spirit and the Blessed Hope," 22; Ralph M. Riggs, "Looking for that Blessed Hope," *PE*, September 12, 1965, 2–4.

[39] Horban, "Holy Spirit and the Blessed Hope," 22.

[40] Horban, "Holy Spirit and the Blessed Hope," 22. Also, George Holmes, "Till He Come," *PE*, April 22, 1962, 7; Cox, "Rapture Facts and Fancies," 5.

[41] Robert B. Larter, "Why I Believe In the Second Coming," *PE*, January 7, 1968, 5.

[42] Horban, "Holy Spirit and the Blessed Hope," 22.

Some things we receive from Christ *now.* Some things are reserved for a future *then.* These two stages are kept in proper perspective by the tension involved in the words *not yet.* . . . To sustain us in the not yet period, we have the hope of the future glory (Romans 8:23, 24), the help of the indwelling Spirit (Romans 8:26), and the sure knowledge that all things are going to contribute to our final glorification.[43]

Third, the Spirit is the source that illuminates and reveals the things to come. But this function is not limited to simply the script of the future. The Holy Spirit keeps the focus on the things that matter to the kingdom and shapes the believer's affections toward the resurrection, the kingdom, and heirship with Christ.[44] When the Spirit is neglected, the values of the kingdom fall into neglect. Fourth, the Spirit empowers believers to be a witness of the Gospel, which will "hasten the day" and fulfill the great commission. As Marlon Jannuzzi comments, "It is not prophetic technicalities nor satanic opposition that delays our Lord's return. . . . He waits for us to see the need of a lost world and accept the challenge to meet that need."[45] The final and most powerful work of the Spirit is through the resurrection of the body.[46] Horban says, "The residence of the Holy Spirit in the heart is a pledge and foretaste of a glorious resurrection because He is the same Spirit that raised Christ from the dead."[47] Through the Spirit, the believer's hope is aligned with the Spirit's hope, namely the fullness of cosmic salvation. Horban says,

> In Romans 8:14–25 this thought is beautifully developed. The whole creation was effected by man's fall and everywhere we see decay, disease, suffering, and death. However, nature also shares our hope and longingly, patiently waits for resurrection morning when it, too, will be delivered from the bondage of this curse. We who have the first fruits of the Spirit sigh for the redemption of the body, for then we shall receive our full adoption, and we shall enter into the full privileges of our sonship and heirship. This is our hope and we with patience wait for it.[48]

---

[43] Melvin L. Hodges, "Now, Not Yet, Then," *PE,* October 20, 1974, 9.

[44] Horban, "Holy Spirit and the Blessed Hope," 22. Also, Ralph Riggs, "Looking for that Blessed Hope," *PE,* September 12, 1965, 2–5.

[45] Marlon Jannuzzi, "Why Jesus Tarries," *PE,* April 14, 1963, 22.

[46] Horban, "Holy Spirit and the Blessed Hope," 23. Also, Cox, "Rapture Facts and Fancies," 5; G. D. Watson, "Our Resurrection Bodies," *PE,* April 14, 1963, 7–8.

[47] Horban, "Holy Spirit and the Blessed Hope," 23.

[48] Horban, "Holy Spirit and the Blessed Hope," 22.

These five emphases represent a return to the type of pneumatic eschatology that was present in the first half of the century. The Holy Spirit is not just revealing facts about the Second Coming, but is transforming the affections in light of the Second Coming.

Signs of the Times

The decade of the 1950s was marked by an increase in pessimism, some of which carried over into the decade of the 1960s as humanity increased its capacity for destruction. As Robert Cunningham comments, "Once those prophecies seemed far-fetched and fantastic. Suddenly they have become plausible, practical, and disturbingly up-to-date."[49] The AG continued to have little hope in the human ability to bring about peace in a time of growing threats to human existence. W. E. Kirchke sums up this anxiety ably.

> Time and again have foreign ministers sat around peace tables with burdened hearts and gigantic barriers, trying to mold a policy of peace of the pieces left by selfish and warring men. They have been powerless to lift the oppression and bondage that grind the subjected peoples of the world with a barbaric tyrannical slavery that is the concoction of demented minds. While men talk "peace," they continue to build their stockpiles of munitions, spy systems, and secret police. They are afraid that one or the other will light the fire for a nuclear attack that will all but destroy this present situation.[50]

During the 1960s–1970s, the Vietnam War, civil and racial unrest, and the prospect of the breakdown of societal norms meant a resurgence of pessimistic prophecy teachings. Looking at the world in 1976, Gordon Chilvers laments,

> How can we survive? That is man's number one question. . . . In the darkest hours of history the hope of Christ's return will revive discouraged men. The best way to meet the despair in the world is to confront it with a confident faith in the promise of Jesus' return.[51]

By the 1980s, prophetic speculation was once again at a fever pitch. The Pentecostal Evangel published three "Prophecy Editions" during this period of unrest.[52]

---

[49] R. C. Cunningham, "When Will Christ Return," *PE*, September 10, 1961, 5.
[50] W. E. Kirchke, "The World's Greatest Space Event," *PE*, March 15, 1964, 18–19.
[51] Gordon Chilvers, "The Only Antidote for Despair," *PE*, October 31, 1976, 5.
[52] *PE*, July 9, 1967; *PE*, January 7, 1968; *PE*, January 5, 1975.

The primary problem with human solutions to the world's problems is that people are inherently sinful. Governments, politics, and the best intentions of leaders will never be enough to solve the world problems. Richard Orchard comments, "Man has tried to govern himself by monarchies, democracies, dictatorships, parliaments, councils, tribal customs, and other forms of jurisdiction; but through all these forms he has not been able to lift himself out of the moral chaos to which his nature bends."[53] America was not exempt during the 1970s from the problems that other counties faced. Orchard comments "America, for all its enlightened system of government, is a land where inequities exist, where innocents sometimes suffer, and where justice does not always prevail."[54] Food and gas shortages were just as much were signs of the "birth-pangs of a new age" as were wars and worldwide famine.[55] C. M. Ward recognized income inequality as a sign of the "beginning of sorrows." He says, "Another 'sorrow' is developing. It's the increasing disparity between rich and poor. The middle class, the spine that has been America, is shrinking."[56]

At the same time during this period, the world was witnessing the height of human achievements in the exploration of space. For the first time, satellites and television made it possible for humanity to imagine the possibility of apocalyptic events being broadcast to the whole world.[57] Articles used clever space-themed terminology such as referring to Jesus as the "Man of Space" who will make his "re-entry" into earth to rapture his "space travelers."[58] As much as this new era of technological advancement had to offer, Al Rediger reminds believers, "Although we all recognize many marvelous achievements, and wonderful advantages in this Space Age, we are not deceiving ourselves into thinking science and learning are creating a utopia where all men's problems will be solved."[59]

---

[53] Richard Orchard, "Better World is Coming," *PE*, September 11, 1977, 4–5.

[54] Orchard, "Better World is Coming," 4–5.

[55] R. C. Cunningham, "The Birth-pangs of the New Age," *PE*, January 26, 1975, 31.

[56] C. M. Ward, "Beginning of Sorrows," *PE*, May 25, 1975, 11.

[57] Donald A. Tanner, "Telstar Points To Christ's Return," *PE*, January 20, 1963, 2–3; Raymond L. Cox, "Killer Star," *PE*, April 2, 1978, 4–5, notes that the incident in 1978 when a Russian satellite, which contained 100 pounds of radioactive uranium 235, could be interpreted as the Revelation 8 account of the star "wormwood" falling from the sky and poisoning the planet.

[58] Kirchke, "The World's Greatest Space Event," 19; Raymond Phillips, "Invasion from Outer Space," *PE*, January 25, 1959, 3; Al Rediger, "Christian Faith for the Age of Space," *PE*, December 13, 1964, 2–3.

[59] Rediger, "Christian Faith for the Age of Space," 2–3.

Just as the threat of war and nuclear weapons brought about more pessimistic views of humanity, discoveries made during space exploration had a positive impact on their eschatology. When the first pictures of the earth from space by NASA were shared with the world, Zelma Argue remarked, "The planet earth. No other generation has ever seen it as we have peeping over the rim of the moon … Earth! Our home! God cares about our planet!"[60] This new glimpse into space gave Argue a new appreciation of the uniqueness of earth in the universe and shaped her expectation of the destiny of the earth. If the earth is this glorious, she wondered, how could it possibly be God's plan for it to be annihilated? Instead she predicts, "What glorious views await us. What scenes of triumph, of renewal, of rejuvenation! … And the earth shall be full of the glory of the Lord. That will be Earth's finest hour!"[61]

The Problem of Israel

During the 1960s–1970s, idealism about the establishment of the state of Israel began to diminish. AG writers certainly supported Israel and believed that a Jewish Nation was crucial to end times prophecy.[62] Harry Steil called the Jewish people "two million signs" that Jesus was coming soon.[63] However, some began to recognize that support for Israel was becoming increasingly complicated. One factor they wrestled with was that Israel had returned without faith in the Messiah. Frank Boyd, one of the most ardent apologists for Israel, recognizes this dilemma.

> I readily agree that Israel is apostate, that they have been under the chastening hand of God, and that they still hate our Lord Jesus Christ; but it is not through this apostate element that God's final purpose for them is to be realized. It will be through a faithful remnant of the last days who will not be deceived by Antichrist.[64]

---

[60] Zelma Argue, "Earth's Finest Hour," *PE,* October 4, 1970, 5.

[61] Argue, "Earth's Finest Hour," 7.

[62] Cunningham, "When Will Christ Return," 6; R. C. Cunningham, "Signs of His Return," *PE,* January 7, 1968, 4; C. M. Ward, "Israel Will Survive," *PE,* June 8, 1975, 22.

[63] H. J. Steil, "Two Millions Signs," *PE,* July 30, 1967, 2–4, recognizes three "healthy shoots" that were pointing to the growth of the fig tree: A territorial root, a political root, and a financial root. Each of these roots was necessary in order for God to complete his plan for Israel. However, that plan will not be fully realized until he removes the Church in the rapture.

[64] F. M. Boyd, "Israel's Glorious Future," *PE,* January 7, 1968, 2.

This meant that for many, support for Israel was a qualified support. Even those who encouraged believers to pray for the peace of Jerusalem were skeptical that peace was possible because of Israel's perpetual conflict with Palestinians. C. M. Ward argued that if peace is Israel's goal, they must "break out of the vicious cycle of terror, retaliation, more terror, and more retaliation."[65] Ward criticized Israel's tactics of retaliation in the conflict with Palestinians. He says, "The inevitable intensification of such measures as 'collective punishment' (the dynamiting of houses), 'administrative arrests' without charge, and deportations will not work any better for the Jews than they worked for the British or the Germans."[66] Ward reminded readers that the only hope for true peace in the Middle East would be under reign of the Messiah. He concludes, "Earth groans politically for that moment."[67]

Another challenge to the AG's perspective on Israel was the growing anti-Christian sentiment from the government. Missionary L. V. Tiller notes that after 1948, no new Christian churches were allowed in Israel.[68] Evangelism was prohibited and social institutions, such as missions, hospitals, and schools, were closed to Christian workers. The hostility toward evangelistic efforts within Israel forced Tiller to focus his efforts on Mulism Arabs outside Hebrew territories. Despite the resistance, Tiller reported that the Holy Spirit was still moving in Israel.

> In the last few years many church leaders and missionaries have been filled with the Holy Spirit, representing all denominations. Probably there are more baptized in the Holy Spirit in Jerusalem today than at any time since the Day of Pentecost. It is felt that God is preparing us for something we do not yet see. This has included many Arab Christians.[69]

As long as the Spirit was being poured out and Israel was still in rebellion, they knew the Gentile Period was still in effect and the work of evangelism should continue.

---

[65] C. M. Ward, "Pray for the Peace of Jerusalem," *PE*, January 26, 1975, 30.
[66] Ward, "Pray for the Peace of Jerusalem," 30.
[67] Ward, "Pray for the Peace of Jerusalem," 30.
[68] L. V. D. Tiller, "What is God Doing in Israel," *PE*, February 9, 1975, 10.
[69] Tiller, "What is God Doing in Israel," 10.

The Millennium

During the 1960s, amillennialism gained in popularity within the AG ranks due to a growing number of AG clergy being educated in Protestant universities. As a result, a resolution was offered at the 1969 General Council that included amillennialism to the "Eschatological Errors."[70] However, there were few articles that actually addressed the millennium.[71] However, the articles that do address the millennium gave some additional details about the characteristics of the millennium. One aspect that was emphasized was the concept of universal justice. Since they rejected the notion that humanity can improve the world, social issues such as poverty, war, and injustice would have to wait until the righteous reign of Christ for final resolution. But in the millennium, writers envisioned a society that would be truly just. Ian MacPherson says, "Poverty is one of the great problems of the world today. Every time the clock ticks, somebody dies because he is too poor to obtain the necessities of life. But in Christ's kingdom it will be different. There will be a period of prodigious plenty."[72] MacPherson imagined a time when the curse would be lifted and the earth would produce abundantly for its citizens. Similarly, Richard Orchard argued that when Christ rules, war will be banished and the world's resources will be used properly for the benefit of all humanity. He says, "The billions now spent for defense can be channeled into education, homes, food, elimination of poverty, and the advancement of that research which will upgrade living conditions throughout the world."[73] C. M. Ward also anticipated Christ's answer to economic injustice.

> Twenty-four hours after Jesus returns to earth, there will be total disarmament and the absolute security. . . . Jesus Christ will disturb the economic injustices upon earth. He will deal with cartels, industrial monopolies, price fixing, surplus profits, unemployment, interest rates, taxes and high cost of living. Peter calls it "a new earth, wherein dwelleth righteousness" (2 Peter 3:13).[74]

The millennial age will be a time of economic justice and a renaissance of creativity, culture, and humanities. Orchard says, "The cultivation of talents,

---

[70] *GC Minutes* (August 21–26, 1969), 81–82.

[71] Ian MacPherson, "Millennium," *PE,* June 29, 1975, 20–22. Authors like Ian MacPherson engaged the different views of the millennium and argued that the premillennial position was the view most consistent with biblical testimony.

[72] Ian MacPherson, "Marks of the Millennium," *PE,* July 13, 1975, 5.

[73] Orchard, "Better World is Coming," 4–5.

[74] C. M. Ward, "An End to Darkness," *PE,* 3172 (February 23, 1975), 5.

architecture, industry, knowledge, and travel shall be so unbounded that our present day will seem very primitive by comparison."[75] The key element that will produce this utopian vision of kingdom will be Christ's righteous rule and the lifting of the curse on the whole order of creation.

Visions of the millennial government included earthly institutions that will execute theocratic rule throughout the earth, utilizing advances in technology in order to enforce his rule.[76] Christ's rule will be so perfect and just that Ian MacPherson believes, "Many who submit to the regal authority of Christ during the Millennium will doubtless do so for prudential reasons."[77] Richard Orchard imagines the impact of Christ's worldly government will be restorative, not punitive.

> The program of God does not include the destruction of this world, but its redemption and restoration to a holy condition. He has not given up on this planet. Jesus died to redeem, to destroy the works of the devil, to bring back, to reconcile, and when He sees the final accumulated results of His obedience to the Father, He shall be satisfied. Earth will once again be beautiful. Sin will be forever eliminated.[78]

The focus on Christ's earthly reign hindered their ability to believe that humanity can work to solve the issues of the world. At the same time, that skepticism also kept them from trusting political solutions. Although the NAE was committed to influencing political and social institutions, the AG's eschatology helped them to resist the temptation to align themselves with any forms of government or political persuasions.[79] During the 1980s, AG members were encouraged to remember

---

[75] Orchard, "Better World is Coming," 4.

[76] MacPherson, "Marks of the Millennium," 4–7, says, "For the first time in history, the world is ready for global sovereignty. Radio, the telephone, television, communication satellites, and high-speed travel have made universal government a viable possibility."

[77] Ian MacPherson, "The End of the World is Near," *PE*, July 27, 1975, 5.

[78] Orchard, "Better World is Coming," 5.

[79] Despite the focus on the signs of the times and the condition of American culture, this research found little encouragement for believers to politically align with any American political party. After the election of Ronald Reagan and the appointment of AG member James G. Watt to the position of Secretary of Interior, the AG's perspective on society and government began to shift to encourage more participation in American politics. See James G. Watt, "... In a Town Nearby," *PE*, October 10, 1983, 6, 11–12. Cf. A. W. Argue Jr., "Should a Christian Be Involved in Politics," *PE*, October 24, 1976, 6–7; Robert P. Dugan, Jr., "Bless the Politicians," *PE*, October 26, 1980, 8–9; Abby Tuttle, "The Christian's Attitude Toward His Government," *PE*, July 1, 1984, 3–4. W. Dennis Huber, "Christian Involvement in the Electoral Process," *PE*, October 14, 1984, 12–13.

when voting, "Do not confuse patriotism, national pride, and Western Culture with Christian faith and practice.... Do not confuse secular political activity with the purpose of the church, nor campaigning with witnessing and preaching."[80]

The New Creation

The redemptive nature of the millennium naturally led writers to argue for continuity between the millennial earth and the new heavens and earth. As earlier noted, Ward compared the promise of a "new earth" to the millennial kingdom.[81] If Christ will invest his earthly government to the renewal of the earth, why would he destroy it all only to create a new one? Ian MacPherson argued that the new creation would be a new chapter of the redeemed earth, not a completely new version.

> The Scriptures proclaim that the world's ultimate destiny is not destruction but reconstruction. On page after page they dwell rapturously on that thrilling theme. The Greek word *telos*, end, signifies not only cessation but consummation, not simply conclusion but completion. God will not just write "finis" but "final" to human history in order to begin a new and inconceivably wonderful chapter.[82]

The telos of the millennium is the beginning of the new creation. Those who held to this perspective of the new creation envisioned a process of renewal that begins with the salvation of creation through sharing in the resurrection of the body (Romans 8).[83] The second phase is the sanctification and the renewal of earth under the jurisdiction of Christ and the saints.[84] The third phase is complete glorification culminating in Christ making "all things new."[85] The future is imagined as a restoration of the original creation. Collin Campbell calls this the "The Eden Connection" in which creation is waiting and groans in expectation for a return to Eden.[86]

---

[80] "10 Guidelines for Christian Voters," *PE*, October 14, 1984, 13.

[81] Ward, "An End to Darkness," 5.

[82] Ian MacPherson, "The New Heavens and New Earth," *PE*, September 21, 1975, 4–5.

[83] Horban, "Holy Spirit and the Blessed Hope," 22.

[84] Orchard, "Better World is Coming," 4–5.

[85] Argue, "Earth's Finest Hour," 7, declares, "What scenes of triumph, of renewal, of rejuvenation!"

[86] Colin Campbell, "The Eden Connection," *PE*, October 31, 1976, 19.

10

MODERN PERIOD (1985–PRESENT)

By the 1980s, the AG had become an influential denomination in American Christianity. Many churches modernized and began to move toward contemporary expressions of evangelicalism and some moved away from traditional Pentecostal spirituality.[1] Modernization also affected how ministers approached the subject of eschatology. Throughout the Modern Period, the fatigue of prophetic speculation and the controversies surrounding eschatological views resulted in the doctrine of the Second Coming entering a period of neglect. This once vital doctrine on which the fellowship was founded was facing several challenges that were leading to a de-emphasis of the Second Coming.[2] First, the rising education level of AG ministers led to more differences in opinion on eschatological positions. The controversy surrounding "eschatological loopholes" in 1980 revealed that many ministers and educators were open to other positions, which often meant that they were not defending the official positions to a new generation.[3] In 2010, a survey of AG ministers found, "while 58 percent reported accepting a dispensationalist interpretation of Scripture, 42 percent rejected this approach."[4] Rather than openly undermining popular eschatological positions, many ministers simply avoided the topic all together. In response, the leadership recruited some educated pastors and

---

[1] See, Poloma, *Assemblies of God at the Crossroads,* which argues that as the AG mainstreamed, it also lost its emphasis on the charismatic manifestations traditionally associated with Pentecostal worship.

[2] David A. Lewis, "War on Prophecy," *PE,* December 17, 1989, 6–7; Michael P. Horban, "The Second Coming—Why Don't We Talk About It?," *PE,* October 14, 1990, 5, comments, "We live in a world that is running out of hope. Yet among Christians there seems to be a lethargy regarding this momentous teaching of the Bible. Prophecy conferences, popular in the middle decades of this century, have all but disappeared. Few evangelists devote a series of messages to the subject of our Lord's return. Pastors seldom address the second coming of Christ. And many Christians have grown cool toward prophetic teaching."

[3] *GP Minutes* (August 13–15, 1979); Blumhofer, *Assemblies of God*, Vol. 2, 183–85. See Chapter 3 for details on the Committee on Loopholes controversy.

[4] Poloma and Green, *The Assemblies of God*, 82.

scholars to defend AG positions in the Pentecostal Evangel.[5] The second challenge effecting eschatological emphasis in this period was the date setting controversy, particularly in 1988 and 2000. Ester Ilnisky, a missionary to Lebanon, criticized the "prophets for profit" who were treating the future like a game and who were arbitrarily deciding which people and nations were expendable in God's plan.[6] She says, "Doomsdayers propagate a message of half-truths. They are opportunists with Satan-entered tidings, making prophecy smack of sensationalism. But the Antichrist is not center stage in these last days. Jesus Christ is."[7] Instead of "following the frenzy," Ilnisky admonishes believers to stay on task and "remain sensitive to the heart-cry of desperate people, victims of injustices."[8] Robert Coleman also criticized prophecy teachers for speculating about how many will die during the tribulation rather than "how many will be lost" and meet eternal damnation because the church is preoccupied with prophecy rather than reaching the lost.[9] Paul Gutkey reminds ministers, "We can be experts in 'rapturology,' but miss the essence of Christianity."[10]

The biggest issue that led to the neglect of eschatology was the embarrassment over speculation about 1988 in Bible prophecy. When Hal Lindsey and Edgar Whisenant convinced believers that Jesus was going to return in 1988, Michael Horban called their books an "embarrassment" that was detrimental to the cause of Bible prophecy.[11] In fact, during this period, few articles focused on sign-based eschatology and even fewer addressed Israel's role in the end times after the 1988 controversy.[12] Although the *Pentecostal Evangel* articles avoided this type of speculation, many AG pastors utilized these materials and were made to look

---

[5] AG College professors include Stanley Horton, Gary B. McGee, Wave Nunnally, James Railey, Zenis Bickett, Maurice Lednicky, Jimmy D. Brewer, as well as British AG scholar David Allen.

[6] Ester Ilnisky, "Christian Life-style in the End Time," *PE*, April 14, 1991, 4–6, comments "Prophecy is not the name of a game. Human beings are not pawns in the hands of self-appointed prophets to be manipulated at will. Countries are not mere geographical locations to be included or excluded from the face of the earth. Prophecy is God's way of communicating to mankind that His sovereignty is perpetually operating on earth to accommodate His plan for man's salvation. Human beings are His highest creation–precious in His sight."

[7] Ilnisky, "Christian-lifestyle in the End Time," 5.

[8] Ilnisky, "Christian-lifestyle in the End Time," 5.

[9] Robert E. Coleman, "How Many Will Be Lost?," *PE*, July 12, 1987, 6–7.

[10] Paul C. Gutkey, "The Rapture: Who's Going?," *PE*, February 23, 1986, 4.

[11] Horban, "The Second Coming—Why Don't We Talk About It?," 5.

[12] Ian MacPherson, "Biblical Weather Forecasting," *PE*, February 1, 1987, 4–5.; Kenneth Barney, "Understanding the Times," *PE*, July 12, 1987, 8–9; Jimmie D. Brewer, "New World Coming," *PE*, July 16, 1989, 4–5. Stanley M. Horton, "The Great Tribulation," *PE*, October 29, 2000, 21.

foolish for it.[13] David Lewis comments, "Pastor, no one expects you to be an eschatological expert. Preach simple biblical messages on the end times. Don't concern yourself with fantasies, date setting, or naming the Antichrist. Stick to the basics."[14] Out of caution to being caught up in all of the speculation, the *Pentecostal Evangel* did not publish a single article on eschatology in 1988.[15] During the Modern Period, there was only one "Prophecy Edition" dedicated to the subject of the Rapture.[16] By 1990, the AG knew they needed to defend their position and did so with several polemical articles defending the rapture and encouraging AG members to once again preach his coming. As the world approached the new millennium in Y2K, the *Pentecostal Evangel* was relatively silent about the significance of this reality compared to the rest of the prophetic community.

The Rapture

As in previous periods, the emphasis on the two-phase coming made the doctrine of the rapture essential. James K. Bridges reemphasized to a new generation why the separation of the two phases was important.[17] First, he argued the purpose is different. The rapture is for deliverance from wrath; the revelation is for appointment to wrath. Second, the timing is different. The rapture occurs before the tribulation; the revelation occurs after the tribulation (a seven-year difference). Third, he argued that the place is different. The rapture occurs in the air; the revelation occurs on the Mount of Olives in Jerusalem. Bridges summarizes the hope that the Rapture gives believers:

> It is a blessed hope (Titus 2:13). It is a purifying hope (1 John 3:3). It is a comforting hope (1 Thessalonians 4:13). It is a glorious hope (Philippians 3:20). It is a hope of deliverance (Galatians 1:4; 1 Thessalonians 1:10; Romans 8:21, 23).[18]

As Bridges' summary demonstrates, hope for the believer is most evident in deliverance from the wrath to come. Correspondingly, there are only a couple

---

[13] Wave Nunnally, "Looking Back at Y2K," *PE,* March 25, 2001, 15.

[14] Lewis, "War on Prophecy," 6.

[15] The only exception is two articles on the Kingdom Now controversy.

[16] *PE,* March 31, 1996. It should also be noted that although not a full issue dedicated to prophecy, *PE,* May 28, 2000, featured Tim LaHaye and the *Left Behind* novels.

[17] James K. Bridges, "The Second Coming of Jesus Christ," *PE,* July 22, 2001, 13.

[18] Bridges, "The Second Coming of Jesus Christ," 13.

articles in which the resurrection of the body has a prominent role in the purpose of Christ's return.[19] Once again, the emphasis on the rapture had detrimental effects on emphasis on the resurrection.

Although the two-phase theology was still present, as the period moved forward articulations of Christ's coming became more ambiguous and some authors blurred the definitions and emphasis between the two-phases. For example, Michael Horban also blurs the distinctions when he says, "The Second Coming of Christ is rightly called the 'blessed hope' because it is the ultimate event and will consummate God's plan of redemption."[20] Also James Railey, professor at AGTS, does not make escape the primary emphasis. He says, "The future for the believer contains the promise of being either raised from the dead or being taken directly into the presence of God. What a blessed hope."[21] Richard Orchard defines the Blessed Hope as the "manifestation of the sons of God," at the same time he also includes "coming of Jesus with great glory" and "lifting of the curse of corruption from creation," which are typically understood as the part of revelation from heaven at the end of the tribulation.[22] Even the General Superintendent, Thomas Zimmerman, emphasizes the "promise of Christ's coming" will be the institution of Christ's kingdom on earth without mention of the rapture.[23]

Unlike the consistent inclusion of the Holy Spirit in eschatology during the previous periods, there is little emphasis on the "latter rain" aspects of their eschatological orientation. There are only a couple occasions when AG writers refer to the latter rain. James K. Bridges says,

> For more than a century, the latter-rain outpouring of the Spirit in power has been experienced by millions of people in every land. . . . We can be sure that during this third millennium the Holy Spirit will be gathering a bride for Christ who will be filled with the Spirit and ready to meet her Lord in the air.[24]

---

[19] Spencer Jones, "Jesus is Coming Again," *PE,* October 29, 1989, 6–7; James Railey, "What Does the Future Hold," *PE,* September 8, 2002, 26–27.

[20] Horban, "The Second Coming—Why Don't We Talk About It?," 4–5.

[21] Railey, "What Does the Future Hold," 27.

[22] Richard E. Orchard, "Plans for This Planet," *PE,* December 28, 1986, 6–7.

[23] Thomas F. Zimmerman, "The Future is Bright," *PE,* June 9, 1985, 7.

[24] James K. Bridges, "The Holy Spirit in the Third Millennium," *PE,* June 11, 2000, 29, is the only article that emphasizes the eschatological "latter rain."

The reluctance to use "latter rain" orientation for the Pentecostal outpouring was most likely due to the growth of the continuationist view of the charismatic gifts.[25]

Avoiding the Tribulation

Only three articles offered any apologetic for the pretribulation rapture during the Modern Period. Richard Orchard, writing during the cold war argued that the world was in the "shadow" of the coming tribulation.[26] In 1992, following the race riots in Los Angeles, Larry Bryan warned readers that the "anarchy" of the tribulation will be infinitely worse and on a global scale when the church is removed from the world.[27] The only detailed apologetic of the tribulation during this period came from several articles by Stanley Horton. When asked how the AG arrived at the pretribulational position, Horton answered, "the vast majority of those who received the Spirit became premillennialists and pre-Tribulationists. This was the Spirit's work, not Darby's, for the Plymouth Brethren were very anti-Pentecostal."[28] Horton claims that there are a "small minority" in the AG that hold a mid-tribulation position," but that the pre-tribulation position "best fits" the AG emphasis on being ready.[29] Horton focuses on 2 Thess. 2:1–17 as the main Scripture passage that affirms the events of the tribulation. He comments, "This passage teaches that the Church will rise to meet Jesus before the Antichrist appears; that is, before or at least by the middle of the Great Tribulation."[30] He also notes that Daniel 7 and Revelation 11 both teach that the antichrist will be revealed "at least before the middle of the tribulation." Once the restraining influence of the Holy Spirit in the Church is removed, the antichrist will be revealed. However, he believes other verses, mainly Rev. 3:10 and Luke 21:28, teach that Christians will be raptured before the wrath to come. The antichrist will "gain great power politically, commercially, and religiously." He will make a covenant with Israel that

---

[25] Though this process is difficult to chart, however, it is articulated well by Craig L. Keener, *Spirit Hermeneutics* (Grand Rapids: Eerdmans, 2016), 49–56, who notes the difficulty in the Pentecostal hermeneutic of the "latter rain." He says, "God did not pour out the Spirit on Pentecost, pull the Spirit back for most of history and then pour out the Spirit again in their own day. . . . The early Pentecostal restorationist approach simply adopted contemporary cessationism and modified it by making the cessation temporary" (50).

[26] R. E. Orchard, "Tribulation Shadows," *PE,* November 9, 1987, 6–7.

[27] Larry Bryan, "When Anarchy Rules," *PE,* August 16, 1992, 4–5.

[28] *PE,* February 23, 1992, 15.

[29] *PE,* September 20, 1992, 23.

[30] Stanley M. Horton, "The Great Tribulation," *PE,* October 29, 2000, 21.

will "lull them into a false sense of security and permit them to rebuild a temple and re-institute a sacrificial system."[31] At the end of the Tribulation, Jesus will appear with his saints to destroy the antichrist at Armageddon and will cast the enemies of God in the lake of fire. Horton's article does not assume to speak for the AG and leaves room for tribulational views to vary but argues for what he believes are the strengths of the pretribulation position. Outside Horton's article, there is little to suggest that adherence to tribulational details was a priority in this period.

The reluctance to emphasize the pretribulation position and conciliatory tones in dealing with eschatological controversies are definitely reflected in articles in the *Pentecostal Evangel*. This suggests that current sentiments toward eschatology are leaning toward a general affirmation of premillennialism, similar to the early days. David Lewis comments, "It is not the purpose of this article to get into the pre-Tribulation, mid-Tribulation or post-Tribulation Rapture arguments. It is time for all who believe in the Rapture to close ranks, stop fighting each other, and realize what the enemy is trying to do."[32] Still others in the AG were not ready to give in to such generalizations. Dan Betzer declares, "The rapture has not been called off. . . . Let the would-be theologians write their mocking treatises on what they term 'the Rapture hoax.' It doesn't change a single fact about the reality of His coming."[33]

Escapism and Social Engagement

One of the primary objection raised with pretribulational eschatology is that it encourages escapism. As demonstrated in this chapter, the more that the AG focused on signs of the times, the more they viewed Christ's coming as a way of escape. James Bridges replies, "Without apology we say to those who accuse us of escapism—yes. It is an escape from a world system that has become anti-Christ and a race of people whose sins have ripened to judgment and in their rejection of Christ they race toward the day of wrath."[34] Others were not comfortable being labeled "escapist." David Lewis comments, "Escapism? I don't know what it is ... If Jesus comes today, hallelujah! But if not, then tomorrow we will be on the front

---

[31] Horton, "The Great Tribulation," 21.
[32] David A. Lewis, "The Rapture of the Church," *PE*, March 23, 1986, 7.
[33] Dan Betzer, "Has the Rapture been Called Off?," *PE*, December 30, 1990, 10–11.
[34] James K. Bridges, "The Second Coming of Jesus Christ," *PE*, July 22, 2001, 13.

lines working for our Lord in His kingdom here and now."³⁵ Lewis argued that the desire to escape wrath was similar to the argument that "divine healing is an escape from sickness."³⁶ Paul Lowenberg wonders how one can make the charge against the AG considering the effective missions work around the world. He comments "The truth of the Rapture puts urgency into our efforts, inspiring people to leave all to obey the call of the Master of the harvest."³⁷

Inherent in the charge that the AG was eschatologically escapist was the criticism that Pentecostals are not socially conscious. To that charge, Lewis replied that early Pentecostals did not have the ability to minister to the poor because they were themselves poor. He declares, "Are we to be indicted for lack of social consciousness in those days? We were those that others should have been socially conscious about." However, he does note that "along with education came wider perception of the world's ills. Social consciousness was born in our midst."³⁸ Lewis concludes,

> Does [the rapture doctrine] make us escapists? I say it doesn't. Premillenarians are some of the most active people in the kingdom of God here and now. Most premillenarians are as socially and politically active as any other sector of evangelical Christianity regardless of eschatological views. I see my premillenarian brothers and sisters at the vanguard of world evangelization, drug rehabilitation, political activism, protest against social evils, feeding and clothing the poor, etc.³⁹

For Lewis and others, the Spirit that inspires believers to hope for Christ's return is the same Spirit that inspires evangelism and other social ministries such as Teen Challenge, orphanages, and compassion ministry.⁴⁰ During the Modern Period,

---

³⁵ David A. Lewis, "Premillenarian Rapture Believers: Are They Socially Irresponsible Escapists?," *PE*, August 16, 1987, 12–13.

³⁶ Lewis, "The Rapture of the Church," 23.

³⁷ Paul Lowenberg, "Message Under Siege," *PE*, July 5, 1987, 6–8.

³⁸ David A. Lewis, "Premillenarian Rapture Believers: Are They Socially Irresponsible Escapists?," 12–13.

³⁹ Lewis, "Premillenarian Rapture Believers: Are They Socially Irresponsible Escapists?," 12.

⁴⁰ Lewis, "Premillenarian Rapture Believers: Are They Socially Irresponsible Escapists?," 13, comments, "Before you charge premillenarians with social irresponsibility, ponder the fact that it was a premillenarian, David Wilkerson, who launched the Teen Challenge ministry, the most successful drug rehabilitation program ever known. Consider Mark Buntain, a premillenarian who built a magnificent hospital for the poor in Calcutta; who daily feeds thousands of starving children; who weeps for the soul of India."

AG ministers were more likely to see the Holy Spirit as a resource to address these injustices. As Gary McGee notes, the Spirit motivates believers to work diligently in the love of God. He says, "In a world filled with people alienated from God and from each other, Jesus' love delivers people from the chains of sin, introduces healing, builds relationships, demonstrates compassion, expresses concern for justice, and offers hope where none exists."[41]

The Kingdom Now and Not Yet

Three-quarters of a century after the AG began, articles were still skeptical of humanity's ability to solve the world's problems. Richard Orchard shares the opinion of his forbearers: "Man's efforts will never usher in Christ's kingdom. The Church will not convert the world, though it is her task to reach as many as possible for Christ."[42] It is clear to David Lewis that amillennial and postmillennial positions are undermined by the present conditions of the world. He comments, "Look at the present climate of war, violence, hate, abuse, immorality. Is this the Millennium? If the binding of Satan described in Revelation has already taken place, the devil must be on a long chain."[43] They maintained their belief that true justice and societal transformation will only come in through the millennium. Thomas Zimmerman declares,

> When Christ comes the second time, He will come to reign in righteousness (Isaiah 32:1). Injustice will cease. Man's inhumanity to man will no longer exist. Swords and implements of war will be beaten into plowshares and implements of peaceful productivity. Universal and local economic chaos will disappear.[44]

Christ alone will not accomplish the work of the millennium; Spirit filled people will aid in the glorious transformation of the future age.[45] During the millennium, "Jesus will take a devastated, polluted remnant of an earth and transform it into a beautiful paradise."[46] In the same way that the rapture was good news for the believer, the Second Coming is good news for the creation. Orchard declares, "God has not forsaken the earth. He could not forsake it after letting His Son die for it.

---

[41] Gary B. McGee, "A New World Order," *PE*, June 30, 1991, 6–7.

[42] Orchard, "Plans for This Planet," 6–7.

[43] Lewis, "War on Prophecy," 6–7.

[44] Zimmerman, "The Future is Bright," 7.

[45] Orchard, "Plans for This Planet," 7.

[46] Samuel J. Bush, "Scared to Death?," *PE*, November 29, 1987, 7.

God has a glorious goal in mind—the exaltation of His lovely Son to glory and honor before the intelligentsia of all the universe."[47]

While the millennium is considered to be the kingdom "not yet," controversies over the "Kingdom Now" teaching led to articles that focused on defining the kingdom "already." David Allen argued that Jesus came to inaugurate two aspects of the kingdom. The first is the Kingdom "in hearts of men and women," which is the "rule of Christ in the lives of men and women, continues and grows to the present time."[48] Allen emphasized the "priority" of Jesus' reign in the Spirit now, though he is convinced "the Kingdom will not be manifested in its fullest, final form until the King returns and sets up His terrestrial rule."[49] Dwight Fearing argues, "The Kingdom Now is that God is working on is in the hearts and lives of all of us … through allowing the kingdom of God to be alive and functioning within me."[50] The danger in emphasizing the kingdom now is that it could negate a desire in believers for the kingdom "not-yet." The most important thing believers can do while waiting for the true kingdom is to "be filled with the Spirit and be witnesses unto Him. His kingdom shall be manifested in due time."[51] For Gary McGee, Spirit-filled believers should live "between the 'now' of the advancing kingdom of God and the 'not yet' of the future Millennial Reign of Christ."[52]

---

[47] R.E. Orchard, "Tribulation Shadows," *PE,* November 29, 1987, 6–7.
[48] David Allen, "It's here-and it's Coming," *PE,* February 7, 1988, 6–7.
[49] Allen, "It's here-and It's Coming," 6–7.
[50] Dwight Fearing, "The Kingdom: Now or Later?," *PE,* October 30, 1988, 13.
[51] Orchard, "Plans for This Planet," 6–7.
[52] McGee, "A New World Order," 6–7.

11

Toward an Assemblies of God Eschatology

The previous chapters explored how AG adherents received eschatological beliefs as expressed through the official statements and the popular literature. Each of the four eschatological tenets have experienced a variety of expressions conditioned by the various historical contexts in which they were received. Yet, at the same time, some fundamental threads have emerged showcasing the heart of AG eschatology commitments. This chapter will synthesize these findings and formulate some conclusions about what makes for an authentic AG eschatology that will become the basis for projecting a future for AG eschatology.

A Pentecostal Eschatology

This study has corroborated William Faupel's assessment that eschatology was the overarching theme of the Pentecostal movement.[1] For the AG, eschatology was embedded in their message and received considerable attention in the resources they produced. All of the other elements of the full gospel were considered subordinate to and dependent upon the truth of the nearness of Christ's return. As D. H. McDowell famously comments, "The second coming of the Lord Jesus Christ is not a feature of a program, it is THE program."[2] They believed the Holy Spirit was being poured out because it was the last days. This allowed the early adherents to emphasize the centrality of the Holy Spirit as the primary sign in their narrative of the unfolding of the future. What the Spirit was doing in the altars of the local assembly was proof that these were the last days.

The AG understood eschatology to be intimately linked to their pneumatology. This was primarily expressed through the motif of the latter rain, which was the most common expression throughout their history. The Spirit was linked to the prophetic message that Jesus is coming, illuminated the events to come, and oriented the believer's affections toward his coming and the kingdom

---
[1] Faupel, *The Everlasting Gospel,* 20.
[2] D. H. McDowell, "The Purpose of the Coming of the Lord," *PE,* May 2, 1925, 2.

of God. However, this pneumatological emphasis was often conditioned by the level of cultural disruptions taking place in the world around them. The cultural lens by which they saw the world often created a definite ebb and flow between emphasis on empirical "sign eschatology," such as Israel, wars, earthquakes, and the pneumatological emphasis on the Spirit or "sigh eschatology" that saw tongues, gifts, and the groaning of creation as signs of the end.

In the beginning, the AG viewed the manifestations of the Spirit as the primary "signs" of Christ's coming. In the first few months following the first General Council in April 1914, articles in the *Pentecostal Evangel* boldly proclaimed that Jesus was coming, but there was little attention given to the prophetic and signs of the times. Two years later in 1916 when the AG codified their doctrinal position on eschatological topics, they chose four key premillennial commitments that were thematically centered in a hopeful imagination of the future.

However, over the next three years, the world had become embroiled in a worldwide conflict, which captured the eschatological imagination and fueled apocalyptic rhetoric and religious zeal. Believers watched Biblical prophecies unfold as nations were realigned, human violence reached its zenith, and Zionist hopes of a state of Israel began to become a reality. The power of these social-political images began to take control of the narrative and became a more powerful sign of the end times than the latter rain of the Spirit. At the same time, internally the AG was engaged in its own controversy as the New Issue was causing division and sectarianism that led them to reluctantly adopt a statement of faith. The pessimism from the war and the self-imposed isolation of the AG contributed to the waning of Pentecostal fervor that characterized Azusa.

For the next two decades, the AG wrestled with a growing sense of permanence that came with the delay in Christ's coming. By the beginning of the Scholastic Period (1927), events happening around the world, especially in Israel, started to carry equal weight in the eschatological imagination of the AG. When the *SFT* was revised in 1927, a new generation of AG leaders shifted the articulation of the official statements toward a more chronological orientation. By focusing on the world, they had lost their focus on what made them unique: the outpouring of the Spirit. These subtle shifts in emphasis were accompanied by an internal stirring as AG adherents sought to recapture the early fervency by emphasizing the Holy Spirit and the Second Coming. Fears that the AG had become too institutional and had lost its Pentecostal identity led to the controversy of the New Order of the Latter Rain. The criticisms led the leadership to intentionally emphasize their identity as a latter rain end time fellowship.

Just as the AG re-embraced the Spirit as their primary sign, another monumental turning point took place in the establishment of the nation of Israel in 1948. Israel's birth as a nation naturally led to a resurgence of dispensational expressions. Although there was enthusiasm over the new prophetic reality, there was also a level of concern, as the spiritual conditions in Israel did not align with their idyllic prophetic expectations. For all its prophetic significance, the establishment of a state for Israel led to some question if the new nation was truly a sign. Meanwhile, a renewed pneumatological emphasis emerged during the 1950s–1960s coinciding with the healing revivals and charismatic movement.

At the same time, the growing nuclear threat and start of the Cold War turned the AG's attention to apocalyptic visions of the future and the pneumatic emphasis was short lived. By 1961, eschatology became a topic of controversy and the leadership revised the *SFT* in ways that fossilized the chronological orientation in a way that controlled the perception of its orientation during the Evangelical Period. Although the dispensational expressions continued to enjoy acceptance in popular AG culture, the fatigue of speculation and the fundamentalist orientation inspired a new generation of educated AG ministers to raise questions about the validity of the dispensational system.

The long-standing tension surrounding speculation reached a head in the Modern Period and as a result the AG eventually avoided all forms of sign-based eschatology. Many in the AG were longing to find an eschatology that placed a priority on the Spirit. As AG leadership faced questions and controversies concerning its eschatological orientation, it struggled to maintain its commitment to the four truths in a way that satisfied the scholars without undermining the doctrine. Consequently, the AG has been at a theological impasse since the beginning of the Modern Period as little emphasis has been placed on the Second Coming in the *Pentecostal Evangel* and few books have been produced.

The current efforts among AG scholars to "revision" Pentecostal eschatology is primarily a reaction to decades of neglect and lack of pneumatological orientation in the way the AG has expressed it eschatology. Most of the critiques focus on the co-option of fundamentalist dispensationalism as the primary factor that contributed to this lack. However, this study has demonstrated that these critiques are only partially correct. It is true that the AG has often articulated an eschatology that was indistinguishable from fundamentalist dispensationalism and completely devoid of any pneumatological elements; but, this study has also shown that there were also periods in which the AG actively proclaimed the type of pneumatologically focused eschatology that many of Pentecostal scholars have desired to see.

The survey of periodical literature demonstrated ten distinctly pneumatological characteristics that have been present to varying degrees and in various periods in the AG's history:

1. The baptism in the Holy Spirit is an eschatological sign of the last days and recipients often emphasized "Jesus is coming soon,"

2. The Spirit prepares the bride for the coming of the Bridegroom through acts of sanctification,

3. The Spirit is the revealer of the events to come and enables believers to interpret the "signs of the times,"

4. The baptism in the Spirit is the down payment of the promise of the resurrection of the body,

5. The Spirit hopes with creation for the resurrection and the final act of cosmic salvation,

6. The Spirit enables believers to shape their affections to hope, groan, long, and patiently wait for Christ's return,

7. The Spirit enables the end time impulse to reach the lost and engage in compassion ministry,

8. The Spirit is a demonstration of the kingdom of God through eschatological signs of tongues, healing, signs and wonders,

9. The Spirit is the "restraining" influence on society that is holding back the evil of the last days, and

10. The Spirit will be poured out during the millennium in order to facilitate the process of renewal and rejuvenation of the earth under the Messiah's rule.

Each of these pneumatological elements represent uniquely Pentecostal modifications to the common tenets of premillennial and dispensational systems.

These modifications are consistent emphases present in each period of the past century, although they exist to greater or lesser degrees.

Sign vs. Sigh Eschatology

Despite this strong pneumatological orientation, over the last century AG eschatology has vacillated back and forth between distinctly Pentecostal expressions and those indistinguishable from fundamentalist dispensationalism. Because of this, what scholars have seen as "uneasy tensions" created by the "co-option" of fundamentalism is better understood to be the presence of two parallel trajectories in pneumatological emphasis. The first trajectory places a priority on the outpouring of the Spirit the primary sign as of the last days. This "sigh eschatology" placed more emphasis on what God was doing in the altars of AG churches than what was taking place in the newspapers. It is reminiscent of Peter's message on Pentecost of "this is that" in that the Spirit coming on all flesh was the sign of the last days (Acts 2:16–17). This is what I would term "sigh eschatology" because it focused on the Spirit's "sighing" or groaning for redemption within the believer as the primary sign of the nearness of Christ's coming (Rom. 8:18–27). Many of these articulations emphasized the Spirit's affective work in loving and waiting for his coming, longing for redemption and resurrection, discerning the times, and being empowered to witness. They were deeply pneumatological in that the Spirit inspired hope of the coming of Christ transformation of all creation.

The second eschatology trajectory places an emphasis on the Holy Spirit, only in a way that defines the Spirit's role as interpreter signs taking place in the world. This "sign eschatology" is a more traditional understanding of Biblical prophecy that also employed an empirical approach animated by a cultural hermeneutic by which events in the local newspaper were correlated with biblical prophecy in order to determine the nearness of Christ's coming.[3] In this form of "this is that"

---

[3] The empirical approach was common in the works of Frank Boyd, *The Budding Fig Tree* (Springfield: Gospel Publishing House, 1925); Stanley Frodsham, *Things Which Must Shortly Come To Pass*, (Springfield: Gospel Publishing House, 1928); Frank Boyd, *Signs of the Times*, (Springfield: Gospel Publishing House, 1950); C. M. Ward, *Waiting...* (Springfield: Gospel Publishing House, 1959). This approach attempts to prove the nearness of the return of Christ by correlating the signs of the times from Jesus' apocalyptic discourse in Matthew 24 with current events. Scripture takes a secondary role to empirical evidences such as the number of earthquakes, crime statistics, the amount of money spent on alcohol, political situations, divorce rates, war and death statistics, and other cultural indicators of moral and spiritual decay. This approach was popular in the earlier years but by 1960, no other works used this approach.

trajectory, the more signs one could document, the closer one was felt to be to the end. Often, this approach led to an emphasis on knowing how close the believer is to being delivered from the world through the rapture. With escape being the primary motivation, there was a greater emphasis placed on heaven and consequently the importance of the resurrected body was diminished.

What these two trajectories demonstrate is that rather than being a linear progression through AG history from a pneumatic orientation to fundamentalist oriented eschatology, it would be more accurate to argue that the AG vacillated like a pendulum between a preoccupation with dispensationally oriented subjective cultural signs and pneumatically oriented objective "sighs" of the Spirit's encounters in people's lives. These two forces pushed against each other and interpreters never completely adopted one over the other.

FIGURE 4: VACILLATING EMPHASIS BETWEEN SIGHS AND SIGNS

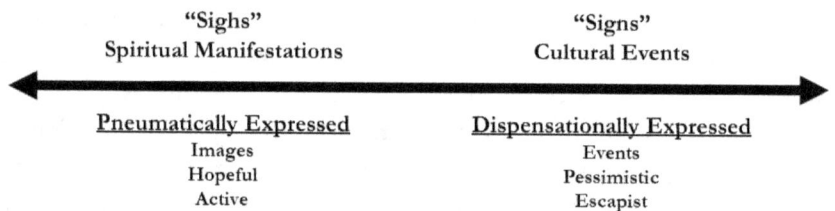

To be fair, when one evaluates AG eschatology simply by comparing the script and order of events, there is little difference from fundamentalist expressions of dispensationalism premillennialism. However, I am suggesting that the order of events was not the determining factor of what made their eschatology Pentecostal or non-Pentecostal; it was whether the Spirit was the foundational orientation and the primary sign of the last days.

When interpreters in the AG employed a Spirit-hermeneutic, they imagined the future optimistically based on what the Spirit was doing in people's lives. They looked to the altars rather than the newspapers for signs that Jesus was coming. The baptism in the Spirit, healing, and miracles generated a sense that God doing positive things in the world through the outpouring of the Spirit. But, when they employed a cultural hermeneutic, they often interpreted the future pessimistically because they were focusing primarily on what is wrong with the world. When negative signs were emphasized, they were more pessimistic and more likely to see the Second Coming as a way of escape.

Therefore, it should be recognized that the script alone is not necessarily sufficient justification for a new model, since there were periods of hopeful and pneumatic expressions of eschatology despite maintaining the basic script of the future. Rather, the challenge for the AG is to maintain the positive and pneumatological orientation embedded in the eschatology. How can AG ministers stay rooted in the work of the Spirit and avoid the endless speculation and obsession with the negative view of culture? To this, we turn to the latent expressions of the "theology of hope."

A Theology of Hope

Dispensationalism is criticized for its pessimism, withdrawal mentality, and hope of escape from the world. Because of this, as we have seen, many Pentecostal scholars recommended revisioning towards a "theology of hope" over apocalyptic options of fundamentalist eschatology. And yet, this study has revealed that a hope-filled eschatology is not something foreign to the AG's historical expressions. There are three important hopeful aspects that are consistent with these calls for more hopeful revisions of AG eschatology. First, for a century Second Coming tenet has remained titled "The Blessed Hope." Over and again, the Second Coming is portrayed as a blessed hope because it is the promise of the future salvation of the believer: body, soul, and spirit. Even with the changes made to the SFT, nothing in this statement indicates that the AG places their hope in escaping from the world. This is not to say that some did not focus on the rapture as a hope of escape from God's wrath on those left behind. But it is important to note that this escapist attitude was particularly noticeable when AG writers were focused on defending pretribulational positions.[4] But for the most part, it was the hopeful aspects of Christ's coming—the promise of redemption—that were foremost AG's eschatological imagination Even for Stanley Horton, the AG's most ardent defender of pretribulationism, hope is defined as, "our resurrection, our new bodies, our reigning with Christ and our eternal future."[5]

Second, the AG emphasizes hope as an essential aspect of their picture of God. In this survey, there are few of the wrathful and fiery warnings about judgment that often accompany popular portrayals of apocalyptic eschatology. Instead, one sees and emphasis on God as a "God of hope" who fills his people with hope.[6]

---

[4] When articles emphasized escape from coming wrath, the concepts of rapture, escape, and heaven were at the forefront. This was particularly the case during the Evangelical Period when, fueled by the impulse to defend eschatological AG positions.

[5] Horton, "Last Things," 598.

[6] J. W. Welch, "Looking for the Glorious Hope," *WE*, November 13, 1915, 2.

The ultimate source of that hope was the Holy Spirit, who was cherished as the deposit of God's promise of resurrection and who inspired believers to wait in eager anticipation of their glorification.

Finally, the Blessed Hope is relational in that as Pentecostals, they often drew from the bridal imagery of eschatological passages to emphasize the Spirit as the primary bond between Christ and his bride. So, while the propositional truth that Jesus is coming was certainly important, the Spirit elicited in these believers a strong affective response to "love his appearing" and look forward to when they will "forever be with the Lord." It is the believer's love for Jesus, brought about by the Spirit, which stirs the heart to cry out, "Come, Lord Jesus!" This relational nearness to Christ through the Spirit also empowers the preaching of the gospel, holy living, and willingness to stay faithful to Christ.

Premillennialism

The primary hallmark of AG eschatology over the past century has been its unswerving commitment to premillennial eschatology. Because they rejected the myth of progress found in postmillennialism and the over-spiritualization of Scripture in amillennialism, in their minds, premillennialism was the only option that took the Bible's statements about the future "as literal as possible" and fit with their dispensational understanding of the latter rain.[7] The expectation of a literal kingdom is based on more than a futurist and literalist interpretation of Revelation. In their Luke-Acts orientation, the AG fully expects that the Lord will "restore the Kingdom to Israel" (Acts 1:4). Without the literal future kingdom, there would be no reason for Christ to return in the same manner he left (Acts 1:11). The commitment to the premillennial return of Christ is the starting point for all the subsequent eschatological doctrines. The millennial kingdom is therefore the beginning of God's eschatological process toward cosmic salvation.

The second way the millennium functions in AG eschatology is as a transitional period of sanctification. The rapid decline of the world before the return of the Lord will leave the world in chaos. However, Jesus will return to set up his kingdom and "will take a devastated, polluted remnant of an earth and transform it into a beautiful paradise."[8] The millennium will be a period of Sabbath and Jubilee and the primary beneficiary of this time of renewal will be creation itself. This process of sanctification is made possible because the curse

---

[7] Horton, "The End Times," 622.

[8] Samuel J. Bush, "Scared to Death?," *PE*, November 29, 1987, 7.

will be reversed, and the Spirit will renew all aspects of human existence. The nations of the world will come under his rule and humanity will enjoy life free from sickness and death, economic prosperity, ideal agricultural conditions, political prosperity under the rule of Christ, and the flourishing of human creativity and culture. Although the Pentecostal movement is the fulfillment of the promise of the latter rain, it is only a foretaste of the outpouring of the Spirit that will take place during the millennium. Unhindered by sin in their resurrected state, believers will rule and reign in the fullness of the Spirit. The eschatological end will culminate after the millennium when the kingdom will be delivered unto the Father and God will become all in all. So, in the AG's eschatological imagination, the renewal of creation is the work of the Spirit, which begins creation's salvation at the resurrection, sanctification during the millennial reign, and glorification in the new heavens and new earth.

The third way the millennium functions in AG eschatology is with regard to the future of Israel and the fulfillment of the OT promises concerning the kingdom. The 1916 *SFT* emphasized the church's role during the millennium rather than Israel's role, but the details about the actual nature of the millennium were rarely discussed. The Balfour Declaration in 1917 and the possibility of a restored Israel impacted the way they imagined the reign of Christ. Consequently, when the *SFT* was revised in 1927, the AG added the expectation of the "salvation of Israel" to its vision of the millennium. Over the next four decades, progress toward establishing an official state of Israel not only became a primary sign of the nearness of Christ's return, but also became the primary purpose of the millennium. By 1961, the AG's position concerning the coming salvation of the Jews closely mirrored a dispensational understanding of Israel's role in the future and the *SFT* was revised to clearly articulate that position.

Support for a future for Israel was based on two primarily pneumatological premises. First, the latter rain orientation of AG eschatology was built on the premise that what was happening physically in Israel corresponded to what was happening spiritually in the Pentecostal movement. The sign of Israel and the sign of the Holy Spirit were often parallel signs that pointed to the nearness of the return of Christ. However, in times when there was greater political movement within Israel, the AG's eschatology favored Israel as the primary sign and often led to more dispensational articulations. Second, the AG understood their experiences in the Spirit as foreshadowing the realities of the Messianic kingdom to be fulfilled in the millennium. The "salvation of national Israel" found in the *SFT* affirms that Israel will only be saved when Jesus is revealed as Israel's Messiah. They believed Israel would eventually be fully restored as a nation, but this would not happen fully until the millennium. So then, the AG's concept of a restored Israel is one that is dependent upon the outpouring of the Spirit on Israel.

While supporting Israel on eschatological grounds, they did not confuse the political state of Israel with the eschatological Israel that will be saved during the millennium. This differentiation allowed many AG writers to feel justified in raising theological and ethical questions about the present social-political issues surrounding Israel. To further complicate Israel's legitimacy, AG writers were concerned about the Jewish hostility toward Christians and missionaries, the treatment of Arabs in occupied territories, and the attempts to restore the Jewish sacrificial system. Eric Newberg contends that during the period of the late 1950s to 1970s, the AG's dispensational eschatology caused them to abandon their missions efforts to Jewish people in Palestine and focused their efforts on evangelizing Arabs and non-evangelical Christians.[9] While Newberg's argument has merit, this study demonstrated that evangelism of Jews remained a priority, and some of the greatest criticisms of Israel came from ministry to Jewish people.[10] According to some writers, the evangelistic mission to the Jewish people was hindered by Israel becoming a nation, not by philosemitism inherent in the AG's eschatological orientation. In a recent position paper on Israel and Palestine, the AG admits "warm feelings" for Israel, but denies that being "pro-Israel" means having to be "anti-Palestinian."[11] Furthermore, it discourages "extremists" who are trying to "help God" fulfill prophecy by helping the Jews. The paper concludes "Though we have emotional ties and affections with Israel, we cannot endorse and approve every action of a particular country whether right or wrong. Our faith calls us to pray for peace and seek to share the gospel message with all who are lost and without a Savior."

Even with a strong "futurist" orientation, the AG did not relegate the kingdom entirely to the future as fundamentalist dispensationalism does. The concept of the "already/not yet," which is popular among Pentecostal scholars

---

[9] Newberg, *The Pentecostal Mission in Palestine*, 127–53, argues that Pentecostal missionaries in Palestine contributed to philosemitism in the AG by enabling the importation of eschatological Zionism and by exporting Islamophobia to the US through missionary reports. This led to a shift in Pentecostal missionary activity from evangelizing Jews and Muslims in favor of neglecting outreach to Muslims, evangelizing Arab Christians, and supporting Jews instead of evangelizing them.

[10] Morris Zeidman, "Restoration of the Kingdom," *PE*, May 1, 1948, 2; Louis Hauff, "A Sign of the Times," *PE*, February 5, 1956, 6–7, "The Gravest Danger," *PE*, October 16, 1948, 9.

[11] This position is made clear in a paper issued called, "Israel - the Church's Response," https://ag.org/Beliefs/Topics-Index/Israel-the-Churchs-Response (accessed 26 December 2017).

today, was present from the beginning in AG writings. As one writer noted, the kingdom of God is present through "salvation, baptism in the Holy Ghost, healing for the sick, and spiritual gifts."[12] The tension between the "now and not yet" was first articulated when AG leaders cautioned the use of the *Scofield Bible* due to its promotion of a "postponed kingdom" and argued that the baptism in the Spirit was proof that the kingdom of God is available today. At times, the AG would place more emphasis on the future kingdom when Israel took center stage. But the revival of Spirit-oriented eschatology in the 1960s and the emergence of Ladd's already/not yet concept in educated circles revived the emphasis on the proleptic aspects of the kingdom. The 1988 position paper on the Kingdom of God set forth in the clearest possible terms the AG position that the kingdom is already in the Spirit demonstrated by signs, wonders, and miracles and that there will be a literal kingdom in the future.

Modified Dispensationalism

The previous chapters demonstrated that the AG consistently used dispensational eschatology as the framework for the understanding of end time events. Articles in the *Pentecostal Evangel* were not overly concerned with articulating the niceties of "dispensational truth," but the script of dispensational events was followed. In one sense, this study has agreed with McQueen that the AG adopted the dispensational script from the beginning without much variation and was not "gradually adopted" with the rise of Fundamentalism.[13]

Throughout this study, the basic characteristics of a literalist and futurist premillennial and dispensational eschatology were present: (1) the secret rapture of the church most often portrayed as prior to the tribulation, (2) the return of the Jews to Palestine prior to Jesus' return, (3) the rise of the Antichrist during the tribulation, (4) the return of the Christ at the end of the tribulation (5) The establishment of a literal 1000 year millennium, (6) the establishment of the kingdom in fulfillment of OT prophecies about Israel, (7) the final judgment followed by the eternal states of heaven and hell, and (8) the new heavens and the new earth.[14] Ideas from Darby and Scofield dispensationalism are present,

---

[12] C. W. Doney, "The Gospel of the Kingdom," *WW*, March 1914, 2; "The Kingdom," *PE*, Second Coming Supplement, September 10, 1920, 6.

[13] This conclusion disagrees with the "gradual adoption" concept found in Sheppard, "Pentecostals and the Hermeneutics of Dispensationalism," 10; Althouse, *Spirit of the Last Days*, 41; Althouse, "The Landscape of Pentecostal and Charismatic Eschatology," 15.

[14] This confirms the "dispensational script" in McQueen, *Toward a Pentecostal Eschatology*, 172.

such as the two-fold rapture and the division between the church and Israel, but many of the elements were equally held by historic premillennialists of the day.

Furthermore, the *SFT* began as a general script of events but eventually became more specific in articulating the fundamentalist dispensational script. But there are also many details that are missing such as the tribulation, the role of antichrist, and the battle of Armageddon. In the end, the AG statements of faith present the order of events clearer than the theology behind the events.

However, a significant contribution made by this study is to point out the need to nuance and perhaps even reconsider the claim that the AG uncritically adopted the fundamentalist models of dispensationalism wholesale. This study agrees with W. Menzies that the AG intentionally modified their particular brand of dispensationalism in ways that resolved the tensions to fit their pneumatology.[15] The key theological presupposition that allowed the AG to modify this dispensational theology was the concept of the latter rain. The dispensational orientation of the latter rain predates the founding of the AG and was the primary theology of the whole Pentecostal movement.[16] By employing the latter rain motif, the AG adopted the chronological script of dispensationalism but made six significant pneumatological modifications to its theology: (1) a modified cessationist parenthesis that explained the latter rain philosophy of history, (2) a modified concept of "signs" that prioritized the restorationist phenomena of the baptism in the Spirit, speaking in tongues, and spiritual gifts, (3) at times a Pentecostal view of the Spirit-baptized bride, (4) a modified ecclesiological separation of the Church and Israel in which there is an ethnic and prophetic separation but not a soteriological one, (5) a modified concept of the kingdom of God in which the kingdom is present now in the manifestations of the Spirit which anticipate the kingdom to come, and (6) a modified vision of the Spirit's work to renew the creation which was non-apocalyptic and emphasized the continuity between the present and future creation. In light of these pneumatological modifications reflecting decidedly Pentecostal beliefs and practices, perceptions about the pneumatological orientation of AG eschatology need to be reconsidered.

In a sense, all Pentecostal eschatology, historically understood, cannot avoid being at minimum a form of dispensationalism because of its adoption of the "latter rain" philosophy of history. As restorationists, they were dependent on a

---

[15] Menzies, *Anointed to Serve*, 329. It is somewhat ironic that Menzies assessment, which likely inspired Sheppard to conduct his research, has been shown by this study to be the most accurate portrayal of the type of dispensational eschatology found in the AG.

[16] Yong, *In the Days of Caesar*, 321; Thompson, *Kingdom Come*, 53.

dispensational and partly cessationist view of the Spirit's work in history in order to justify the belief that the Pentecostal movement was the renewal of Apostolic Christianity in preparation for the Second Coming of Christ. Although their dismal view of the church fit well their conception of the bride of Christ, this position became less tenable for some modern AG historians who downplayed the latter rain philosophy of history in favor of a continuationist position.[17] A continuationist orientation allows for the Spirit to be present at various times in history while at the same time recognizing the unique expression of Pentecostal phenomenon.[18] By placing all of church history into the "Age of the Spirit," it opens up the possibility of a sovereign latter rain outpouring that culminates with the Pentecostal movement without being a-historical or holding to complete cessationism. This is why historians William Menzies and Carl Brumback speak of the Pentecostal movement as an "eschatological continuation and completion of the historical work of God" rather than a latter rain restoration.[19] This model is also preferred by modern scholars such as Craig Keener, who prefers to see history as an "ebb and flow" of spiritual activity in the form of periods of revival and apostasy.[20]

In light of these modifications, I am convinced that the AG adopted not fundamentalist or even Scofieldian dispensationalism; rather what evangelical scholars term "progressive dispensationalism."[21] Progressive dispensationalism differs from classical dispensationalism in that although it uses the same script of

---

[17] B. F. Lawrence, *Apostolic Faith Restored*, (Springfield: Gospel Publishing House, 1916); Stanley Frodsham, *With Signs Following* (Springfield: Gospel Publishing House, 1926). Both Lawrence and Frodsham give an apologetic for the experience of Spirit–baptism but more so they draw on occurrences throughout history where charismatic gifts and glossolalia have been present to validate the movement's legitimacy as from God. Both historians recognize the various places prior to Azusa where the Spirit was poured out during the mid and late 1800s.

[18] Vondey, *Beyond Pentecostalism*, 153.

[19] Menzies, *Anointed to Serve*, 57–78, frames the Pentecostal movement in terms of a revival of apostolic Christianity rather than a last days restoration. This allows him to see the Spirit at work in various times while at the same time recognizing the unique expression of Pentecostal phenomenon. Brumback, *Suddenly…From Heaven*, 349–50, holds a similar position and in his time, as the revival was thought to be waning, he says, "One thing which we trust has been made clear by this historical record is that however this revival may end, it began in the Spirit!"

[20] Craig L. Keener, *Spirit Hermeneutics* (Grand Rapids: Eerdmans, 2016), 50.

[21] The term "progressive dispensationalism" is a modern term, but I am arguing that the type of modifications contemporary progressive dispensationalists employ are similar to AG modification. For a brief discussion of the difference in ecclesiology between classical and progressive dispensationalism see Alan Hultber, Craig A. Blasing, and Douglas J. Moo, *Three Views on the Rapture: Pretribulation, Prewrath, or Postribulation* (Grand Rapids: Zondervan, 2010), 68–72; Craig A. Blaising and Darrell L. Bock, *Progressive Dispensationalism* (Grand Rapids: Zondervan, 1993).

events, there is a different theology that orients the script. In progressive dispensationalism, the rapture does not function as a way to dispensationally separate the Jews from the church, nor does it restrict the saving activity of the Spirit during the tribulation. It does make a distinction between Israel and the church in terms of organization, ethnicity, politically, and historically but does not separate them for soteriological purposes. Salvation is possible in the same way for both Jews and Gentiles through the gospel of Jesus Christ. At the same time, Israel is a distinct ethnic people who have a prophetic destiny that will fulfill the OT promises about the millennium. These differences fit perfectly into the AG's Pentecostal and dispensational orientation. The script may have much in common with what was popularized by Scofield, but the theology came from the latter rain eschatology grounded in the outpouring of the Spirit. The AG did not need to adopt fundamentalist forms of dispensationalism because they had their own Pentecostal form of dispensational assumptions that governed the way they imagined the future.

When it comes to the central tenet of dispensationalism, the pretribulation rapture, this survey has confirmed the assertion of Sheppard, as well as Menzies and Anderson, that the AG doctrinal statements do not necessarily officially endorse a tribulational position.[22] The term "rapture" was present in the Blessed Hope article in 1916, but was curiously removed in 1927 in favor of the term "translation" and has remained absent ever since. The term returned in 1961 in the millennium article but was not coupled with any statement on the tribulation. The only official document that affirms a position on the tribulation is the Rapture Position Paper, which is decidedly pretribulational. Even in the controversies that created the 1980 "Committee on Loopholes," the AG declined to make the pretribulation position the official position. The ambiguous nature of the AG's position on this central doctrine by itself should alert us to the fact that AG eschatology did not blindly accept classical or fundamentalist eschatology.

The openness to tribulational variety is also illustrated by the 1937 "Allowance Clause," which allowed ministers to hold post-tribulational positions as long as they didn't teach it. The expansion of the "Allowance Clause" in 1961 to include all eschatological errors meant that AG ministers are allowed by the AG constitution to hold pre- and mid-tribulation positions openly as well as post-tribulation and amillennial views privately. While it is uncertain if, at the popular level, the AG would be comfortable with this position, from a legal

---

[22] Sheppard, "Pentecostals and the Hermeneutics of Dispensationalism," 8; Menzies and Anderson, "D. W. Kerr and Eschatological Diversity," 15.

standpoint the official AG position remains sufficiently open to allow diversity of opinion. As J. R. Flower commented, "There is so much room for speculation here that it behooves none of us to be dogmatic."[23] Regardless of the diversity of opinion on when the church will be raptured out of the tribulation—pre, mid, or both—the assumption that there will be a tribulation is not really in question. A firmly established commitment to the two-phase coming assured that a period must exist between the two comings. Their "finished work" theology could not allow Christians to endure the wrath of God. Even though they believed Christians would certainly endure "tribulation" in this life, the earthly trials and persecutions cannot be equated to the wraths of judgment predicted in a futurist interpretation of Revelation.

Another popular tenet of dispensationalism is the idea that the Holy Spirit will be removed from the earth before the tribulation. But this position presents multiple problems for both the ubiquitous nature of the Spirit and the soteriological and phenomenological operation of the Spirit. Instead, several AG writers modified this position to argue that the Spirit will not only remain on earth during the tribulation, but the Spirit will be essential to the sanctifying work of the tribulation.[24] Elizabeth Sisson believed the tribulation was a "remedy" of the Spirit and an act of God's love that will sanctify the Church, the Jews, and the nations before Jesus returns.[25] She says, "A new expression of his love! Judgment is His second remedy when His first has proved ineffectual."[26] The tribulation serves to revive the Church who is left behind, bring Israel to repentance, and prepare the nations for the rule of Christ in the millennium. This sanctifying concept is imbued with pneumatological imagery found in the Lukan pronouncement that the Spirit will baptize "with fire."[27] To conceive of the tribulation as restorative rather than punitive offers a powerful pneumatic alternative to the traditional views of the tribulation as God's wrath and opens up the Spirit to work in sanctification, repentance, and renewal (John 16:8–11).

---

[23] J. R. Flower, "Living in Momentous Days," *WE* July 14, 1917, 8, where he notes that there are different interpretations of whether the rapture will happen at the beginning of the tribulation and concedes that the coming could be at the beginning or middle of the tribulation.

[24] Richard W. Klinge, "The Work of the Spirit in the Tribulation," *Paraclete* 19, no. 2 (1985): 24–27. Cf. Riggs, *The Path of Prophecy*, 113.

[25] Elizabeth Sisson, "These Wars! Why?" *LRE*, July 1916, 16.

[26] Sisson, "These Wars! Why?," 16.

[27] Macchia, *Baptized in the Spirit*, 99, argues for a similar concept in that the metaphor of "baptism in the Spirit" implies a divine spiritual work of "purgation and restoration" in preparation for the kingdom of God.

Each of these examples of the fundamental concepts found in dispensationalism were modified based on pneumatological considerations that gave AG eschatology a unique Pentecostal expression. Although the basic structure mirrored fundamentalist dispensationalism, to say the AG adopted fundamentalist dispensationalism fails to appreciate the true character of their doctrine. Though some might argue that the AG did not differentiate enough from the basic framework of dispensationalism, they certainly wrestled with the tensions and found ways to place a priority on their Pentecostal theology.

Transformationalist Eschatology

One of the biggest concerns expressed by AG scholars is the fear that dispensational eschatology has encouraged escapism and quietism about social, political, economic, and ecological issues. While the AG persistently rejected the postmillennial vision of reform in favor of premillennialism, this study has confirmed Murray Dempster's research in that although the rapture doctrine has the "potential" for escapism, which at times the AG engaged in, there were also streams of resistance within the AG that rejected the attitudes of neglect and withdrawal.[28] Escapist attitudes certainly existed, however, escapism was simply one response to this orientation; there was equal potential within their eschatology to promote active engagement. The imminence of Christ's return fueled the AG's missionary impulse, not just to "snatch from the fire," but also to meet felt human needs at practical levels through compassion ministry, orphanages, and rescue homes.[29]

There are three primary ways to understand how social issues fit into the AG's eschatological imagination. First, they rejected the postmillennial vision that human effort, whether secular or religious, can ultimately reform society. The myth of human progress and achievement was exposed as the world's most

---

[28] Dempster, "Eschatology, Spirit Baptism, and Inclusiveness," 157; Lewis, "Premillenarian Rapture Believers: Are They Socially Irresponsible Escapists?," 12. It should be pointed out that escapism is a potential attitude based on the reality of the nearness of Christ's return whether one is committed to a dispensational concept of a tribulational period or not. If one believes in imminence, that Christ could come at any moment, then the present order is near to the end. So it is not the adoption of dispensationalism that creates this potential, but the doctrine of imminence, which is present in both historic premillennialism as well as dispensational premillennialism.

[29] Dempster, "Eschatology, Spirit Baptism, and Inclusiveness," 158, argues "Responding to human need within a global context with its various cultural matrixes became a practical component in gaining a hearing for the 'good news' of God's salvation and has generated a staggering proliferation of social programs in all sectors of the Pentecostal movement."

advanced societies were also responsible for some of the greatest destruction of human life the world had witnessed. At the same time, whatever reluctance they expressed about relying upon human effort, they did not encourage passivity in meeting people's felt needs.

Second, they prioritized evangelism over social effort, but not to the exclusion of it. Most of the problems of the world were really sin issues that education and enlightenment do not have the power to overcome. The AG relied heavily on the gospel of the kingdom to address society's issues. As one writer noted, saved people become better people, which is the "shortest path to all social reform."[30] While social welfare was not their priority, they did acknowledge social injustice such as exploitation, human trafficking, war, poverty, and ecological destruction and acknowledged the Christian responsibility to work to save the exploited, feed the poor, work in addiction recovery, and in later years engage in compassion ministry. Even so, the AG was often selective in the types of social issues they chose to engage in. The AG's silence on racial issues, its checkered past concerning the roles of women, and its suspicion of public education justifiably leaves questions about the AG's overall commitment to social justice.

Third, this study found no evidence that AG eschatology advocated a reckless attitude toward the environment. There is little apocalyptic language in the official statements apart from the tenet of the final judgment. On the contrary, writers held a tranformationalist vision of the future, one in which they imagined the renewal of the earth and the reversal of the effects of sin upon creation. The apocalyptic notions of annihilation present in the popular literature were a minority position that was most visible during times when the possibility of massive destruction was at the forefront of their eschatological imagination. Particularly in the 1970s, writers were aware of the ecological dangers that pollution, global warming, and exploitation have caused and believed they were the direct consequences of humanity's sin, greed, and corruption. Even with these convictions, the AG stopped short of becoming advocates for conservation because of the persistent fear that "social gospel" solutions would take priority over spiritual issues.[31]

---

[30] R. M. Russell, "Prophecy and Present Events," *PE*, April 16, 1921, 9.

[31] In 2005, in a growing recognition of the need to emphasize compassion ministry, the General Council voted to expand its prerogatives to include "to respond to human need with ministries of compassion." *GC Minutes* (August 2–5, 2005), 32. While the issue of social engagement has garnered support, at the most recent GC in 2017, Resolution 3 on "Compassion, Justice, and Peacemaking" was withdrawn because it was controversial in its orientation toward "social justice." http://generalcouncil.ag.org/Business (Accessed 14 December 2017). Minutes have not yet been published.

With each of these insights from the past concerning the history of AG expressions of Second Coming of Jesus, we now will turn our attention to the question, "What is the future of AG eschatology?"

PART THREE

THE FUTURE OF ASSEMBLIES OF GOD ESCHATOLOGY

12

IMAGINING THE FUTURE

This study has sought to understand the origins and development of AG eschatology with the ultimate goal of trying to establish what is unique about the denomination's eschatology. This task has no doubt proved to be challenging because, while the four fundamentals endured, in each generation official statements were revised, the emphasis shifted, and theological reflection matured. This reality exposes the fallacy held by some who have maintained that AG positions have remained unchanged and therefore need no further revision.[1] But this position is also very common at the popular level in those who want the SFT to carry a sense of permanence and inerrancy. However, this study has shown that at both the official and popular levels of expression, there is no consensus concerning these expressions that would argue for any sense of permanence. An originalist might argue that whatever the AG originally believed is the heart of what should be believed today. For them, one only needs to go back to what was in the original statements to understand the "true" AG position. Still others may argue that what constitutes the AG position is what is expressed in their local churches, popular theology, or Bible Colleges. But as Alister McGrath points out, these are naïve understandings that fail to take into account the historical development of doctrines and their function within a Christian community.[2] Alternatively, it is equally problematic for contemporary scholars to argue the AG needs alternatives outside of what have historically been held by the community. This would be to strip the community of its distinctive identity and demarcation from other communities. To me, all the aforementioned options are ultimately privileging one

---

[1] Menzies, *Anointed to Serve*, 317, states that "no changes whatsoever were made until the General Council in 1961" and the changes were only a "minor rewording." Similarly, Thomas Zimmerman in the *AG Minister Letter*, November 6, 1961, 2, comments, "By this action the General Council of the Assemblies of God has told the world that its faith in the Full Gospel as declared forty-five years ago is still unchanged and unwavering. In some points the Statement of Fundamental Truths was actually strengthened and the emphasis which we have placed previously upon precious truths became even more intense."

[2] McGrath, *The Genesis of Doctrine*, 37–52.

particular expression against the broader variations that have been present through the entire history. Therefore, I agree with Peter Althouse when he argues, "Neither a simple re-institution of the doctrines of the early movement, nor the wholesale abandoning of Pentecostal heritage is helpful, but rather a re-thinking of Pentecostal eschatology in a contemporary way which does justice to both."[3]

However, in the attempt to "do justice to both," what one may posit as an alternative may not necessarily be helpful in expressing what it means to be AG. For example, simply dispensing with dispensational eschatology in favor of other models of premillennialism (or having no position at all) would only be seen as a move to abandon an essential part of the denominational identity. Therefore, whatever alternatives are suggested, if they are not grounded in what it has historically meant, they cannot help but move AG eschatology away from its core identity and will never convince those within the community that such moves are needed. In the same way that current scholars lament the adoption of fundamentalist theological presuppositions, attempts to adopt other theological frameworks could have similar results. Alternative theologies can inform and deepen one's understanding of the doctrines, but they cannot replace them. True doctrinal development occurs by listening to those outside the tradition, but in a way that gives greater depth to the voice of the already established community.

The better way forward in projecting a future for AG eschatology is to engage in a conversation with those who identify with the community, both past and present, leadership and laity, official and popular. The community that makes up the AG is, by nature of its ecclesiastical polity, a confessional community. The concept of the "cooperative fellowship" is based on the assumption that the collective whole is equal to, rather than greater than, the sum of the parts. Therefore, the collective voice of the official statements, its various ministers, and those in the academy all work together to constitute the whole of the AG. In order to construct an eschatology that represents the fellowship faithfully, the dialogue partners must have a vested interest in the community. In owning the process as a community, the goal of demarcating the boundaries of what it means to be AG are reinforced and identity is affirmed. There has yet to be a suggestion for developing AG doctrinal formulations that focuses on drawing from its "own wells."

This chapter will attempt to assess the imagination's role in theology as a way of constructing a theology of the future and explore the role of the Spirit in the imagination as a uniquely Pentecostal way of constructing the future. Those insights will be used as a basis to construct a contemporary pneumatological

---

[3] Althouse, *Spirit of the Last Days*, 61.

eschatology grounded in the each of the four images contained in the eschatological fundamental truths. This attempt will seek to develop AG eschatology in a way that will dialogue with the AG academic community and is consistent with the testimony of the past century.

The Crisis of Imagination

During the past century, Protestant theology has been in the process of trying to free itself from what Wolfgang Vondey has called "a crisis of imagination."[4] For much of its history, the church has struggled to view imagination as a resource for theological reflection without embracing subjectivism.[5] Particularly since the Reformation, theological reflection has been rooted in enlightenment epistemological assumptions that the world was built on a system of universal laws and "self-evident" truths.[6] Using Common Sense Realism and Baconian principles, Protestants adopted a scientific approach to the study of the Bible, one in which rationality took precedence over other perceived subjective approaches. Liberal scholars used modernist assumptions to explain away the supernatural elements of the Scripture, which resulted in higher criticism. Conservatives, observing how higher criticism was undermining Christian truths, used modernist assumptions to make arguments for Christian evidences and verifiable truths, which resulted in Fundamentalism.[7] Although these two approaches were in opposite directions, both were ultimately employing the same modernist assumption that something is only true if it can be verified empirically.[8]

---

[4] Wolfgang Vondey, *Beyond Pentecostalism* (Grand Rapids: Eerdmans, 2010), 16.

[5] Vondey, *Beyond Pentecostalism*, 16–34, sketches a history of the varied relationship between imagination and the Christian community all the way back to the garden where the serpent gave Adam and Eve an invitation to imagine what it would be like to become like God. Because of this story, the Hebraic concept of imagination was perceived as the power to create possibilities, both positive and negative. Following the rise of the apocalyptic genre, the imagination became associated with the Holy Spirit and functioned as a divine way to communicate details about God's future dealings with Israel. The prophetic imagination was also employed by Jesus and the NT writers to communicate about the coming of the Son of Man. The apocalyptic imagination saw its climax in the Book of Revelation. The patristic fathers embraced the role of imagination, however, over the next few centuries, the role of imagination began to be diminished as medieval scholastics elevated reason above imagination as the primary epistemological function.

[6] Marsden, *Fundamentalism and American Culture* (New York: Oxford University Press, 2006), 14–15.

[7] Marsden, *Fundamentalism and American Culture*, 16–17.

[8] Marsden, *Fundamentalism and American Culture*, 54.

Conservative evangelicals turned to Princeton Theology, which emphasized a literal reading of Scripture, Christian evidences, and an essentially empirically based faith.[9] This assumption turned the Bible into a book of self-evident facts to be scientifically studied and theological reflection into simply making propositional statements of what was viewed as universally held truths. By the turn of the twentieth century, Protestant theology was built on a simplistic "Bible doctrine" methodology that made propositional statements that lacked hermeneutical and theological depth.[10]

In recent years, newer hermeneutical methodologies emerged that are not bound to modernist assumptions and are more open to the experiential and practical aspects of the Pentecostal faith.[11] Pentecostals, in particular, have developed pneumatological approaches that read Scripture in a way that is in conversation with the Spirit and the community.[12] By opening up the hermeneutical process beyond empirical methodologies, imagination has once again emerged as a resource for understanding truth, God, and the meaning of the Scripture.

---

[9] Kenneth Richard Walters, Jr., *Why Tongues? The Initial Evidence Doctrine in North American Pentecostal Churches* (JPTSup 42; Blandford Forum: Deo Publishing, 2016), argues that Common Sense Realism provided the philosophical foundation of their epistemology, which encouraged the need for verification of spiritual experiences in revivalist movements.

[10] For a discussion of the role of Pentecostal theological hermeneutics and "Bible doctrine" methodology, see, Christopher A. Stephenson, *Types of Pentecostal Theology: Method, System, Spirit* (Oxford: Oxford University Press, 2013) and Frank D. Macchia, "The Struggle for Global Witness: Shifting Paradigms in Pentecostal Theology," in Murray W. Dempster, Byron D. Klaus, Douglas Peterson, eds., *The Globalization of Pentecostalism: A Religion Made to Travel* (Carlisle: Regnum Press, 1999), 8–29.

[11] L. William Oliverio Jr., *Theological Hermeneutics in the Classical Pentecostal Tradition* (Leiden, Netherlands: Brill, 2012), 87–88, 136–42.

[12] L. William Oliverio Jr., "Introduction," in Kenneth J. Archer and L. William Oliverio Jr., eds., *Constructive Pneumatological Hermeneutics in Pentecostal Christianity* (New York: Pelgrave Macmillan, 2016), charts the recent developments in hermeneutics in the Pentecostal tradition. Perhaps the most promising Pentecostal approach is the "reader-centered" narrative approach proposed by John Christopher Thomas, *The Spirit of the New Testament* (Blandford Forum, UK: Deo Publishing, 2005), 14–15, which focuses on the way the Scripture shapes the readers affections. See also Lee Roy Martin, "Psalm 63 And Pentecostal Spirituality: An Exercise in Affective Hermeneutics," in Lee Roy Martin, ed., *Pentecostal Hermeneutics: A Reader* (Boston: Brill, 2013), 263–86 and Jacqueline Grey, "When the Spirit Trumps Tradition: A Pentecostal Reading of Isaiah 56:1-8," in Archer and Oliverio Jr., eds., *Constructive Pneumatological Hermeneutics in Pentecostal Christianity*, 146–48.

The Pneumatological Imagination

Richard Kearney has argued that imagination is fundamental to constructing any theology of God.[13] Theology at its basic level is the process of thinking about God.[14] Since God is by nature metaphysically and empirically inaccessible, the human imagination must project images about God in the mind, filling in the gaps between what is cognitively apprehended in Scripture and what we know exists but have never seen. Through the imagination, we create concepts of truth by reproducing and applying existing images as well as creating new images that support our concepts of truth.[15] This cognitive act of creativity is inherent in our humanity and a reflection of the imago dei.[16] As James K. A. Smith points out, human beings are not simply thinking beings that apprehend and analyze data; they are powerfully emotional beings shaped by images and prone to constructing metanarratives about reality.[17] Because of this, Smith argues that the process of world-making is culturally shaped through what Charles Taylor calls the "social imaginary."[18] Taylor's epistemological assumptions begin with the notion that the world is far too complex and socially contextualized for any one person to ascertain the vast realm of factors that shape human reality. In effort to order our thoughts about the world, humans naturally fill in the blanks through the imagination to create a narrative about reality. This means that concepts of truth are shaped in part by "how we imagine the world before we ever think about it."[19]

The ability to draw concrete concepts of truth from imagined realities is crucial to a faith that is grounded in a historical event such as the Day of Pentecost. The past is not available to us except in the words of Scripture. However, we can recall realities common to the human experience and use them to imagine what is not present to us.[20] The imagination helps us to envision the past in ways that are shaped by our present realities but are mediated by the Spirit.

---

[13] Richard Kearney, *The Wake of Imagination* (London: Routledge, 1998), 16.

[14] Kay, *Pentecostalism*, 214.

[15] Amos Yong, *Spirit-Word-Community* (Eugene: Wipf & Stock, 2002), 126.

[16] Kearney, *The Wake of Imagination*, 39.

[17] James K. A. Smith, *Desiring the Kingdom* (Grand Rapids: Baker Academic, 2009), 66.

[18] Smith, *Desiring the Kingdom*, 66.

[19] Smith, *Desiring the Kingdom*, 66.

[20] Trevor Hart, "Imagination for the Kingdom of God," in Richard Bauckham, ed., *God Will Be All in All* (Edinburgh: T&T Clark, 1999), 55, defines imagination as the ability "to call to mind objects, person or states of affairs which are other than those which appear to confront us in what, for want of a better designation, we might call our present actuality."

What results from this process is a new set of information in the form of narratives, images, icons, and visions, all which exist to frame reality. The story of Pentecost uses familiar images of fire and wind to invite the imagination to connect with the biblical narrative in a way that stirs the affections toward a transformational encounter.[21] When readers use their imaginations, they not only see the disciple's experience of the Spirit in their minds, they can imagine themselves experiencing the Spirit alongside the disciples.[22] Rational theology provides cognitive information about God, but images have the multidimensional ability to shape a person's experience. Without the imagination, the living words of Scripture "flatten into book words."[23] So, rather than being detrimental to the task of theology, I would argue that without the imaginative faculties of the human mind, theology is an epistemological impossibility.

The potential of imagination to be a resource for theological reflection is becoming attractive to Pentecostal scholars. As Frank Macchia points out, many Pentecostal scholars have become unsatisfied with the "dispassionate objectivity and absolute certainty that characterized both modernism and older liberals and fundamentalists."[24] By placing an emphasis on narrative theology and experience, Pentecostals have found that they have more in common with pre-modern methodologies than they do with their Protestant forbearers. By adopting the epistemological assumptions of Protestant theology, Pentecostals have become in danger of undermining their distinctives as a theological community.[25] Furthermore, as Stian Ericksen argues, this primarily first world methodology is in many ways inconsistent with global nature of the Pentecostalism that often

---

[21] Jacqueline Grey, *Three's a Crowd: Pentecostalism, Hermeneutics and the Old Testament* (Eugene: Pickwick, 2011), 16.

[22] Daniel Albrecht, *Rights in the Spirit: A Ritual Approach to Pentecostal/Charismatic Spirituality* (Sheffield, UK: Sheffield Academic Press, 1999), 246, comments, "Pentecostals consciously attempt to understand the biblical messages and appropriate them to their community. Biblical terms and biblical images abound in the liturgy, the language and the lifestyles of Pentecostals. . . . In other words, biblical symbols provide the primary medium through which the community understands itself and communicated that understanding; biblical images contain and carry the Pent/Char spirituality."

[23] Eugene Peterson, *Reversed Thunder: The Revelation of John & the Praying Imagination* (San Francisco: Harper & Row, 1988), 13–16.

[24] Macchia, "The Struggle for Global Witness," 12.

[25] Kenneth J. Archer, "A Pentecostal Way of Doing Theology: Method and Manner," *IJST* 9, no. 3 (2007): 306, argues, "I believe that part of the problem of 'explaining' our theology has been the uncritical adoption of theological methods and forms which contain epistemological and theological perspectives that undermine the Pentecostal spirituality which shaped its story."

views rationalistic epistemology as "reductionist, predetermined Eurocentric and intellectually paternal."[26]

As an alternative to the prevailing modernist epistemology, Amos Yong offers Pentecostals a different epistemic framework rooted in the foundation of the Holy Spirit in what he calls the "pneumatological imagination."[27] For Yong, the pneumatological imagination presupposes that all knowledge of God begins with an experience of Holy Spirit, who is "the divine mind that illuminates the rationality of the world to human minds."[28] Rather than being separated from reason, the imagination is a function of the divine reason communicated by the Spirit. The Spirit communicates concrete truths about God, but does so through a number of "root metaphors" that experientially shape our understanding of the world.[29] Pentecostals express their theology through metaphors such as "baptism in the Spirit," "latter rain," and the "full gospel."[30] These metaphors are not just biblical truths; they are images, signs, and symbols, all of which must be mediated pneumatologically in order to convey divine realities.[31] In other words, "biblical symbols provide the primary medium through which the community understands itself and communicated that understanding; biblical images contain and carry the (Pentecostal) spirituality."[32] The connection between the Spirit and imagination is very natural in that the Spirit is almost exclusively referred to in the Scripture through images such as "baptism," "fire," "a dove," "rain," "water," and "power," and the Spirit's work is described in terms such as "filling," "baptizing," "cleansing," "falling," "coming upon," and "hovering."[33] Consequently, the baptism in the Spirit is not just a truth taught in the Bible, it is also a multi-dimensional experience that engages the imagination in visualizing

---

[26] Stian Eriksen, "The Epistemology of Imagination and Religious Experience," *Studia Theologica* 69, no. 1 (2015): 45–73.

[27] Amos Yong, *Spirit-Word-Community* (Eugene: Wipf & Stock, 2002), 129.

[28] Yong, *Spirit-Word-Community*, 123.

[29] Yong, *Spirit-Word-Community*, 134–36.

[30] Archer, "A Pentecostal Way of Doing Theology," 311–14.

[31] Yong *Word-Spirit-Community*, 208, explains, "To say that theological reflection is mediated semiotically is to affirm that religious knowledge is communicated through a variety of forms-i.e. . . . Put experientially, the first Christians experienced the Spirit through the violent rushing wind, through the tongues of fire which alighted on each of them, through stammering lips and strange tongues, all of which were interpreted or understood, at least in part, through the sacred writings. . . . Put theologically, Christians experience Jesus through the pneumatically constituted body of Christ."

[32] Albrecht, *Rights in the Spirit*, 246.

[33] Elizabeth A. Dreyer, *Holy Power, Holy Presence: Rediscovering Medieval Metaphors for the Holy Spirit* (New York: Paulist Press, 2007), 25–34.

the experience with the Spirit. In appealing to the pneumatological imagination as a source for truth, I am not saying that doctrine is ultimately subjective. The imagination helps form one's understanding of truth, but it does so in ways that are tested against the Spirit's revelation in Scripture and conforms within the context of the confessional community. This ensures that the images are biblical (Word), pneumatic (Spirit), and demark the boundaries of shared experience (Community).[34] All three aspects work together to shape the Pentecostal movement, its narratives, and its theological reflection.[35]

The Eschatological Imagination

Drawing on the concept of the pneumatological imagination, I would suggest that the root metaphors of the Pentecostal imagination could be employed as a resource for constructing a narrative about the future.[36] As a root metaphor, the "latter rain" is not just a way of talking about the doctrine of Spirit baptism; it is also an image that conveys a grand metanarrative explaining God's eschatological plan. As Vondey comments, "The Pentecostal imagination envisioned the last days as the unfolding of a cosmic drama of hope and judgment that constituted an irreversible break with the world and became the heartbeat of the Pentecostal self-understanding."[37] The latter rain, therefore, is an eschatological image that conveys the complex theological framework by which Pentecostals understand the work of the Spirit in the world.

In assessing potential within the pneumatological imagination for developing eschatology, it is helpful to remember that imagination is not something foreign to eschatology. John J. Collins has called apocalyptic literature a "revolution of the imagination" that uses "symbols and imagery to articulate a sense or feeling about the world."[38] Through apocalyptic literature, an alternative world is

---

[34] Yong *Word-Spirit-Community,* 217, comments, "Theological knowledge can therefore be said to emerge semiotically by way of the pneumatological imagination's quest for truth as constrained normatively by the object(s) of engagement. Theological hermeneutics and theological method are thereby inherently triadic as well, both with regard to the activity of interpretation, which is semiotically structured, and with regard to the three moments of imagination (Spirit), engagement (Word), and truthful normativity (Community)."

[35] Vondey, *Beyond Pentecostalism*, 26–28.

[36] My intention in using the language of "pneumatological imagination" is not to adopt Yong's epistemological approach to theological hermeneutics per se, rather to draw his emphasis on metaphor as an inherently Pentecostal way of communicating truth.

[37] Vondey, *Beyond Pentecostalism*, 28.

[38] John J. Collins, *The Apocalyptic Imagination* (Grand Rapids: Eerdmans, 1998), 228.

presented in a way that is shaped by images, poetry, and symbols that communicate divine reality. This is especially the case in the Book of Revelation, where imaginative symbols convey theological truths about the future in ways that also provide alternative interpretations of the present world.[39]

The reluctance to utilize the eschatological imagination as a source for truth is understandable considering the AG began during the anti-modernist era. Despite their theological differences, the AG considered themselves more akin to Fundamentalists than modernists and utilized similar methodological approaches.[40] This meant that they adopted a literalist approach to Revelation and assumed that the images were "history written in advance."[41] AG interpretations, despite the consistent push back in the *Pentecostal Evangel*, could not help but employ a cultural hermeneutic.[42] This kind of prophetic interpretation is a version of the Pentecostal "this-is-that" hermeneutic in that it affirms the narrative orientation by seeking to correlate the future with the present events in the world.[43] The irony in this approach is that although they rejected imagination in their readings of prophetic literature, their literal accounts of the future became the source of a new genre of eschatological fiction, which imagined the future in narrative form.[44] The problem with eschatological fiction is that instead of employing the imagination to interpret the symbols of the book,

---

[39] Collins, *The Apocalyptic Imagination*, 282, argues that apocalyptic symbols are not intended to give descriptive details about the future as much as they are intended to assign meaning to the present world in contrast to the hope of the world to come.

[40] For the discussion of the AG relationship to Fundamentalism see, Isgrigg, "The Pentecostal Evangelical Church," and Zachary M. Tackett, "More than Fundamentalists: fundamentalist Influences within the Assemblies of God, 1914–1942," a paper presented at the 26th Annual Meeting of the Society for Pentecostal Studies (March 13–15, 1997). See also R.E. McAlister, "The Pentecostal Movement," *PE*, May 13, 1922, 5; E. N. Bell, "Q&A," *PE*, December 27, 1919, 5.

[41] McQueen, *Toward a Pentecostal Eschatology*, 179, believes that dispensational eschatology was "a ready made eschatology" for the finished work tradition because of the way they viewed prophecy as history written in advance complemented by the finished work on the cross.

[42] Some examples of the push back by the AG in times of speculation can be seen in Ralph Riggs, "The Second Coming of Christ," *PE*, March 4, 1950, 2; Forrest Smith, "So Many Kinds of Voices," *PE*, March 9, 1975, 10–11; Daniel E. Johnson, "Please Don't Tamper With The Blessed Hope," *PE*, August 24, 1980, 4; "Ready for His Any Moment Coming," *PE*, December 26, 1982, 3–4.

[43] Vondey, *Beyond Pentecostalism*, 63. As John E. Thiel, "For What May We Hope? Thoughts on the Eschatological Imagination," *Theological Studies* 67 (2006): 520, points out, "Eschatology requires a special hermeneutics precisely because the objects of its knowledge are unavailable, and unavailable in a way that encourages error in their interpretation."

[44] Althouse, "Left Behind—Fact or Fiction?," 193–94.

they simply fictionalized their literal interpretation of Revelation.[45] As Peter Althouse comments, "The literal interpretation advocated in *Left Behind* is not a nuanced understanding of the *sensus literalis* that gives priority to the literal and includes multiple layers of understanding, but a narrowing of literary genres to articulate to univocal propositions."[46] By the 1970s and 1980s, "eschatological fiction" had become the primary way evangelicals imagined the future.[47]

The pneumatological imagination offers a very different approach to the cultural hermeneutic, one that reverses the hermeneutical process and in which the images of the Spirit take a primary role. In contrast to the often dogmatic and speculative cultural interpretations, this approach takes a posture of humility, fallibility, and is self-critical.[48] Instead of entrenching immutable visions of the future, it admits that knowledge of the future is profoundly limited and can only be seen "through a glass darkly." John demonstrated this approach in the Apocalypse when he was asked to interpret the image of the saints in white robes (Rev. 7:14). Rather than imposing his own limited and culturally shaped interpretations upon this image, John's response was, "Sir, you know!" John's deflection of the angel's question demonstrates his awareness of the limits of his knowledge and his openness to dialogue with the angel in order to more properly understand the image.[49] A two-fold emphasis on limited knowledge (fallibility) and openness to dialogue, I would argue, is a proper attitude toward interpreting the future consistent with the biblical narrative.

By allowing the Spirit to guide the discernment process, eschatological images can be pneumatically discerned in a way that informs the social imagination but

---

[45] This is a point I bring out in Daniel D. Isgrigg, *Why I Want To Be Left Behind* (Tulsa: Word & Spirit Press, 2008).

[46] Althouse, "Left Behind—Fact or Fiction?," 194.

[47] In 2000, the *Pentecostal Evangel* ran a series of stories about the *Left Behind* novels including an interview with Tim LaHaye. In, "Prophecy–based Fiction," *PE*, May 8, 2000, 6, LaHaye describes his novels as "the first fictional portrayal of events that is true to the literal interpretation of Bible prophecy." Another article, "*Left Behind* Triggers Quest for Jesus," *PE*, May 28, 2000, 8, describes how powerful the imagination can be when employed through eschatological fiction. One reader testifies, "It touched my heart so deeply, as I visualized every scene."

[48] Yong, *Spirit Poured Out on All Flesh*, 29, argues that these three values are "distinctive" to Pentecostal theology because of the limitations it puts on post-Enlightenment reason, its contextual multi-cultural expression, and pre-critical hermeneutical methodology.

[49] Thomas and Macchia, *Revelation*, 172; Stephen S. Smalley *The Revelation to John* (Downers Grove: IVP, 2005), 195.

is not controlled by it.⁵⁰ This type of pneumatic discernment allows the biblical narrative to interpret the contemporary world through symbols, narrative plot, and meaning.⁵¹ Richard Bauckham comments,

> Once we begin to appreciate their sources and their rich symbolic associations, we realize that they cannot be read either as literal descriptions or as encoded literal descriptions, but must be read for their theological meaning and their power to evoke response.⁵²

Seeing these symbols as eschatological images, rather than solely literal events, opens up the possibility for discernment to take place in any time or location. McQueen comments, "By engaging with the spiritual truths to which the images of the Apocalypse point, we become aware of the spiritual truth that exists within our own flesh-and-blood world."⁵³ So in one sense, the images are future realities that will ultimately come to pass. But for those who are not living in that eschatological moment, the images become the grammar for discerning and interpreting realities in the present.⁵⁴

The principal advantage of conceiving eschatology through pneumatological imagination is that it provides a way of articulating doctrine that is open to the Spirit's shaping of the future of doctrine.⁵⁵ Prophetic images have a way of being culturally interpreted by each generation as believers strive to express eschatological convictions in response to their present conditions. However, the more doctrine is expressed in these cultural parameters, i.e., as events, the more doctrine will be irrelevant to future generations who face a different set of circumstances.⁵⁶ In a rapidly changing world, the potential for neglect and

---

⁵⁰ John Christopher Thomas, "Mystery of the Great Whore: Pneumatic Discernment in Revelation 17," in *Perspectives in Pentecostal Eschatologies*, 111–36, argues that the Pentecostal practice of pneumatic discernment is a welcome alternative to end times speculation and is more faithful to the methodology given by the Spirit for understanding the images in the Apocalypse.

⁵¹ Yong, *In the Days of Caesar*, 323.

⁵² Richard Bauckham, *The Theology of the Book of Revelation* (Cambridge: Cambridge University Press, 1994), 20.

⁵³ McQueen, *Toward a Pentecostal Eschatology*, 291.

⁵⁴ Hart, "Imagination for the Kingdom of God," 57.

⁵⁵ Pinnock, *Flame of Love*, 221, argues that because both progression and regression occur in the development of our understanding, it is therefore necessary that "the Spirit leads us" because of "our fallibility and proneness to error." Openness to the future should be a byproduct of the openness of the Spirit's ability to bring revelation in the present.

⁵⁶ This is the heart of McGrath's thesis in *Genesis of Doctrine* in which he argues that in the case of Roman Catholic Canon law, doctrinal permanence created by propositional understandings

irrelevancy is high when truth is inextricably connected to social contexts. Some in past generations exerted considerable energy identifying present conditions as "proof" of the Lord's coming, only to have those conditions drastically change. The regrettable results of the decades of speculation have been demonstrated in the denominational and ministerial neglect of the AG's most prominent doctrine. As former General Superintendent, George O. Wood, recognizes, "Many people in our churches have become burned out by all the speculative scenarios and dates put forward for the Second Coming. . . . We need to put aside all the speculative scenarios and get to the core of the doctrine . . . 'Jesus is coming.'"[57] When cultural interpretations become entrenched, ministers who may have other perspectives are forced to remain silent on eschatological topics in order to avoid falling into disfavor.[58] On a denominational level, the *Pentecostal Evangel* and GPH simply chose not to publish new books in the past few decades, presumably to avoid controversy.[59]

The AG's avoidance of the topic does not mean that belief in the Second Coming has diminished. As Poloma and Green found over a decade ago, 94 percent of AG ministers agree or strongly agree that the Bible clearly teaches a "premillennial" view of the future but only 58j percent reported accepting a dispensationalist interpretation of Scripture, while 42 percent rejected dispensationalism altogether.[60] A large number of AG ministers have clearly rejected the emphasis on end time events, but at the same time remain fully committed to the core images of the AG's premillennial views. In a similar study William Kay found among Pentecostal minsters in Britain, nearly all those surveyed (99%) affirmed the return of Christ, the rapture of the church, and the belief in the coming millennium.[61] But, when it comes to tribulational positions, a larger number are unsure (30%) compared to those who are certain Christians

eventually become irrelevant to new situations and hinders the process of development. Such was the case for the Reformation, which became viewed as a threat to the institution. Because they were unable to reconcile the developments in doctrine, the only option was either submission or division.

[57] George O. Wood, *Core Values* (Springfield: Gospel Publishing House, 2007), 28. Wood himself admits being influenced by his education at Fuller Theological Seminary where the kingdom is defined as "the tension between the already and not yet" and that perspective has informed how he understands the coming of Christ.

[58] Blumhofer, *Restoring the Faith*, 270–71.

[59] Since 1975, only seven books on prophecy have been published by GPH. Only two were by authors other than Horton, of which the last one was published in 1996.

[60] Poloma and Green, *The Assemblies of God*, 82.

[61] William K. Kay, "Premillennial Tensions: What Pentecostal Ministers Look Forward To," *Journal of Contemporary Religion* 14, no. 3 (1999): 361–73.

will escape the tribulation (47%). He concludes those who expect to go through tribulation are more likely to be educated and more likely to emphasize the Pentecostal gifts.[62] What this tells us is that the core images have lasting value in creating the foundation for truth in every generation and allow the Spirit to be a resource for discerning the future in each generation. For younger Pentecostals, premillennial eschatology and commitment to Pentecostal theology are perfectly compatible.

Images of the Spirit

As I have already suggested, the SFT is already constructed in a way that lends itself to the pneumatological imagination rather than a chronological interpretation. By orienting AG eschatology through pneumatological images, the four fundamental truths can be viewed thematically and a natural chiastic symmetry emerges.[63] Read as images rather than chronological events, there is a chiastic structure and literary parallelism linking image 1 with 4 and 2 with 3.

>   a. Blessed Hope (1)
>   b. Millennium (2)
>   b. Final Judgment (3)
>   a. New Heavens & Earth (4)

Situated within the doctrine of the Blessed Hope is the image of the resurrection of the body, which encompasses the concepts of complete salvation, wholeness, and healing. Resurrection is the ultimate image of the old becoming new, implying a continuity between the old body and the new body. In the EFT,

---

[62] Kay, "Premillennial Tensions," 361, 366. Of those who held that the church would go through the tribulation (termed "tribulationist" (T) by Kay), 63% were less than forty years old. By contrast, of those who held pre-tribulational positions, only 33% were under forty years old. This suggests that there has been a recent shift in eschatological beliefs of Pentecostal ministers in the last forty years from pre-tribulational positions to either tribulational or agnostic positions. He also found that 73% of those who held the tribulationist (T) position had ministerial training, suggesting that education was a significant influence on tribulational view. This exposure made them more likely to have a tribulationalist view of the future, yet at the same time holding firmly to premillennial positions.

[63] It is certainly difficult to propose that the chiastic structure was intentional among the crafters of the *SFT*. However, the AG certainly believed that the Holy Spirit was involved in crafting these four doctrines. This is not to suggest there is a sort of infallibility to the construction of these four tenets, only to propose that the literary characteristics used in apocalyptic texts are evident here. For a discussion of chaisms in Johannine literature, see John Christopher Thomas, *A Pentecostal Commentary on The Johannine Epistles*, (London: T&T Clark, 2004), 56.

the image of resurrection of humanity is paralleled by the image of the resurrection of the rest of creation in the doctrine of the New Heavens and Earth. Like the body, the resurrection of the cosmos implies bringing new life to that which was in decay and implies continuity between the first creation and the new creation. Resurrection is the final act of salvation for humanity on the micro scale and the new creation on the cosmic macro scale. Both doctrines are grounded in the eschatological work of Christ and are pneumatically linked in the promise of individual and cosmic salvation found in Romans 8.

        a. Hope of Individual Resurrection (1)
           b. Hope of Earthly Justice (2)
           b. Hope of Cosmic Justice (3)
        a. Hope of Cosmic Resurrection (4)

If resurrection is the ultimate act of salvation for humanity and all of creation, the Millennium and Final Judgment provide the second correlating parallel. For the AG, the millennium is a time of earthly justice, in which Christ will rule with perfect justice over the nations, the curse of sin will be reversed, and injustice will be purged from the earth. In the Final Judgment, cosmic justice will be exacted upon the principalities and powers in heavenly realms, and the whole cosmos will be purged of evil, not just earth. So, the millennium is characterized by the image of earthly justice, while the final judgment is focused on cosmic justice. The consequences of salvation are resurrection and life; the consequences of sanctification are peace and justice. Salvation and judgment are parallel images of the Messiah's eschatological coming commonly found in apocalyptic literature.[64] Both the images and their corresponding concepts provide a pneumatological orientation consistent with the witness of the AG and are capable of sustaining a future for AG eschatology.

Similar to a thematic conceptualization, there is also a way in which the four fundamental truths represent images that describe the eschatological work of the Spirit. Because the Holy Spirit is the Spirit of the last days, the progress toward the eschatological consummation can be viewed in terms of the future work of the Spirit. Each of the four doctrines of the AG (blessed hope, millennium, judgment, new heavens and new earth) could also be conceived as four images of the Spirit's eschatological work (resurrection, restoration, recompense, renewal). By seeing these four doctrines in terms of images of the Sprit's work, it adds a

---

[64] Bauckham, *The Theology of the Book of Revelation*, 63–67, argues that the image of the coming of the Son of Man in apocalyptic literature is always expressed in terms of both salvation for the righteous and judgment for the unrighteous, which are essentially "two sides to one coin.".

layer of meaning to these events that is not apparent by a simple chronological ordering of events. It is this approach to the four eschatological fundamental truths that will be explored in the next few chapters.

13

IMAGES OF HOPE: TOWARD A PNEUMATOLOGICAL ESCHATOLOGY

In this chapter, I will propose a constructive contribution to AG eschatology rooted in the pneumatological imagination. Each Eschatological Fundamental Truth will be explored as a pneumatological image expressed as an eschatological longing that is a characteristic of Pentecostal spirituality. The goal of this contribution is not to construct a comprehensive Pentecostal eschatology for the AG; it is rather to develop these doctrines with new layers of theological depth by integrating the various voices of the community in a way that is faithful to the past, is Spirit-oriented, and is in conversation with contemporary theological reflection.[1]

A principle challenge in developing the AG's vision of the future is the overly propositional nature of the *SFT*. The limited statements could create a propensity for the truths about the Second Coming of Christ to be something that is assented to without any regard for what actions should accompany this conviction. As Frank Macchia points out, the only way to keep eschatological beliefs from being solely propositional is to expand the reaches of doctrine to engage the Spirit in the process of imagining our vision of the kingdom.[2] If eschatology is defined by what the Spirit is doing now in anticipation of the future, it opens up the conversation to more transformational reflections. As Stephen Land argues, this type of eschatological vision requires theology to be in terms of "orthodoxy, orthopraxy and orthopathy, or belief, actions, and affections, respectively."[3] When the Spirit shapes eschatological doctrine, truths (orthodoxy) have a way changing our affections (orthopathy) and inspiring our actions (orthopraxy). The affections engendered by the Spirit are more than just

---

[1] Since AG eschatology should be rooted in the voices within the community, there will be a priority to the periodical literature, which will be supplemented with the voices from AG's doctrinal books that have not been consulted to this point.

[2] Macchia, *Baptized in the Spirit*, 112.

[3] Steven J. Land, *Pentecostal Spirituality: A Passion for the Kingdom* (Sheffield: Sheffield Academic Press, 1993), 41–48.

feelings; they are passions that shape the believer by the values of the kingdom.[4] This is why Land has defined Pentecostal eschatology in terms of "a passion for the kingdom."[5] The coming of the Spirit upon the Church at Pentecost created an eschatological community whose mission it is to live out the message of the kingdom.[6] As Murray Dempster frames it, "From an eschatological perspective, the mission of the church is to witness to the truth that the kingdom of God which still belongs to the future has already broken into the present age in Jesus Christ and continues in the world through the power of the Holy Spirit."[7] Sadly, Pentecostals are not as well known for their engagement in social issues as they are for missionary enterprises.[8] The answer to this challenge, as Dempster point out, "lies in the Pentecost-Kingdom framework in which the doctrine of the return of Jesus Christ is to be interpreted in the eschatological and ethical context of Jesus' kingdom teaching."[9] In other words, what the kingdom shall be in the future should shape the way the kingdom is lived out now. In this way, the Second Coming is more than a doctrine, it is a Spirit-inspired vision of the kingdom motivated by a passion for the kingdom and modeled after the mission of the Coming King.

Based on this paradigm, each doctrine will be examined by the images produced by the pneumatological imagination (orthodoxy), the pneumatological affection the Spirit engenders (orthopathy), and the pneumatological response that it should inspire (orthopraxy). In fusing together the image, the affection, and the practice, it will not only produce a holistic understanding of AG spirituality, but will also provide insulation from the temptation toward quietism and escapism. In developing a pneumatological eschatology, this chapter will propose a future for AG eschatology that could reinvigorate these doctrines to ensure their centrality to the AG for future generations. The end goal is to construct a contemporary, yet contextual eschatology that reflects the past and at the same time imagines the future.

[4] Dale M. Coulter and Amos Yong, eds., *The Spirit, the Affections and the Christian Tradition* (Notre Dame: University of Notre Dame Press, 2016).

[5] Land, *Pentecostal Spirituality*, 148.

[6] Dempster, "Eschatology, Spirit Baptism, and Inclusiveness," 155–56.

[7] Murray W. Dempster, "Evangelism, Social Concern, and the Kingdom of God," in M. W. Dempster, B. D. Klaus and D. Petersen, eds., *Called and Empowered: Global Mission in Pentecostal Perspective* (Peabody: Hendrickson, 1991), 23–24.

[8] Daniel D. Isgrigg, "Interpreting the Signs of the Times: How Eschatology Shaped Assemblies of God Social Ethics," a paper presented at the 47th Society for Pentecostal Studies (March 8–10, 2018).

[9] Dempster, "Christian Social Concern in the Pentecostal Perspective," 59.

The Spirit of Hope: Imagining Resurrection

The AG was founded on two theological convictions: the baptism in the Holy Spirit and Second Coming of Jesus.[10] These two pillars were intimately connected and theologically dependent upon each other. As one early member wrote, "The most important of all messages, and one which the Holy Ghost emphasizes above everything else is this: 'Jesus is coming soon.'"[11] The SFT refers to the coming of Jesus as the "Blessed Hope," which is defined as "the resurrection of those who have fallen asleep in Christ and their translation together with those who are alive and remain unto the coming of the Lord."[12] In this section, I will explore the importance of the resurrection as a powerful image that has the potential to shape the future of the eschatological imagination of the Second Coming of Jesus.

The image of the "Blessed Hope" is derived from four supporting verses in the *SFT*: 1 Thess. 4:16–17, Rom. 8:23, Tit. 2:13, 1 Cor. 15:52–53.[13] My intention in looking at these passages is not to engage in detailed exegesis, but to explore the eschatological images they portray. For a century, the AG has referred to the return of Jesus as "the blessed hope." This title is taken from Paul's admonishment to Christians to stay faithful to Christ as they "wait for the blessed hope—the appearing of our great God and Savior Jesus Christ" (Tit. 2:13).[14] Paul's description of the appearing of Jesus is expressed by two affective images. First, it is "blessed." For believers, the coming of Jesus is not something to be feared; instead, it is an event that should be met with a full anticipation and joy. As P. C. Nelson points out, the appearing of Jesus is a blissful, happy, and hopeful image.[15] However, as Cecil Robeck has noted, the return of Christ has also been used as a "not so blessed hammer" and a fear-based tool for motivating believers toward holiness.[16] Yet, in Paul's imagination, no such motivation exists. Rather, the future is good and should be welcomed. Second, Paul refers to Christ's

---

[10] *GC Minutes* (April 2–12, 1914), 1.

[11] "How Long," *WE*, April 20, 1918, 8.

[12] *GC Minutes* (October 1–7, 1916), 13. The 1927 version removed the term rapture in favor of "translation."

[13] *GC Minutes* (October 1–7, 1916), 13. 1 Cor. 15.51, 52 was added in *GC Minutes* (September 16–22, 1927), 5–8.

[14] Despite its role in the title given to the second coming doctrine, Horton, *Our Destiny*, 141, Williams, *Systematic Theology*, 190, and Horton, "The Last Things," 603, each have only one passing reference to this verse.

[15] Nelson, *Bible Doctrines*, 141.

[16] Robeck, "Faith, Hope, Love, and the Eschaton," 3.

appearing as "hope." Hope is an emotional response that can only be generated by the expectation of something good in the future. Paul hopes for Christ to appear in all of his glory and for believers to "appear with him in glory" (Col. 3:4). The use of the term "appearing" is informative to this hope because it is typically associated with what the AG would consider to be the second phase of Christ's return.[17] Christ's return in power and glory is the ultimate image revealing the "Coming of God" to all creation and declaring that Jesus is God, Savior, and the awaited Messiah.[18] This is the "blessed" hope.

N. T. Wright argues that the power behind the language of Christ's appearing is rooted in the reality that Christ is now absent from the world.[19] To speak of Christ's presence/absence is not just a statement about his current location; it is a relational description of his proximity to believers. Following his resurrection from the dead, Jesus gathered his disciples and told them to wait in Jerusalem until they were baptized in the Holy Spirit. Still perplexed at what Christ meant, the disciples asked him if now was the time he would "restore the kingdom to Israel" (Acts 1:6). Rather than restoring the kingdom, Jesus promised that the Spirit would be poured out and the kingdom would be present by the Spirit of God. As the disciples watched the resurrected Jesus ascend into heaven, two angels appeared and made a promise: "This same Jesus who has been taken from you to heaven, will come back in the same way you have seen Him go into heaven" (Acts 1:10). Luke's narrative communicates two realities. First, in the absence of Jesus from this earth, he promised he would be present with them through the outpouring of the Holy Spirit. Second, he promised that his absence would only be temporary in that just as he ascended to heaven, he will also descend from heaven to earth once again. The way he left provided the disciples an image for the manner in which he would return: in the clouds.[20]

---

[17] Pearlman, *Knowing the Doctrines of the Bible*, 390. Furthermore, Williams, *Systematic Theology*, 190, says, "We must not insist that the Greek word *parousia*, which some expositors say refers specifically to the rapture ... it is often used in connection with Christ's coming in the revelation from the heaven in the glory of His divine presence (parousia) to reign." See also Caleb V. Smith, "7 Reasons for Loving His Appearing," *PE*, October 18, 1953, 3; J. S. Eastman, "The Rapture of the Church," *PE*, April 29, 1973, 30.

[18] Moltmann, *The Coming of God*, 24. The concept of eschatology in Jewish dimensions is often communicated as the "coming of God" and "the day of the Lord."

[19] N. T. Wright, *Surprised by Hope* (New York: HarperOne, 2014), 123–36.

[20] Craig S. Keener, *Acts: An Exegetical Commentary* I (Grand Rapids: Baker Academic, 2012), 731–32, argues that Luke's image of Jesus departing "in a cloud" was in order to invoke the messianic image of the Son of Man from prophetic literature and confirms Jesus' apocalyptic declaration that the Son of Man will come with "clouds of glory" (Matt. 24:5–8).

Peter Althouse argues that Luke holds the presence/absence dialectic together through the ascension, Pentecost, and the *parousia*.[21] Pentecost is not just a historical event, nor is it simply the inauguration of the "Church age'; Pentecost inaugurates, mediates, and will eventually consummate the "Eschatological-Spirit Age."[22] The absence of Jesus is accompanied by the presence of Jesus in the Spirit because he is "exalted to the right hand of the father and having received the promise of the Holy Spirit has poured out this that you both see and hear" (Acts 2:33). The fact that Jesus is absent now, but the Spirit is present serves as a powerful reminder of the promise that although he ascended, he will "appear" once again.[23] Without the ascension of Jesus and absence from his disciples, there can be no Pentecost.[24] Without Pentecost, there is no reminder of his future appearing or assurance of our future resurrection. It should therefore be no surprise that passion for the Holy Spirit would correspond with passion for the coming of Jesus.[25]

The second passage used to support the Blessed Hope is 1 Thess. 4:13–16, which is arguably the most important image in this passage in the AG's eschatological imagination. Paul concludes from Christ's own words that believers on earth will be "caught up together with them in the clouds to meet the Lord in the air" (1 Thess. 4:17). The image of the "catching way" or "rapture" is so central to the eschatological imagination it even has its own grammar rooted in affective language usually used for an emotional experience.[26] Because of the similar affective characteristics associated with terms "blessed hope" and "rapture," it is no wonder these labels have become the preferred language of the coming of Christ. Similar to Luke's account of the ascension, Paul imagines the coming of Christ using the apocalyptic image of clouds as a way of portraying

---

[21] Peter Althouse, "Ascension, Pentecost, Eschaton," in John Christopher Thomas, ed., *Toward a Pentecostal Ecclesiology* (Cleveland, TN: CPT Press, 2010), 225–45.

[22] Yong, *Renewing Christian Theology*, 45.

[23] Stanley M. Horton, *The Promise of His Coming* (Springfield: Gospel Publishing House, 1967), 49.

[24] Carl Brumback, *Accent on the Ascension* (Springfield: Gospel Publishing House, 1955), 131–40. Brumback considers the ascension to be the most neglected doctrine in Christian theology. Just as Jesus was resurrected and ascended into heaven to prepare for the kingdom, when Jesus comes, believers will be resurrected and "carried body and soul to heaven to prepare for his return and establishment of the kingdom." He says, "The descent of the Spirit was absolutely dependent upon the Ascent of Christ" (98).

[25] Land, *Pentecostal Spirituality*, 66, comments, "The longing for the Lord to come, for the Holy Spirit, and for the kingdom of God are part of the same things: it is one passion."

[26] Horton, *Our Destiny*, 82; Horton, *The Promise of His Coming*, 99.

Christ "in the midst of the saints."[27] Paul draws a connection here between the risen Christ who ascended into the clouds after his resurrection in bodily form and the resurrection of the saints who will ascend into the clouds in bodily form.

It is clear that for many in the AG, this passage teaches the concept of "the rapture" of the church, which is typically seen as the means by which the church escapes to heaven during the tribulation.[28] However, the concept of the "rapture" has been growing in disfavor among a new generation of Pentecostal scholars not only because of its dispensational origin, but also because of the exegetical issues that seem to convey the exact opposite interpretation of this passage. Scholars point out that Paul's use of the phrase "caught up to meet him" in 1 Thess. 4:17 usually "connotes the image of a public and visible event" in which a king or dignitary would be "ceremonially escorted back into the city."[29] In this interpretation, the image here is of Christ and his saints returning to earth descriptive of the "appearing" rather than the "rapture." AG scholar Stanley Horton does not dispute this interpretation, but he navigates this problem by arguing that Paul does not mention where the believers go after the resurrection.[30]

The ambiguity of this passage leaves the reader with two options: will the living saints welcome Jesus and the departed saints back to earth, or will Jesus and the departed saints welcome the living saints to heaven? From the perspective

---

[27] Horton, *The Promise of His Coming*, 97, suggests that the image of Christ coming "with the saints" can be translated "in the midst of the saints" indicative of Christ's desire to be "among the saints." Rebecca Skaggs and Priscilla C. Benham, *Revelation: Pentecostal Commentary* (Blandford Forum: Deo Publishing, 2009), 23, also point out that the image of the cloud in the OT suggests God's presence in the midst of the saints. But unlike OT narratives where God is not seen in the cloud, here the cloud reveals Christ in all of his glory.

[28] Cf. Williams, *Systematic Theology*, 192, defines the rapture as "Christ's coming for the Church to take her to be with Him during the time between His coming for His own and the time when He comes to manifest himself to the world." Williams's treatment of the resurrection is the near the end of his chapter on eschatology and undervalues its place as the blessed hope (238–48). Menzies and Horton, *Bible Doctrines*, 211–19, emphasizes the priority of the resurrection as the "real hope" of Christ's coming, but like Williams defines the rapture as the "catching away" to heaven.

[29] Bertone, "Seven Dispensations or Two-Age View of History," in Althouse and Waddell, eds., *Perspectives in Pentecostal Eschatologies*, 75–80, rightly points out that this passage uses the word *apantesis*, which connotes the image of a public and visible event in which "dignitaries who would be ceremonially escorted back into the city." See also McQueen, *Toward a Pentecostal Eschatology*, 266–68.

[30] Horton, *The Promise of His Coming*, 99–100, notes, "Paul does not say anything directly at this point about escorting the Lord back to earth after we meet Him in the air." See also Horton, "The Last Things," 623–24. Ambiguity about the destination of believers is also expressed by E. N. Bell, "Questions and Answers," *WE*, November 24, 1917, 8, who notes that the marriage supper "takes place after the Rapture and in the air, before Jesus comes on earth to take possession." See also, "The Future Life," *CE*, September 6, 1919, 12.

of Pentecostal tradition, the answer is both. Early Pentecostals imagined the rapture in terms of the bride being "caught up" to greet the Bridegroom in the air and accompanying him into heaven for the marriage supper of the Lamb.[31] But this trip to heaven will only be temporary, lasting at most seven years. At the same time, scholars rightfully point out that this passage suggests that the account is describing the Lord coming with his saints to reign on earth. Furthermore, if the resurrection and translation take place simultaneously, the AG slogan that the rapture is Christ coming "for the saints" and revelation is Christ coming "with the saints" breaks down. Either way, what it important to note is that whatever view one takes of the tribulation (whether pre, mid, post, or even a-trib), the goal is still the same: Christ is coming to reign on earth with his saints.[32]

In light of this perspective, the use of the term "rapture" by the AG need not be a stumbling block because of its association with an escapist mentality. Historically, the rapture is not a statement about the destination of believers or the belief that the church will escape as much as it is a term that is synonymous with resurrection. The way the *SFT* was written in 1916 declares the "resurrection" is what happens to the dead in Christ; the "rapture" is what happens to the living when Christ comes.[33] The word "rapture" is simply describing the future transformation of the body from death to life where "mortality puts on immortality," rather than describing the time of the tribulation or the location of the believer after Jesus comes. Because of the difference in the ontological state of these two sets of believers, the eschatological act of resurrection is different: the dead must come completely to life in unifying the body and soul while the living need only to be transformed. This is seen clearly when Myer Pearlman says, "After the resurrection and the rapture they will attain immortality; that is, they will have glorified bodies."[34] The revision in 1927 supports this idea when the term "rapture" was changed to "translation" perhaps in order to keep from encouraging escapist mentality and confusing the emphasis on the resurrection.[35] Understood in this way, Horton describes the

---

[31] Cf. Macchia, *Baptized in the Spirit*, 274.

[32] As Riggs, "The Second Coming of Christ," 2, comments, "the whole objective of the resurrection and translation is to meet the Lord in the air and to be with Him forevermore, a grand reunion with One whom we love dearer than life itself."

[33] *GC Minutes* (October 1–7, 1916), 13.

[34] Pearlman, *Knowing the Doctrines of the Bible*, 369.

[35] See 3.3.2. By broadening the definition, the AG made their statement inclusive to various forms of tribulational positions and downplayed the two-phase emphasis. To this day, the "rapture" remains absent from this definition.

"rapture" as the "resurrection, our new bodies, our reigning with Christ, and our eternal future," a position consistent with the historic testimony of the Church.[36]

The third supporting verse for the Blessed Hope is Rom. 8:23. This verse has received plenty of emphasis in the history of the AG, but has often been overlooked by interpreters both inside and outside the tradition. Paul declares, "Not only so, but we ourselves, who have the firstfruits of the Spirit, groan inwardly as we wait eagerly for our adoption to sonship, the redemption of our bodies" (Rom. 8:23). There are several important images conveyed within this passage. First, Paul describes the Spirit in terms of the "firstfruits" of the resurrection of the body, a biblical image describing an early portion of a full blessing.[37] The image of the first fruits calls to mind Paul's concept of a "down payment" of future glory (Eph. 1:14).[38] The future harvest anticipated by the "firstfruits of the Spirit" is not the hope of a future total spirituality in some platonicistic sense, rather for Paul, the harvest is the resurrection of the body and the consummation of full eschatological redemption. This is demonstrated in Paul's image of Jesus as the "firstfuits" of the resurrection (1 Cor. 15:23) the embodiment of the "life giving Spirit" (1 Cor. 15:45).[39] Jesus was "justified in the Spirit" (1 Tim. 3:16) in that his resurrection proleptically accomplishes the full redemption. What is anticipated is the fullness of glory in our "adoption as sons, the redemption of the body." The Spirit is the Spirit of Life and the Spirit of Resurrection, who "raised Christ from the dead" and is our promise that the Spirit will also "quicken our mortal bodies" (Rom. 8:11).[40] As the penultimate work of the Holy Spirit, the resurrection brings together both eschatological and pneumatological images in a way that imagines the future through the image of the baptism in the Spirit.

Too often Pentecostals have limited the scope of the Spirit's work to a personal level. However, Rom. 8:23 expands the operation of the Spirit to encompass all

[36] Horton, "The Last Things," 598.

[37] Wright, *Surprised by Hope*, 163, comments, "This Spirit, already present within Jesus' followers as the first fruits, the down payment, the guarantee of what is to come, is not only the beginning of the future life, even in the present time, but also the energizing power though which the final transformation will take place."

[38] Althouse, "Ascension, Pentecost, Eschaton," 239–40, believes that Paul does not describe the portion of the Spirit as a way of anticipation of the fullness of the Spirit in a future time as much as it is the Spirit that anticipates the fullness of the eternal state of eschatological life. However, I follow Macchia, *Baptized in the Spirit*, 90–91, in the belief that eternal life of the future is precisely because the Spirit is poured out without measure and baptizes all creation in the Spirit.

[39] Horton, "The Last Things," 605.

[40] Pearlman, *Knowing the Doctrines of the Bible*, 375; Horton, "The Last Things," 603.

of creation. Because all of creation suffers under the weight of sin, all of creation also benefits from the redemption of Christ's death and resurrection. Richard Orchard declares, "God has not forsaken the earth. He could not forsake it after letting His Son die for it. God has a glorious goal in mind—the exaltation of His lovely Son to glory and honor before the intelligentsia of all the universe."[41] Paul's metaphor of the groaning of the Spirit harkens to the creation narrative where the Spirit "broods" over the water and breathes life into Adam.[42] Drawing on this image, Paul envisions the reversal of the Edenic fall in which both the body and the creation that was subjected to frustration will experience glorious freedom.[43] Since sin has "contaminated" the spiritual and physical world, Paul imagines that "all creation" is groaning with the Spirit in hope to receive the breath of life. As Caleb Smith beautifully expresses,

> The sounds of nature, the cries of animals, and the songs of birds are all pitched in a minor key. Earth, sea, and sky are full of fierce pursuit and crude capture, breathless escape and haunting fear. But then the misery of nature will be transformed into a jubilee.[44]

In this way, Spirit baptism becomes a powerful metaphor for the coming of the Spirit to fill believers with the eschatological Spirit and the coming of Jesus to fill the whole creation with the eschatological Spirit.[45]

The fourth supporting verse for the Blessed Hope is 1 Cor. 15:51–52. In this passage Paul brings to the forefront the importance of the doctrine of the resurrection of the dead. The resurrection is so central to New Testament

---

[41] R. E. Orchard, "Tribulation Shadows," *PE*, November 29, 1987, 6–7. The connection between sin-redemption in creation is also found in Frank Boyd, *The Budding Fig Tree* (Springfield: Gospel Publishing House, 1925), 24. He says, "Redemption covers not only the individuals who accept its provisions, but the 'whole creation'—the earth and all of God's universe upon which the ugly hand of sin has been laid."

[42] Yong, *The Spirit Poured Out on All Flesh*, 280–83.

[43] Bruce R. Marino, "The Origin, Nature, and Consequences of Sin," in Stanley M. Horton, ed. *Systematic Theology*, 255–90.

[44] Caleb V. Smith, "7 Reasons for Loving His Appearing," *PE*, October 18, 1953, 3, 20.

[45] Macchia, *Baptized in the Spirit*, 90–91. Sisson, *Foregleams of Glory*, 50–51, believes the latter rain outpouring of the Spirit "on all flesh" also includes the creation, which intensifies the groaning of creation in the same way that the baptism in the Spirit intensifies the longing in believers for the return of Christ.

theology that Brian Robinette calls it the "grammar" of the gospel.[46] Paul declares,

> For if the dead are not raised, then Christ has not been raised either. And if Christ has not been raised, your faith is futile; you are still in your sins. Then those also who have fallen asleep in Christ are lost. If only for this life we have hope in Christ, we are of all people most to be pitied (1 Cor. 15:16–19).

The Jewish expectation of resurrection emerged out of the recognition that by nature humanity does not have the capacity to survive death.[47] During the period of Judah's exile when the Jews were experiencing death as a people because of their rebellion and sin, the prophets began to envision a future time when the dead would be raised to life.[48] Images such as the valley of dry bones in Ezekiel 37 gave Israel hope that their rebellion and death would not be permanent, believing that the coming Messiah will bring about a resurrection of Israel in anticipation of the restitution of the kingdom of the Messiah. The coming of the Messiah was seen not only in terms of eschatological salvation of God's people, but also as a time of eschatological judgment upon God's enemies.[49] These corporate concepts of salvation and judgment continued to be developed until NT times when the expectation of resurrection became individualized, emphasizing the unification of the body and the soul.[50] Resurrection became seen as the ultimate act of salvation, which reversed the conditions of sin and death and initiated the process of renewal of Israel and the whole earth. Therefore, what the promise of the *parousia* is primarily concerned with is the fate of the dead, not the living.

In 1 Corinthians, Paul uses the image of resurrection in this way. He declares, "We shall not all sleep, but we shall all be changed, in a moment, in the twinkling of an eye, at the last trumpet. For the trumpet will sound, the dead will be raised

---

[46] Brian D. Robinette, *The Grammars of Resurrection* (New York: Crossroad Publishing Company, 2009).

[47] Richard Bauckham, *The Theology of the Book of Revelation* (Cambridge, UK: Cambridge University Press, 1994), 48.

[48] Joseph E. Coleson, "Israel's Life Cycle from Birth to Resurrection," in Avraham Gileadi, ed., *Israel's Apostasy and Restoration* (Grand Rapids: Baker, 1988), 237–49, argues that the prophets, particularly Ezekiel and Isaiah, set for the metaphor of the life cycle of the Bride (Israel) from conception to natural death. The "stages of life" cast as infancy, election, apostasy, and death will culminate in a promise of resurrection as the bride is restored to covenant relationship.

[49] Hart and Bauckham, *Hope Against Hope*, 118–20.

[50] Moltmann, *The Coming of God*, 68.

imperishable, and we will be changed" (1 Cor. 15:51–52). Paul uses several contrasting images to describe the transformation that will take place at the resurrection.[51] The body that is perishable, humiliated, weak, and natural, will be raised imperishable, glorified, powerful, and of the Spirit.[52] For Paul, resurrection is the final act of salvation that is traced all the way back to the sin of Adam (1 Cor. 15:22) as death is "swallowed up in victory." The transformation of the body from a "natural body" to a "supernatural body" is vital to salvation because "flesh and blood cannot inherit the kingdom of God" (1 Cor. 15:50).[53] So in Paul's imagination, the resurrected body is a reversal by the Second Adam of what was lost by the first Adam.

By elevating the importance of the bodily resurrection, significance is placed on the dignity of the body, which guards against the platonistic emphasis on the soul rather than the body. Unfortunately, emphasis on the rapture rather than the resurrection has too often resulted in a greater emphasis on heaven than on earth. But this is symptomatic of a deeper dualism in the evangelical imagination in which heaven is seen as a spiritual and perfect place and the physical earth as non-spiritual and impure.[54] The problem with this understanding of the world is it has subtly engrained the idea of heaven being the eternal home for believers and the earth the temporal home.[55] As N.T Wright notes, "This attitude has been reinforced again and again in hymns, prayer, monuments and even quite serious works of theology and history. It is simply assumed the word heaven is the appropriate term for the ultimate destination, the final home."[56] If heaven is the

---

[51] Roy E. Ciampa and Brian S. Rosner, *The First Letter to the Corinthians* (Grand Rapids: Eerdmans, 2010), 810–17.

[52] Craig Keener, *1–2 Corinthians* (Cambridge, UK: Cambridge University Press, 2005), 130–35, argues that Paul's use of the term *pnuematikos* refers to "spiritual" or "of the Spirit" as is the case earlier in 1 Cor. 12:1.

[53] Gordon D. Fee, *The First Epistle to the Corinthians* (Grand Rapids: Eerdmans, 1987), 786, argues that the transformed body is not "spiritual" in composition, in contrast to the physical and "immaterial" body. The *pneumatikos* is the spirit-supernatural body that is transformed by the power of the Spirit just as Jesus in his resurrected state is a "life-giving Spirit."

[54] Gary Scott Smith, *Heaven in the American Imagination* (New York: Oxford University Press, 2011), 171–72, 177–81, argues that following the 1950s, an explosion of evangelical emphasis on heaven took place, particularly in religious literature. A likely reason for this is the emergence of the mass crusade evangelism efforts and methodologies of Billy Graham to encourage believers to be born again in order to gain access to heaven.

[55] This is a point that I make in Isgrigg, *Why I Want to be Left Behind*, 65–75, where I have an entire chapter called, "Heaven is Not My Home."

[56] Wright, *Surprised by Hope*, 19.

believer's home, the purpose of the coming of Jesus is changed from hope of salvation in the physical realm (resurrection) to an act of liberation of believers from the physical realm.[57]

For the AG, the true hope of Christ's coming has not been to "fly away" to a spiritual heaven as much as it is the anticipation of the resurrection in preparation of the millennium.[58] Articles on heaven as the "home" of believers in the *Pentecostal Evangel* did not emerge until the mid-twentieth century.[59] In fact, Elizabeth Sisson openly rejected the common affinity with heaven as the ultimate goal for the believer. She says, "The popular notion that at the death of the body each saint comes into full bliss and the full powers of the eternal life, is nowhere taught in the Word."[60] However, as more emphasis was placed on the rapture in support of the pretribulational position, the image of Christ's coming shifted to an emphasis on heaven rather than establishing the kingdom on earth. The irony of this shift is that the "heaven is our home" emphasis is antithetical to the core commitment to premillennialism. If Jesus were coming to take believers to heaven eternally, there would simply be no need for the millennial reign on earth. Furthermore, it disassociates salvation from the physical body, making the resurrection an unnecessary doctrine.[61] The AG does not advocate such duality.[62] S. A. Jamieson argues, "The resurrection is a necessity for the soul needs a body."[63] This is why the emphasis on the resurrection is so vital to the AG's doctrine of the Second Coming. The resurrection holds together all of the aspects

[57] Wright, *Surprised by Hope*, 13–30, outlines the reasons for confusion about heaven and the various consequences of the Christian emphasis on heaven over resurrection.

[58] Some AG doctrinal texts have confused the doctrine of heaven for the blessed hope. For example, Nelson, *Bible Doctrines*, (1948), 142–47, teaches that the dead in Christ will be raised with a "spiritual body" that is "adapted to live in a spiritual world." The way he frames his understanding gives the impression that heaven (the land of eternal life) is the ultimate goal of the rapture.

[59] There are only a few articles in each decade that emphasized heaven as the final home. However, in the 1940s to 1950s, heaven became a regular subject and was held out as the final destination rather than earth. See A. H. Argue, "Heaven—The Future Home of the Saints," *PE*, March 8, 1959, 6–7; Frank Insensee, "Our Heavenly Inheritance," *PE*, June 17, 1951, 6; *PE*, April 26, 1953, 10; *PE*, January 17, 1954, 12; E. S. Williams, "Our Heavenly Inheritance," *PE*, June 1, 1958, 12; "I'll Be Home Soon," *PE*, June 12, 1960, 24.

[60] Sisson, *Foregleams of Glory*, 50.

[61] Bauckham and Hart, *Hope Against Hope*, 126.

[62] An example is J. N. Gortner, "Some Last Things," *PE*, January 22, 1921, 2–3, who is highly committed to dispensationalism yet comments, "God is interested in our bodies while we live here amid these scenes of time, and He does not forget them when our spirits take their departure from this world. They are His bodies now, and even though they may die they will be His bodies still."

[63] S. A. Jamieson, *Pillars of Truth* (Springfield: Gospel Publishing House, 1927), 103.

of Christ's coming into a coherent whole, emphasizing the work of the Spirit, the value of material creation, and the future kingdom.

The Pneumatological Affection: Spirit of Hope

Despite the pessimism inherent in premillennialism, the AG has primarily framed the Second Coming in terms of a "theology of hope." But how is it that both pessimism and hope can coexist in the same eschatological imagination? Fraser Watts is able to solve this dilemma by making an interesting distinction between hope and optimism.[64] Optimism is the "attitudinal" outlook created when a person expects something based on empirical evidence that points to the likelihood of that thing taking place.[65] The more likely something is, the more optimistic one becomes. This is precisely why sign-based empirical approaches to the signs of the times were so popular.[66] The more signs they could point to, the more certain they were that the return of Jesus was very soon. These signs also fueled the conviction that the world was not progressing. This sort of pessimism should not be seen as unreasonable considering that the "progress" achieved in areas such as technology, education, and science in the twentieth century also produced considerable "moral regress" exhibited by modernism's exploitation of power and use of technology to threaten human existence.[67] Premillennialists and dispensationalists are not the only ones who share this conviction. Modern theologians such as Emil Brunner and Jürgen Moltmann saw first-hand the chaos the myth of progress had created in the modern world.[68] The depravity of the twentieth century also did not escape

---

[64] Fraser Watts, "Subjective and Objective Hope," in John Polkinghorn and Michael Welker, eds., *The End of World and the Ends of God* (Harrisburg: Trinity Press International, 2000), 47–60.

[65] Watts, "Subjective and Objective Hope," 57.

[66] The most common approach to Bible prophecy was the sign-based empirical approach that attempted to prove the nearness of Christ's return by correlating the signs of the times from Jesus' apocalyptic discourse in Matthew 24 with current events. AG prophecy books were filled with an "array of historical facts" intended to inspire the reader to believe in the nearness of the Lord's return. This approach can be seen in Frank Boyd, *The Budding Fig Tree* (Springfield: Gospel Publishing House, 1925); Stanley Frodsham, *Things Which Must Shortly Come To Pass*, (Springfield,: Gospel Publishing House, 1928); Frank Boyd, *Signs of the Times*, (Springfield,: Gospel Publishing House, 1950); and C. M. Ward, *Waiting...* (Springfield: Gospel Publishing House, 1959).

[67] Hart and Bauckham, *Hope Against Hope*, 15.

[68] Emil Brunner, *Eternal Hope* (Philadelphia: Westminster Press, 1954), 15–40, juxtaposes the Christian hope for the future with the progress of human achievement. He says, "This is the lesson which humanity has had to learn in recent decades, and in awful contemplation of the nothingness of its optimistic hopes of progress. The monstrous increases in the scientific means of conquering nature have been exposed as dangerous possibilities of universal suicide ... the charm of the idea of progress

the attention of the leading scientific and social minds that struggled to envision anything other than future apocalyptic scenarios.[69] Based on these empirically assessed images of the future, it is no wonder that the "signs of the times" failed to engender any sort of optimism.

However, as Watts points out, hope is something altogether different. Hope is an objective reality that is not dependent upon the likelihood of a set of circumstances to inspire it.[70] Hope derives its epistemic value from objective promises, not from empirical potentialities and statistical probabilities. Hope is an affective response, engendered by the Spirit based on God's promise that the future will be good. As Hart and Bauckham explain, "From an eschatological perspective, the more improbable the better! . . . The only credible eschatology, given the failure of the myth of progress, is a transcendent one, which looks for a resolution of history that exceeds any possible imminent outcome of history."[71] Transcending the rational realm, hope operates in the affective realm generated within the imagination. The capacity to trust in this future is facilitated by the ability to imagine a moral future—one that is good. It is a "wager on transcendence" that is risky but is made possible by the one who is in control of the future.[72] This kind of hope is not a false optimism that depends on the human ability to progress; it is faith in God's ability to be faithful to his promise to "make all things new."

Because hope is a moral evaluation about the future, it is always framed in terms of what *should* or *ought* to be.[73] The recognition that the future is good involves recognizing that there is a sense in which the present is broken and in

---

has vanished and humanity, in the full flower of its development, has fallen a prey to the panic of nihilism" (p. 23). Also, Moltmann, *The Coming of God*, 192–202.

[69] William R. Stoger, "Scientific Accounts of Ultimate Catastrophes in Our Life-Bearing Universe," in Polkinghorn and Welker, eds., *The End of the World and the Ends of God*, 19–28.

[70] Watts, "Subjective and Objective Hope," 57.

[71] Hart and Bauckham, *Hope Against Hope*, 15.

[72] Hart and Bauckham, *Hope Against Hope*, 50.

[73] Michael G. Lawler, *What Is and What Ought to Be* (New York: Continuum Press, 2005), 25–43, argues that the tendency of systematic theologians to operate solely in the realm of "ought to be" needs to be tempered by a realistic and sociological description of "what is" when discussing transcendent concepts within certain contexts. Practical theology and the study of religious phenomenon could be considered more concrete than the idealism of Western theological expression because of the way they are sociologically accurate to the beliefs of a community. A balance between what is and what ought to be provides a balanced methodology, which from an eschatological position, seeks to balance a realistic apprehension of the present (the realistic and pessimism) with what should be (the ideal and optimistic).

need of redemption.[74] To argue for disengagement from the present would be to judge what humanity has become as somehow acceptable and would serve to justify the entrenchment of exploitation. In this way, a vision of the future should have the ability to "transfigure every empirical present."[75] The great irony of present day evangelicalism is that although many evangelicals hold premillennial views of eschatology; they often hold postmillennial visions of culture that portray America as a Christian nation and the government as a function of the manifest destiny.[76] The very reason why the AG rejected the postmillennial vision was because of its propensity to associate the present kingdoms of the world with the divine kingdom.

The Spirit of hope offers an alternative vision to the one the world can provide because the Spirit's hope is based on a promise rather than empirical data. Hope is the affection encouraged by the Spirit who waits and longs for Christ's return based on the promise that in the last days God will pour out his Spirit. The Holy Spirit, then, is the ultimate and only truly necessary sign of Christ's return. The Spirit is our "down payment" of that promise, and the baptism in the Spirit is our "seal" that reminds us of the eschatological future kingdom. Paul even uses similar terms to describe the baptism in the Spirit when he prays for the Spirit to cause hope to "fill" and "overflow" believers (Rom. 15:13).[77] If the Spirit is the true fountain of hope, then what we are actually talking about is the Spirit's hope, not the believer's hope. As J. W. Welch proclaimed, "He establishes in us the glorious hope, thus making Himself the God of Hope to us."[78] The hope the Spirit inspires within believers is the hope of resurrection, which includes the redemption of all creation. As Moltmann has argued, when one experiences the Spirit, one inevitably experiences "the eschatological longing for the complete salvation, redemption of the body and new creation of all things."[79]

Paul describes the believer's response to this salvific hope with the beautiful pneumatological image of "groaning." Groaning is an image that speaks of

---

[74] Macchia, *Baptized in the Spirit*, 281, argues that tongues is a transcendent sign which both reminds humanity of its brokenness and assures believers of a transcendent future.

[75] Hart and Bauckham, *Hope Against Hope*, 56.

[76] The fruits of manifest destiny were the expansion of the west, the subjugation of Native Americans, and the economic forces that empowered the slave trade of the American South. Studebaker, *A Pentecostal Political Theology for American Renewal*, 22–37.

[77] Horton, "Last Things," 597–98.

[78] J. W. Welch, "Looking for the Glorious Hope," *WE* November 13, 1915, 2.

[79] Jürgen Moltmaan, *Spirit of Life: A Universal Affirmation* (Minneapolis, MN: Fortress Press, 2001), 73.

struggle and suffering, concepts not often found in Pentecostal theology. Chris Green has identified three "groanings" that Paul refers to in Rom. 8:13–30: the groaning of creation (v. 19–22), the groaning of the believer (v. 23–25), and the groaning of the Spirit (v. 26–27).[80] Green defines groaning as "a *longing* for the eschatological fulfillment of all things, a *travailing* in effort to give life to the new age, and an *agonizing* under the burden of interior frailty and exterior oppression by the forces of sin, death, and injustice."[81] All three of these metaphors—longing, travailing, and agonizing—carry the sense of suffering and are manifested as groans "too deep for words."[82] Steven Torr rightly points out that Pentecostals need a better theology of lament, one in which the Spirit works in hopeful anticipation so that believers can endure the times of difficulty.[83] However, I would suggest that the groaning of the Spirit in Romans is not so much a groan of mourning in the expectation of a death as it is the groan of the Spirit in creation in expectation of new life. This type of groan is a hopeful longing for redemption and the promise that "death will be swallowed up in victory." As early AG missionary Alice Luce proclaims,

> The suffering and groaning of nature in this time of the dominion of sin, is not a hopeless mourning over something irrevocably lost. On the contrary, it is a suffering in hope, a death which is only the gateway of entrance into new life . . . the whole creation, though it suffered with him in this fall, will ultimately be redeemed and restored to greater beauty and fertility than ever.[84]

---

[80] Chris E. Green, "The Crucified God and the Groaning Spirit," *JPT* 19 (2010): 124–42.

[81] Green, "The Crucified God and the Groaning Spirit," 137.

[82] Similar to Green, Harry J. Steil, *What Will Happen Next* (Springfield: Gospel Publishing House, 1938), 57–60, identifies "three groans" that are taking place in anticipation of the coming of Jesus: the animal creation that is "praying for deliverance," the earth that is in pain because of disease, war, and natural disasters, and the Christian who is "groaning with sympathy for the sufferings of the world." But he adds, "the three groans shall soon change to three cheers!"

[83] Stephen C. Torr, *A Dramatic Pentecostal/Charismatic Anti-Theodicy: Improvising on a Divine Performance of Lament* (Eugene: Pickwick Publishing, 2013).

[84] Alice Luce, *Little Flock and the Last Days*, (Springfield: Gospel Publishing House, 1927), 47–48.

The groans of the Spirit as eschatological longings are expressed as "sighs" of waiting, not sorrows of loss.⁸⁵ The creation is not asking "why?" in complaint against injustice; it is asking "how long?" in a hopeful expression of faith.⁸⁶

Frank Macchia draws a natural parallel between the groans of creation and speaking in tongues as an eschatological sign that points to the hope of the *telos* of salvation.⁸⁷ Stephen Torr adds, "The act of lamenting in tongues thus contains the lament, but also, by very nature of it being in tongues, is a sign of the promise of what is to come—a manifestation of the redeemed future in the present."⁸⁸ This act of lament is more than a way to cope with the unredeemed world; it is a powerful prayer of intercession expressed in a way characteristic of the "hastening prayers" of early Pentecostals. The phenomenon of speaking in tongues is an eschatological protest of the present order and a longing for the future order.⁸⁹ As Macchia comments, "Glossolalia is not only a yearning for liberation and redemption to come, it is an 'evidence' that such has already begun and is now active."⁹⁰ Tongues are often referred to in the AG as the "initial evidence" of the baptism in the Spirit. But tongues are also a continuing sign and reminder for believers that the fullness of Christ's presence (his *parousia*) is coming.⁹¹

⁸⁵ Frank D. Macchia, "Jesus is Victor," in Althouse and Waddell, eds., *Perspectives in Pentecostal Eschatologies*, 388–89, notes that in the eschatology of Johann Blumhardt, the inbreaking of the Kingdom in the Spirit means that "groaning is not a cry of helplessness but a positive yearning for the liberation of all things from suffering and bondage."

⁸⁶ H. K. Harrington, "Lament or Complaint? A Response to Scott Ellington, Risking Truth: Reshaping the World Through Prayers of Lament," *JPT* 18 (2009): 177–81.

⁸⁷ Frank D. Macchia, "Sighs Too Deep For Words," *JPT* 1 (1992): 47–73.

⁸⁸ Stephen C. Torr, "Lamenting in Tongues: Glossolalia as a Pneumatic Aid to Lament," *JPT* 26, no. 1 (2017): 46.

⁸⁹ Modern theologians outside the Pentecostal movement are also embracing the eschatological function of glossolalia. Jeffrey Lamp, "N. T. Wright—Right or Wrong for Pentecostals?" in Janet Meyer Everts and Jeffrey S. Lamp (eds.), *Pentecostal Theology and The Theological Vision of N.T. Wright* (Cleveland: CPT Press, 2015), 25, demonstrates that N. T. Wright has developed a theology of glossolalia in which "heaven and earth overlap and interlock in the present in anticipation of the ultimate coming together of the heaven and earth in the present." Althouse, *Spirit of the Last Days*, 137, points out that Moltmann's openness to the Spirit of Life allows him to create space for the charismatic gifts to characterize the present age. Although never experiencing glossolalia personally, Moltmann sees speaking in tongues as personal and corporate charismata flowing from "Christ's liberating lordship." See Moltmaan, *Spirit of Life*, 180–86.

⁹⁰ Macchia, "Sighs Too Deep For Words," 70.

⁹¹ Aaron Friezen, *Norming the Abnormal* (Eugene: Pickwick, 2013), 135, discusses the AG's distinctive doctrine of "initial evidence" and the AG's expansion of that doctrine to include the idea of the tongues as a "continuing evidence" of the Spirit-filled life. See the AG position paper, "The

The Pneumatological Response: Tarrying in the Spirit

If longing is the proper affection engendered by the Spirit of resurrection, what sort of praxis should these longings inspire? For the answer, I want to revisit the parable of the ten virgins that was so essential to the early Pentecostal eschatological imagination. Early Pentecostals looked to the parable of the foolish virgins to imagine Spirit baptism as the "minimum requirement" for the rapture. However, with the delay of the Second Coming, second-generation AG writers drew from this parable instructions for waiting. Although they were zealous for his coming initially, the delay became a test to see if Pentecostal people would be able to wait patiently. As the parable of the virgins demonstrates, the believer's pneumatological response to the promise of resurrection requires the Spirit's fruit of patience, a virtue that must accompany a true eschatological longing in order to endure with passion for his coming. The problem with the five foolish virgins was not that they weren't ready. They were dressed and prepared to meet the bridegroom just as was the five wise virgins. What separated the two companies was the amount of oil needed to patiently wait for as long as the delay might persist.[92] The impulse to want to escape the world that is so common in evangelical eschatological culture is a carnal desire of the flesh and not a fruit of the Spirit. Fleshly eschatology looks at present conditions and seeks to escape, which is motivated by a desire for immediate relief. But true patience requires the "oil" of the Holy Spirit to stay ready in the delay. The essential principle is this: the longer the wait, the more oil is needed for the waiting. Because of this, Pentecostal eschatology by nature, if it draws upon the resources of the Spirit, should be incapable of being escapist because the fruit of the Holy Spirit's work is patience and maturity.[93]

In order to be pneumatological, Pentecostal eschatology needs to re-discover the value of "tarrying." As a hallmark of Pentecostal spirituality, tarrying is a deeply Spirit-oriented practice that requires patience, repetition, letting go of one's own self, and holding on to God.[94] In cultivating the practice of tarrying,

Baptism in the Holy Spirit: The Initial Experience and Continuing Evidences of the Spirit-Filled Life," adopted by General Presbytery the General Council of the Assemblies of God, August 11, 2000.

[92] William J. Seymour, "Behold the Bridegroom Cometh," *AF,* January 1907, 2, notes that all the virgins were "pure," and that each had oil. Although they started out to meet the bridegroom, they ran out of oil as they waited. See also "The Ten Virgins," *AF,* November 1906, 4; "Rebecca; Type of the Bride of Christ," *AF,* February 1907, 2.

[93] Daniel Castelo, "Patience as a Theological Virtue: A Challenge to Pentecostal Eschatology," in Althouse and Waddell, eds., *Perspectives in Pentecostal Eschatologies,* 232–46.

[94] This process of tarrying, which has been preserved in the black Pentecostal church, is described beautifully in David D. Daniels III, "'Until the Power of the Lord Comes Down': African American

Pentecostals can re-engage the virtues of waiting, longing, and preparing for the Bridegroom to come, while at the same time cultivating patience and endurance, not impatience and escape.[95] The sanctifying practice of Pentecostal prayer (tarrying at the altar) should also be mirrored by how one lives (tarrying in patient endurance).[96] Each of the Pentecostal sacraments, such as speaking in tongues, praying for healing, the Lord's Supper, and tarrying at the altar, are daily and weekly practices that encourage patient hope and eschatological longing.[97]

The Spirit of Peace: Imagining the Millennium

The AG's commitment to premillennialism is based on the overwhelming conviction that Jesus will return to set up his kingdom on earth. The SFT states: "The revelation of the Lord Jesus Christ from heaven, the salvation of national Israel, and the Millennial Reign of Christ on the earth is the Scriptural promise and the world's hope (2 Thess. 1:7; Rev. 19:11–14; Rom. 11:26, 27; Rev. 20:1–7)."[98] Although the scriptural basis for the millennium is derived from Revelation 20, AG doctrinal formulations actually glean very little details from this passage. Instead, the visions of this period are shaped by OT promises that portray a future world marked by idyllic conditions under the Messiah. The prominent image within the concept of the millennium is that of peace between God, humanity, the world, and creation. In contrast to the "otherworldly" emphasis of heaven, the millennium is earth-centered, marked by activity, ordered and structured, and mutually beneficial for all inhabitants of the earth. The SFT describes the reign of Christ in terms of a reign of "universal peace (Isa. 11:6–9)."[99] Christ's rule will bring about a peaceful political rule (Isa. 2:4; Mic. 4:3). One prominent image that controls the concept

---

Pentecostal Spirituality and Tarrying," in Clive Erricker and Jane Erricker, eds., *Contemporary Spiritualties* (London: Continuum Press, 2001), 173–88.

[95] Daniel Castelo, "Tarrying on the Lord: Affections, Virtues and Theological Ethics," *JPT* 13, no. 1 (2004): 49.

[96] Vondey, *Pentecostal Theology*, 64.

[97] Wesley Scott Biddy, "Re-envisioning the Pentecostal Understanding of the Eucharist: An Ecumenical Proposal," *Pneuma* 28, no. 2 (Fall 2006): 228–51, notes that Pentecostal ordinances represent eschatological "signs" of the work of God in the life of the believer and are sacramental in nature even if they are not conceived as such. Also, Macchia, "Tongues as a Sign," 51–76, and Kenneth J. Archer, "Nourishment for our Journey: The Pentecostal *via Salutis* and Sacramental Ordinances," in Chris E. W. Green, ed., *Pentecostal Ecclesiology* (Boston: Brill, 2016), 141–60, make similar arguments.

[98] *GC Minutes* (September 16–22, 1927), 8.

[99] The phrase "universal peace" was not in the original statement. It was added to the *SFT* in *GC Minutes* (August 23–29, 1961), 23.

of the millennium is Peter's expectation that Christ will return to bring about the "restoration of all things" (Acts 3:21).[100] The AG imagined it as a time of "renewal" of the earth and "reconstruction" of the present order under the lordship of Jesus through peace and justice.[101] The resurrection of body and the created world will usher in a new epoch for creation in which the curse of sin will be lifted, sin will be restrained, agriculture will flourish, and human life will experience restored longevity and divine health (Isa. 11:6–8; Ezek. 36:30).[102] The nations will benefit from universally prosperous economic conditions (Ezek. 34:26–27) and will experience an educational renaissance (Isa. 2:2).[103] The ultimate goal is for all nations to willingly submit to his Lordship (Ps. 72:11; Zec. 14:16).

Is a literalist vision of the future kingdom still a viable option for today? In the past few decades a growing number of ministers have become uncomfortable with the literalist hermeneutic for interpreting Revelation and have gravitated toward an amillennialist position.[104] While there are certainly scholars who support this idea, for the AG, a commitment to a future kingdom on earth cannot not be dismissed in favor of the kingdom now (as in postmillennialism) or spiritually in Christ (as in amillennialism).[105] Amos Yong, one the most prolific Pentecostal scholars in the fellowship, maintains that premillennialism is still vital to the theology of the Pentecostal movement.[106] Yong recognizes that belief in the millennium is simply affirming the expectation that Jesus will literally return to reign on earth. While the specific belief that Christ's reign on earth will be a literal 1,000-year timeframe is dependent upon a literal interpretation of Revelation 20; the general belief in the future literal reign of

[100] Williams, *Systematic Theology*, 206, 233–34; Horton, *Promise of His Coming*, 53–55.

[101] "The Shaking of the Nations," *PE*, Second Coming Supplement, September 10, 1920, 8; D. H. McDowell, "The Purpose of the Coming of the Lord," *PE*, May 2, 1925, 3.

[102] Menzies and Horton, *Bible Doctrines*, 250; E. N. Bell, "Questions and Answers," *WE*, March 30, 1918, 9.

[103] Myer Pearlman, *Windows into the Future* (Springfield: Gospel Publishing House, 1941), 160; Williams, *Systematic Theology*, 206–208, Ralph M. Riggs, *God's Calendar of Coming Events* (Springfield: Gospel Publishing House, 1962), 58–59; Menzies and Horton, *Bible Doctrines*, 238–39.

[104] Blumhofer, *Restoring the Faith*, 223–38. See also section 3.4.2.

[105] Nearly every AG Bible doctrine text outlines the three millennial positions. Horton, "The End Times," 620–22, and Menzies and Horton, *Bible Doctrines*, 231–36, offer simplistic engagements with the strengths and weaknesses of each millennial view. Nelson, *Bible Doctrines*, 151–56, defends the premillennial coming but does not engage other views. Pearlman, *Knowing the Doctrines of the Bible*, 294, gives only one passing mention of millennium in the very last page of his book. The common thread is the commitment to interpret Revelation "as literally as the context allows" and to facilitate the fulfillment of OT promises concerning Israel.

[106] Yong, *Renewing Christian Theology*, 51.

Christ on earth is not.[107] Throughout much of Church history, the expectation of the literal return of Christ and his earthly kingdom was affirmed in the creeds of the church despite holding non-futurist views of Revelation.[108] For the AG, belief in the millennium is a belief in messianic eschatology rooted in Paul's discussion of Israel in Romans 9–11.[109] There will come a day when Israel is restored and the Messiah will reign on earth as the OT has promised. But is affirming a millennium that is a literal 1,000 year period vital to the AG position? Not necessarily, considering that from 1927–1961 the *SFT* did not specify the length of time but affirmed the reign of Christ on earth. The actual length of time is not as important as the affirmation that Jesus will return to the earth to rule his eschatological kingdom. As Yong points out, "The actual nature of the thousand years may not be resolvable on this side of the eschaton, but Christians across the evangelical-ecumenical spectrum ought to be able to agree that eschatological salvation includes creaturely involvement in divine rule."[110] By taking this position, the millennium can still be affirmed even amidst a growing number of non-literal hermeneutical approaches to Revelation.

The second reason that Amos Yong values the concept of the millennium is because it affirms the imminent coming of Christ; a belief prominently displayed in the *SFT* and throughout AG literature.[111] The AG rejected other millennial views primarily because they are dependent upon earthly circumstances in order to bring about the coming of Christ.[112] This is why the concept of prophecy as

---

[107] Thomson, *Kingdom Come*, 126–27, sees the literal 1000-year period as non-essential because "the millennium lies beyond history in the eschatological Kingdom of glory, it is the time of eternity, not of historical time."

[108] George Eldon Ladd, *The Blessed Hope* (Grand Rapids: Eerdmans, 1984), 19–34, points out that the prevailing view of most early church fathers was futuristic post-tribulational millennialism. It should also be noted that not all premillennialists are futurists. The historicist sees the Book of Revelation as a description of the struggle between the church and the world throughout history except for the consummation of the eternal state. See Stanley J. Grenz, *The Millennial Maze* (Downers Grove: InterVarsity Press, 1992), 127–47.

[109] Moltmann, *The Way of Jesus Christ*, 28–37, outlines his Messianic eschatology based on Paul's teaching that the Christian "Yes" to Christ and Israel's "no" means that time of universal redemption is still to come when Israel will become the Messianic community God intended.

[110] Yong, *Renewing Christian Theology*, 50–51.

[111] Yong, *Renewing Christian Theology*, 52.

[112] *GC Minutes* (September 2–9, 1937), 46, "We recommend that all our ministers teach the imminent coming of Christ, warning all men to be prepared for that coming, which may occur at any time, and not to lull their minds into insecurity by any teaching that would cause them to feel that certain events must occur before the Rapture of the saints." The doctrine of imminence, although they profess it to be vital to pretribulationism, is actually inherent in premillennialism and a rejection of

"history written in advance" is problematic. A deterministic vision of the future makes the coming of Christ dependent upon prophetic circumstances to transpire in the world before the coming of Christ is possible.[113] By implication, this would mean that prior to 1948 (or other perceived prophetic fulfillments) the doctrine of imminence would be a prophetic impossibility. However, if there is "no event that must take place" before the coming of Jesus, then speculation and prediction is an empty exercise. The very fact that there has been a delay in Christ's coming should suggest that the future is more open than this prophetic hermeneutic suggests. The time set for the restoration of the kingdom is subject to the openness of God and the future of Jesus Christ.[114] Until then, Jesus must "remain in heaven until the time comes for God to restore everything" (Acts 3:20). The unknown-ness of the time of Christ's *parousia* suggests that the particular time is not yet determined, rather than simply the information has not yet been revealed.[115] Moltmann explains,

> The parousia of Christ and the end of this world-time belong together. They do not belong together in the sense that we could talk about a "coming of Christ at the end of times," as if this end were fixed once and for all. The relation between the parousia and the end is the very reverse of that: we have to talk about the end of time in the coming of Christ. It is not the "end of the world" that would bring with it Christ's parousia. It is the parousia of Christ, which will bring the wretchedness of "this world time" to its end in the glory of his eternal kingdom.[116]

postmillennialism. Support for the any moment return is predicated on the belief that there is no event that must take place before the rapture can occur.

[113] Many in the AG mistakenly assume that one must hold a pretribulational view of the rapture in order to believe in imminence. This is not the case. All premillennial positions maintain that Christ could come at any moment and that what is happening in the world has no controlling interest in deciding when he will come.

[114] Moltmann, *Theology of Hope*, 194–95, argues the future is not determined by the calendar; it is determined by the freedom of God and the coming of Jesus. The openness of the future is God's openness to act outside of time. However, there are limits to that openness, being that an expected future is still to come. Otherwise, the future would be empty of hope. So, while the coming of Jesus is certain, the future is not certain as to when that coming will take place.

[115] There is symmetry here between Christ who waits in heaven until he is sent by the father (Acts 3:20) and Matthew's declaration that Jesus is waiting until the Father declares it is time (Mt. 24:36). The Father sets the time of restoration by his own authority (Acts 1:7).

[116] Jürgen Moltmann, *The Way of Jesus Christ: Christology in Messianic Dimensions* (New York: Harper Collins, 1990), 321. This assertion by Moltmann is contingent upon his view that the millennium does not belong to historical time. The parousia ushers in eschatological time, which

What Moltmann is arguing is that the end does not come because it is time; the end comes because Jesus comes when the Father decides it is time. This is why it is impossible to know the day or the hour. The Father's eschatological patience is motivated by his love for humanity and his willingness to extend grace as long as needed (2 Pet. 3:9).[117] The possibility of an "open" eschatology should be attractive to Pentecostals, whose pneumatology and concept of God is one of possibility, change, and non-deterministic.[118] Understood this way, the fact that Jesus has not returned despite nearly 2000 years of expectation is inconsequential to biblical prophecy. As long as the Spirit is still crying out "come!" believers still expect his "soon" coming.

Third, Yong argues that the millennium encourages creaturely participation in the divine rule of the Kingdom.[119] Jesus' kingdom will achieve its utopian goal in cooperation with his saints and by the power the Spirit. This image of the millennium is vital to Christ's future and his fulfillment as Lord and Messiah (Rev. 11:15).[120] For Myer Pearlman, Jesus fulfilled his role as Prophet and Priest in his first coming; the millennium will be the fulfillment of Jesus' role "as King beginning at his coming and continuing throughout the Millennium."[121] The

---

breaks with the current epoch and ushers in a new era. However, this conception of time is not consistent with the AG which sees the millennium as the culmination of time, after which begins the period of eternal time. Despite this disagreement, Moltmann's conviction that the *parousia* is not waiting for the present time to end is an important correlating concern with the AG.

[117] Stanley M. Horton, *The Book of Acts* (Springfield: Gospel Publishing House, 1981), 56–57, suggests that the promise of his coming restoration (times of refreshing) are conditional on Israel's acceptance and repentance. This fact, which likely contributes to the delay in the *parousia*, makes Christ's coming and the fulfillment of prophecies necessarily contingent upon Israel's repentant response. This is also consistent with Peter's suggestion that God is waiting on people to repent before bringing about the end (2 Pet. 2:9). This is what Clark Pinnock, *Most Moved Mover* (Grand Rapids: Baker Academic, 2001), 57–58, refers to as the "partly settled and partly unsettled future" of God.

[118] Pinnock, *Most Moved Mover*, 12, notes that sympathy towards openness views has been within "Wesleyan, Arminian and Pentecostal evangelical circles." However, the topic of an "open eschatology" has yet to be fully explored. The only attempts to date to discuss an open eschatology are in David W. Baker, ed., *Looking into the Future* (Grand Rapids: Baker Academic, 2001), in which articles by Clark Pinnock, Stephen C. Roy, John Sanders, and Steven R. Tracy, explore the concepts of foreknowledge, theodicy, universal salvation, and assurance in the context of Open Theism, but none of them address particular issues of eschatology or the hermeneutics of prophetic interpretation.

[119] Yong, *Renewing Christian Theology*, 51.

[120] Moltmann, *The Way of Jesus Christ*, 321–36, argues that the coming of Jesus wrapped up into Christ's Messianic future envisioned as the "coming one," the "Lord," the "Messiah" and the "Son of Man." Each of these titles invokes images of Christ's rule in an earthly kingdom.

[121] Pearlman, *Knowing the Doctrines of the Bible*, 394.

image of Christ as the perfect Messianic King is central to this eschatological vision.

What kind of rule will this be? The *SFT* describes it as a reign of "universal peace (Isa. 11:6–9)."[122] This political image is meant to communicate Christ's universal and absolute righteous rule over all nations as King of Kings and Lord of Lords. Macchia points out that the reign of peace of the Messiah over the nations dwarfs the time of wrath on the nations, demonstrating that God's grace "much more abounds" than his judgment. In contrast to the image in Revelation of the beast who rules by threat of death, Christ does not force the nations to obey, demonstrated by the fact that some are even led astray at the end of the millennium.[123] Christ's judgment upon the nations is "not to annihilate them, but in order to rule them in justice and in peace!"[124] The goal is for all nations to willingly submit to his Lordship (Ps. 72:11; Zec. 14:16).

During the millennium, when the Spirit is finally poured out upon Israel, "the whole nation – contrite, cleansed, and clothed with the Spirit of God – will be ready to fulfill their mission to all the nations of the earth."[125] The saints who faithfully witness about the Messiah will be resurrected and will reign with Christ in this kingdom ruled by the Spirit of Peace (Rev. 20:4–6).[126] But they will not do it alone, as the salvation of national Israel will also result in salvation for all the nations. The work of restoration in all facets of creation will be accomplished in cooperation with the saints as the Spirit is poured out on all flesh (Isa. 32:15; Joel 2:28–30).[127] As Wonsuk Ma points out, "As the spirit is lavishly poured out

---

[122] The phrase "universal peace" was not in the original statement. It was added to the *SFT* in *GC Minutes* (August 23–29, 1961), 23.

[123] Thomas and Macchia, *Revelation*, 621.

[124] Thomas and Macchia, *Revelation*, 620.

[125] Alice Luce, *Little Flock and the Last Days*, (Springfield: Gospel Publishing House, 1927), 70–71.

[126] Hart and Bauckham, *Hope Against Hope*, 135, note that the mention of "martyrs" in Rev 20:4 commonly focuses scholars on this group being a special group. However, AG writers do not see it that way. Stanley M. Horton, *The Ultimate Victory*, (Springfield: Gospel Publishing House, 1991), 294, argues that this company includes the saints of all ages, including the martyrs, since Jesus promises that those who overcome will reign with Christ (Rev. 3:21–22). It could also be suggested, such as is the case in Thomas and Macchia, *Revelation*, 356, that this is a universal designation for "overcomers" who have demonstrated "identification and solidarity with Christ" even unto death. Skaggs and Benham, *Revelation*, 206, make a similar claim that the phrase "those who are beheaded" is "probably a general turn representing all those who have wholly committed themselves to Christ." A more general interpretation is consistent with the AG claim of the Bride being identified as "overcomers."

[127] Horton, "The End Times," 630; Horton, *The Ultimate Victory*, 295; A. D. Millard, "The Prophecy of Joel," *Paraclete* 17, no. 2 (Spring 1983): 10–12. The work of the Holy Spirit in the

upon the members of the restored community, they will experience the reversal of fortunes for Israel: agricultural abundance, physical and emotional security, and moral restoration."[128] Under the reign of the Spirit-filled Messiah, the poor and the needy will receive justice as the abundance of the earth meets the needs of the vulnerable (Isa. 11:2–4). The Spirit will work through God's eschatological people (both Jew and Gentile), increase the Messiah's government of Peace (Isa. 9:6–7), and all nations will be reconciled to God.[129]

In addition to Yong's three compelling reasons for sustaining a vibrant millennial doctrine, I offer several additional rationales. First, there is a strong emphasis among Pentecostal scholars concerning the "already/not yet" tension found in the concept of the kingdom of God.[130] This concept, made popular in the academy in last half of the twentieth century, has been part of the AG's understanding of the kingdom of God from the beginning. The concept of the "already/not yet" is descriptive of the inner logic of Pentecostal theology and affirms the kingdom is present now in the manifestations of the Spirit and is still to come in the full consummation of the kingdom at the return of Christ. In order to maintain this concept, both aspects of the kingdom must be affirmed. As Peter Althouse points out, "The tension between the now and the not yet cannot be resolved in favor of the now as with realized, existential or mystical eschatologies, nor can it be resolved in favor of the future with thorough-going, futurist or dispensation eschatologies."[131] Were this tension to be resolved either way, the Pentecostal mission would be hindered and Pentecostal theology would be undermined.[132] Through the Spirit of God, the kingdom is experienced not only in the various experiences in the Pentecostal *via salutis*, but also in

---

millennium is a regrettably neglected topic in AG eschatology. Although its often commented that the Joel 2 will have its ultimate fulfillment in the millennium, few writers spend any time or give any support for this view.

[128] Wonsuk Ma, *Until the Spirit Comes: The Spirit of God in the Book of Isaiah* (JSOTSup 271; Sheffield, UK: Sheffield Academic Press, 1999), 211.

[129] Ma, *Until the Spirit Comes*, 211, notes that for Isaiah, the blessing of the Spirit upon Israel will have a corresponding influence on the reconciliation of the Gentiles to Yahweh.

[130] Althouse, "The Landscape of Pentecostal and Charismatic Eschatology," 13; Dempster, "Eschatology, Spirit Baptism, and Inclusiveness," 164; Horton, "Last Things," 605, Thomas and Macchia, *Revelation*, 501; Waddell, "What Time is it?," 147; Wood, *Core Values,* 28; Yong, *Renewing Christian Theology*, 15–16.

[131] Althouse, "Ascension, Pentecost, Eschaton," 242–45.

[132] Land, *Pentecostal Spirituality*, 97–99.

Pentecostal manifestations characteristic of the kingdom.[133] The church is indwelt with the Spirit "in order to function as a sign and instrument of the Kingdom in the world."[134] This sign would have no significance if it did not affirm the nature of the future kingdom.

A second significant contribution to the strength of premillennialism comes from Jürgen Moltmann's concept of eschatological millenarianism.[135] As Peter Althouse has documented, Moltmann has become a significant theological resource for many of the leading Pentecostal scholars.[136] Like Pentecostals, Moltmann rejects historical millennialism, which is the postmillennial vision that believes secular or religious institutions can be equated with the kingdom of God. Instead, he argues in favor of eschatological millenarianism, which is the belief that the present order will end and will usher in the messianic kingdom in its fullness.[137] Moltmann argues that eschatological millenarianism is not only the best millennial option; it is a "necessary picture of hope" that speaks powerfully against the tyranny of the present order, is rooted in the Christological hope of resurrection, and represents the hope of a future for Israel.[138] Pentecostals should be encouraged that the leading eschatological mind of the twentieth century holds similar convictions to that which the AG has held.

A third reason that premillennialism is preferred by Pentecostal scholars is the Luke-Acts orientation of the movement.[139] Reinforced throughout Luke-Acts is the emphasis on the Spirit in connection with the expectation of the coming

---

[133] Matthew Thompson, "Eschatology as Soteriology" in Althouse and Waddell, eds., *Perspectives in Pentecostal Eschatologies*, 198–204, argues that each of the crisis moments in the Pentecostal *via salutis* of the five-fold gospel anticipate the eschatological fullness of complete cosmic salvation in reverse order. See also Thompson, *Kingdom Come*, 128–43.

[134] Frank D. Macchia, "Church of the Latter Rain," in J.C. Thomas, ed., *Toward a Pentecostal Ecclesiology*, 255. Elizabeth Sisson, "A Sign People," *PE*, January 11, 1919, 2–3 makes a similar claim that Pentecostals are a "sign people," signaling to the world that the Latter Rain has come and the end is near.

[135] Jürgen Moltmann, *The Coming of God* (Minneapolis, MN: Fortress Press, 2004).

[136] Althouse, *Spirit of the Last Days*, studied four prominent Pentecostal theologians, Steven Land, Eldin Villafane, Miroslav Volf, and Frank Macchia, all of which have been highly influenced by Moltmann.

[137] Moltmann, *The Coming of God*, 192. Althouse, *Spirit of the Last Days*, 123, points out that early Pentecostals fit into Moltmann's concept of eschatological millenarianism because they "rejected the triumphalism of America's 'manifest destiny' and 'success' orientation and saw themselves as a 'chosen people' or 'remnant' empowered by the charismatic gifts of the Spirit."

[138] Moltmann, *The Coming of God*, 192–202.

[139] Yong, *Renewing Christian Theology*, 44–49.

kingdom.[140] Luke's infancy narratives of Zechariah, Simeon, Anna, John the Baptist, and Mary all include the Spirit prophesying the coming messianic kingdom.[141] Further, the key passage that drives the Pentecostal mission (Acts 1:8) is preceded by the disciple's question, "Lord, is now the time you will restore the kingdom to Israel?" This close relationship between the mission of the Spirit and the messianic expectation of the coming kingdom in Luke is vital in the Pentecostal imagination.[142] As Pentecostals, we cannot affirm the tension of the "already/not yet" without both a present and future aspect to the kingdom.[143]

One final benefit of the AG's affirmation of the millennium is that it provides the rationale for the place of Israel and the future Messianic kingdom. From nearly the day the AG was created, believers watched the seemingly miraculous return of the Jews and the establishment of a national–political state of Israel. What was only speculation for premilllennialists in the nineteenth century became a reality and unfolded through every stage of development in the AG. Contemporary AG scholars, despite concerns about the way in which Israel is seen within dispensational eschatology, have not abandoned a future for Israel. Beyond simply affirming a literalistic hermeneutic, premillennialism is ultimately about envisioning a future for Israel. Moltmann says, "The fact that this messianic hope of those who believe in Christ opens up an analogous future for Israel, seems to be a special mark of Christian premillennialism. It is the Christian dream of the Jews—not for their conversion to the Church, but for their resurrection into the kingdom of their Messiah."[144] Contemporary Evangelical scholars, regardless of whether or not they accept dispensationalism, have recognized the need for a theology of Israel that takes the OT promises seriously

---

[140] Blaine Charette, "Restoring the Kingdom to Israel: Kingdom and the Spirit in Luke's Thought," in Althouse and Waddell, eds. *Perspectives in Pentecostal Eschatologies,* 49–60.

[141] Horton, *Our Destiny,* 161–74. These passages were instrumental in the messianic expectations for the AG. See examples in, "This Present Crisis," *WE,* July 1, 1916, 7; "Impending World Judgment and The Only Place of Shelter," *PE,* January 25, 1919, 9; Myer Pearlman, "Watchful Waiting," *PE,* September 1, 1928, 1, 6–7; Edith Armstrong, "The Welcoming Committee," *PE,* December 22, 1963, 11.

[142] Horton, *Our Destiny,* 194–97.

[143] This disagrees with Charette, "Restoring the Kingdom to Israel," 59, who argues that the restoration of Israel and the establishment of the Kingdom is re-interpreted by Luke as the operation of the power of the Spirit. He says, "Through the Spirit's power God is now bringing all people the benefits of the Kingdom." While I agree with his expansion of the kingdom to include the present work of the Spirit, this cannot be at the expense of the kingdom in the future. See Land, *Pentecostal Spirituality,* 99.

[144] Moltmann, *The Coming of God,* 151.

without embracing the extremes or overemphasis often found in evangelical eschatology.

For the AG, belief in a future for Israel is expressed by the *SFT* and declares the millennium will bring about the "salvation of national Israel." But, in what way should a commitment to the "salvation of national Israel" be understood? Amos Yong believes the inclusion of a future for Israel is inherent in the Pentecostal understanding of the universal outpouring of the Spirit.[145] For Yong, the restoration of Israel in Luke-Acts is tied to eschatological inauguration of the last days in the Spirit at Pentecost. This means that the messianic mission "includes rather than excludes Israel as part of the people of God."[146] Therefore, the diasporic promise that the Spirit will be poured out on "all flesh" must include Jews, Arabs, and Gentiles in the last days. Because the mission of proclaiming the death and resurrection of the Messiah has not ceased, in a dispensational sense, the missional mandate to reach the "Jew first" with the gospel of the Messiah is still in effect.[147] Rather than negating the ethnic separation of Jew and Gentile, it argues for an eschatological union of both into one people under the Messiah in the kingdom. Larry McQueen takes a similar approach in that the messianic implications of being "in Christ" means that Church does not replace Israel, but that "Israel itself has been transformed into a global community."[148]

Frank Macchia solves the ecclesiastical tension between the Church and Israel by arguing that the church does not replace Israel; Israel's election ultimately finds its fulfillment in Christ. He says, "Israel and the church find their destiny in him."[149] In Revelation, the crucified Lamb is the "fulfillment of Israel's mission," which the church prophetically proclaims to the nations. He says, "There is no Israel ultimately without the church and the nations to whom the church as the eschatological Israel of the Lamb is called to bear witness."[150] Macchia rejects a dispensational understanding of the Church and Israel, noting that in Revelation the church is ascribed all of the titles of Israel including "priests," "a kingdom," and "a city" (New Jerusalem).[151] Because the church is rooted in OT concepts of Israel, he says, "The church is the 144,000 from the tribes of Israel that find their way through the wilderness of trials of the latter

[145] Yong, *In the Days of Caesar*, 332–42.
[146] Yong, *In the Days of Caesar*, 337.
[147] Horton, *Our Destiny*, 196.
[148] McQueen, *Toward a Pentecostal Eschatology*, 230.
[149] Thomas and Macchia, *Revelation*, 534–35.
[150] Thomas and Macchia, *Revelation*, 502.
[151] Thomas and Macchia, *Revelation*, 506, 532–35.

days to the New Jerusalem."[152] By expanding the church to include the eschatological Israel, Macchia in turn, includes Israel in the eschatological church.[153] This eschatological understanding of Israel and the Church is consistent with the AG's understanding of the Church, Israel, and the coming messianic kingdom. The church is considered "spiritual Israel," not in a dispensational sense, but in a sense of the prophetic distinction as the people of God.[154] As Moltmann asserts, the church is eschatologically "parallel to Israel, and over against Israel."[155]

The AG's position toward eschatological Israel is further clarified by their understanding of the nature of the present State of Israel. As Chapter 4 demonstrated, Israel as a political entity is not the same as Israel the eschatological people of God.[156] AG writers did not easily dismiss the Jewish hostility to Christians and missionaries, the treatment of Arabs in occupied territories, and the attempts to restore the Jewish sacrificial system. This sort of caution was deeply embedded in a millennial theology that would question the legitimacy of any kingdom of Israel that has not first welcomed the Messiah. Further, their stance on the theological affirmation of Israel is not to be interpreted as "anti-Palestinian" or any other ethnic group in the Middle East. The AG has chosen to take an official "apolitical stance in matters of government and nations" and "cannot endorse and approve every action of a particular country whether right

---

[152] Thomas and Macchia, *Revelation*, 506, 532–35.

[153] This is consistent with Moltmann, *The Coming of God*, 199 who points to Revelation 7 in which "sealed" Christians will be joined together with the "sealed" Jews who together constitute the "messianic people of the messianic kingdom." Horton, "The Last Things," 630, takes a similar position arguing "the two groups are joined to reign with Christ for the thousand years."

[154] Williams, *Systematic Theology*, 91–97, briefly discussed the differentiation between Israel and the Church according to the promises of God, but also notes the similarities in designations as "the assembly," which leads him to take a "broad view" of the meaning of the church to include all the people of God. None of the bible doctrine books of the AG argue for an ecclesiastical differentiation between the Church and Israel, nor do they argue for a covenantal separation of the two peoples. The distinction between the Church is eschatological and related solely to God's prophetic plan for the Jewish people.

[155] Moltmann, *The Coming of God*, 199.

[156] Chapters 7 and 8 demonstrates that many in the AG had questions not only about the legitimacy of Israel's restoration but also the theological tensions that came with their presence as a nation that returned in unbelief. This attitude is contra D.J. Wilson, "Eschatology, Pentecostal Perspectives," in *DPCM*, 265, who claims, "(Pentecostals) have applauded the restoration of Israel, no matter what the means employed."

or wrong" even if some within the fellowship would do otherwise.[157] The doctrinal affirmation of "the salvation of the Israel" is not an endorsement of present-day Israel; it is an eschatological statement about the future when the Messiah is revealed from heaven and the kingdom is restored to Israel in the millennium. Blaine Charette says, in the present, Israel cannot claim the rights as true Israel because; "The nationalistic aspirations have been replaced by new realities created by the eschatological spirit, which benefit all peoples."[158] When Christ does return, Israel will "be redeemed through the seeing of Christ of the parousia."[159] Holding together a separation of the state of Israel from the eschatological Israel guards the AG against advocating for a divine endorsement of the actions of a secular manifestation.

In the debate about how to understand the relationship between present Israel and eschatological Israel, Robert Jenson asserts that any attempt to talk about Israel needs qualification.[160] Jenson makes a distinction between what he calls "Canonical Israel" and religious/secular Israel. Canonical Israel is the biblical and national political entity that was established through Moses but whose existence ceased when the temple rituals ended under Rome. That Israel does not exist today. What does exist is the religious institution called Judaism, which claims the right to be called Israel but does so without the ethnic and cultic realities that defined Canonical Israel. The State of Israel may consist of the political, rabbinical, or cultural aspects centered in the synagogue, however, none of these entities can claim to be Israel based on the canonical, covenantal, and messianic parameters in Scripture. However, the Church, which is in a sense the Spiritual Israel and who has been grafted into Israel, shares in the promises made to Israel by accepting the Messiah. This claim allows the Church and Israel to enjoy a parallel existence.[161] Jenson therefore proposes an eschatological and messianic concept of Israel in the "already/ not yet" framework. The Israel of political and religious claim is the "not yet" Israel that awaits eschatological fulfillment. The Church exists as the Israel "already" in partaking of the promises of the Messianic kingdom now but is not the kingdom's full expression. Both await the promises of "resurrection" (Gentiles bodily, Israel politically) and live in the tensions that await the Messiah's return. Jenson proposes an ecclesiastical distinction that is

---

[157] This position is made clear in a paper issued called, "Israel - the Church's Response," https://ag.org/Beliefs/Topics-Index/Israel-the-Churchs-Response (accessed 26 December 2017).

[158] Charette, "Restoring the Kingdom to Israel," 56.

[159] Moltmann, *The Coming of God*, 199.

[160] Robert W. Jenson, "Toward A Christian Theology of Judaism," in Carl E. Braaten and Robert W. Jenson, eds., *Jews and Christians: People of God* (Grand Rapids: Eerdmans, 2003), 1-13.

[161] Jenson, "Toward A Christian Theology of Judaism," 5.

eschatologically shaped and does not restrict the activity of the Spirit in the present in the same way as dispensationalism does. Jenson's distinction, coupled with the AG's testimony, should convince us that whatever Israel is geo-politically in the present, it should not be confused with the eschatologically redeemed Israel of the Messiah's future kingdom.

The Pneumatological Affection: Righteousness, Peace, and Joy

The strength of the doctrine of the millennium is the hope that into a world of sin, corruption, and death, Jesus will return and establish a kingdom of righteousness and peace. This vision of the future imagines a utopian time of economic and social equality, the absence of warfare, and universal justice for all humanity. Paul describes the nature of Christ's pneumatological rule: "For the kingdom of God is not eating and drinking, but righteousness, peace, and joy in the Holy Spirit" (Rom. 14:17). These three values of the kingdom, which are descriptive of the present work of the Spirit, are based on the expectation of the fullness of righteousness, peace, and joy in Christ's future kingdom. They are the "bylaws of the kingdom," which are proclaimed by the gospel of the kingdom and they will find their fullness in Christ's rule.[162] Paul's vision of the kingdom is not based on hedonistic impulses or the fancies of human delights; they are realized "in the Holy Spirit."[163] Righteousness, peace, and joy are not only the benefits of those who are part of the kingdom; they are the missional goal of the kingdom that require believers to live out the values of the kingdom in the power of the Spirit. In his first coming, Jesus engaged in the Spirit's mission of liberation through charismatic power and compassionate engagement with those who needed liberating.[164] Following Christ's example, our passion for the kingdom should be evidenced by our passion to "love your neighbor as yourself." As Dempster declares, "Where God reigns, justice is established for the poor, the sick, the powerless, and the disinherited."[165] This vision of the kingdom is one in which love transcends all ethical and cultural barriers in order to promote peace, righteous actions, and true joy to all people. This is not an endorsement of postmillennial visions; it is simply the way of living out the gospel of the

---

[162] "Crisis," *WE*, April 21, 1917, 7.

[163] Thomas and Macchia, *Revelation*, 621, comments, "Dreams of eternal wealth, mansions, and political power hardly reflect the values of the kingdom of God."

[164] Moltmann, *Spirit of Life*, 61–62.

[165] Dempster, "Eschatology, Spirit Baptism, and Inclusiveness," 174.

kingdom.[166] The life of the kingdom is therefore characterized by the life of the Spirit, as the eschatological Spirit baptizes all creation and brings about the final eschatological transformation.[167]

The Pneumatological Response: Peacemaking

If the kingdom of God is ultimately a vision of the reign of peace governed by the Holy Spirit, let me suggest three practical pneumatological responses the AG should have to this vision. First, the image of the coming reign of the Prince of peace should be paralleled by a Pentecostal impulse toward peacemaking. Early Pentecostals believed that agenda of the millennium will be implementing Christ's rule as the Prince of Peace aided by his saints who have lived as "blessed peacemakers" in the kingdom (Mt. 5:9).[168] AG leaders were some of the greatest proponents of non-violence within the Pentecostal movement and the AG adopted a pacifist position in 1917. It declared,

> We, as a body of Christians, while purposing to fulfill all the obligations of loyal citizenship, are nevertheless constrained to declare we cannot conscientiously participate in war and armed resistance which involves the actual destruction of human life, since this is contrary to our view of the clear teachings of the inspired Word of God, which is the sole basis of our faith.[169]

The AG maintained an ethic of honor towards government, but at the same time believed that participation in the willful destruction of human life for government was antithetical to their Pentecostal faith. As one writer wrote, God will not bless "those who delight in war, but those who are so permeated by the Spirit of the Prince of Peace."[170] Paul Alexander pointed out that commitment has been all but reversed since World War II.[171] However, there has been a resurgence of the AG's

---

[166] Brunner, *Eternal Hope*, 72, comments, "All who, impelled by the love of Christ, have made an effort at some point to improve matters, whether it be in the church itself, in education, in shaping of law, in care for the weak of all kinds—they have done it in the certainty that thus some leavening of secular life by the leaven of the Gospel would take place. ... This faith in the possibility of a better future through the effectual action of the Holy Ghost belongs to the very foundations of the Christian faith."

[167] Macchia, *Baptized in the Spirit*, 97.

[168] Alexander, *Peace to War*; Paul Nathan Alexander, "Speaking in the Tongues of Nonviolence: American Pentecostals, Pacifism and Nationalism," *Brethren Life & Thought* (Spring 2012): 1–16.

[169] *AG Combined Minutes* (1914–1917), 11–12; Martin W. Mittelstadt, "Spirit and Peace in Luke–Acts," *Didaskalia* (Fall 2009): 17–40.

[170] "Crisis," *WE* 186 (April 21, 1917), 7.

[171] Alexander, *Peace to War*, 207.

commitment to non-violence among a new generation of scholars.[172] Yet most of the literature overlooks the fact that it was their millennial expectation of the reign of the Prince of Peace that motivated this conviction.[173] The peace of Christ's kingdom is not garnered by political power like the Pax Romana; it is established by the Spirit of God and maintained by the Prince of Peace.[174] As Spirit-filled people, this vision of peace motivates believers to advocate for peace even if the possibility of total peace will not be fully realized until the millennium.[175] If the Spirit of Peace is going to reign in the AG, there must be a renewed commitment to non-violence; not only for the unborn, but for all human life.[176]

The second area this vision of peace informs is attitudes about national identity. The development of the AG has coincided with a period of the development of American nationalism. Early AG leaders were cautious about ascribing any spiritual identity to America and its democratic ideas. Their primary motivation for such caution was the belief that all governments and political systems, even America, had the potential to give rise to the antichrist. Because of this belief, they also rejected the notion that any nation could be classified as "a Christian nation" since the Church is a mystical body scattered throughout all nations.[177] Today, sentiments among Pentecostals are quite

[172] Brian Pipkin and Jay Beaman, eds., *Early Pentecostals on Nonviolence and Social Justice* (Eugene: Pickwick, 2016); Paul Alexander, ed., *Pentecostals and Nonviolence: Reclaiming a Heritage* (Eugene: Pickwick, 2010); Jay Beaman, *Pentecostal Pacifism* (Eugene: Wipf & Stock, 2009).

[173] Michael Beals, "Toward a Pentecostal Contribution to the Just War Tradition," in Paul Alexander, ed., *Pentecostals and Nonviolence,* 248, is the only one that mentions the role of premillennialism but admonishes Pentecostals to have a responsible premillennialism that that does not use it as an excuse to not care about the world.

[174] Martin W. Mittelstadt, "Spirit and Peace in Luke–Acts," *Didaskalia* (Fall 2009): 17–40, points out that the messianic orientation of Luke-Acts anticipates a kingdom of peace intended to be in direct contrast of the Roman claim of the *Pax Romana*.

[175] The objection that peace will only come in the millennium was common in the AG. For example, John Goben, "The Millennial Reign," *PE,* February 21, 1925, 2, comments, "We are living in a time when the churches are advocating no more war. I don't like war: but, my brother, there will be war as long as the devil is loose and rules in the hearts of men."

[176] Paul Alexander, "Seeking Peace with Justice," in Craig S. Keener, Jeremy S. Crenshaw, and Jordan D. May, eds., *But These Are Written … Essays on Johannine Literature in Honor of Professor Benny C. Aker* (Eugene: Pickwick Publishers, 2014), 150.

[177] "Light on the Present Crisis," *PE,* July 1, 1916, 6–9. The author further declares, "In this great European war the strife is not between two companies of God's people, but between various world powers whose doom is sealed. … A little clear and logical thinking, accompanied by an intelligent knowledge of God's Word, will easily dispose of the fallacy that this war is being waged between Christian nations, for it is impossible for us to find in this dispensation a whole Christian town, village or congregation, not to mention a Christian Nation."

different. American exceptionalism has encouraged a new generation to unwittingly adopt postmillennial attitudes toward the supremacy of American identity.[178] As was the case in the early Pentecostal movement, the image of millennium should militate against these attitudes. Whatever national and racial identity believers possess now will ultimately be overpowered by identification with Christ and his kingdom. The book of Revelation describes the eschatological reality in the inclusive image of God's people, united as one people from "every tribe, people and language" (Rev. 7:9). Furthermore, the global nature of the kingdom of God should have implications on how Spirit-filled believers identify themselves. Although we are citizens of our native country, we are more so citizens of God's kingdom, which is multi-national and includes citizens of nations considered to be national enemies. As Alexander points out, prioritizing the kingdom of God should "subordinate other claims of *ethnos*, such as race or nation."[179] In Christ's kingdom there is no place for feelings of national or racial superiority.[180] The kingdom of God transcends artificial geographical boundaries, many of which were arbitrarily drawn following WWI. Instead, as a 1980s *Pentecostal Evangel* voting guide reminds AG members, it is a sin to "confuse patriotism, national pride, and Western Culture with Christian faith and practice."[181] If the Spirit of Peace is going to reign in the AG, all nationalistic and ethnic barriers need to be broken down through the redemptive work of Christ and all the "deepest divisions" of cultural, social, economic, and gender divisions must be overcome in the local church.[182]

The third response engendered by the millennial vision of the reign of peace should be that of peace between races. Much in the same way that the Spirit engenders an alternative political identity, the kingdom should also suggest an

---

[178] Studebaker, *A Pentecostal Political Theology for American Renewal*, 22–37.

[179] Paul Nathan Alexander, "Speaking in the Tongues of Nonviolence: American Pentecostals, Pacifism and Nationalism," *Brethren Life & Thought* (Spring 2012): 1–16; Tackett, "The Embourgeoisement of the Assemblies of God," 226–30.

[180] One of the reasons Charles Parham has been rejected by the modern Pentecostal movement is because of his eschatological racial views on British-Israelism. See Charles F. Parham, *A Voice Crying in the Wilderness* (Baxter Springs, KS: 1902), 108; Leslie D. Callahan, "Redeemed or Destroyed: Re-evaluating the Social Dimensions of Bodily Destiny in the Thought of Charles Parham," *Pneuma* 28, no. 2 (Fall 2006): 203–27; Tony Richie, "Eschatological Inclusivism: Exploring Early Pentecostal Theology of Religions in Charles Fox Parham," *JEPTA* 27, no. 2 (2007): 138–52.

[181] "10 Guidelines for Christian Voters," *PE*, October 14, 1984, 13.

[182] Pearlman, *Knowing the Doctrines of the Bible*, 345, recognizes, "The church is a spiritual brotherhood or fellowship in which all divisions that separate mankind have been abolished. "There is neither Jew nor Gentile"."

alternative racial identity from which we were born. The AG's vision of the future is imagined as a time when "all nations will stream to Jerusalem" to be part of God's kingdom. No matter the tribe or tongue, all racial divisions are erased in this millennial vision. This eschatological vision of reconciliation was evident at Azusa, when the Spirit of God erased the distinctions between black and white, rich and poor. Unfortunately, there has not been racial peace in the Pentecostal movement.[183] The lack of impulse toward racial integration and reconciliation in the AG was a failure to catch the eschatological vision of the millennium.[184] Although they expected the kingdom to include all races, they were perfectly satisfied to relegate that work to the future. Although there is little overtly racist language in AG literature, there also is a complete absence of the type of racial vision present at Azusa Street.[185] In occupying a place of privilege as a white Pentecostal fellowship, they were able to build a racially monolithic theological community in isolation from black Pentecostals.

In more recent years, the AG has taken steps to acknowledge its own racial isolation and have expanded its ethnic representation.[186] This greater awareness has produced dividends in recapturing the eschatological nature of the multi-racial vision of Azusa. During a 2005 dialogue on the AG and its racial history, Thomas Trask declared, "We desire the multi-racial model of Azusa Street, not so we can be an anomaly of modern Pentecostal history, but so we can become the prototype for what the Holy Spirit expects of the church in the years ahead."[187] One place to start in achieving this goal is for Spirit-filled people to

[183] Derrick R. Rosenior, "The Rhetoric of Pentecostal Reconciliation," in Michael Wilkinson and Steven M. Studebaker, eds., *The Liberating Spirit: Pentecostals and Social Action in North America* (Eugene: Wipf & Stock, 2010), 53–84.

[184] Thomas Trask, "Response to A Paper Presented by Dr. Leonard Lovett," *Cyberjournal for Pentecostal-Charismatic Research* 14 (May 2005), admits, "Our record of race relations indicates that we failed to keep the dream and example of an integrated Christian community, composed of all races, as modeled at Azusa Street … We cannot undo the history of racism that followed the Azusa Street revival, but we can, with the Lord's help, write a new and better chapter. And, with His grace, and the help of your forgiveness, encouragement, and favor—we shall!'

[185] One of the few racially based comments in AG literature was by W. F. Carothers, "Attitude of Pentecostal Whites to the Colored Brethren in the South," *CE*, August 14, 1915, 2. Carothers was a close associate of Parham who shared his views against racial mixing. Carothers argued that different races were "God's intention," a claim he believed was not motivated by "prejudice nor any other evil intent" but is intended to "preserve racial purity and integrity." He argued that the South "selfishly" mixed the races for their own financial gain, which ultimately instituted the racial tensions in America.

[186] Darrin Rodgers, "The Assemblies of God and the Long Journey Toward Racial Reconciliation," *AG Heritage* 28 (2008): 50–61.

[187] Trask, "Response to A Paper Presented by Dr. Leonard Lovett."

acknowledge the sin of national idolatry. Slavery existed because Christians chose the economic and political welfare of nation over the welfare and dignity of human beings. If the Spirit of Peace is going to reign in the AG, its members must join in the hard work of repentance and reconciliation inherent in the Pentecostal imagination of the future.

How can the AG overcome these current political, national, and racial tendencies? Amos Yong argues that Pentecostals need an alternative view of political powers.[188] He points out that all powers exercised by the *polis* are essential elements of the political, economic, and social make-up of any community or society. Because of this, he argues that it is right to recognize that all powers are ordained of God and have been established for the common good of all humanity, both religious and secular. A Pentecostal political theology must recognize the powers of the present, yet not in a way that demonizes them. The beast of Revelation is a political image representing the antitype of Christ's millennium and certainly guards the Christian against aligning with the powers of this world.[189] But this is not to say that all powers and intuitions are satanic in nature; but neither are they divine.[190] They are human institutions that are fallen in which subjection, exploitation, and injustice can become entrenched. In this way, the Spirit has the opportunity to restrain evil systems with kingdom principles.[191] The Pentecostal response to the powers is therefore the gospel proclamation of the Kingdom, which critiques injustice. The Spirit must empower believers to see these systems for what they are—fallen powers—and can provide the prophetic vision needed to properly discern and critique them in light of Christ's kingdom.

The Spirit of Justice: Imagining the Final Judgment

The third eschatological fundamental truth is the image of the final judgment. Within this image are a number of important eschatological concepts. The image of the lake of fire is not found in the Old Testament, but was likely developed from

---

[188] Yong, *In The Days of Caesar*, 162–63.

[189] Hart and Bauckham, *Hope against Hope*, 114–15.

[190] The testimony in the AG against giving divine status to the United States is clear. See "Light on the Present Crisis," *PE*, July 1, 1916, 6–9, and "The Good News of the Lord's Appearing," *PE*, July 23, 1921, 8, which critique the notion of any country being considered to be sacred precisely because of eschatological assumptions that the powers of the world are tools of the Antichrist.

[191] Yong's concept of the restraining of the gospel is one that is common in AG views of the "restrainer" in their eschatological vision.

the apocalyptic tradition of the valley of Gehenna.[192] The lake of fire is imagined in Revelation as the eternal destination of the cosmic unholy trinity of evil that usurps God's place as King on earth and persecuted his saints. The devil, the beast, and the false prophet are not only the prime enemies of God; they are the enemies of all humanity. This is precisely why the 1916 SFT placed the priority on judgment of God's enemies above rebellious humanity.[193] The wicked that have joined in the enemy's rebellion are judged by their works and share the fate of God's enemies (Rev. 20:12). As Thomas and Macchia comment, "The implications cannot be clearer. If one identified with Satan and the beast and the false prophet in this life, that one will suffer eternal death with them."[194]

The righteous will be judged by a very different standard; they are saved by their inclusion in the Book of Life through identification with the Lamb and by his blood (Rev. 3:5; 13:8).[195] As Horton comments, "As for the believer, his sins—both known and confessed sins and unknown and therefore unconfessed sins (1 John 1:7, 10; 2:1)—have been blotted out."[196] In this way, the wrath of God is not something arbitrary or subject to moments of God's anger. Judgment is rooted in the Lamb's sacrificial death and implements "only what has been decided once and for all at the cross."[197] The fire is "everlasting" which gives a sense of permanence to God's judgments. In one sense, it is a somber image for those who have rebelled against God. In another, it is an image of comfort for those who faithfully held to the testimony of Jesus even to the point of death, but will have no part in eschatological death.[198] In fact, death itself will experience "death" as the temporal consequences of sin (death and the grave) are cast into the lake of fire, permanently purging death itself from any possibility of being a part of the new creation.[199] Through the final judgment, the entire cosmos will be sanctified and prepared in anticipation of the *telos* of God's indwelling of the new creation.

---

[192] Skaggs and Benham, *Revelation: Pentecostal Commentary*, 202.

[193] This is particularly evident in the 1916–1927 version of the *SFT*. The unfortunate reversal of emphasis in later revisions placed a priority of judgment on humanity.

[194] Thomas and Macchia, *Revelation*, 363.

[195] Thomas and Macchia, *Revelation*, 363; Skaggs and Benham, *Revelation: Pentecostal Commentary*, 212.

[196] Horton, *Ultimate Victory*, 302.

[197] Hart and Bauckham, *Hope Against Hope*, 145.

[198] Thomas and Macchia, *Revelation*, 363.

[199] Thomas and Macchia, *Revelation*, 362–63; Menzies and Horton, *Bible Doctrines*, 251.

The Pneumatological Affection: Spirit of Justice

In the biblical narrative, justice involves two major concepts. First there is the concept of punitive justice, which concerns itself with punishing the perpetrators of evil and doling out the consequences for that act of injustice. This is the image presented in the doctrine of the final judgment. However, this concept, while sufficing the need for justice for the perpetrator, offers little solution for the damage done to the victim.[200] For the victim, justice requires what Meredith Kline refers to as "redemptive judgment."[201] Redemptive acts of justice engage the victim and offer acts of love, reconciliation, and provision for the consequence suffered as a result of injustice. These acts of justice are rooted in the biblical idea of distributive justice, which is established on the premise that true justice is "equal rewards for equal merits."[202] In other words, injustice exists when individuals are not treated fairly or opportunities are not equal in society. This vision of justice is one that requires society to maintain justice for the poor, the oppressed, the economically disadvantaged, and the racially marginalized.[203] Only when basic welfare is ensured for the vulnerable in society is justice truly possible.

Murray Dempster argues Jesus' vision of the final judgment is based on this concept of redemptive justice. He points out that in Jesus' parable of the sheep and goats (Matt 25:31–46), eternal judgment will be exacted based on the believer's actions toward Jesus, the one who identifies with the poor, hungry, thirsty, sick, prisoner, and foreigner.[204] In this way, the fate of humanity rests on the degree to which a person is willing to live by the principle: "love your neighbor."[205] Miroslav Volf argues that because this is a public mandate, final justice will be a social event in which individuals, nations, and generations will

---

[200] Miroslav Volf, *Exclusion and Embrace: a theological exploration of identity, otherness, and reconciliation* (Nashville: Abingdon Press), 197.

[201] Meredith G. Kline, *God, Heaven, and the Har Magedon: A Covenantal Tale of Cosmos and Telos* (Eugene: Wipf & Stock, 2006), 115.

[202] Christofer Frey, "The Impact of the Biblical Idea of Justice," in Henning Graf Reventlow and Yair Hoffman, eds., *Justice and Righteousness: Biblical Themes and their Influence* (JSOT 137; Sheffield, UK: Sheffield Academic Press, 1992), 96.

[203] Alexander, "Seeking Peace with Justice," 141.

[204] Dempster, "Eschatology, Spirit Baptism, and Inclusiveness," 178–79, notes that obedience to the "six corporal works" are not the basis for judgment. Instead, Jesus will say "I never knew you" to those who failed to "recognize" that he is in "solidarity with the least of these."

[205] Miroslav Volf, "The Final Reconciliation," *Modern Theology* 16, no. 1 (January 2000): 91–113.

partake in the public adjudication of the offences of the world.[206] For Volf, the public nature of this event is redemptive towards the victim in two ways. First it acknowledges that it was the violation of justice toward the victim that is being judged, affirming the role of punitive justice. But in including the victim, Volf also imagines the possibility for the Spirit of God to work reconciliation by allowing the victim to offer forgiveness rooted in God's grace rather than justice. He comments,

> With mutual embrace made possible by the Spirit of communion and grounded in God's embrace of sinful humanity on the cross, all will have stepped into a world in which each enjoys the other in the communion of the Triune God and therefore all take part in the dance of love freely given and freely received.[207]

By envisioning the final judgment as a final sanctifying work of the Spirit, it opens the possibility for judgment to be reconciliatory, as Volf suggests. As perpetrators stand before God for their crimes, they also stand before the Lamb, who has "reconciled the world to himself," as a mediator of grace on that day.[208] In holding together the retributive and redemptive aspects of justice, it "leaves room for an understanding of the final social reconciliation as the Holy Spirit's perfecting of the inter-human reconciliation which God has accomplished in Christ and in which human beings have been involved all along in response to God's call."[209]

Imagining a pneumatological vision of the final judgment is vital to a coherent Pentecostal eschatology. Throughout the Scriptures, the Spirit is portrayed as the Spirit of Justice.[210] The Spirit enabled the leaders of Israel to judge according to God's righteousness (Num. 11:17, Judg. 3:10, 6:34, 11:29). OT prophetic books portray the Spirit as the one who "uncovers and condemns all that is wrong, and as the Spirit of burning, purges it out."[211] OT prophecies of the Messiah envision the Spirit of justice resting upon the Spirit-filled Messiah in order to rule in righteousness and to seek for justice for victims.[212] The Spirit of justice is also implied in the concept of the Spirit as advocate (Jn. 14:26).[213] In suffering injustice, the Spirit is the "advocate" who intercedes and

---

[206] Volf, "The Final Reconciliation," 103.
[207] Volf, "The Final Reconciliation," 103.
[208] Thomas and Macchia, *Revelation*, 437–42.
[209] Volf, "The Final Reconciliation," 106.
[210] Moltmann, *Spirit of Life*, 123–43.
[211] Ralph M. Riggs, *The Spirit Himself* (Springfield: Gospel Publishing House, 1949), 23.
[212] Moltmann, *Spirit of Life*, 129.
[213] Moltmann, *Spirit of Life*, 123, 129.

accompanies believers in their weaknesses (Rom. 8:26). When the church hears cries of those who are suffering injustice, they are responding to and acting on the Spirit's inner groan for the justice of God's coming reign (Rev. 6:10).

Jonathan Kienzler argues that the baptism in the Spirit is itself an image of eschatological judgment. When John declared that Jesus would baptize "with the Spirit and fire," he was describing one pneumatological and eschatological event. Kienzler says, "It is not necessary to see it as two aspects of one baptism: "Holy Spirit" and "fire"; rather it should be pictured as hendiadys: "fiery Holy Spirit", with the emphasis on the Holy Spirit's purging and dividing work."[214] The "tongues of fire" present at Pentecost foreshadows the fiery eschatological judgment.[215] He says, "In Luke's historical framework, judgment begins at Pentecost, pointing forward to the final judgment when temporal division is made permanent."[216] The cleansing that takes place in judgment is a "purifying work that will restore Israel in fulfillment of God's promises."[217] By using the image of fire in the concept of the final judgment, we can say that the work of eschatological purgation is the work of the Spirit. The fire that purifies is not imagined as apocalyptic fire of God's wrath that destroys the creation; it is the purifying fire of the Spirit that in God's mercy and grace will sanctify the earth and the whole cosmos in preparation of the New Heavens and Earth.

The Pneumatological Response: Prophetic Discernment

The doctrine of the final judgment is vital to the eschatological imagination because it envisions the eschatological work of sanctification through the fiery Holy Spirit. Because it is the Spirit of judgment who reveals, convicts, and judges on matters of righteousness (Jn. 16:8–9), the fiery Holy Spirit is essential to retributive justice executed by the Coming Judge, as well as enabling redemptive justice, that works for the liberation and empowerment of the victims of injustice. In order to properly judge according to the Spirit, believers must operate in pneumatic discernment in order to identify and critique injustice around them. No book of the Bible models this type of discernment better than the Book of Revelation in which the readers are encouraged to pneumatically discern the

---

[214] Jonathan Kienzler, *The Fiery Holy Spirit: The Spirit's Relationship with Judgment in Luke-Acts* (JPTSup 44; Blandford Forum, UK: Deo Publishing, 2015), 61.

[215] Kienzler, *The Fiery Holy Spirit*, 71.

[216] Kienzler, *The Fiery Holy Spirit*, 210.

[217] Kienzler, *The Fiery Holy Spirit*, 63.

images, not just to predict their order correctly.[218] This prophetic hermeneutic is empowered by what Walter Brueggemann calls the "prophetic imagination."[219] In the OT, Spirit-filled prophets operated in prophetic discernment as they proclaimed the truth of YHWH's true kingdom to those who were part of the Jerusalem establishment.[220] Through the Spirit, they were able to critique the current establishment by appealing to the ancient narratives of YHWH's covenantal people. In the same way, the Spirit of Justice should empower Pentecostal believers to exercise the prophetic imagination needed to discern the power structures, racial attitudes, and political platforms of any nation in which they are found.

There are two particular images in Revelation that require prophetic critique that have contemporary application today. First, pneumatic discernment should empower the church to operate in the spirit of self-critique. It is easy for the church to use its prophetic voice to condemn the world, the culture, or the spirituality of a nation. And yet, the Book of Revelation opens with prophetic critiques of the people of God.[221] John prophetically imagines Jesus as the coming one "who walks among" the churches and offers words of encouragement/critique for "those who have ears to hear" in the church. In each opportunity for compromise the seven churches faced, Jesus called them to operate in pneumatic discernment in order to stay faithful to Christ.[222] As Mellissa Archer points out, "The Spirit who mediates Jesus' words and message will help the church in discerning his world. The church, then, is charged with the task of *hearing* in the Spirit."[223] The way that the Church "hears the Spirit" is by being obedient in "keeping the words of prophecy" and operating as a prophetic community in the world.[224] When the Spirit's voice is not discerned, the church can easily lose its missional purpose, lose heart in persecution, give into idolatry, be careless with false teaching, descend into spiritually lifelessness,

---

[218] Thomas and Macchia, *Revelation*, 244, 299, 486–89.

[219] Walter Brueggemann, *The Practice of Prophetic Imagination* (Minneapolis: Fortress Press, 2012), 25.

[220] Brueggemann, *The Practice of Prophetic Imagination*, 24–39.

[221] Thomas and Macchia, *Revelation*, 80.

[222] Melissa L. Archer, "*'I Was in the Spirit on the Lord's Day': A Pentecostal Engagement with Worship in the Apocalypse* (Cleveland: CPT Press, 2015), 139–42.

[223] Archer, "*I Was in the Spirit on the Lord's Day*," 140.

[224] John Christopher Thomas, *The Apocalypse* (Cleveland: CPT Press, 2012), 122–23.

grow weary, or become completely worthless.²²⁵ Pneumatic discernment calls the church to self-critique, knowing "if we were more discerning with regard to ourselves, we would not come under such judgment" (1 Cor. 11:31 NIV).

The second object of prophetic critique that requires pneumatic discernment highlighted in Revelation is that of power. This critique is portrayed most evidently in the image of the mark of the beast (Rev. 14:11–18). The readers are admonished to use discernment in calculating the "number of his name" and in identifying the images of the beast's seven heads and ten horns (Rev. 17:9). The interpretation of the mark of the beast is not of particular concern at this point, but the way one discerns the image is certainly important to proper pneumatic discernment of the world.²²⁶ It is, however, necessary to note that the reason the reader needs pneumatic discernment in identifying the beast is in order to avoid aligning themselves with the beast, who is portrayed as a political and religious image symbolizing both an individual and a system of power that universally controls systems of governments and economics.²²⁷ Indiscriminate of a person's station in life or place in the world, believers cannot escape the seductive reach of the beast's rule. Although there is debate about the correct interpretation of what power(s) to which these images refer, for the AG's imagination, the fact that that beast can potentially emerge from any government means that all interpretations have a contemporary element. Loyalty to the beast requires accepting his mark; loyalty to God requires rejecting that mark and being sealed by God (Rev. 7:14). The message that is discerned in these images is clear: "Too

---

[225] Archer, "*I Was in the Spirit on the Lord's Day,*" 135–64. The Church in Ephesus was careful to discern their works yet failed to discern their motivation for their works and were called to recover "Christlike compassion" as their primary motivation. Smyrna was commended for discerning the work of Satan in their midst and was encouraged to stay faithful in persecution. The Church at Pergamum had failed to discern the doctrine of the Nicolaitans and was called to pneumatically discern "their public and private witness and to reject any teaching that does not align itself with Jesus' teaching." The church at Thyatira was called to repent for allowing the false teacher Jezebel to lead the church astray. Pneumatic discernment was needed to identify the idolatry and to lead the church to repentance. Whereas faithful churches were experiencing death for faithful witness, Sardis was an active church but was dying. Only through hearing the Spirit's call to communal repentance would they be able to experience life again. Philadelphia was a faithful church that "kept" Jesus' words and received no condemnation. However, they were called to trust that they would be "delivered" from the trial they were enduring and must discern Jesus' promises and not grow weary. Jesus rebuked the Church of Laodicea for not discerning that they had become "neither hot nor cold" and self-deluded.

[226] McQueen, *Toward a Pentecostal Eschatology*, 290, comments, "By engaging with the spiritual truths to which the images of the Apocalypse point, we become aware of the spiritual truth that exists within our own flesh-and-blood world."

[227] Thomas and Macchia, *Revelation*, 242.

much attachment to and/or dependence upon a world order or its systems that may be connected to the beast is futile. . . . Any temptation to compromise with the world and its systems is seen for the false choice that it is."[228]

The role of pneumatic discernment in the critique of powers works in two trajectories. First, the Holy Spirit should inspire discernment in order to judge against injustices in the powers and systems. Paul Alexander points out that Jesus was a "threat to the status quo, to establishments, and to powers."[229] Although the AG has a history of recognizing the injustices, prophetic critique requires more of a response than simply identifying injustice. I agree with Dempster that as a prophetic community the Church has a responsibility to "unmask systemic injustice in laws governing institutional life." [230] The primary means for advocating justice in society is prophetic critique and faithful witness. The church in Revelation overcame injustice by faithful witness. Injustices must be spoken to, evil institutions must be challenged, and principalities must be engaged. However, this leads to the second trajectory to work and advocate against injustice within the systems, which also requires the wisdom of pneumatic discernment. Too often, calls for justice are focused on reforming unjust systems to reflect the kingdom of God. Institutions and powers, such as governments, can seek to enforce justice, but they will always do so imperfectly and pragmatically. True justice has few options in the present because there is only a "closed list" of institutions available to humankind.[231] The lack of options in the present certainly gave AG leaders pause in attributing divine status to any such powers in the present.

Revelation reminds us that even the best of political systems are the beast, which if are aligned with too closely, will ultimately demand our allegiance. Christians need the Spirit of discernment because often the beast is not the remedy for injustice; it is often the primary means by which injustice is enforced.[232] McQueen comments, "The beast is all around us, beckoning us to

---

[228] Thomas and Macchia, *Revelation*, 243.

[229] Alexander, "Seeking Peace with Justice," 145.

[230] Dempster, "Eschatology, Spirit Baptism, and Inclusiveness," 183–85.

[231] Ivan Petrella, *The Future of Liberation Theology: An Argument and Manifesto* (New York: Taylor and Francis, 2016), 93–95, here is referring to the options of economic systems within the "deep structures" of society that could allow for true expressions of social justice, but the same could be said of all aspects of institutions and powers.

[232] Thomas and Macchia, *Revelation*, 229–42. The beast is always depicted in Revelation as a "parody" of the Spirit of justice in that as the spirit of injustice is the constant source of the persecution and suffering of the saints.

take its mark and acknowledge the salvific qualities of its promises that political power and the pursuit of wealth is the path to ultimate salvation. Where is the beast? The beast is within our own tradition, perhaps even within our own hearts…"[233] The church cannot deceive itself into believing that if only God's people were to be in power then the kingdom could be established within political structures. As Tony Richie admonishes, "The politics of the Spirit indicate that Christians do not fear political involvement in the world, though they must always guard against the seduction of 'Constantinianism,' or the pull of worldly power wrapped in the disguise of religious garb."[234] The church should be an advocate for the powerless, oppressed, and exploited, but must do so in a way that does not seek to become the powerful. The call for justice is for the Church to embrace a social ethic, not a political theology.[235] The Church should provide ministry to victims of injustice rather than relying on the strategy of aligning with political powers to accomplish social goals.[236] Such a strategy fails to heed the words of the Spirit to discern the beast and resist being absorbed into its mission. The kingdom of God exists neither in "the right's effort to recover Christendom and the left's effort to establish the kingdom of social justice."[237] Both approaches forget what early members of the AG understood: the kingdoms of the world are not yet the kingdoms of our Lord and of his Christ. Until then, Christians must remain an alternative *polis*, a kingdom awaiting the King.[238]

---

[233] McQueen, *Toward a Pentecostal Eschatology*, 291.

[234] Tony Richie, "Can Anything Good Come Out of Premillennialism? A Response to Robert O. Smith," *Dialog* 48, no. 3 (Fall 2009): 297.

[235] Dempster, "Eschatology, Spirit Baptism, and Inclusiveness," 177.

[236] Christopher Norris and Sam Speers, *Kingdom Politics: In Search of a New Political Imagination for Today's Church* (Eugene: Cascade Books, 2015), 95–97, offers a different idea how to accomplish this task. They point out that advocacy can take two forms. The first form is a type of political advocacy in which the church engages in the lobbying for change in the form of speaking to representatives, making policy statements, and circulating petitions with the end of changing unjust laws. The judgment of the success of such endeavors is based on the outcome of elections. However, political solutions are not the only solutions to human problems of injustice. They advocate a different kind of advocacy that responds to human justice by using the church as a vehicle to empower victims of injustice without aligning with the political establishment. They comment, "This is a structural alternative to state and national politics, ordered around a different set of convictions, a different set of political practices, and ultimately, a different allegiance."

[237] Studebaker, *A Pentecostal Political Theology for American Renewal*, 203.

[238] James K. A. Smith, *Awaiting the King: Reforming Public Theology* (Grand Rapids: Baker Academic, 2017).

The Spirit of Life: Imagining the New Creation

Of the four eschatological doctrines, the New Heavens and New Earth has been the most neglected. Despite three major revisions to the EFT, this doctrine remains to this day only a partial quote of 2 Pet. 3:13, "We, according to His promise, look for new heavens and a new earth, wherein dwelleth righteousness" (2 Peter 3:13; Revelation 21, 22)." The doctrinal books of the AG have shown equal ambivalence towards this doctrine.[239] Considering this fact, its inclusion in the list of "fundamental" truths is a bit of a mystery.[240] Because of the AG's lack of emphasis on the doctrine of the New Heavens and New Earth (NHNE), there is confusion among its members about the future creation and its relation to the present. There have been some in the AG's history that have taken an apocalyptic approach to the creation, imagining that it will ultimately be destroyed and replaced with a "new heavens and new earth."[241] No one was more supportive of this position than Stanley Horton, who argues that completely new creation is an act of love.[242] Because this book has exerted a high level of influence over AG ministers, it might be assumed that this is the AG's primary position. However, this study has demonstrated the testimony of the past century in the AG in the Pentecostal Evangel is overwhelmingly in favor of the creation being renewed at Christ's coming, not destroyed.[243] As was noted earlier, the renewal of creation fits the

---

[239] Nelson, *Bible Doctrines*, (1948), 165–70, spends his whole chapter further explaining the millennium without discussing the NHNE at all. Pearlman, *Knowing the Doctrines of the Bible*, makes no mention of the doctrine. Williams, *Systematic Theology*, 260–64, recognizes the importance of this image as the culmination of God's plan to "renovate" and "renew" the earth. Menzies and Horton, *Bible Doctrines*, 255–62, gives the NHNE much needed attention and envisions the new creation as a "replacement" for the old, which will be torn down and destroyed.

[240] I argue the inclusion of the NHNE was likely because of an early doctrinal statement made by E. N. Bell, "For Strangers. Who Are We?," *WW,* May 20, 1914, 1–2.

[241] "New Heavens and A New Earth," *WE,* February 9, 1918, 5; "Our Lord's Unveiling of Things to Come," *PE,* September 22, 1928, 3.

[242] Menzies and Horton, *Bible Doctrines*, 255–62, argues that the new creation will be "replacement" for the old, which will be torn down and destroyed. See also, Horton, *The Ultimate Victory,* 310. I attribute this attitude to Horton and not Menzies because *Bible Doctrines* is a revision of William W. Menzies, *Understanding Our Doctrine* (Springfield: Gospel Publishing House, 1971), which only contained one chapter on "Last Things." Stanley Horton published a revised and updated version of Menzies' work as *Bible Doctrines*, where he added several complete chapters on eschatology that Menzies failed to cover, including the New Heavens and New Earth.

[243] Leaders who argued that God will not destroy the creation include Sisson, *Foregleams of Glory*, 66; S. A. Jamieson, "A New Heavens and A New Earth," *PE,* September 30, 1922, 5; Nelson, *Bible Doctrines,* (1948), 168; J. N. Gortner, *Studies in Revelation* (Springfield: Gospel Publishing House,

chiastic inner logic of the AG's emphasis on the resurrection in that the resurrection of the body is paralleled by the resurrection of the creation and is held together by the pneumatic concept of the groaning of the Spirit found in Romans 8. The new heavens and new earth is the culmination and glorification of that process.

What is at stake can be seen in two contrasting visions: *creation ex nihilo* and *creation continua*.[244] The *ex nihilo* vision is a cataclysmic one in which the new creation replaces the old. Although a minority position in the AG literature, it should be noted that it is not without support among some Pentecostal scholars.[245] The primary reason many Pentecostals reject this idea is that it might encourage irresponsible attitudes toward creation. It is, of course, possible that one might expect the annihilation of the world and at the same time argue for responsibility for the present creation.[246] Still, there is a tendency to use biblical visions of the earth passing away as justification for the view that the new heavens and earth will be entirely new creations. Robby Waddell argues that 2 Pet. 3:10–13, which envisions the creation being "destroyed by fire," is notoriously difficult to interpret in favor of his continuationist interpretation.[247] However, he argues for an alternative rendering of "destruction by fire" as an image of prophetic judgment meant to encourage the pursuit of holiness rather than advocating for the annihilation of creation.[248] Other verses such as Col. 1:20 argue that Christ holds creation together and will ultimately "reconcile" heaven and earth, not annihilate it.[249] Apocalyptic and cataclysmic views of the future are in discord with this vision, offering no hope for creation and only making a groaning creation a victim of complete death.

The vision of *creation continua,* on the other hand, is the expectation that the new creation will be a perfected and resurrected version of the old much in the same way as human resurrection. As Waddell points out, the promise of God is

1948), 253; John L. Meredith, "Does the Second Coming of Christ Mean the End of the World?," *PE,* August 26, 1956, 15; Zelma Argue, "Earth's Finest Hour," *PE,* October 4, 1970, 5; Ian MacPherson, "The New Heavens and New Earth," *PE,* September 21, 1975, 4–5, C. M. Ward, "An End to Darkness," *PE,* February 23, 1975, 5.

[244] A. J. Swoboda, *Tongues and Trees: Toward a Pentecostal Ecological Theology* (JPTSup 40; Blandford Forum, UK: Deo Publishing, 2013), 230.

[245] Thomas and Macchia, *Revelation,* 363; Thomas, *The Apocalypse,* 617–18; Skaggs and Benham, *Revelation: Pentecostal Commentary,* 212. These commentaries agree that the hearers would have expected the "disappearance" of the former creation in order to usher in the new creation.

[246] Waddell, "Apocalyptic Sustainability," 103.

[247] Waddell, "Apocalyptic Sustainability," 105.

[248] Waddell, "Apocalyptic Sustainability," 106–107.

[249] Studebaker, *A Pentecostal Political Theology for American Renewal,* 160.

that he will make "all things new," not "all new things."[250] One of the most important concepts that enable the continuity between the present creation and the future creation is the millennium. The renewal of creation begins in the millennium as the curse is reversed and creation undergoes the process of sanctification by the Spirit. The whole creation that has been groaning will enter a time of Sabbath rest as the Spirit re-creates the paradise once lost in Eden.[251] In renewing the earth, the Holy Spirit gives value and dignity to creation and empathizes with the creation as a "wounded Spirit" that it is at risk of total annihilation.[252] Instead of annihilation, the image of the New Jerusalem fuses together the dwelling of God (heaven) and the dwelling of man (earth) together into one image.[253] The AG's vision of the old creation being saved and resurrected during the millennium is certainly contrary to many assessments of prevailing attitudes about Pentecostal eschatology.[254]

The Pneumatological Affection: Spirit of Life

In the opening verses of Genesis, the Holy Spirit is described as "hovering over the waters" as new life explodes into being. The Spirit is also present at the culmination of creation when God breathes life into Adam (Gen. 2:7). The symmetry between the Spirit at both the initiation and culmination of creation indicates that the Spirit and creation share a close relationship.[255] The Spirit is the Spirit of life, who fills the earth with life and brings vitality to all the material creation.[256] As Clark Pinnock points out, the Spirit is the Creator Spirit who is not subject to the creation; he is Lord of creation, the Lord and giver of life.[257] As the Lord of creation, the Spirit indwells creation with his presence and is the steward of the work of God on the earth.[258] Pinnock describes the stewarding work of the Spirit: "As shaper of

[250] Waddell, "Apocalyptic Sustainability," 108, fn. 52.

[251] Wonsuk Ma, "Isaiah," in Trevor J. Burke and Keith Warrington, eds., *A Biblical Theology of the Holy Spirit* (Eugene: Cascade Books, 2014), 42.

[252] Veli-Matti Karkkainen, *Pneumatology* (Grand Rapids: Baker Academic, 2008), 164.

[253] Waddell, "Apocalyptic Sustainability," 102.

[254] The continual prevalence of the narrative that Pentecostals support the apocalyptic end to the creation demonstrates how essential a comprehensive assessment is to this conversation. See Jeffrey Lamp, "New Heavens and New Earth," *Pneuma* 36, no. 1 (2014): 64–80, and Waddell, "Apocalyptic Sustainability," 105.

[255] Yong, *Spirit Poured Out on All Flesh*, 281.

[256] Moltmann, *The Spirit of Life*, 83–89.

[257] Pinnock, *Flame of Love*, 87.

[258] Wonsuk Ma and Julie C. Ma, *Mission in the Spirit: Towards a Pentecostal/Charismatic Missiology* (Oxford, UK: Regnum Books International, 2010), 18–20.

environment, the Spirit is ecologist par excellence, forming and sustaining all habitable space."²⁵⁹ In light of the intimate relationship between the Spirit and creation, it is not surprising that Paul connects the resurrection of creation with the work of the Spirit (Rom. 8:11–24). As the Spirit of creation, the fall of Adam not only subjected creation to "frustration," but also that frustration is vocalized by the Spirit, who "has been groaning as in the pains of childbirth right up to the present time" (Rom. 8:22). Creation itself, indwelt by the Spirit, groans in pneumatological hope of redemption. In fact, as Yong points out, the resurrection "grants us insights into God's intentions to restructure (re-create) the laws of nature infected by sin.²⁶⁰ The intimate Spirit-body-creation connection allows Frank Macchia to speak in terms of a future baptism of all creation in the Spirit. He says,

> In Pauline terms, the kingdom of God and the divine indwelling of creation converge in the final deliverance of creation from the dominion of death (bondage to sin and death) unto the liberating of dominion of life. The ultimate goal of Spirit baptism is thus also the goal of the kingdom of God: the final dominion of life over death as all of creation becomes the dwelling place of God's Holy Spirit.²⁶¹

Spirit-baptism foreshadows the coming baptism of all creation. In the same way that the resurrection gives dignity to the body, the renewal of all creation affirms the goodness of creation and God's plan for creation.

The Pneumatological Response: Stewardship

Waddell points out that one of the greatest challenges to this vision of creation is that most evangelicals see the future as merely anthropological.²⁶² Although humanity enjoys a special place in God's creation, it is not valuable to the exclusion of the rest of creation.²⁶³ The close relationship between the creation and the

---

²⁵⁹ Clark Pinnock, *Flame of Love*, 87.

²⁶⁰ Amos Yong, *The Spirit of Creation: Modern Science and Divine Action in the Pentecostal Charismatic Imagination* (Grand Rapids: Eerdmans, 2011), 91.

²⁶¹ Macchia, *Baptized in the Spirit*, 103.

²⁶² Robby Waddell, "Revelation and the (New) Creation: A Prolegomenon on the Apocalypse, Science and Creation," a paper presented at the 35th Annual Meeting of the Society for Pentecostals Studies (2008), 2.

²⁶³ The essential differences between the humanity and other elements of creation should not be seen as defining the value of those elements. For example, Yong, *The Spirit of Creation*, 200, argues, "Human beings have a complexity to their experiences that rocks do not have, but to conclude that rocks have no experiences at all means both that they do not exert causal influence in the world (which

human body, which is itself part of the creation, guarantees that it is God's intention that "we shall be redeemed with the world, not from it."[264] If the human body will survive the transition from the present order to the future, why would it be any different for the rest of creation? Furthermore, what value would a resurrected body serve without a material creation for humanity to dwell in? Yong concludes, "Human beings are symbiotically related not only to the animal world but also to the environment in its many layers of complexity;" therefore, creation invites us to "care for the world, to the best of our abilities."[265] Augustinus Dermawan has argued that the lack of ecological engagement by the AG has more to do with models than eschatological convictions.[266] Pentecostals have primarily focused their research on the charismatic functions of Spirit and have honestly, but naively, failed to consider the subject of the Creator Spirit.[267] Because few Pentecostals have ventured into the field of ecotheology, there are few models for Pentecostals to draw from. Dermawan comments, "It is clear that we need a model that is theologically and biblically appropriate and at the same time is able, even powerful to change perception and move on people's hearts and hands to care for their environment."[268]

The AG has held the majority position that creation will be renewed and restored by the Spirit. And yet, little of that conviction has led to any particular attempt by the AG to provide a model that values creation in a way that is consistent with their renewalist eschatology. In the AG imagination, Jesus' kingdom will operate in restorative peace with creation. The eschatological vision of the messiah's kingdom involves a harmony with the created world where the "lion will lay down with the lamb" (Isa. 11:6). And yet, peace with creation was established first in the various ways Jesus encountered creation and creation responded to his lordship.[269] It is unfortunate that the AG has a reputation of

they do) and that they are incapable of being experienced." While admitting that rock cannot experience in the same way as humans, the human experience is shaped by rocks and cannot be understood without their existence.

[264] Moltmann, *The Spirit of Life*, 89.

[265] Yong, *The Spirit of Creation*, 228.

[266] Augustinus Dermawan, "The Spirit in Creation and Environmental Stewardship: A Preliminary Pentecostal Response Toward Ecological Theology," *AJPS* 6, no. 2 (2003): 199–217.

[267] Dermawan, "The Spirit in Creation and Environmental Stewardship," 208–09.

[268] Dermawan, "The Spirit in Creation and Environmental Stewardship," 214.

[269] Jesus' connection to the creation is seen not only in his portrayal as the creator (Jn. 1:1), but also in how the creation responds to him. Some examples are his ability to command stones to turn to bread (Matt. 4:3), the wild animals attend to him (Mk. 1:13), the wind and waves obeying him (Matt. 8:26–27), the use of ecologically based parables, and creation seemingly pouring forth bodies from the

being careless with the environment, considering there is little to substantiate that claim.[270] Not even the fact that John McConnell, Jr., the original founder of Earth Day, was the son of an AG minister has been able to change that narrative.[271] The issue of environmental stewardship has certainly captured the AG's attention in recent years. In 2014, the Pew Forum found that 46% of AG adherents felt that stricter environmental rules were needed in order to protect the environment, while 46% felt that such regulations were too costly.[272] The 46% who favored these actions were not just the sentiments of younger generations; it was shared across generations.[273] Even the leadership of the AG has felt it important to address the subject of environmental stewardship in a recent position paper called "Environmental Protection," which declares,

> The Assemblies of God believes everyone needs to be good a steward of *all* God's creation–including the earth. . . . We feel Christians must act responsibly in their use of God's earth as we rightly harvest its resources. As stated in Genesis 1:27–30, we believe God has given mankind alone complete dominion (authority) over the earth's resources. These resources include the land, the water, the vegetation, and the earth's minerals; as well as the animals, fish, and fowl. Like the earth, we acknowledge these to be gifts from God to mankind; and as gifts they are to be appreciated and cherished. As Christians

---

grave at the death of Jesus (Matt 27:52–53). This idea is explored fully in Richard Bauckham, *Living with Other Creatures: Green Exegesis and Theology* (Waco, TX: Baylor University Press, 2011).

[270] The only example given by scholars to substantiate this claim is the legend of the ecothology of Secretary of Interior James Watt. As was demonstrated in Chapter 4, the claims about Mr. Watt were fabricated and his own statements contradict the attitudes attributed to him.

[271] Nicole Sparks and Darrin J. Rogers, "John McConnell, Jr. and the Pentecostal Origins of Earth Day," *AG Heritage* 30 (2010): 16–25, 69. See also John McConnell, Jr. and John C. Munday, Jr. *Earth Day: Vision for Peace, Justice, and Earth Care: My Life and Thought at age 96* (Eugene: Resource Publications, 2011). McConnell was passionate about advocating "a climate of peace and justice as a prerequisite for ecological preservation" and coined the term "Earth Day" in 1968. He managed to orchestrate the first governmental observance of Earth Day in San Francisco, CA, in 1970. Earth Day was later adopted by the United Nations, without McConnell's permission, and the date was moved to April 22.

[272] www.pewforum.org/religious-landscape-study/religious-denomination/assemblies-of-god/views-about-environmental-regulation/ (accessed 1 January 2018). This statistic was up from 2007 when 40% supported the regulations.

[273] The 2014 statistic report that of the 46% who advocated greater regulation, (% by age group) 22% were 18–29, 31% were 30–49, 27% were 50–64, 20% were 65+.

we believe dominion requires good stewardship of our temporary home–earth.²⁷⁴

Despite the growing place in the AG's "heart" for the environment, there is yet to be an AG model for a Pentecostal eco-theology that could mobilize the "hands" of AG adherents.

The Pentecostal community as a whole is beginning to inch toward this goal. The most comprehensive attempt at an ecotheology to date is by A. J. Swaboda.²⁷⁵ In his book *Tongues and Trees,* Swaboda identifies several concepts that have potential for constructing a Pentecostal ecotheology.²⁷⁶ He argues that Jesus' mission in the NT transcends the personal dimension, having ramifications for the whole of creation. In the same way that Spirit baptism means indwelling of humanity, Swaboda argues that the metaphor implies a relationship between the Spirit and creation who groans for redemption.²⁷⁷ Swaboda argues that a "sustainable eschatology" must be engendered which promotes responsibility and attentiveness to the needs of creation.²⁷⁸ Rather than seeing ecological disaster as an eschatological sign that the world is "right on track" toward a predicted apocalyptic end, Pentecostals must view violence against nature as groans that are waiting to be redeemed. This approach should emphasize the human role in preparing the creation for Christ's return rather than abandoning it in hopes of Christ's return.

Another appeal to a Pentecostal view of ecology is by Peter Althouse, who draws parallels between the doctrine of healing and creation care.²⁷⁹ In the doctrine of healing, humans wrestle with the effects of sin, but lean into the Lord and to the power of the Holy Spirit to reverse these effects and provide healing now. This does not mean that humans can expect to be eternally healthy; healing is simply a temporary sign of an eschatological reality. Caring for creation should be understood in a similar way as physical healing. We recognize that sin has caused pollution and the exploitation of nature's resources. Rather than resigning the world to decay, we should work to bring healing to the suffering creation. The creation suffers "by no will of its own," but calls out in the Spirit in its suffering in hopes of glorification. The exploitation of the creation is an injustice

---

²⁷⁴ https://ag.org/Beliefs/Topics-Index/Environmental-Protection (accessed 1 January 2018).

²⁷⁵ A. J. Swoboda, *Tongues and Trees: Toward a Pentecostal Ecological Theology* (JPTSup 40; Dorset: UK, Deo Publishing, 2013).

²⁷⁶ Swoboda, *Tongues and Trees*, 192–237.

²⁷⁷ Swoboda, *Tongues and Trees*, 203.

²⁷⁸ Swoboda, *Tongues and Trees*, 236.

²⁷⁹ Althouse, "Pentecostal Eschatology in Context," 213.

that deserves our attention and our affection. As Spirit-filled believers, we can work to reverse the effects of sin upon creation. Though this work will only be temporary relief for creation, it is an expression of faith in an eschatological future in which creation will be fully healed. If the Spirit is vital to the mission of relieving the suffering of the vulnerable humanity, would not the Spirit not also seek to rescue creation from pollution, resources from exploitation, and beauty from destruction? For those who proclaim freedom for the captive, it is incongruous to advocate for the oppression and subjugation of creation. If the AG is going to reflect the Spirit of Life, it must capture the eschatological vision of the future redemption and renewal of creation in a way that motivates the work of conservation and preservation in anticipation of that day.

14

THE FUTURE OF THE ESCHATOLOGICAL FUNDAMENTAL TRUTHS

Whatever developments toward a more pneumatological eschatology warranted by this study, the AG is still faced with the monumental task of forging a path for the developments to be implemented. Too often, suggestions for development are left in the realm of the theoretical but have no practical suggestions for ways that doctrine can be re-formulated to reflect these ideas. Therefore, drawing from Alister McGrath's concept of doctrine development, I want to suggest ways in which the concepts embedded in AG eschatological statements can be developed and the statements themselves can be revised. This is a risky proposition for anyone, no doubt. But if there is to be a future for AG eschatology, there must be a process for developing doctrine that continues to cast these doctrines in a relevant light to a new generation.

The Possibility of Eschatological Development

I want to suggest that latent in the AG ethos and ecclesiological structure are several values that could be employed as a methodology for doctrinal development that could provide a way to forward. The "Introduction" to the Constitution that was adopted at the first General Council provided a proto-doctrinal presupposition that the General Council, which consists of all those who hold credentials, is a "cooperative fellowship" centered on the two-fold theological emphasis of the "latter rain" outpouring of the Spirit and the coming King.[1] When the SFT was adopted two years later, they expanded upon these two pillars by offering seventeen points of doctrine, creating a standard for the unity of the faith. Although these were considered "Bible truths" recognized as doctrines "surely believed among us," they adopted them with a particular methodology for the way in which they would function. The introduction to the SFT declares:

---

[1] *GC Minutes,* (April 2–12, 1914), 2.

> The Statement of Fundamental Truths is not intended as a creed for the Church, nor a basis of fellowship among Christians, but only as a basis of unity for the ministry alone. . . . The human phraseology employed in such a statement is not inspired nor contended for, but the truth set forth in such phraseology is held to be essential to a full Gospel ministry. No claim is made that it contains all truth in the Bible, only that it covers our present needs as to these fundamental matters.[2]

This methodological statement provides the framework for how its members are to understand the role of AG doctrine. First, the *SFT* was not created as a complex doctrinal treatise; it was a collection of limited doctrinal positions based on what they perceived as generally accepted truths. The task of summarizing biblical truth into simple propositional statements was difficult, yet they were able to navigate that difficulty by appealing to the value of unity.[3] The minimalist statement was important because of the way it fostered the unity of the Spirit. They did not intend to draw artificial lines that limited fellowship among believers. These statements were meant to state what is "essential to a full Gospel ministry" among a cooperative body.

Therefore, in projecting the future of AG doctrine, we must conclude that a minimalist statement should be preferred to more precise statements.[4] The recent addition of position papers by the Executive Presbytery has narrowed the articulations beyond what is deemed essential by the General Council. Narrow statements reduce the opportunity for unity by narrowing the criteria by which someone is considered to be an adherent to the faith.[5] If AG doctrine is going to develop, a move toward broader, rather than narrower, statements must be embraced. Particularly in the case of eschatological doctrine, the arguments are almost always over the details. What has divided the AG concerning eschatology

---

[2] *GC Minutes*, (October 1–7, 1916), 12.

[3] J. R. Flower, "The Spirit of the General Council," *WE*, October 21, 1916, 8 admits, "We know that it is impossible for a large body of men to gather together to discuss doctrinal matters without there being differences of opinion ... Fortunately, the spirit of 'we the brethren' ran all through the Council, and though some grew vehement in the presenting of their side of the questions involved, yet the general attitude of all was courteous and Christlike."

[4] The controversy over the language of "initial evidence" is proof that precise statements lead to fracturing of the movement rather than unity. See Glen Menzies, "Tongues as 'The Initial Physical Sign' of Spirit Baptism in the Thought of D. W. Kerr," *Pneuma* 20, no. 2 (Fall 1988): 175–89.

[5] Robeck, "An Emerging Magisterium? The Case of the Assemblies of God," 251, argues that the position papers, changes to the doctrinal portions of the ministerial application, and the limitations placed on educators were intended to "narrow" the identity of the AG, which ultimately resulted in alienating of some of the best minds, pastors, and educators the fellowship has to offer. Cf. Blumhofer, *Restoring the Faith*, 254.

has not been the general acceptance of premillennialism, which is affirmed by the *SFT* and has been widely held by AG scholars, it is the imposition of the details of the dispensational script on these statements that have caused scholars to critique the theology behind the script and the exegetical validity of those interpretations. The *SFT* is best served as a minimalist statement that provides a tent big enough for diversity without undermining the four main premillennial commitments.

Second, the *SFT* was intended to be "a basis of unity for the ministry alone" and not a tool for excluding others from the fellowship. The founders envisioned doctrine as a means of fostering a sense of community identity in service to its mission. J. W. Welch comments, "The one purpose of the Council is the unifying of the Children of God. One-accordness is the sure precursor of Pentecost. Revivals will only follow the brethren who labor in perfect unity with their living Head and with one another."[6] The "General Council" model the AG adopted allows the members to participate in a dialogical approach that emphasizes listening to the member's voices, the Spirit, and the Word. In fact, the 1916 Council that created the *SFT* was intended to be a "Bible Council" out of a desire to discuss, clarify, and unify on Scriptural teaching.[7] If differing ideas exist, there must be a discussion of those ideas in order to help advance the development of the AG's theological identity.[8] Conversely, if there are ideas that serve to undermine that speech act of the body, they must also be evaluated. But that process of evaluation must be the possession of the community rather than the privilege of the leadership alone. Only through dialogue in which the community values both speaking and listening can development take place.[9] Hearing is a Pentecostal value as the community heeds the call of Jesus to "Hear what the Spirit is saying to the Church."[10]

Third, the *SFT* was intended to be a fallible statement. It says, "The human phraseology employed in such statement is not inspired nor contended for, but the truth set forth in such phraseology is held to be essential to a full Gospel

---

[6] S. Frodsham, "Notes From An Eyewitness," *WE,* October 21, 1916, 4.

[7] J. N. Welch, "Editorial," *WE,* June 24, 1916, 3, 7.

[8] This point is made ably by Heyduck, *The Recovery of Doctrine,* 1–7, who laments the divisive role that doctrine has often played within his own denomination and argues that the failure to develop doctrine can be equally problematic as entrenched ideas become sacred cows that often drive ministers to leave a denomination to find solace.

[9] Heyduck, *The Recovery of Doctrine,* 74, says, "When we see doctrine as a dialogical act, we see it as a function of the church united-not merely institutionally or structurally, but primarily in terms of common life in the Christian narrative."

[10] Revelation 2–3.

ministry." They intentionally avoided adopting a rigid, restrictive, and creedal statement that would place undue authority on the human phraseology. They certainly meant them to reflect the truths found in the Scripture, but they also acknowledged that the statements themselves were human and fallible. Because of their fallibility, squabbles over what they were "intended" to mean only undermines the very purpose for which they were created. As E. S. Williams insisted, no one person can "infallibly interpret" the *SFT* for the whole fellowship, not even the General Superintendent!

> It is not the prerogative of any one person to infallibly interpret for the entire General Council its doctrinal declaration. . . . Neither can a lone individual, though elected to office in the General Council, speak infallibly for the entire Council Fellowship in endorsing the work of one person who seeks to interpret the meaning of the Fundamental Truths adopted by the body.[11]

The SFT are not ex cathedra, they are catholukos, having their origin from the whole of the community. The founders were brave enough to conceive of a system in which unity can exist even in the midst of disagreeing positions. J. R. Flower reflects, "It was thought best at the time to agree on principle that the Scriptures themselves are the all-sufficient rule for faith and practice, with freedom for interpretation and development of truth left to the individual minister."[12] They trusted the Spirit to reveal truth, to encourage unity, and to generate good faith among ministers. If AG doctrine is going to have a future it must take a position of fallibility rather than inerrancy in its doctrinal expressions.[13] When the statements are seen as fallible, it allows the community to engage in conversation and allows doctrine to be open to development. Humility is a spiritual exercise that both the AG magisterium and the populace of the church must learn. Ralph Riggs argues for this approach to prophecy when he says, "Differing viewpoints can be respectfully listened to, compared with various statements of the Divine body of Prophecy, spread before the Lord in prayer, and accepted to that degree to which they harmonize with the Scripture and received the witness of the Spirit."[14] If the

---

[11] Nelson, *Bible Doctrines*, introduction.

[12] J. R. Flower, *The Origin and Development of the Assemblies of God*, (Springfield: Gospel Publishing House, 1938), 8.

[13] Amos Yong, *Spirit Poured Out on All Flesh* (Grand Rapids: Baker Academic, 2005), 29, argues that in order for Pentecostal theology to expand and develop to include the global perspective, it needs to be fallibilistic, multi-perspectival, self-critical and dialogical.

[14] Ralph M. Riggs, *The Path of Prophecy* (Springfield: Gospel Publishing House, 1937), 26–28, 110–11.

statements are fallible in their construction, then the Holy Spirit is allowed to revise as greater light is discovered. As Flower further comments, "The statement is simple enough to permit elaboration based on further light which may be received from the Holy Spirit in the future."[15] Doctrinal development requires an openness toward the future that allows the Spirit to bring new light and new emphasis as needed.[16] Further, through the sanctifying work of the Holy Spirit, doctrine can be purged of elements that may have become fossilized in the heart of the AG.[17]

Fourth, the *SFT* was intended to be a contextual statement. It was not intended to have a response for every theological question that could be asked. It says, "No claim is made that it contains all truth in the Bible, only that it covers our present needs as to these fundamental matters."[18] The "present needs" they were addressing had to do with questions being raised within a particular historical context.[19] Because the context is always changing, doctrine should be open to the possibility of re-stating, re-visioning and re-presenting by the community to fit a new context.[20] The truths may be permanent, but wording is subject to the fallibility of those who wrote them and are reflective of the historical situation in which the statement was crafted. Therefore, a doctrine has the possibility of being restated in modern times with modern contextual understandings without destroying the truth claim.[21] History has shown that not all developments have been positive; being subject to both progression and regression.[22] The concept of the "full gospel" was seen as a revival of truths that

---

[15] Flower, *The Origin and Development of the Assemblies of God*, 8.

[16] Clark H. Pinnock, *Flame of Love* (Downers Grove, IL: IVP Academic, 2016), 221.

[17] Pinnock, *Flame of Love*, 218.

[18] *GC Minutes*, (October 1–7, 1916), 12.

[19] Lonergan, *Method in Theology*, 325, recognizes that doctrine originates "not in some vacuum of pure spirit but under concrete historical conditions and circumstances that developments occur, and a knowledge of such conditions and circumstances is not irrelevant in the evaluation of history that decides on the legitimacy of developments."

[20] Lonergan, *Method in Theology*, 322–23, says dogma has a permanence of meaning because they are declared by the church and cannot be separated from the verbal formulation of the doctrines because "the permanence attaches to the meaning and not to the formula."

[21] McGrath, *The Genesis of Doctrine*, 8, argues, "Doctrinal criticism obliges us to ask what specific theological insights lie behind a specific doctrinal formulation, and what historical contingencies influenced both those insights and the manner in which they were thus being articulated, with a view to restating (if necessary) that formulation."

[22] A. J. Gordon, "The Recurrence of Doctrine," *PE,* September 26, 1914, comments, "Nature constantly changes her garments, lest she weary us by her monotony, so with Truth. Its cycles of doctrine are ever revolving. New scenery and a varying climate for each succeeding generation of the

were given special expression in the Pentecostal movement. Stanley Horton suggests that the Holy Spirit has an active role in emphasizing truth in the present age that was not prominent in generations before.[23] He is not suggesting that truth is evolving, rather the Spirit is presently active in the church to illuminate truth because "the Spirit still desires to guide us into all truth."[24] If AG doctrine is going to have a future, a Spirit-inspired process of evaluation, discernment, and reform must exist in order to meet the needs of a new historical situation. Through listening to the Spirit's voice in the academy, the leadership, and the General Council the present needs of the fellowship can be assessed and addressed.

Re-Imagining the Eschatological Truths

In the previous section, I argued that a methodology is present in its Constitution and Bylaws that provides a way for doctrinal development to take place. In light of those established principles, I will make a modest attempt at proposing a revision to each of the four EFT based on the existing statements and informed by the research in this study. These suggestions will be offered in the spirit of the original statement and in honest reflection on the core commitments that were developed in this study. Pursuant to this task are a number of considerations about offering these revisions according the *SFT* methodology. First, I will attempt to pick the basic wording from the various versions: 1916, 1927, 1961, or 2015. The decision for choosing which version will be based on its suitability to the key elements reflective of the "present needs" of the fellowship. Second, this task will require me to make additions and revisions that will allow the integration of ideas that reflect the AG's pneumatological orientation. However, these statements cannot be exhaustive to reflect all that was discovered in this study, which means they will continue to be limited in scope. Finally, in keeping with the original *SFT*, the truth behind each statement should be biblical, but the wording should not be considered as infallible. This is simply one person's attempt at recasting each of the fundamental truths in ways that capture the ethos of AG eschatological expression. The result, I hope, will be a twenty-first century

---

Church is the result. Progress in doctrine there cannot be since there is one truth; but recurrence of doctrine there must be."

[23] Stanley Horton, *Into All Truth*, (Springfield: Gospel Publishing House, 1955), 13, notes, "These four teachings have received special emphasis and illumination by the Holy Spirit during the present-day Pentecostal revival. He has delighted to bring all of them into prominence."

[24] Horton, *Into All Truth*, 13.

revision of these statements that is hopeful, pneumatological, and affective, while at that same time unifying and inclusive.

The Future of the Blessed Hope

In light of the pneumatological orientation of the doctrine of the Second Coming, I suggest some revisions to the "Blessed Hope" that will prominently feature the image of hope expressed through the Spirit. To begin with, the 1916 statement provided a fundamental foundation because it set the expectation that the Blessed Hope is the "resurrection and the rapture." The 1927 version kept the same focus but improved the wording in a way that would make the statement inclusive by removing the term "rapture." The current version reflects the 1927 wording with minor modifications to its dated terminology in recent years. It is this current version that I will seek to develop.

13. The Blessed Hope (2015)[25]

> The resurrection of those who have fallen asleep in Christ and their translation together with those who are alive and remain unto the coming of the Lord is the imminent and blessed hope of the Church (1 Thessalonians 4:16, 17; Romans 8:23; Titus 2:13; 1 Corinthians 15:51, 52).

What is needed in this statement is for the Holy Spirit to take a primary role. In emphasizing the Spirit's work in both the act of resurrection and the affective response, this statement can transcend its propositional value to include the necessary orthopathy and orthopraxy. First, since the statement assumes the title but reads as an incomplete sentence, I would add the phrase, "The Blessed Hope is . . ." This would also lend more force to the definition that we have established in this study. Second, the Holy Spirit's role should be emphasized both in the resurrection and in the pneumatological response of groaning and waiting. Since the Blessed Hope includes hope for the body and all of creation, the connection between the body-Spirit-creation is warranted in the definition.

13. The Blessed Hope (Proposed)

> The Blessed Hope is the promise that at the imminent Second Coming of Jesus Christ, the dead shall be resurrected and the living shall be transformed by the Holy Spirit, who inspires believers to wait patiently and groan inwardly with all

---

[25] *GC Minutes* (August 3–7, 2015), 99–100.

creation for redemption (Tit. 2:13, 1 Thess. 4:16, 1 Cor. 15:51–52, Rom. 8:11–23).

The Future of the Millennial Reign

The Millennial Reign is the expectation that Jesus Christ will return to establish his kingdom on earth and will rule in peace. The 1916 statement was designed to be a summary of premillennial eschatology rather than a statement on the millennium. The 1927 revision was therefore needed in order to focus its content as such. However, it left out an important detail that 1961 added; the millennium will be a reign of peace. While re-writing this statement, they took the opportunity to reemphasize the rapture and the two-phase concept. These additions, while certainly reflecting positions within the AG, are unwarranted and only narrowed the potential of their acceptance by giving the impression that the AG has a specific stance on the tribulation. Therefore, I suggest that the 1927 and 1961 be combined and revised.

14. THE MILLENNIAL REIGN OF JESUS CHRIST (1927)[26]

The revelation of the Lord Jesus Christ from heaven, the salvation of national Israel, and the millennial reign of Christ on the earth is the Scriptural promise and the world's hope. (2 Thess. 1:7; Rev. 19:11–14; Rom. 11:26, 27; Rev. 20:1–7).

14. THE MILLENNIAL REIGN OF JESUS CHRIST (1961)[27]

The second coming of Christ includes the rapture of the saints, which is our blessed hope, followed by the visible return of Christ with His saints to reign on the earth for one thousand years (Zech. 14:5; Matt. 24:27, 30; Revelation 1:7; 19:11–14; 20:1–6). This millennial reign will bring the salvation of national Israel (Ezekiel 37:21, 22; Zephaniah 3:19–20; Romans 11:26, 27) and the establishment of universal peace (Isaiah 11:6–9; Psalm 72:3–8; Micah 4:3, 4).

The principle need for a future revision is additional language that connects the reign of Christ with the kingdom of God and emphasizes the Spirit's role in establishing the reign of peace. In light of the messianic importance of Israel, I suggest that the "salvation of national Israel" should remain as part of the new

[26] *GC Minutes* (September 16–22, 1927), 8.
[27] *GC Minutes* (August 23–29, 1961), 23.

statement, although omitting it could make the statement more inclusive. I would suggest eliminating the non-essential or non-explicit verses that support each idea.

THE MILLENNIAL REIGN OF JESUS CHRIST (Proposed)

The Millennial Reign is the fulfillment of the hope that Jesus Christ will return with His saints to establish the kingdom of God on earth (Zech. 14:5; Matt. 24:30; Rev 1:7; 20:1–6). During the millennium, the Holy Spirit will be poured out on all flesh (Joel 2:28–32), Israel will be saved (Ez. 37:21–22; Zeph. 3:19–20; Rom. 11:26–27), and universal peace and justice will be established (Isa. 11:6–9; Ps. 72:3–8; Mic. 4:3–4).

The Future of the Final Judgment

The Final Judgment envisions the cosmic act of sanctification in which the enemies of God and those who join in their rebellion are purged from creation in order to prepare for the new creation. The wording of the 1916 statement put the emphasis on the judgment of God's enemies as the primary purpose of the lake of fire. The 1927 version made a helpful change by eliminating the list of sins, lending further force to the emphasis on the judgment of God's enemies rather than the sins of humanity. The 1961 version changed the title from "Lake of Fire" to "The Final Judgment," while giving the impression of an event rather than an eschatological image which can also serve as a powerful image of future justice. However, the 1961 rewrite of the statement did shift the emphasis of eschatological judgment upon believers. The reversal of the order of humanity and God's enemies was unfortunate, since the lake of fire was never intended for humanity.

15. THE LAKE OF FIRE (1927)[28]

The devil and his angels, the Beast and the false prophet, and whosoever is not found written in the Book of Life, shall be consigned to the everlasting punishment in the lake which burneth with fire and brimstone, which is the second death. (Rev. 19:20; Rev. 20:10–15).

15. THE FINAL JUDGMENT (1961)[29]

There will be a final judgment in which the wicked dead will be raised and judged according to their works. Whosoever is not found written in the Book

---

[28] *GC Minutes* (September 16–22, 1927), 8.
[29] *GC Minutes* (August 23–29, 1961), 23.

of Life, together with the devil and his angels, the beast and the false prophet, will be consigned to everlasting punishment in the lake which burneth with fire and brimstone, which is the second death (Matt 25:46; Mark 9:43–48; Revelation 19:20; 20:11–15; 21:8).

In order to offer a future statement, a rewrite is justified in which the value of justice is emphasized and a priority is placed on the judgment of God's enemies. There should also be an emphasis on the final judgment as the final act of sanctification.

THE FINAL JUDGMENT (Proposed)

The final judgment is the hope that the Spirit of justice will purge from creation the cosmic enemies of God and the wicked that follow in their rebellion and consign them to everlasting punishment in the lake of fire, which is the second death (Matt. 25:46; Mk. 9:43–48; Rev. 19:20, 20:11–15, 21:8).

The Future of the New Heavens and New Earth

Since the New Heavens and New Earth has received virtually no revisions, I will use the most current version as my starting point. However, some helpful editions found in the *Condensed Fundamental Truths* statement also have potential for this revision.

16. The New Heavens and the New Earth (2015)

"We, according to His promise, look for new heavens and a new earth, wherein dwelleth righteousness" (2 Peter 3:13; Revelation 21,22).

16. WE BELIEVE... and look forward to the perfect New Heavens and a New Earth that Christ is preparing for all people, of all time, who have accepted Him. We will live and dwell with Him there forever following His millennial reign on Earth. "And so shall we forever be with the Lord!"[30]

This statement requires a couple of additions that would allow it to better reflect the pneumatic orientation of the AG position. First, the NHNE is considered to

---

[30] "Assemblies of God Fundamental Truths Condensed," (March 2010) http://ag.org/top/Beliefs/Statement_of_Fundamental_Truths/sft_short.cfm (accessed 11 January 2017). The origin of this statement is unknown. There is no record in the General Secretary office about the origin of this statement. It appears to have been created sometime in the 2000s by the office of Public Relations for a pamphlet called, "Our 16 Doctrines," (Springfield MO: Office of Public Relations, 2004).

be the culmination of the sanctifying process that began in the millennium and was completed at the final judgment. Therefore, a statement about the concept of renewal and the emphasis on continuity between the first creation and the new creation is warranted.

16. The New Heavens and the New Earth (Proposed)

The New Heavens and New Earth is the hope that following the Spirit's renewal of the earth in the millennium and the purging of sin at the final judgment, God will restore creation to the glorified state in which God's dwelling will once again be with humanity. (Rom. 8:21; 2 Pet. 3:13; Rev. 21:1–4).

These four revisions could provide a future for AG eschatology, one that is rooted in the historic fundamentals, expressed with the pneumatological imagination, and speaks to relevant issues within the AG today. With the methodology proposed in the previous chapter, the AG has the opportunity to develop its doctrine for a new generation of Pentecostal believers who believe in the outpouring of the Spirit and the soon return of Christ.

15

Conclusion

In 1993, AG historian Edith Blumhofer sounded a warning that a new generation of ministers were questioning the fellowship's core belief in the Blessed Hope.[1] Writing on the heels of a decade that endured the preoccupation with end times Bible prophecy culminating in the debacle of 88 Reasons Why Jesus is Returning in 1988, the whole subject of eschatology left a bad taste in the mouth of some young AG ministers. It was becoming clear that AG clergy were simply done with the dispensational charts of yesteryear and were seeking more meaningful models of eschatology found in other theological communities. In the local church, pastors simply avoided the topic altogether rather than face the minefield of wading into the final four AG fundamental truths. Meanwhile, scholars blamed the theologies of fundamentalist dispensationalism as the source of the whole mess. But it was perhaps the Y2K frenzy that finished the job once and for all for this generation. The new century began with a deeply felt exhaustion about the whole topic. Sadly, one of the AG's most distinctive doctrines became simply a memory of the past.

Ironically, just a couple years after Blumhofer's warning, the AG published its last full work eschatological work: *Our Destiny* (1996) by Stanley Horton, the person most responsible for articulating AG eschatology over the last half-century.[2] While Horton's final book was the most careful and in-depth eschatological text to date, this book ultimately signaled a symbolic end for the AG. For the next three decades, the AG avoided publishing end times books that had once been some of the most frequent publications. In some ways, this was the final exhale of an outdated model that saw eschatology as simply a puzzle to solve by reading the news side-by-side with the Bible. It was an end to the hobby of studying of prophecy in order to final all the "keys" to the end times. It was a harbinger that signaled the last days of an eschatology that turned the miracle-believing people, who should be Christianity's greatest optimists, into hopeless pessimists who grumble at the fallen world they are waiting to escape. In its place, a new generation began to groan for a different set of eschatological signs, ones

---

[1] Blumhofer, *Restoring the Faith*, 270–71.
[2] Horton, *Our Destiny: Biblical Teachings on Last Things*.

that inspire hope and dreams of the world that is to come and instill deeper meaning into the coming of Jesus beyond nostalgic sentimentality found in gospel songs for those who were tired of this world.

Believers who have lived in these three generations probably could not imagine how the dry bones of Pentecostal eschatology could live again in the hearts of this fellowship. I certainly know I did not. I began this study a decade ago with hopes of rapturing the AG out of dispensationalism by deconstructing the old paths of what I thought were the AG's views and replacing it with something deeper that reflected my Pentecostal orientation. Ignorantly, I assumed the eschatology of the past was a hopeless cause that should be abandoned for safer eschatological shores. However, the Spirit was planning something different with this study. The Spirit wanted to use this research to call my generation to awaken again to his coming. Little did I know that by going back to the voices of the past, I would discover what I had been looking for all along: a Blessed Hope. Day after day, as I read the writings of these women and men whose shoulders I stand on today, the Spirit led me to discover elements of a richer, deeper, and more hopeful Spirit-focused view of the future than I ever dreamed. The evidence convinced me that deep within the wells of Spirit-filled believers in this fellowship, there are resources in the Pentecostal ethos and founding passion for the coming kingdom that we can draw from today.

What this book imagines is a future for AG eschatology. It was an honest attempt to be faithful to the past, while also offering fresh insights and deeper revelation to the truths this fellowship has cherished. To those who have serious questions and have been tempted to abandon it all, perhaps this study will give you new ways of understanding our historic eschatological identity and inspire a vision for where we can go in the future. There is still room for you in this tribe. For those who have tended to major on the minors, I pray this study will give you new ways of seeing Christ's coming as more than a puzzle to solve; but as a living and Spirit-filled hope for all believers. To the pastors who avoided the topic altogether, I pray this will inspire you once again to dig deep, to love his coming, and to passionately proclaim the full gospel message that "Jesus is coming soon." And finally, to the scholars in this community, I hope this study has challenged the assumptions about the deficits in its development and has given new ways of seeing how the Spirit has animated the AG's commitments the premillennial coming of Jesus Christ.

By examining the past, we have unearthed the deep pneumatological resources found in the hopes and visions of Spirit-empowered believers who have gone before us. By examining the present, we have diagnosed our current condition and have sought to offer solutions to heal the wounds of misunderstanding and misrepresentation of the AG's commitments. Finally, though the pneumatological imagination, we have found ways to imagine the future in which a contemporary, yet contextual eschatology can re-ignite a passion for Christ's coming. I pray that these contributions will benefit this Pentecostal fellowship and ensure that a new generation of AG ministers and members will continue to love and look for the Blessed Hope, the imminent return of Jesus Christ.

Bibliography

Assemblies of God Publications

Blumhofer, Edith L. *The Assemblies of God: A Chapter in the Story of American Pentecostalism* I and II. Springfield: Gospel Publishing House, 1989.
Boyd, Frank. *The Budding Fig Tree*. Springfield: Gospel Publishing House, 1925.
—*Signs of the Times*. Springfield: Gospel Publishing House, 1950.
Brumback, Carl. *Accent on the Ascension*. Springfield: Gospel Publishing House, 1955.
—*Suddenly ... From Heaven*. Springfield: Gospel Publishing House, 1961.
Burke, Bob. *Like a Prairie Fire: A History of the Assemblies of God in Oklahoma*. Oklahoma City, OK: Oklahoma District Council of the Assemblies of God, 1994.
Flower, J. R. *The Origin and Development of the Assemblies of God*. Springfield: Gospel Publishing House, 1938.
Frodsham, Stanley. *With Signs Following*. Springfield: Gospel Publishing House, 1926.
—*Things Which Must Shortly Come To Pass*. Springfield: Gospel Publishing House, 1928.
Gortner, J. N., *Are the Saints Scheduled to Go Through the Tribulation?* Springfield: Gospel Publishing House, 1930.
—*Studies in Revelation*. Springfield: Gospel Publishing House, 1948.
Horton, Stanley M. *The Book of Acts*. Springfield: Gospel Publishing House, 1981.
—*Into All Truth*. Springfield: Gospel Publishing House, 1955.
—*Our Destiny: Biblical Teachings on Last Things*. Springfield: Gospel Publishing House, 1996.
—*The Promise of His Coming*. Springfield: Gospel Publishing House, 1967.
—*Systematic Theology*. Springfield: Logion Press, 1998.
—*The Ultimate Victory*. Springfield: Gospel Publishing House, 1991.
Jamieson, S. A. *Pillars of Truth*. Springfield: Gospel Publishing House, 1927.
Kendrick, Klaude. *The Promise Fulfilled*. Springfield: Gospel Publishing House, 1961.
Lawrence, B. F. *Apostolic Faith Restored*. Springfield MO: Gospel Publishing House, 1916.
Luce, Alice. *Little Flock and the Last Days*. Springfield: Gospel Publishing House, 1927.

Menzies, William W. *Anointed to Serve: The Story of the Assemblies of God.* Springfield: Gospel Publishing House, 1971.
—*Understanding Our Doctrine.* Springfield, MO; Gospel Publishing House, 1971.
Menzies, William W. and Stanley M. Horton. *Bible Doctrines: A Biblical Perspective.* Springfield: Logion Press, 1993.
Myland, D. Wesley. *The Latter Rain Covenant and Pentecostal Power.* Chicago: Evangel Publishing House, 1910.
Pearlman, Myer, *Knowing the Doctrines of the Bible.* Springfield: Gospel Publishing House, 1937.
—*Windows into the Future.* Springfield: Gospel Publishing House, 1941.
Riggs, Ralph M. *God's Calendar of Coming Events.* Springfield: Gospel Publishing House, 1962.
Riggs, Ralph M. *The Spirit Himself.* Springfield: Gospel Publishing House, 1949.
Sisson, Elizabeth. *Foregleams of Glory.* Chicago: Evangel Publishing House, 1912.
Steil, Harry J. *What Will Happen Next.* Springfield: Gospel Publishing House, 1938.
Ward, C. M. *Waiting…* Springfield: Gospel Publishing House, 1959.
Where We Stand. Springfield: Gospel Publishing House, 2001.
Wood, George O. *Core Values.* Springfield: Gospel Publishing House, 2007.

Documents and Correspondence

Gohr, Glenn. "The Statement of Fundamental Truths: Chronological History compiled by Glenn Gohr." 2000. Flower Pentecostal Heritage Center, Springfield, MO.
Kerr, D. W. "Fundamentals of the Faith "Plus.'" CBI Correspondence Course 8, 1926, Flower Pentecostal Heritage Center, Springfield, MO.
Kerr, D. W. "Correspondence to J.W. Welch." July 22, 1925, Flower Pentecostal Heritage Center, Springfield, MO, Transcription by Daniel D. Isgrigg, October 2015.
"Our 16 Doctrines." Assemblies of God Office of Public Relations, Springfield, MO, 2004.
Pierce, Willard C. "Outline Studies in the Chart of the Ages." Central Bible College, 1924, Flower Pentecostal Heritage Center, Springfield, MO.
World Assemblies of God Fellowship Constitution and Bylaws, August 2014.

Journals

Alexander, Paul N. "Speaking in the Tongues of Nonviolence: American Pentecostals, Pacifism and Nationalism." *Brethren Life & Thought* (Spring 2012): 1–16.
Archer, Kenneth J. "A Pentecostal Way of Doing Theology: Method and Manner." *IJST* 9, no. 3 (2007): 301–14.

Biddy, Wesley Scott. "Re–envisioning the Pentecostal Understanding of the Eucharist: An Ecumenical Proposal." *Pneuma* 28, no. 2 (Fall 2006): 228–51.

Bratton, Susan P. "The Ecotheology of James Watt." *Environmental Ethics* 5 (1983) 225–35.

Callahan, Leslie D. "Redeemed or Destroyed: Re-evaluating the Social Dimensions of Bodily Destiny in the Thought of Charles Parham." *Pneuma* 28, no. 2 (Fall 2006): 203–27.

Cerillo, Augustus Jr. "Interpretive Approaches to the History of American Pentecostal Origins." *Pneuma* 19, no. 1 (Spring 1997): 29–54.

Coulter, Dale M. "The Spirit and the Bride Revisited: Pentecostalism, Renewal, and the Sense of History." *JPT* 21, no. 1 (2012): 289–319.

Cunningham, Robert. "We Believe: Robert C. Cunningham Recalls the Origin of the Doctrinal Statement that Appears Regularly in the Pentecostal Evangel." *AG Heritage* 15, no. 3 (Fall 1995): 15.

Dempster, Murray, W. "Social Concern in Pentecostal Perspective." *JPT* 1, no. 2 (1993): 51–64.

Dermawan, Agustinus. "The Spirit in Creation and Environmental Stewardship: A Preliminary Pentecostal Response Toward Ecological Theology." *AJPS* 6, no. 2 (2003) 199–217.

Dresslehaus, Richard. "What Can The Academy Do For The Church." *AJPS* 3, no. 2 (2000): 319–23.

Eriksen, Stian. "The Epistemology of Imagination and Religious Experience." *Studia Theologica* 69, no. 1 (2015): 45–73.

Fudge, Thomas A. "Did E. N. Bell Convert to the 'New Issue'?" *JPT* 18 (2001): 122–40.

Gohr, Glenn. "The Historical Development of the Statement of Fundamental Truths." *AG Heritage* (August 2012): 61–66.

Green, Chris E. "The Crucified God and the Groaning Spirit." *JPT* 19 (2010): 124–42.

Harrington, H.K. "Lament or Complaint? A Response to Scott Ellington." *Risking Truth: Reshaping the World Through Prayers of Lament." JPT* 18, no. 2 (2009): 117–81.

Isgrigg, Daniel D. "The Latter Rain Revisited: Exploring the Origins of the Central Metaphor in Pentecostalism." *Pneuma* 41, nos. 3–4 (2019): 439–57.

Kay, William K. "Premillennial Tensions: What Pentecostal Ministers Look Forward To." *Journal For Contemporary Religion* 14, no. 3 (1999): 361–73.

—"Three Generations On: The Methodology of Pentecostal History." *JEPTA* 6, nos. 1–2, (1992): 58–70.

Larson, Duane. "An Ecumenical "Council" Revisited." *Dialogue* 44, no. 4 (Winter 2005): 389–400.

"The Legacy of James Watt." *Time Magazine*, October 24, 1983, 25.

Ma, Wonsuk. "Pentecostal Eschatology: What Happened When the Wave Hit the West End of the Ocean." *AJPS* 12, no. 1 (2009): 95–112.

Macchia, Frank D. "Sighs Too Deep For Words." *JPT* 1 (1992) 47–73.

—"Tongues as a Sign: Towards a Sacramental Understanding of Pentecostal Experience." *Pneuma* 15, no. 1 (1993): 61–76.

Marsden, George. "Lord of the Interior." *The Reformed Journal* 31, no. 6 (June 1981): 2–3.

Menzies, William W. The Influence of Fundamentalism." *AJPS* 14, no. 2 (2001): 199–211.

—"The Reformed Roots of Pentecostalism." *PentecoStudies* 6, no. 2 (2007) 78–99.

Menzies, Glen and Gordon L. Anderson. "D. W. Kerr and Eschatological Diversity in the Assemblies of God." *Paraclete* 27, no. 1 (1993): 8–16.

Millard, A.D. "The Prophecy of Joel." *Paraclete* 17, no. 2 (Spring 1983): 10–12.

Mittlestadt, Martin W. "Spirit and Peace in Luke–Acts." *Didaskalia* (Fall 2009): 17–40.

Molenaar, William. "The World Assemblies of God Fellowship: United in the Missionary Spirit." *AG Heritage* 31 (2011): 43.

Nestor, Charles. "Position Papers." *Agora* 2, no. 3 (Winter 1979): 10–11.

Richie, Tony. "Can Anything Good Come Out of Premillennialism? A Response to Robert O. Smith." *Dialog* 48, no. 3 (Fall 2009): 292–300.

—"Eschatological Inclusivism: Exploring Early Pentecostal theology of Religions in Charles Fox Parham." *Journal of the European Pentecostal Theological Association* 27, no. 2 (2007): 138–52.

Robeck, C. M. "An Emerging Magisterium." *Pneuma* 25, no. 2 (Fall 2003): 164–215.

— "Faith, Hope, Love, and the Eschaton." *Pneuma* 14, no. 1 (Spring 1992): 1–5.

Sheppard, Gerald T. "Pentecostals and the Hermeneutics of Dispensationalism: The anatomy of an Uneasy Relationship," *Pneuma* 6, no. 2 (Fall, 1984): 5–33.

Rodgers, Darrin J. "The Assemblies of God and the Long Journey Toward Racial Reconciliation." *AG Heritage* 28 (2008): 50–61.

Sparks, Nicole and Darrin J. Rogers. "John McConnell, Jr. and the Pentecostal Origins of Earth Day." *AG Heritage* 30 (2010) 16–25, 69.

Studebaker, Steven M. "Pentecostal Soteriology and Pneumatology." *JPT* 11, no. 2 (2003): 248–70.

Thiel, John E. "For What May We Hope? Thoughts on the Eschatological Imagination." *Theological Studies* 67 (2006) 517–41.

Thomas, John C. "Pentecostal Theology in the Twenty–First Century," *Pneuma* 20, no. 1 (Spring 1998): 3–19.

Torr, Stephen C. "Lamenting in Tongues: Glossolalia as a Pneumatic Aid to Lament." *JPT* 26 (2017): 30–47.

Trask, Thomas, "Response to a Paper Presented by Dr. Leonard Lovett." *Cyberjournal for Pentecostal-Charismatic Research* 14 (May 2005).

van der Laan, Paul. "What is Left Behind? A Pentecostal Response to Eschatological Fiction." *JEPTA* 24, no. 1 (2004): 49–70.
Volf, Miroslav. "The Final Reconciliation." *Modern Theology* 16, no. 1 (January 2000): 91–113.
—— "On Loving with Hope: Eschatology and Social Responsibility," *Transformation* 7, no. 3 (1990): 28–31.
Waddell, Robby C. "What Time is it? Half-past Three: How to Calculate Eschatological Time." *JEPTA* 2 (2011): 141–52.
Watt, James. "Ours is the Earth." *The Saturday Evening Post.* January–February 1982. 74–75, 104.

Secondary Literature

Albrecht, Daniel. *Rights in the Spirit: A Ritual Approach to Pentecostal/Charismatic Spirituality.* Sheffield, UK: Sheffield Academic Press, 1999.
Alexander, Estrelda. *Black Fire: One Hundred Years of African American Pentecostalism.* Downers Grove, IL: Intervarsity Press, 2011.
Alexander, K.E. *Pentecostal Healing: Models in Theology and Practice.* Dorset, UK: Deo Publishing, 2006.
Alexander, Paul N. ed. *Christ at the Checkpoint.* Eugene, OR: Pickwick Publishing, 2012.
——*Peace to War: Shifting Allegiances in the Assemblies of God.* Telfor, PA: Cascadia Publishing House, 2009.
——ed. *Pentecostals and Nonviolence: Reclaiming a Heritage.* Eugene, OR: Pickwick, 2010.
——"Seeking Peace with Justice." In *But These Are Written ... Essays on Johannine Literature in Honor of Professor Benny C. Aker,* edited by Craig S. Keener, Jeremy S. Crenshaw, and Jordan D. May, 139–52. Eugene, OR: Pickwick Publishers, 2014.
——"What Can Pentecostals and Charismatics do for Peace with Justice in Israel and Palestine." In *Christ at the Checkpoint,* edited by Paul N. Alexander, 61–74. Eugene, OR: Pickwick Publishing, 2012.
Althouse, Peter. "Ascension, Pentecost, Eschaton." In *Toward a Pentecostal Ecclesiology,* edited by John Christopher Thomas, 225–45. Cleveland, TN: CPT Press, 2010.
Althouse, Peter. "The Landscape of Pentecostal and Charismatic Eschatology: An Introduction." In *Perspectives in Pentecostal Eschatologies,* edited by Peter Althouse and Robbie Waddell, 1–21. Eugene, OR: Pickwick Publishing, 2010.
—— "Left Behind – Fact or Fiction: Ecumenical Dilemmas of the Fundamentalist Millenarian Tensions in Pentecostalism." *JPT* 13.2 (2005) 187–207.

— "Pentecostal Eschatology in Context: The Eschatological Orientation of the Full Gospel." Peter Althouse and Robbie Waddell. eds. *Perspectives in Pentecostal Eschatologies* (Eugene, OR: Pickwick Publishing, 2010), 205–31.

—*Spirit of the Last Days: Pentecostal Eschatology in Conversation with Jürgen Moltmann* (JPTSup 25; London: T&T Clark International, 2003).

Althouse, Peter and Robbie Waddell. eds. *Perspectives in Pentecostal Eschatologies* (Eugene, OR: Pickwick Publishing, 2010).

Anderson, R. M. *Vision of the Disinherited*. New York: Oxford University Press, 1979.

Archer, Kenneth J. "Nourishment for our Journey: The Pentecostal *via Salutis* and Sacramental Ordinances." in Chris E.W. Green, ed. *Pentecostal Ecclesiology* (Boston, MA: Brill, 2016), 141–60.

—*A Pentecostal Hermeneutic for the Twenty–First Century* (London, New York: T& T Clark).

Archer Kenneth J. and L. William Oliverio Jr. eds., *Constructive Pneumatological Hermeneutics in Pentecostal Christianity*. New York: Pelgrave Macmillan, 2016.

Archer, Melissa L., "*'I Was in the Spirit on the Lord's Day': A Pentecostal Engagement with Worship in the Apocalypse*. Cleveland, TN: CPT Press, 2015.

Astley, Jeff and Leslie J. Francis. eds. *Exploring Ordinary Theology*. Farnham, UK: Ashgate Publishing, 2013.

Baker, David W., eds. *Looking into the Future*. Grand Rapids, MI: Baker Academic, 2001.

Bauckham, Richard, ed. *God Will Be All in All*. Edinburgh: T&T Clark, 1999.

—*Living with Other Creatures: Green Exegesis and Theology*. Waco, TX: Baylor University Press, 2011.

—*The Theology of the Book of Revelation*. Cambridge, UK: Cambridge University Press, 1994.

Bauckham, Richard and Trevor Hart. *Hope Against Hope*. Grand Rapids, MI: Eerdmans, 1999.

Beals, Michael "Toward a Pentecostal Contribution to the Just War Tradition." in Paul Alexander, eds. *Pentecostals and Nonviolence: Reclaiming a Heritage* (Eugene, OR: Pickwick, 2010), 229–49.

Beaman, Jay. *Pentecostal Pacifism*. Eugene, OR: Wipf & Stock, 2009.

Bebbington, David W. *The Dominance of Evangelicalism: the Age of Spurgeon and Moody*. Downers Grove, IL: Intervarsity Press, 2005.

Bertone, John A. "Seven Dispensations or Two–Age View of History." In *Perspectives in Pentecostal Eschatologies,* edited by Peter Althouse and Robby Waddell, 61–94. Eugene, OR: Pickwick, 2010.

Blaising Craig A. and Darrell L. Bock. *Progressive Dispensationalism*. Grand Rapids: Zondervan, 1993.

Bloomberg, Craig L., and Sung Wook Chung, eds. *The Case for Historic Premillennialism*. Grand Rapids: Baker Academic, 2009.

Blumhofer, Edith. *Restoring the Faith.* Urbana, IL: University of Illinois Press, 1993.

—"William H. Durham: Years of Creativity, Years of Dissent," In *Portraits of a Generation,* edited by James R. Goff Jr. and Grant Wacker, 23–42. Fayetteville, AR: University of Arkansas Press, 2002.

Blumhofer, E., R. Spittler, and G. Wacker, eds. *Pentecostal Currents in American Protestantism.* Urbana, IL: University of Illinois Press, 1999.

Braaten, Carl E. and Robert W. Jenson, eds. *Jews and Christians: People of God.* Grand Rapids: Eerdmans, 2003.

Bruggemann, Walter. *The Practice of Prophetic Imagination.* Minneapolis, MN: Fortress Press, 2012.

Brunner, Emil. *Eternal Hope.* Philadelphia: Westminster Press, 1954.

Burke, Trevor J., and Keith Warrington. *A Biblical Theology of the Holy Spirit.* Eugene, OR: Cascade Books, 2014.

Burgess, Andrew. *The Ascension in Karl Barth.* Burlington, VT: Ashgate Publishing, 2004.

Burgess, S. M. and E. M. van der Maas, eds. *New International Dictionary of Pentecostal and Charismatic Movements.* Grand Rapids: Zondervan, 2003.

Cartledge, Mark J. *Testimony in the Spirit: Rescripting Ordinary Pentecostal Theology.* Farnham, UK: Ashgate Publishing, 2010.

Castelo, Daniel, "Patience as a Theological Virtue: A Challenge to Pentecostal Eschatology." In *Perspectives in Pentecostal Eschatologies,* edited by Peter Althouse and Robby Waddell, 232–46. Eugene, OR: Pickwick Publishing, 2010.

Ciampa, Roy E. and Brian S. Rosner. *The First Letter to the Corinthians.* Grand Rapids: Eerdmans, 2010.

Charette, Blaine. "Restoring the Kingdom to Israel: Kingdom and the Spirit in Luke's Thought." In *Perspectives in Pentecostal Eschatologies,* edited by Peter Althouse and Robby Waddell, 49–60, Eugene, OR: Pickwick Publishing, 2010.

Coleson, Joseph E. "Israel's Life Cycle from Birth to Resurrection." In *Israel's Apostasy and Restoration,* edited by Avraham Gileadi, 237–49. Grand Rapids: Baker, 1988.

Collins, John J. *The Apocalyptic Imagination.* Grand Rapids: Eerdmans, 1998.

Couch, Mal, ed. *Dictionary of Premillennial Theology.* Grand Rapids: Kregel Publishing, 1997.

Coulter, Dale M. and Amos Yong, eds. *The Spirit, the Affections and the Christian Tradition.* Notre Dame, IN: University of Notre Dame Press, 2016.

Crutchfield, Larry V. *The Origins of Dispensationalism: The Darby Factor.* Lanham, MD: University Press of America, 1992.

Daniels III, David D. "Until the Power of the Lord Comes Down." In *Contemporary Spiritualties,* edited by Clive Erricker and Jane Erricker, 173–88. London: Continuum Press, 2001.

Dayton, Donald W. *Discovering An Evangelical Heritage.* New York, Harper & Row: 1976.

—"From Christian Perfection to the 'Baptism of the Holy Ghost.'" *Aspects of Pentecostal–Charismatic Origins,* edited by Vinson Synan, 41–52. Plainfield, NJ: Logos, 1975.

—"Pentecostal Studies." In *From The Margins: A celebration of the theological work of Donald W. Dayton,* edited by Christian T. Collins Winn, 147–75. Eugene, OR: Pickwick Publishing, 2007.

—*Theological Roots of Pentecostalism.* Peabody, MA: Hendrickson Publishers, 1987.

Dempster, Murray W. "Eschatology, Spirit Baptism, and Inclusiveness: An Exploration into the Hallmarks of a Pentecostal Social Ethic." In *Perspectives in Pentecostal Eschatology,* edited by Peter Althouse and Robby Waddell, 155–88. Eugene, OR: Pickwick Publishing, 2010.

—"Evangelism, Social Concern, and the Kingdom of God." in *Called and Empowered: Global Mission in Pentecostal Perspective,* edited by M. W. Dempster, B. D. Klaus and D. Petersen, 23–59. Peabody, MA: Hendrickson, 1991.

Dreyer, Elizabeth A., *Holy Power, Holy Presence: Rediscovering Medieval Metaphors for the Holy Spirit.* New York: Paulist Press, 2007.

Drummond, Henry, *A Defense of the Students of Prophecy in Answer to the Attack of the Re. Dr. Hamilton.* London: James Nisbet, 1828.

Ehlert, Arnold D., *A Bibliographic History of Dispensationalism.* Grand Rapids: Baker, 1965.

Erricker, Clive and Jane Erricker, eds. *Contemporary Spiritualties.* London: Continuum Press, 2001.

Ervin, Howard M. *Healing Sign of the Kingdom.* Peabody, MA: Hendrickson, 2002.

Everts, Janet Meyer and Jeffrey S. Lamp, eds. *Pentecostal Theology and The Theological Vision of N.T. Wright.* Cleveland, TN: CPT Press, 2015.

Faupel, D. W. *The Everlasting Gospel.* JPTSup 10; Sheffield: Sheffield Academic Press, 1996.

Fee, Gordon D. *The First Epistle to the Corinthians.* Grand Rapids, MI: Eerdmans, 1987.

Frey, Christofer, "The Impact of the Biblical Idea of Justice," in *Justice and Righteousness: Biblical Themes and their Influence,* edited by Henning Graf Reventlow and Yair Hoffman, 91–104. Sheffield, UK: Sheffield Academic Press, 1992.

Friezen, Aaron. *Norming the Abnormal.* Eugene, OR: Pickwick, 2013.

Gannon, Raymond L. *The Shifting Romance with Israel.* Shippensburg, PA: Destiny Image, 2012.

Gibson, Scott M. *A. J. Gordon, American Premillennialist.* Lanham, MD: University Press of America, 2001.

Gileadi, Avrahameds. *Israel's Apostasy and Restoration.* Grand Rapids: Baker, 1988.

Goff Jr., James R. and Grant Wacker, eds. *Portraits of a Generation.* Fayetteville, AR: University of Arkansas Press, 2002.

Green, Chris E., eds. *Pentecostal Ecclesiology.* Boston: Brill, 2016.

Grenz, Stanely J., *The Millennial Maze.* Downers Grove, IL: InterVarsity Press, 1992.
Grey, Jacqueline. *Three's a Crowd: Pentecostalism, Hermeneutics and the Old Testament.* Eugene, OR: Pickwick, 2011.
—"When the Spirit Trumps Tradition: A Pentecostal Reading of Isaiah 56:1–8." In *Constructive Pneumatological Hermeneutics in Pentecostal Christianity*, edited by Kenneth Archer and William Oliverio Jr, 143–58. New York: Pelgrave Macmillan, 2016.
Hart, Trevor. "Imagination for the Kingdom of God." In *God Will Be All in All*, edited by Richard Bauckham, 49–76. Edinburgh: T&T Clark, 1999.
Heyduck, Richard. *The Recovery of Doctrine in the Contemporary Church: An Essay in Philosophical Ecclesiology.* Waco, TX: Baylor University Press, 2002.
Hultber, Alan, Craig A. Blasing, and Douglas J. Moo, *Three Views on the Rapture: Pretribulation, Prewrath, or Postribulation.* Grand Rapids: Zondervan, 2010.
Isgrigg, Daniel D. "The Latter Rain Revisited: Exploring the Origins of the Central Metaphor in Pentecostalism." *Pneuma* 41, no. 3–4 (2019): 439–57.
—, Martin W. Mittelstadt, and Rich Wadholm, Jr., eds., *Receiving Scripture in the Pentecostal Tradition.* Cleveland, TN: CPT Press, 2020.
—*Why I Want To Be Left Behind.* Tulsa, OK: Word & Spirit Press, 2008.
Jacobsen, Douglas, "Knowing the Doctrine of Pentecostals: The Scholastic Theology of the Assemblies of God." In *Pentecostal Currents in American Protestantism*, edited by E. Blumhofer, R. Spittler, and G. Wacker, 90–95. Urbana, IL: University of Illinois Press, 1999.
Jenkins, Philip. *The Great and Holy War.* San Francisco, CA: HarperOne, 2014.
Jenson, Robert W. "Toward A Christian Theology of Judaism." In *Jews and Christians: People of God*, edited by Carl E. Braaten and Robert W. Jenson, 1–13. Grand Rapids: Eerdmans, 2003.
Karkkainen, Veli-Matti. *Pneumatology.* Grand Rapids: Baker Academic, 2008.
Kay, William K. *Pentecostalism.* London: SCM Press, 2009.
—*Pentecostals in Britain.* Carlisle, UK: Paternoster Press, 2002.
Kearney, Richard. *The Wake of Imagination.* London: Routledge, 1998.
Keener, Craig S. *1–2 Corinthians.* Cambridge, UK: Cambridge University Press, 2005).
—*Acts: An Exegetical Commentary* vol. 1. Grand Rapids: Baker Academic, 2012.
—*Spirit Hermeneutics.* Grand Rapids: Eerdmans, 2016.
Keener, Craig S., Jeremy S. Crenshaw, and Jordan D. May. eds. *But These Are Written…Essays on Johannine Literature in Honor of Professor Benny C. Aker.* Eugene, OR: Pickwick Publishers, 2014.
Kienzler, Jonathan. *The Fiery Holy Spirit: The Spirit's Relationship with Judgment in Luke-Acts.* Dorsett, UK: Deo Publishing, 2015.
King, Gerald W., *Disfellowshipped: Pentecostal Responses to Fundamentalism in the United States 1906–1943.* Eugene, OR: Pickwick Publishing, 2011.

Kline, Meredith G. *God, Heaven, and the Har Magedon: A Covenantal Tale of Cosmos and Telos*. Eugene, OR: Wipf & Stock, 2006.
Ladd, George Eldon. *The Blessed Hope*. Grand Rapids, MI: Eerdmans, 1984.
Lamp, Jeffrey. "N. T. Wright—Right or Wrong for Pentecostals?" In *Pentecostal Theology and The Theological Vision of N.T. Wright*, edited by Janet Meyer Everts and Jeffrey S. Lamp, 7–26. Cleveland, TN: CPT Press, 2015.
Land, Steven J., *Pentecostal Spirituality: A Passion for the Kingdom*. JPTSup 1; Sheffield: Sheffield Academic Press, 1993.
Lawler, Michael G. *What Is and What Ought to Be*. New York: Continuum Press, 2005.
Lindbeck, George. *The Nature of Doctrine*. Philadelphia: Westminster Press, 1984.
Lonergan, Bernard. *Method in Theology*. New York: Seabury Press, 1979.
Ma, Wonsuk. "Isaiah." In *A Biblical Theology of the Holy Spirit*, edited by Trevor J. Burke and Keith Warrington, 34–45. Eugene, OR: Cascade Books, 2014.
—*Until the Spirit Comes: The Spirit of God in the Book of Isaiah*. Sheffield, UK: Sheffield Academic Press, 1999.
Ma, Wonsuk and Julie C. Ma. *Mission in the Spirit: Towards a Pentecostal/Charismatic Missiology*. Oxford, UK: Regnum Books International, 2010.
Macchia, Frank D. *Baptized in the Spirit: A Global Pentecostal Theology*. Grand Rapids: Zondervan, 2006.
—"Church of the Latter Rain," in *Toward a Pentecostal Ecclesiology*, edited by J. C. Thomas, 248–58. Cleveland, TN: CPT Press, 2010.
—"Jesus is Victor." In *Perspectives in Pentecostal Eschatology*, edited by Peter Althouse and Robby Waddell, 375–400. Eugene, OR: Pickwick Publishing, 2010.
—'The Struggle for Global Witness: Shifting Paradigms in Pentecostal Theology." In *The Globalization of Pentecostalism: A Religion Made to Travel*, edited by Murray W. Dempster, Byron D. Klaus, Douglas Peterson, 8–29. Carlisle, UK: Regnum Press, 1999.
—"Theology, Pentecostal." In *NIDPCM*, edited by S. M. Burgess, and E. M. van der Maas, 1138–40. Grand Rapids: Zondervan, 2003.
MacPherson, Dave. *The Incredible Coverup*. Plainsfield, NJ: Logos 1975.
Mangum, R. Todd and Mark S. Sweetnam. *The Scofield Bible: Its History and Impact on the Evangelical Church*. Colorado Springs, CO: Paternoster, 2009.
Marino, Bruce R. "The Origin, Nature, and Consequences of Sin." In *Systematic Theology*, edited by Stanley M. Horton, 255–90. Springfield: Logion Press, 1998.
Marsden, George, M. *Fundamentalism and American Culture*. New York: Oxford University Press, 2006.
Martin, Lee Roy, ed. *Pentecostal Hermeneutics: A Reader*. Boston: Brill, 2013.
— "Psalm 63 And Pentecostal Spirituality: An Exercise in Affective Hermeneutics." In *Pentecostal Hermeneutics: A Reader*, edited by Lee Roy Martin, 263–86. Boston: Brill, 2013.

McConnell, Jr., John and John C. Munday, Jr., *Earth Day: Vision for Peace, Justice, and Earth Care.* Eugene, OR: Resource Publications, 2011.
McGee, Gary B., "Historical Background," In *Systematic Theology,* edited by Stanley M. Horton, 9–38. Springfield MO: Logion Press, 1995.
—*Initial Evidence.* Eugene, OR: Wipf & Stock, 1991.
— "Pridgeon, Charles Hamilton," In *Dictionary Pentecostal and Charismatic Movemements,* edited by Stanley M. Burgess and Gary B. McGee, 727. Grand Rapids: Zondervan, 1988.
McGrath, Alister E. *The Genesis of Doctrine: A Study in the Foundation of Doctrinal Criticism.* Grand Rapids: Eerdmans, 1997.
McQueen, Larry D. *Toward a Pentecostal Eschatology.* Dorset, UK: Deo Publishing, 2012.
Moltmann, Jürgen. *Spirit of Life: A Universal Affirmation.* Minneapolis, MN: Fortress Press, 2001.
—*The Way of Jesus Christ: Christology in Messianic Dimensions.* Translated by Margaret Kohl. New York: Harper Collins, 1990.
Moore, David. "Discerning the Times: The Victorious Eschatology of the Shepherding Movement." In *Perspectives in Pentecostal Eschatologies,* edited by Peter Althouse and Robbie Waddell, 273–92. Eugene, OR: Pickwick Publishing, 2010.
Newberg, Eric. *The Pentecostal Mission in Palestine.* Eugene, OR: Pickwick Publishing, 2012.
Noll, Mark A. *Turning Points: Decisive Moments in the History of Christianity.* Grand Rapids: Baker Academic, 2012.
Norris, Christopher and Sam Speers. *Kingdom Politics: In Search of a New Political Imagination for Today's Church.* Eugene, OR: Cascade Books, 2015.
Olena, Lois E. *Stanley M. Horton: Shaper of Pentecostal Theology.* Springfield: Gospel Publishing House, 2009.
Oliverio Jr., L. William. "Introduction." In *Constructive Pneumatological Hermeneutics in Pentecostal Christianity.* edited by Kenneth J. Archer and L. William Oliverio Jr. New York: Pelgrave Macmillan, 2016.
Peterson, Eugene. *Reversed Thunder: The Revelation of John & the Praying Imagination.* San Francisco: Harper & Row, 1988.
Petrella, Ivan. *The Future of Liberation Theology: An Argument and Manifesto.* New York: Taylor and Francis, 2016.
Pinnock, Clark. *Flame of Love.* Downers Grove, IL: IVP Academic, 2016.
—*Most Moved Mover.* Grand Rapids: Baker Academic, 2001.
Pipkin, Brian and Jay Beaman, eds. *Early Pentecostals on Nonviolence and Social Justice.* Eugene, OR: Pickwick, 2016.
Poewe, Karla, ed. *Charismatic Christianity as a Global Culture.* Columbia SC: University of South Carolina Press, 1994.

Polkinghorn, John and Michael Welker, eds. *The End of World and the Ends of God.* Harrisburg, PA: Trinity Press International, 2000.
Poloma, Margaret. "Assemblies of God." In *New International Dictionary of Pentecostal and Charismatic Movements,* edited by Stanley M. Burgess, and Eduard M. van der Maas, 333–40. Grand Rapids: Zondervan, 2003.
—*Assemblies of God at the Crossroads.* Knoxville, TN: University of Tennessee Press, 1989.
Poloma, Margaret and John Green. *The Assemblies of God: Godly Love and the Revitalization of American Pentecostalism.* New York: New York University Press, 2010.
Prosser, Peter. *Dispensationalist Eschatology and Its Influence on American and British Religious Movements.* Lewiston, NY: Edwin Mellen Press, 1999.
Reventlow, Henning Graf and Yair Hoffman, eds. *Justice and Righteousness: Biblical Themes and their Influence.* Sheffield, UK: Sheffield Academic Press, 1992.
Robinette, Brian D. *The Grammars of Resurrection.* New York: Crossroad Publishing Company, 2009.
Rosenior, Derrick R. "The Rhetoric of Pentecostal Reconciliation." In *The Liberating Spirit: Pentecostals and Social Action in North America,* edited by Michael Wilkinson and Steven M. Studebaker, 53–84. Eugene, OR: Wipf & Stock, 2010.
Sandeen, Ernest R. *The Roots of Fundamentalism: British and American Millenarianism.* Chicago: University of Chicago Press, 1970.
Scofield, C. I. *Plain Papers on the Doctrine of the Holy Spirit.* Westwood, NJ: Revell, 1899.
—*The Scofield Reference Bible.* New York: Oxford University Press, 1909.
Skaggs, Rebecca and Priscilla C. Benham. *Revelation: Pentecostal Commentary.* Blandford Forum: Deo Publishing, 2009.
Smalley, Stephen S. *The Revelation to John.* Downers Grove, IL: IVP, 2005.
Smith, Gary Scott, *Heaven in the American Imagination.* New York: Oxford University Press, 2011.
Smith, James K. A. *Awaiting the King: Reforming Public Theology.* Grand Rapids: Baker Academic, 2017.
—*Desiring the Kingdom.* Grand Rapids: Baker Academic Press, 2011.
Spittler, Russell, "Are Pentecostals and Charismatics Fundamentalists." In *Charismatic Christianity as a Global Culture,* edited by Karla Poewe, 103–16. Columbia SC: University of South Carolina Press, 1994.
Stephenson, Christopher A. *Types of Pentecostal Theology: Method, System, Spirit.* Oxford, UK: Oxford University Press, 2013.
Stoger, William R. "Scientific Accounts of Ultimate Catastrophes in Our Life-Bearing Universe," in *The End of the World and the Ends of God,* edited by John Polkinghorn and Michael Welker, 19–28. Harrisburg, PA: Trinity Press International, 2000.

Studebaker, Steven M. *A Pentecostal Political Theology for American Renewal: Spirit of the Kingdoms, Citizens of the Cities.* New York: Palgrave McMillan, 2016.

Swoboda, A. J. *Tongues and Trees: Toward a Pentecostal Ecological Theology.* Dorset: UK, Deo Publishing, 2013.

Synan, Vinson, ed. *Aspects of Pentecostal-Charismatic Origins.* Plainfield, NJ: Logos, 1975.

—*The Holiness-Pentecostal Tradition.* Grand Rapids: Eerdmans, 1997.

Matthew K. Thompson. "Eschatology as Soteriology." In *Perspectives in Pentecostal Eschatologies,* edited by Peter Althouse and Robby Waddell, 198–204. Eugene, OR: Pickwick Publishing, 2010.

—*Kingdom Come: Revisioning Pentecostal Eschatology.* Blandford Forum: Deo Publishing, 2010.

Thomas, John C., *The Apocalypse: A Literary and Theological Commentary.* Cleveland, TN: CPT Press, 2012.

— "Mystery of the Great Whore: Pneumatic Discernment in Revelation 17." In *Perspectives in Pentecostal Eschatologies,* edited by Peter Althouse and Robby Waddell, 111–38. Eugene, OR: Pickwick Publishing, 2010.

—*A Pentecostal Commentary on The Johannine Epistles.* London: T&T Clark, 2004.

—*The Spirit of the New Testament.* Dorset, UK: Deo Publishing, 2005.

—eds. *Toward a Pentecostal Ecclesiology.* Cleveland, TN: CPT Press, 2010.

Thomas, John Christopher and Frank D. Macchia. *Revelation.* Grand Rapids: Eerdmans, 2016.

Torr, Stephen C. *A Dramatic Pentecostal/Charismatic Anti–Theodicy: Improvising on a Divine Performance of Lament.* Eugene, OR: Pickwick Publishing, 2013.

Van De Walle, Bernie A. *The Heart of the Gospel: A. B. Simpson, the Fourfold Gospel, and Late Nineteenth Century Evangelical Theology.* Eugene, OR: Pickwick Publishing, 2009.

Vondy, Wolfgang. *Beyond Pentecostalism.* Grand Rapids: Eerdmans, 2010.

Volf, Miroslav. *Exclusion and Embrace: a theological exploration of identity, otherness, and reconciliation.* Nashville, TN: Abingdon Press, 1996.

Wacker, Grant, *Heaven Below.* Cambridge, MA: Harvard University Press, 2003.

Waddell, Robby C. "Apocalyptic Sustainability." In *Perspectives in Pentecostal Eschatologies,* edited by Peter Althouse and Robby Waddell, 95–110. Eugene, OR: Pickwick Publishing, 2010.

— "Revelation and the (New) Creation: A Prolegomenon on the Apocalypse, Science and Creation." A paper presented at the 35th Annual Meeting of the Society for Pentecostals Studies. 2008.

—*The Spirit of the Book of Revelation.* Dorset, UK: Deo Publishing, 2006.

Watts, Fraser. "Subjective and Objective Hope." In *The End of World and the Ends of God,* edited by John Polkinghorn and Michael Welker, 47–60. Harrisburg, PA: Trinity Press International, 2000.

Wilkinson, Michael and Steven M. Studebaker. eds. *The Liberating Spirit: Pentecostals and Social Action in North America.* Eugene, OR: Wipf & Stock, 2010.

Wilkinson, Paul Richard. *For Zion's Sake: Christian Zionism and the Role of John Nelson Darby.* Milton Keynes, UK: Paternoster, 2007.

Wilson, D. J. "Pentecostal Perspectives on Eschatology." In *New International Dictionary of Pentecostal and Charismatic Movements,* edited by Stanley M. Burgess, and Eduard M. van der Maas, 264–65. Grand Rapids: Zondervan, 2003.

Winn, Christian T. Collins, ed. *From The Margins: A celebration of the theological work of Donald W. Dayton.* Eugene, OR: Pickwick Publishing, 2007.

Wright, N.T., *Surprised by Hope.* New York: HarperOne, 2014.

Yong, Amos, *In the Days of Caesar.* Grand Rapids: Eerdmans, 2010.

—*Renewing Christian Theology: Systematics for a Global Christianity.* Waco, TX: Baylor University Press, 2014.

—*The Spirit of Creation: Modern Science and Divine Action in the Pentecostal Charismatic Imagination.* Grand Rapids: Eerdmans, 2011.

—*Spirit Poured Out on All Flesh.* Grand Rapids: Baker Academic, 2005.

—*Spirit-Word-Community.* Eugene, OR: Wipf & Stock, 2002.

Ziefle, Joshua R. *David du Plessis and the Assemblies of God.* Boston, MA: Brill, 2013.

Unpublished Papers and Theses

Jackson, Alicia R. "Ezekiel's Two Sticks and Eschatological Violence in the Pentecostal Tradition: An Intertextual Literary Analysis." Ph.D. thesis. University of Birmingham, 2018.

Isgrigg, Daniel D. "Interpreting the Signs of the Times: How Eschatology Shaped Assemblies of God Social Ethics." A paper presented at the 47th annual meeting of the Society for Pentecostal Studies, March 2018.

—"The Pentecostal Evangelical Church: The Theological Self-identity of the Assemblies of God as Evangelical 'Plus.'" A paper presented at the 46th Meeting of the Society for Pentecostal Studies, March 2017.

—, "'Rescued women:' Early Pentecostal Responses to Sex Trafficking," a paper presented at the 50th Annual Meeting of the Society for Pentecostal Studies, Southlake Texas, March 2021.

Tackett, Zachary M., "More than Fundamentalists: fundamentalist Influences within the Assemblies of God, 1914–1942." A paper presented at the 26th Annual Meeting of the Society For Pentecostal Studies, March 1997.

—"The Embourgeoisement of the Assemblies of God: Changing Perspectives on Scripture, Millennialism, and the Roles of Women." Ph.D. thesis. Southern Baptist Theological Seminary, May 1998.

Websites

ag.org/Beliefs/Topics-Index/Environmental-Protection (Accessed 1 January 2018).
ag.org/top/Beliefs/Statement_of_Fundamental_Truths/sft_short.cfm (accessed 11 January 2017).
Strupp, Joe. "Bill Moyers Apologizes to James Watt for Apocryphal Quote." http://www.editorandpublisher.com/news/bill-moyers-apologizes-to-james-watt-for-apocryphal-quote/ (accessed 13 August 2017).
Watt, James. "The Religious Left's Lies." *Washington Post.* May 21, 2005. http://www.washingtonpost.com/wp-dyn/content/article/2005/05/20/AR2005052001333.html (accessed 15 August 2007).
www.aog.org.uk/about-us/what-we-believe (accessed March 17, 2018).
www.pewforum.org/religious-landscape-study/religious-denomination/assemblies-of-god/views-about-environmental-regulation/ (accessed 1 January 2018).

MAJOR NAME AND SUBJECT INDEX

Althouse, Peter 24, 30-31, 83, 198, 205-206, 217, 237-38, 263
Anderson, Gordon 22-23, 46-47, 51, 96-97, 190,
Baptism in the Holy Spirit, 3, 4, 6, 7, 9-10, 11, 20, 23, 32, 41-44, 46, 54, 69-71, 92, 105, 107, 109-10, 112, 114, 126, 139-42, 180, 182, 186-87, 188, 203-204, 215, 221, 227, 229, 230, 252, 260, 260, 263
Bell, E. N. 43-48, 51, 69, 72-73, 102, 109, 111-13, 115, 121
Blumhofer, Edith 4, 13, 23, 45, 59, 66, 79-80, 137, 141, 156, 277
Boyd, Frank 10, 21, 53, 55, 58, 83, 84, 119, 149, 161, 181, 225
Brumback, Carl 42, 189, 217
Collins, A. P. 43-45, 54
Darby, J. N. 6, 71-72, 171, 187
dispensationalism, 6-8, 10-14, 20-40, 52, 55-56, 58, 71-74, 78, 85, 92-93, 96, 98, 111-14, 123, 138, 145, 151, 153, 155, 156, 167, 179-92, 198, 208, 218, 225, 237, 239-40, 267, 277-78
environmental concerns, 28, 34, 85-87, 147-50, 193, 260-63
escapism 31, 33-34, 51-52, 90-91, 97, 108, 129, 138, 140, 152-54, 170, 172-74, 182-83, 192-, 214, 219
Flower, J. R. 42, 45, 53, 69, 72, 81, 97, 102, 109, 113, 190, 268-69
Frodsham, Stanley 45, 47-48, 75, 82, 106-107, 111-12, 119, 122, 126, 132, 181, 189, 252, 267
Fundamentalism 7-8, 13, 20, 23-24, 26, 30, 31, 38, 42, 137, 181, 187, 199, 205
Gortner, J. N. 53, 58, 70, 77, 105, 110, 116, 126

Horton, Stanley 14, 155-56, 171-72, 183, 218, 220, 249, 257, 270, 277
Israel, 6, 9, 11, 21, 33, 34, 37, 38, 55-56, 60-61, 63-64, 66-67, 73, 90, 95-98, 105-106, 112, 114, 125, 131-32, 135, 138, 140, 142-46, 154, 161-62, 178-79, 184-92, 216, 222, 231, 233, 236-43, 251-52, 272-73
Jamieson, Samuel 46-48, 53, 69, 117, 224
Kay, William ix, 5, 7, 9, 12, 67, 201, 209-209
Kerr, D. W. 22, 44-48, 53-54, 113
Leonard, T. K. 45-47
Luce, Alice 10, 106-107, 114, 116, 228
Macchia, Frank 30-33, 37, 202, 213, 229, 236, 240-41, 249, 260
Menzies, Glen 22-23, 46-47, 51, 96, 190, 266
Menzies, William 10, 19-20, 22, 39, 42, 49, 53, 61, 102, 118, 125, 137, 188, 189, 232, 257
mid-tribulation, 79, 112-13, 171, 172, 190
Moltmann, Jurgen viii, 29-31, 40, 222, 225, 227, 229, 234, 238-41, 252
Nelson, P. C. 21, 133, 215, 224, 232, 257, 268
Pacifism 29, 122-23, 244
Palestine, 56, 75, 131, 142-43, 186, 188
Pearlman, 21, 216, 219, 220, 232, 235, 246, 257
postmillennial, 4-8, 28, 91, 93, 108, 121, 174, 185-86, 192, 227, 232, 238, 243, 246
post-tribulation, 51, 56, 76-77, 78-79, 172, 190

pre-tribulation, 6, 50-51, 79, 80, 89, 97, 113, 131, 142, 153, 156, 171-72, 183-84, 190, 224
Pridgeon, Charles 76
Racism 120-122, 247
Riggs, Ralph 71, 138, 139-40, 146, 146, 148, 268
Scofield, C. I. 7, 10-11, 24-26, 71-75, 187, 188, 190
social, 4, 7-8, 26, 27-29, 31, 39, 93, 118-21, 134-35, 148, 163-64, 172-74, 192-93
Trask, Thomas 247-48
Volf, Miroslav
Waddell, Robby 28-29, 35-36, 259, 260
Ward, C. M. 146, 149, 154-55, 160-63, 165
Watt, James G. 85-86
Williams, E. S. 21, 53, 81, 127-30, 135, 141-42, 268
Wood, George 208
Yong, Amos 30, 33-35, 203, 232-37, 240, 248, 260-61
Zimmerman, Thomas 59, 137, 151, 156, 170, 174, 197

www.ingramcontent.com/pod-product-compliance
Lightning Source LLC
Chambersburg PA
CBHW050312120526
44592CB00014B/1878